CHURCHILL AND SECRET SERVICE

CHURCHILL AND SECRET SERVICE

DAVID STAFFORD

JOHN MURRAY
Albemarle Street, London

© David Stafford 1997

First published in 1997
by John Murray (Publishers) Ltd,
50 Albemarle Street, London W1X 4BD

The moral right of the author has been asserted

A catalogue record for this book is available from the British Library

ISBN 0-7195-5407 1

Typeset in 12.25/13.5 Monotype Garamond by Servis Filmsetting Ltd, Manchester

Printed and bound in Great Britain by
the University Press, Cambridge

To C.M.T.
with love and affection

In the high ranges of Secret Service work the actual facts in many cases were in every respect equal to the most fantastic inventions of romance and melodrama. Tangle within tangle, plot and counter-plot, ruse and treachery, cross and double-cross, true agent, false agent, double agent, gold and steel, the bomb, the dagger and the firing party, were interwoven in many a texture so intricate as to be incredible yet true. The Chief and the High Officers of the Secret Service revelled in these subterranean labyrinths, and pursued their task with cold and silent passion.

Winston Churchill, 'My Spy Story', *Thoughts and Adventures*, 1932

Contents

Illustrations

13. Edward Spears, professional intelligence officer, ally of Savinkov and Churchill's trusted adviser

14. George Lansbury, Churchill's *bête noire* and MI5 target, with 'Captain' Edward Tupper, Churchill's private agent

15. Sir Joseph Ball, MI5 officer on the Lansbury case and mastermind of Conservative 'dirty tricks' in the 1930s

16. Sir Stewart Menzies, head of the Secret Intelligence Service ('C') and Churchill's wartime spymaster

17. Ralph Wigram, secret informant for Churchill against appeasement

18. Desmond Morton, Churchill's intelligence adviser, with Churchill and Admiral Sir Andrew Cunningham, First Sea Lord

19. Hugh Dalton, Churchill's first 'minister for ungentlemanly war'

20. Lord Selborne, Dalton's successor and Churchill's trusted friend

21. Lord Swinton, appointed by Churchill in 1940 to fight 'the Fifth Column'

22. Admiral Darlan with General Franco and Marshal Pétain.

23. Alan Hillgarth, British wartime intelligence officer and secret post-war adviser to Churchill

The author and publisher wish to acknowledge the following for permission to reproduce illustrations: 1, 3, 5, 6, 7, 8, 9, 10, 15, 16, 19, 21 and 22, Hulton Getty Picture Collection; 2, J. P. A. Haldane; 4, University of Edinburgh library; 11, Robin Bruce Lockhart; 12 and 13, Popperfoto; 14, British Library; 17, Patricia Clifton and Sir Martin Gilbert; 18, Imperial War Museum; 20, Public Record Office; 23, Professor Jocelyn Hillgarth

Acknowledgements

The idea for this book began when I was investigating the Special Operations Executive, the secret wartime agency Churchill created to wage subversive war behind enemy lines. Opening a file in the Public Record Office, I discovered that he had responded so powerfully to John Steinbeck's inspirational fable about European resistance, *The Moon is Down*, that he urged the Royal Air Force to make massive airdrops of small arms and sabotage material to the captive peoples of Hitler's Europe. Coming straight from the heart, Churchill's idea died a bureaucratic death. But my own, to explore his enthusiasm for the work of Britain's many secret services in both peace and war, survived. Other books and responsibilities intervened, and only recently was I able to return it. In a project spanning so many years, I have accumulated numerous debts to many people and institutions.

Financially, research was assisted by a grant from the Social Sciences and Humanities Research Council of Canada. Professor Peter Jones of the Institute for Advanced Studies in the Humanities and Professor Malcolm Anderson of the International Social Sciences Institute, both at the University of Edinburgh, kindly provided me with accommodation and research facilities, and I am grateful to them and their staffs for much generosity and support; in particular to Anthea Taylor, Dilys Rennie and Julie Leech. The National Library of Scotland with its courteous and efficient staff has been a pleasure to work in, and the same may be said for the Churchill Archives Centre in Cambridge under its Keeper, Piers Brendon, and Archivist, Alan Kucia. All extracts from the letters, speeches and other writings of Sir Winston S. Churchill are reproduced with permission of Curtis Brown Ltd., on behalf of The Estate of Sir Winston S. Churchill. (Copyright Winston S. Churchill.)

Extracts from the writings of Randolph S. Churchill are reproduced with permission of Curtis Brown Ltd., on behalf of The Estate of Randolph Churchill. (Copyright The Estate of Randolph Churchill.) These extracts are also reproduced with permission of Curtis Brown Ltd., on behalf of C&T Publications Ltd. (Copyright C&T Publications Ltd.) The Public Record Office in Kew has responded to my many demands on its services promptly and efficiently, as has the Scottish Record Office; Crown copyright material in the Public Record Office is reproduced by kind permission of the Controller of Her Majesty's Stationery Office, including letter HW 1/1 that appears on page 192, and material from the Godfrey papers by permission of the Trustees of the National Maritime Museum. Dr Ian Armour and Irene Lynch, who helped with much of the research, exhibited exemplary resourcefulness and perseverance, and I am deeply indebted to them both.

I am most grateful to the Lady Soames and Churchill College, Cambridge, for granting me permission to consult and quote from the Spencer-Churchill papers; to the Rt. Hon. Sir Hector Monro, his grandson, for granting access to and permission to quote from the papers of Major-General Sir John Spencer Ewart deposited in the Scottish Record Office; to Julian Sandys for access to the Duncan Sandys papers; to Glasgow University Library, Department of Special Collections, for permission to quote from the MacCallum Scott Diary; to William Hall, for permission to quote from the papers of his grandfather (Admiral 'Blinker' Hall) deposited in Churchill College, Cambridge; to Michael Foot, for help over many years; to Richard Haldane for kindly welcoming me to Cloan and for insights into the life of his great uncle, Richard Burdon Haldane; to J.P.A. Haldane, for permission to use the photograph of Haldane and Churchill; to Professor Jocelyn Hillgarth, for use of the photograph of his father, Alan Hillgarth, and for permission to quote from his letters and to reproduce the telegram on page 323; and to Sir Martin Gilbert, for the photograph of Ralph Wigram and Churchill in the garden at Chartwell, and other help.

With Dr Paul Addison, Director of the Centre for Second World War Studies at the University of Edinburgh, a good and supportive friend, I have enjoyed countless discussions on Churchill, and he also provided an invaluable critique of the manuscript. Andrew Lownie has been everything an author could expect of an agent and more, bringing his own expertise on intelligence to bear in frequent helpful suggestions as the book developed. Grant McIntyre, my editor, has been a pleasure to work with, as have other members of the staff at 50 Albemarle Street, in particular Deborah Licorish, Caroline Westmore, and Stephanie Allen. I am also grateful to my indexer, Susan Hibbert.

Many friends, colleagues and others on both sides of the Atlantic have also helped. In particular I would like to thank Richard Aldrich, Professor Christopher Andrew, Joan Bright Astley, David Boler, Sir Robin Brook, Anthony Montague Browne, Angus Calder, the late Robert Cecil, Martin Clark, Professor Richard Clogg, Sebastian Cox, Robin Denniston, Professor John Ericson, Professor John Ferris, Alan Francis, Jonathan Frewen, Professor J. L. Granatstein, Professor Michael Handel, Professor Peter Hennessy, Nicholas Hiley, Gerard De Groot, Eunan O'Halpin, Sir David Hunt, Lawrence James, Professor Rhodri Jeffreys-Jones, the Rt. Hon. Lord Jenkins of Hillhead, Carol Kenwright, Tarka King, Richard Langworth, Paul Lashmar, Andrew Lycett, Professor James McConville, the late Sir Fitzroy Maclean, Sir Brooks Richards, Mark Seaman, Professor Sergiu Serebriany, Professor Bradley Smith, Professor Denis Smyth, Professor Wesley Wark, David Watson, Professor Donald Cameron Watt, Sir Peter Wilkinson.

Finally I would like to reserve my warmest thanks to Jeanne Cannizzo, my keenest supporter and critic, who has accompanied me through the toil, tears and sweat of my research and writing.

Edinburgh, March 1997

Introduction

In August 1953 a joint operation by Britain's Secret Intelligence Service and the American Central Intelligence Agency overthrew Iran's Prime Minister, Dr Mohammed Musaddiq. The Shah, who had fled to Rome, returned to Tehran in triumph, and London and Washington celebrated a major intelligence coup. The local commander of this cloak-and-dagger affair was CIA officer Kermit Roosevelt, the 35-year-old grandson of Theodore and cousin to Franklin. A week later, over a celebratory lunch at the Connaught Hotel in London, he gave his British colleagues an exhaustive account of events. Then, still exhilarated by his exploits, he made his way to 10 Downing Street to meet the Prime Minister, Winston Churchill.

Churchill had been returned to office for a second term as Prime Minister in 1951. Now, at 78, he was showing his age. Earlier that summer he had suffered a severe stroke, but characteristically defied his medical advisers and soldiered on. The news from Tehran had caught his imagination. Learning that Roosevelt was in London he wanted a personal account of the overthrow of the man whom in private he had mocked as 'Mussy Duck'. Ushered in by an aide, Roosevelt found Churchill lying in bed propped up by pillows. The two men exchanged reminiscences about the last time they had met, at the White House Christmas Party shortly after Pearl Harbor. Then Roosevelt launched into his tale. From time to time Churchill dozed off, only to awake and grill the American on a point of detail. Finally, when Roosevelt had completed his account, Churchill grinned and shifted himself further up on to his pillows. 'Young Man,' he said, 'if I had been but a few years younger, I would have loved nothing better than to have served under your command in this great venture!'[1]

This scene captures the quintessential Churchill of legend: defiant in adversity, overriding the cautious advice of his counsellors, vicariously reliving the adventures of his youth, exulting in the defeat of Britain's enemies, militant in the defence of imperial interests. His horizons encompassed an era when the nuances of shifting loyalties amongst desert factions counted as much as the movements of the navies and armies of the great powers, and when the Iranian desert, like the North-West Frontier of the Indian Empire, was a vital playing field in the Great Game, that murky struggle between the British and Russian Empires of intelligence and clandestine intrigue waged across Central Asia. To Churchill, Operation 'Boot' – the SIS code name – was but the latest episode in this lifetime shadow war.

It was also an Anglo-American operation, a triumphant vindication of the special relationship that Churchill had forged with Franklin Roosevelt during the Second World War. An extraordinary and elaborate network of secret agreements between the intelligence services of the two countries provided the backbone of Western defence in the Cold War. Churchill had been its principal architect and when the diplomats hesitated over Iran he had thrown his weight decisively behind secret-service action. For an ailing man close to the end of his political life he retained a lively interest in the world of intelligence and covert operations. It could hardly be otherwise. He had, after all, been involved in it for some sixty years.

Winston Churchill – as journalist, soldier, politician, statesman, war leader, grand strategist, liberal, imperialist and reactionary – has presented multiple faces to a still-fascinated world. Yet the Churchill I present here is one barely explored before. The Second World War volumes of Sir Martin Gilbert's official biography reveal his fascination for the 'golden eggs' of Ultra delivered by the code-breakers at Bletchley Park, but remarkably little has emerged about his lifelong contacts with the secret service that began before the First World War and extended into his second term as Prime Minister in the 1950s. For all his own voluminous writings, Churchill remained discreet on the subject. Only recently has the veil of official secrecy been lifted to reveal several important new sources.

Outstanding amongst the recently released records of British twentieth-century code-breaking, for example, are the files of Ultra and other intercepts specifically selected for Churchill's daily consumption during the Second World War. His scribbled notes and queries to 'C', the head of the SIS who delivered them personally in a buff-coloured dispatch box, demonstrate the intensity of his interest. As do hundreds of files of the Special Operations Executive

(SOE), created by Churchill in July 1940 'to set Europe ablaze' with the fires of sabotage, subversion and resistance. Here, too, one can trace Churchill's personal hand in operations. Finally, with the completion of the official biography, Churchill's own voluminous papers are now open to public view. Sir Martin Gilbert has completed a magnificent task in publishing much of the material in the companion volumes to his work, but as Churchill himself believed when it came to intelligence, studying raw material can often deliver unexpected dividends – as I have discovered.

To these new sources on Churchill can be added the perspectives provided by those who have done much over the last decade or so to illuminate both the history of intelligence, and the role played by politics and political leaders in creating and using it. Churchill provides an outstanding example of a leader with a powerful faith in its value and what his secret services could deliver.[2] So much so, indeed, that he often demanded to see raw intelligence, regularly threw himself into operational detail, and even employed agents of his own. This is hardly surprising given that he had been a spy himself in the 1890s and had been personally briefed on Britain's new Secret Service Bureau within weeks of its formation in 1909. His habit of using private sources of intelligence to complement that of the official secret services continued into the 1950s.

Churchill's use of intelligence has not gone entirely unnoticed, however, and critics have frequently cried foul. The most notorious case is Pearl Harbor, where conspiracy theorists have argued that he deliberately withheld information predicting the Japanese attack in order to force the United States into war. A resilient popular myth also maintains that Coventry, the target of a mass bombing raid by the *Luftwaffe* in 1940, was another of his intelligence sacrificial lambs. Warned in advance, the argument goes, he permitted the deaths of hundreds of innocent civilians in order to protect the top-secret source. Such stories are not confined to the Second World War. In 1914 Churchill was First Lord of the Admiralty. The United States under Woodrow Wilson remained determinedly neutral, and to win over American hearts and loosen their purse strings the British mounted a major propaganda offensive to depict the Germans as enemies of democracy and humanity. Then, in May 1915, a German U-boat torpedoed the Cunard liner *Lusitania*, drowning twelve hundred passengers, including over one hundred Americans. American opinion swung heavily against the Germans. Churchill received signals intelligence about U-boat movements. Hence, it has been claimed, he must have deliberately concealed information about the impending attack. None of these conspiracy theories survives the test of evidence, but they reveal a widespread belief in the power of intelligence to shape events and Churchill's willingness to be ruthless in using it.

If the manipulation of intelligence for reasons of callous *realpolitik* is a charge frequently levelled against him, so is that of indulging a romantic fascination with cloak-and-dagger operations as exemplified in his creation of the SOE in 1940 to wage unorthodox war behind enemy lines. Over the next five years he frequently made time in his overcrowded schedule to meet personally secret agents who had parachuted into enemy territory. He was familiar with such dangers, for as a young man he had been shot at by Cuban guerrillas and had faced death in various skirmishes on the fringes of Empire. His daring escape from a prisoner-of-war camp during the Boer War had made him a household name even before he entered Parliament in 1900. British air crew during the Second World War even carried a reminder of his exploits in their escape kit, with instructions on what to do if on the run behind enemy lines.

The adrenalin excitement of action never left him. In Cairo in 1943 his enthusiasm for Marshal Tito and the Yugoslav partisans derived from meeting those who handled intelligence reports from the Balkans, men later parachuted into the hills of Bosnia. When his own son Randolph was dropped into Yugoslavia, Churchill told Tito wistfully how much he regretted not being able to take part himself. Later, when he feared that aid to the French resistance was flagging, one of SOE's legendary secret agents, Wing Commander Forrest Yeo-Thomas (the 'White Rabbit'), engineered a meeting. Granted five minutes, he hypnotised Churchill with his tales of secret service. Over an hour later he emerged with the promise of vastly increased support for the Maquis.

Magnificent, but was it war? – *effective* war, that is. Or was it not a waste of lives and, too often, a foolish betrayal of Britain's true interests? Was Churchill not carried away by his romantic enthusiasm for guerrilla warfare to support Tito and the partisans and thus deliver Yugoslavia into Communist hands? And did his support for resistance not recklessly encourage hopeless acts of bravado – such as the 1944 uprisings in Warsaw, Slovakia and the Vercors, France – that saw the deaths of thousands of brave patriots at trifling cost to German occupiers? As the Second World War has receded in memory such charges against him have moved to the fore. How should we judge this aspect of Churchill's fascination with secret service?

Whatever the verdict, it is undeniable that Churchill combined a creative strategic imagination drawn to the unorthodox with an unerring instinct for the importance of intelligence. An essential part of statecraft, it has been said, is the importance of *knowing*.[3] And of the main three Allied leaders – Churchill, Roosevelt and Stalin – he was by far and away the most effective user of his intelligence services. Hitler trusted only his own intuition, never read agents' reports, and preferred to divide and rule his intelligence chiefs by setting them at each other's throats. Stalin was blinded by ideology, and Roosevelt feasted only fitfully on the rich pickings of American code-breakers. Amongst twentieth-century British politicians – indeed, all leaders of the major powers – Churchill is unique in consistently relishing and realising the potential of intelligence, in all its forms, in both peace and war.

Churchill's intense curiosity about the world around him fuelled a voracious and lifelong appetite for information that would define whatever passion consumed him at the time. As a young officer in the late-Victorian Army he doubled as a journalist, seeking out news that would make sense of his experience – and further his ambitious programme of self-promotion. As a rising-star politician before the First World War he frequently astonished his contemporaries with his obsession. Most politicians of that era took their leisure time seriously, retreating for long periods to the grouse moors or golf links. Not Churchill: he disliked holidays and once declared that he would not mind being condemned to live for ever within the square mile that encompassed Westminster. Even on honeymoon in Venice in 1908 he dismayed his wife by preferring the newspaper stalls to the splendours of the Grand Canal.

As a minister he taxed his civil servants to exhaustion with his relentless demands. To be prepared for often hostile questions across the floor of the House of Commons, he needed the security of proper briefings. When real war raised the stakes to life-or-death, he followed the intelligence files closer than any of his colleagues, and made it his business to know intimately the leading personalities, sources and agencies. He carried this legacy through to peacetime, in the 1920s avidly reading secret intercepts of Soviet communications revealing Communist plots in Britain and the Empire. During the

1930s he established a private intelligence network to track Nazi rearmament which rivalled that of the official government.

Once installed as Britain's war leader in 1940 he immediately revitalised the intelligence services, enthusiastically consumed his 'golden eggs' and masterminded the London–Washington intelligence alliance. This relationship led the Cold War fight against the Soviet Union and he remained in touch with the intelligence world even while in opposition from 1945 to 1951. Then, back in Downing Street, and his old wartime comrade General Dwight D. Eisenhower in the White House, he demonstrated again his appetite for secret intelligence with the coup in Iran, spy flights over the Soviet Union, and other exploits.

Alongside his natural curiosity Churchill possessed a vivid imagination that often led him into dead ends and to make errors. But it also provided great flashes of insight and brilliance. 'There is required for the composition of the great commander', he wrote in *The World Crisis*, 'not only imagination but also an element of legerdemain, an original and sinister touch, which leaves the enemy puzzled as well as beaten.' Desmond Morton, the SIS officer who fed him intelligence in the 1930s and served as his conduit to the secret services during the Second World War, noted how he adored 'funny operations'. Secret intelligence, deception, special operations, double-cross systems, commando raids and guerrilla actions all received his enthusiastic support as complements, and frequently alternatives, to the work of the Armed Forces. Additionally, such stratagems provided that adrenalin buzz. Even before public revelations about Allied triumphs in Ultra intelligence surfaced some twenty years ago, Ronald Lewin, in his study of Churchill as warlord, noted how 'all that was romantic in him . . . thrilled to the excitement of intercepted signals, delphic reports from agents, the broken code, the sense of participation'.[4]

The same impulse also drew him to mavericks and buccaneers, unorthodox figures who defied convention. In politics, it explained his friendship with Beaverbrook and Birkenhead; in strategy, his support for characters such as T. E. Lawrence and Orde Wingate; in the secret war, his fascination for Boris Savinkov, Sidney Reilly and Michael Collins. His attraction to nihilists and terrorists sat ill with his conservative instincts for law and order. But they appealed to his craving for the flamboyant, the adventuresome, the unusual, the unconventional; cloaked in secrecy, their attraction was doubly potent.

If Churchill's fascination for secret war throws light on his character, so it illuminates crucial chapters in the history of Britain's modern secret services. These have grown from a handful of men working from improvised Whitehall offices on the eve of the First World War, into multimillion-pound operations employing thousands of professionals housed in state-of-the-art headquarters linked to networks around the globe. But this bureaucratic growth was never as independent of politicians as they have liked to pretend. 'Plausible deniability' – the principle that ministers should be able to deny knowledge of intelligence operations – should not disguise the fact that the secret services have flourished with their often keen support.

Churchill played a far more important and active part in the creation of Britain's modern intelligence community than is generally recognised. Both as a Liberal and as a Conservative he believed in a strong state and an intelligence service to go with it. As President of the Board of Trade in 1909 he was a member of the Cabinet when the Secret Service Bureau was created, and as Home Secretary he willingly provided Vernon Kell, head of its counter-espionage section (later MI5) with the surveillance weapons he demanded to deal with German spies. It was Churchill who first authorised the clandestine interception of mail through general warrants and who chaired the committee that spawned the draconian 1911 Official Secrets Act. At the Admiralty he keenly supported Kell's war against German spies targeting the Royal Navy and its installations. When war broke out in August 1914 he quickly seized on the importance of Signals Intelligence (SIGINT) and created Room 40 to handle it. From then on it became his lifelong habit to read special intelligence reports whenever he could. If any single politician can be credited with nursing Britain's secret service through its infancy, it is Churchill.

With his contacts thus well established in early and middle age, Churchill entered a familiar world when he assumed the mantle of leader in 1940. It did not make him uncritical of his intelligence advisers. Far from it. He held firmly to the principle that such information should be the servant and not the master of policy. His hunger for it was always shaped to a purpose. This was well expressed by Isaiah Berlin in a compelling portrait he wrote at the time: 'He has an immense capacity for absorbing facts but they emerge transformed by the categories which he powerfully imposes on the raw material . . .'[5] Displeased by MI5 intelligence, one of Churchill's first acts was to fire Vernon Kell. Later on he frequently challenged the judgements of the Joint Intelligence Committee and often dictated unpalatable directives to the Special Operations Executive. Despite this – perhaps because of it – he understood the personalities and machinery of the intelligence world, saw the secret services as vital tools of policy, and effectively harnessed them to the war effort.

Victory brought him personal defeat in the 1945 General Election. During the electoral campaign he had claimed that a Labour government would herald a British Gestapo. Ironically he had done more than most to grant generous powers to the security service. This reflected the darker side to his imagination. For a man so frequently and mistakenly accused of conspiracy, he was prone to suspicion and readily believed in the existence of a foreign spy menace. This was true in both world wars. Before 1914 he uncritically embraced Kell's nightmares of such an army preparing the way for a German invasion. After the Bolshevik Revolution he trembled at the prospect of Communist subversion. And in 1940, so convinced was he of the dangers of a German Fifth Column that he encouraged the internment or shipment overseas of thousands of aliens. Fundamentally a humane man, he soon came to regret this – but not until fear of a German invasion had passed and the defeat of Hitler was in sight.

What Churchill did for intelligence seems clear: out of the Second World War came a centralised apparatus geared fully to serving the interests of the state. But what did intelligence do for him? If it helps a leader, he will use it. If not, he will ignore or suppress it. To what extent did he manipulate intelligence for his own survival and advancement, wielding it against political rivals and opponents? In what ways did he exploit it to his country's advantage, not merely in war against enemies but in conflicts with friends? He forged a great and historic alliance with the United States. But where did intelligence fit into the London–Washington special relationship, and was he as open-handed in sharing secret intelligence with the Americans as he later claimed? And what about other allies such as the Free French, the Soviets, the Commonwealth? How did the intelligence game play there? What, in short, were the mutual benefits at work in Churchill's lifelong passion for secret service?

I

Adventure

When first in the dim light of early morning I saw the shores of Cuba rise and define themselves from dark-blue horizons, I felt as if I sailed with Long John Silver and first gazed on Treasure Island. Here was a place where real things were going on. Here was a scene of vital action. Here was a place where anything might happen. Here was a place where something would certainly happen. Here I might leave my bones.[1]

The date was November 1895. Winston Churchill had just sailed into Havana harbour, dominated by the great El Moro fortress high up on the cliffs commanding the channel to the port. Cuba had begun its final and successful attempt to throw off Spanish rule. In the mountains of central Cuba a guerrilla army led by the veteran rebel General Maximo Gomez was holding down a Spanish army of some 250,000 men under Marshal Martinez Campos. It was already clear that the Spaniards could not crush the insurrection. Two years after Churchill left, the sinking of the US battleship the *Maine* in the same harbour brought the United States into the struggle. It also drew in Theodore Roosevelt who cut a spectacular figure with his 'Rough Riders', a voluntary cavalry unit made up of cowboys, Ivy League footballers, New York policemen and Native Americans. The Spanish-American war won Roosevelt the Governorship of New York, the Republican Vice-Presidency and eventually the White House. It also destroyed the last remnants of Spain's once mighty New World empire, gave Cuba its independence, and brought the Americans on to the world stage as a major power.

Here, indeed, was a scene of vital action and stirring world events. Churchill did not leave his bones in Cuba, but quite apart from discovering the joys of Havana cigars, rum cocktails and afternoon siestas, he first experienced the thrill of war, marched against an enemy, found himself under fire and witnessed violent death. For this instinctive soldier it was his first great adventure and he relished every minute.

Cuba also brought his first encounter with popular revolt against dictatorship, guerrilla warfare, and underground resistance and intelligence. If any single episode captivated the youthful Churchill with the adventure and mystery of secret service, it was his few weeks in what he romantically called 'The Pearl of the Antilles'.

Nor is it irrelevant that it coincided with his first journey across the Atlantic. Despite his aristocratic origins and his own enduring fascination with his English heritage, he was half-American. His Brooklyn-born mother, Jennie Jerome, was the daughter of swashbuckling New York lawyer and financier Leonard Jerome, founder of the American Jockey Club, part owner of the *New York Times* and creator of the Bronx racing track. A society beauty with many admirers, Jennie spent most of her life in Europe, squandered the Jerome fortune, neglected Winston, and left him with an obsessive need to make his own financial way in life. His father, Lord Randolph Churchill, also left scars. The second son of the seventh Duke of Marlborough, he briefly illuminated the political scene as the founder of 'Tory Democracy' and Chancellor of the Exchequer. In 1886 he impulsively resigned and never enjoyed office again. He died just a few months before Churchill arrived in Havana. Arrogant, rude, impulsive, and known as the 'Champagne Charlie of politics', he rarely saw his elder son and often treated him harshly. But Lord Randolph did him one service. After an unhappy time at Harrow, he was sent to the Royal Military College at Sandhurst. He had always been fascinated with soldiers, not unusual for a boy brought up in the heyday of Empire. His nursery was strewn with toy soldiers – 'all British, organised as an infantry division with a cavalry brigade' – and the earliest surviving letter to his mother, written as a 7-year-old, touchingly thanks her for 'the beautiful presents those Soldiers and Flags and Castle'.[2] At Sandhurst he did well, graduating twentieth out of a class of 130 students. A successful military career beckoned. Early in 1895 he was commissioned as a Second Lieutenant in the 4th Hussars cavalry regiment. In anticipation of several years' service in India he was given ten weeks' immediate leave.

Already he was exhibiting one of his major character traits: a horror of boredom. More importantly, he knew what he wanted: to enter politics and expunge the humiliation of his father's career. His strategy was simple, direct and unconcealed in its ambition. He would make his name in war, both as a soldier and as a war correspondent. The reward would be headlines and a record of personal bravery – a sure ticket to Parliament. The strategy was astute, and it worked. Within five years he was in the House of Commons, launched on a fifty-year career that would take him to the summit of politics and the heroic leadership of his country during the Second World War.

The wars he encountered deeply coloured his military outlook and strategic thinking, for these were not the great clashes of European armies. They were frontier battles on the edge of empire where the regular forces met their match at the hands of guerrillas, and science and technology could not win the hearts and minds of rebellious peoples. Churchill knew where his loyalties lay as an ardent patriot sworn to defend Britain's imperial power. At the age of 11 he had shared the national dismay at news of Gordon's death at Khartoum, he had stood in the crowd to celebrate Victoria's Golden Jubilee in 1887, and had avidly read the adventure stories of Rider Haggard and G. A. Henty. But from personal experience he learned a profound respect for the rebellious and an acute awareness of the damage they could inflict on imperial rule. All this was to play its part in his fascination for the secret world.

Casting around for the first small war, he heard news of the Cuban revolt. This, combined with curiosity about his mother's birthplace, drew him across the Atlantic. Before leaving England he contracted with the London *Daily Graphic* to publish his dispatches from the front, gained accreditation with the Spanish Army, and persuaded friend and fellow subaltern Reginald Barnes to go with him.

The two young men sailed from Liverpool. Typically, Churchill barely endured the boredom of several days at sea. In New York things changed dramatically. They were regaled for a week by Bourke Cochran, a wealthy Irish-American lawyer and congressman who had challenged Grover Cleveland for the Democratic nomination in 1892. They met Supreme Court judges, were received by the Vanderbilts, dined at the Waldorf and visited West Point military academy. They also encountered a vibrant and bustling democratic energy that deeply impressed Churchill. 'This is a very great country, Jack', he wrote to his younger brother. 'Not pretty or romantic but great and utilitarian.'[3]

From New York Churchill and Barnes travelled by train to Key West and embarked for Havana. Their visit had been well planned. They met the British Consul-General in Havana and the next day set off by train for Marshal Campos's headquarters at Santa Clara. For the next two weeks they observed guerrilla war at first hand.

Churchill's main task was to provide readers of the *Daily Graphic* with dramatic copy and a name to remember. But he also had another mission. Before leaving London he had paid a visit to Colonel Edward Chapman, the Director of Military Intelligence and a veteran of the Afghan and Burmese wars. Chapman briefed Churchill on the situation in Cuba and provided the two young men with maps. He added that it would be helpful if they could 'collect information and statistics on various points and particularly as to the effect of the new bullet – its penetration and striking power', thus giving their visit a quasi-official status. Thus, Churchill's first overseas mission fell into the well-established tradition of the British amateur spy sent overseas with instructions to keep his eyes and ears open.[4]

The elusive nature of the war quickly impressed him. 'Where are the enemy?' he asked the young Spanish officer delegated to escort them. 'Everywhere and nowhere' came the response. His first report for the *Graphic* captured the mood. His attempts to reach Campos's headquarters at Santa Clara were severely hampered by rebel attacks on the railroad. One of their favourite tricks was to derail passing trains by pulling on wires fastened to loosened rails. They were also using dynamite. The Spaniards responded by attaching pilot engines and armoured cars to the trains. This offered no guarantee. A train carrying Campos's Chief of Staff was blown off the tracks and Churchill's journey had to be diverted via the coast. The alternative route was little safer. Again the line was cut when the rebels destroyed a small bridge and Churchill had to wait for a day while it was repaired. 'These thirty miles of railway are the most dangerous and disturbed in the whole island', he told *Graphic* readers. 'Twenty-eight separate little forts and over 1,200 men are employed in the railroad's protection, but in spite of all these precautions communication is dangerous and uncertain . . .' Only the week before, the rebel leader Maximo Gomez had personally led a raid on one of the forts and forced the garrison to surrender. The luckless Spanish officer in charge faced an official firing squad.

The countryside was littered with evidence of the insurrection. Churchill saw burned houses, broken-down fences, and occasionally sighted on the spur of a hill or on the edge of the forest some lone horseman spying on the Spaniards. Ten days into their visit, after sleeping in the fortified village of Arroyo Blanco, news arrived that

Gomez and 4,000 rebels were encamped a few miles to the east. The column set off in the early-morning mist. Suddenly at the rear firing broke out. Churchill could see smoke and flashes, but it was all some distance away and soon died out. It was the first time that he had heard shots fired in anger. It was also his twenty-first birthday.

More escapades followed. The horse behind him was felled by a shot from a guerrilla sniper. Rebels attacked while he and Barnes were swimming in a river half-dressed; they were forced to scramble away from the bullets. That night a shot came through the thatched roof of the barn in which they were sleeping, while outside several Spaniards were killed or wounded. On the final day there was a small battle with the rebels which Churchill watched from the safety of horseback a few hundred yards away. After much noise and a few wounded, the rebels slipped away into the impenetrable jungle. The insurgents, Churchill concluded, could never be caught or defeated. At the rate Campos was proceeding, he guessed, it would take even the Kaiser and the entire German army twenty years to crush the revolt.

The enemy, indeed, was everywhere and nowhere. Churchill was now witnessing what history had taught him. Napoleon had come to grief in Spain at the hands of guerrillas who sapped the morale of the French armies. Now the Spaniards were suffering: they could rarely pin down the rebels, but the guerrillas always knew where to find them. The reason was good and comprehensive intelligence, due largely to the sympathy of the population. 'Hence they know everything', Churchill observed, 'the position of every general, the destination of every soldier, and what their own spies fail to find out their friends in every village let them know.' Moreover, the rebels were able to paralyse the economy. The sugar cane was ripe and combustible – they only had to give the word and the plantations would go up in flames.

Churchill's youthful heart was with the rebellion, but he also feared it. On the one hand the entire Spanish administration was utterly corrupt. Yet reluctant to dismiss the rebels, as did the Spaniards, as mere banditti, he deplored their tactics and feared their victory might bring a bankrupt government, racial violence and revolution. He desired the end, but flinched from the means. He could only hope for a compromise that would produce a free, prosperous and law-abiding island.[5]

This first great adventure left an indelible mark. Back in the somnolent heat of Bangalore he wrote a revealing novel entitled *Savrola*, at once a typical Victorian Ruritanian romance, a perceptive bio-graphical confession and a revealing glimpse of his political views. Savrola, a young and dashing aristocrat, leads a popular revolt against the aged and autocratic President Molara of the Republic of Laurania. The revolt succeeds and the President is killed, but then Savrola is rejected by the people and leaves the country with Lucille, Molara's beautiful young widow, the only woman he loves. Eventually when order is restored they return, and peace and prosperity descend on Laurania.

Savrola is clearly advertising copy for Churchill. To his brother Jack, Churchill described him as 'the Great Democrat, a wild sceptic with an equally powerful imagination'. But what drives the character is the inner demon of ambition and a spirit that knows 'rest only in action, contentment only in danger, and in confusion [finds its] only peace'. Churchill had already diagnosed the 'Black Dog' of depression that would plague him throughout his life. Politically, the novel echoes the liberal views on rebellion of his Cuban reporting.[6]

Yet there is a rarely noticed sub-plot. Amongst the rebels moves the extremist revolutionary Karl Kreutze – clearly an outsider in this Latin-cum-Balkan paradise – who heads a secret society manipulating the people's discontent for sinister socialist ends. It is Kreutze who murders Molara and, although he in turn is killed, the extremists succeed in forcing Savrola into exile. Here, as in real-life Cuba, Churchill raises the spectre of 'bad' rebels who threaten peace and prosperity. During the Second World War he would lend his enthusiastic support to movements of national revolt against Nazi occupation, such as the Yugoslav partisans and the French Maquis. But he adamantly opposed those he considered to be 'extremists', such as the Greek partisans. Significantly he regularly condemned them as 'banditti' – the contemptuous term used fifty years before by his Spanish hosts.

In the summer of 1897, as Britain celebrated Queen Victoria's Diamond Jubilee, Afghan rebels rose in revolt on the North-West Frontier of India to threaten British control of the Malakand Pass, the gateway to Chitral. The aptly named Colonel Sir Bindon Blood was placed at the head of a punitive expeditionary force and Churchill again rushed to the scene of action. Armed with commissions from the *Daily Telegraph* and the Allahabad *Pioneer* he was soon in the thick of things.

He was immediately struck by the parallels with Cuba. The military problem facing the Spaniards differed little from that presented by the wild Afghan landscape: 'a roadless, broken, and undeveloped country; an absence of any strategic points; a well-armed enemy with great mobility and modern rifles, who adopt guerrilla tactics.'[7]

Everything about the Malakand Field Force engaged his romantic spirit: the breathtaking grandeur of the western Hindu Kush – the high mountain passes and lonely valleys, the snow-covered peaks, the steep and rugged slopes gouged out by the rains – as well as the rugged tribesmen with their ancient carbines. Here for a brief moment he was able to play the Great Game, a world of intrigue where every man was a warrior, every house a fortress, every family waged its vendetta and every clan nourished its feud. Agents and informers for the Indian Army, like Kipling's *Kim*, provided eyes and ears throughout the land, and political officers exploited enmities between rival factions to maintain an uneasy imperial peace.

This time, however, advance intelligence had failed the Indian Army. Partly this was the understandable result of discounting mere rumour, as Churchill noted in *The Malakand Field Force*, his published account of the affair. 'The bazaars of India, like the London coffee houses of the last century, are always full of marvellous tales – the invention of fertile brains. A single unimportant fact is exaggerated, and distorted, till it becomes unrecognisable. From it, a thousand wild, illogical, and fantastic conclusions, are drawn. So the game goes on.'[8] The secular minds of Western intelligence officers were also to blame for failing to appreciate the depth of religious feeling amongst the Muslim population. To the very last, none had expected more than a skirmish. It was Churchill's first lesson in the inevitability of surprise and the fallibilities of even the most experienced intelligence officers.

He learned a good deal more about the intricacies of the Great Game from Captain Henry Stanton, one of Blood's intelligence officers, who proved an invaluable friend and guide, 'a good fellow and full of knowledge of all sorts'. He was certainly an important figure in Churchill's introduction to intelligence work. Long forgotten, Stanton's official report on the work of the Intelligence Department with the Malakand Field Force still resides in War Office files.[9] It is notable for its generous tribute to the intelligence work of local agents such as Abdul Hamid Khan, 'of good Afghan refugee family which for three generations has been conspicuous for its loyalty in Government service'. Fluent in English, Persian, Hindustani and Pushtu, he was, Stanton noted with satisfaction, both intelligent and discreet, and his knowledge of frontier peoples proved crucial to the British. Churchill borrowed some of its conclusions. It was a practice in the Indian Army for political officers under civilian control to be attached to field forces to conduct local negotiations and collect information. Echoing the identical criticism from Stanton's report, Churchill concluded that intelligence should be the exclusive preserve of the Army's Intelligence Department. The collection of information was one of the most important of military duties, he noted, and civilian officers could hardly be expected to understand what a general required. In short, he concluded from his Malakand experience that intelligence and operations were intimately linked, and that the former should be firmly controlled by those who had to act on it.[10]

A different kind of war presented itself in 1898. Sir Herbert Kitchener and the Egyptian Army had been advancing up the Nile towards Khartoum since 1896 and Churchill was desperate to join the expedition. After pulling every string conceivable he arrived in Cairo with a commission in the 21st Lancers and accreditation as a war correspondent from the *Morning Post*. He caught up with Kitchener's army a week before the battle of Omdurman. He found himself in the thick of it, his journalist's eye hard at work. 'The whole scene flickered exactly like a cinematograph picture', he wrote, 'and besides, I remember no sound. The event seemed to pass in absolute silence.'[11] He was appalled by the scenes of carnage. Three days later he reconnoitred the battlefield. Heaps of bodies lay festering in the desert heat, while hundreds of the wounded and dying begged for help and pleaded for water. Here, he realised, was no glory. His massive and compelling two-volume history of the expedition, *The River War* (1899), he aptly described as 'a tale of blood and war'.

Churchill went out of his way to credit Egyptian Army intelligence for its role in Kitchener's victory. In part this was no more than politic. During the march up the Nile he had received generous hospitality from Colonel (later Sir Reginald) Wingate, head of the Intelligence Branch, while in London the Directorate of Military Intelligence provided the maps and plans for his book. Its *Handbook of the Soudan 1898* and *Report on the Nile 1898*, prepared by leading intelligence officer Lord Edward Gleichen, provided him with essential background. But Churchill's praise extended to an enthusiastic appreciation of what intelligence and espionage could contribute to the efforts of regular forces. 'Up the great river', he wrote, 'within the great wall of Omdurman, into the arsenal, into the treasury, into the mosque, into the Khalifa's house itself, the spies and secret agents of the Government – disguised as traders, as warriors, or as women – worked their stealthy way.'[12] He was not merely referring to Wingate's espionage on the Nile in the abstract. Twenty-five miles north of Omdurman, and two days before the battle itself, he had had an extraordinary encounter with a spy.

He was on reconnaisance with a squadron of the 21st Lancers amongst dense bush. A few men armed with carbines dismounted to proceed ahead on foot. After a mile or so, the group halted to take bearings. While they were waiting, Churchill spotted a man in a patched jibbah and armed with several fish-hook spears emerge from the bushes. He immediately ordered a soldier to thrust at the man with a lance, which he skilfully avoided. Then Churchill ordered him to lay down his spears, which he did, and he was marched to the rear. Churchill returned triumphantly to camp with his prisoner. His pride quickly turned to embarrassed humiliation. His captive whom he had almost had killed, it transpired, was no ordinary native but a spy working for Army intelligence in Omdurman. The episode sparked considerable amusement amongst his fellow war correspondents and it took all his persuasion to prevail on the Reuters man not to cable an account of the affair back to London. Not surprisingly, he omitted this misadventure in spy-catching from his later popular memoirs of this period, *My Early Life*.[13] But a year later another escapade brought him headlines and world fame.

War broke out between Britain and the Boers in October 1899. Immediately Churchill sailed for Cape Town. By this time, his ambition clearly set, he had resigned his Army commission and unsuccessfully campaigned for a seat in Parliament. Now, with a lucrative contract from the *Morning Post*, he was headed for Natal and Ladysmith where British troops had been surrounded by the advancing Boers. He got no further on the railway from Durban than Estcourt, where he met an old friend from North-West Frontier days, Captain Aylmer Haldane, who had just been ordered to take an armoured train and reconnoitre up the line in the direction of Ladysmith. Churchill reluctantly agreed to accompany him, and at dawn they set off into Boer territory.

Subsequent events became legendary. Boer saboteurs derailed two of the train's trucks with a boulder laid across the line. Churchill, under heavy fire, succeeded in clearing the line, but then he, Haldane and about fifty men got separated from the engine, were taken prisoner by the Boers and ended up in an officers' camp housed in the State Model School in Pretoria, capital of the enemy Transvaal. After his attempts to win freedom as a war correspondent failed, Churchill joined an escape attempt by Haldane and an Afrikaans-speaking man called Sergeant Brockie. Churchill succeeded in scaling the wall, but his two companions gave up their efforts after the sentry became suspicious.

Without maps, compass or food, and with no knowledge of Afrikaans, Churchill decided to go it alone and headed for the border with Portuguese East Africa and its capital Lourenço Marques, some 300 miles through enemy territory. Making his way through Pretoria's night-time streets and guiding himself by the stars, he found the railway line to the coast. By jumping on and off goods trains and encountering a sympathetic manager who hid him down a mine until the hullabaloo over his escape had died down, he finally reached freedom. By this time the Boers had put a price on his head and the British newspapers had blazoned his escape across the headlines. His arrival back in Durban was greeted with hysteria in the popular press.

Churchill had little doubt what was needed for victory: greater flexibility, more imagination and unorthodox military methods, as well as more men. More irregular corps should join the fight. As for himself he arranged a commission in the South African Light Horse, just the sort of force he had in mind, with whom he experienced the bloody battle of Spion Kop and witnessed the relief of Ladysmith – a campaign he described as one of the happiest memories of his life. The siege over, he hastened to join the final triumphant march from Bloemfontein to Pretoria. By this time the Boers had launched a campaign of partisan warfare, forming hundreds of small commando groups to harass the British. Joining General Sir Ian Hamilton's forces, the next six weeks of adventure provided vivid memories that endured a quarter of a century later. The climax came when Churchill entered Johannesburg even before the Boer forces had left. In advance of the main force, and in the company of a young Frenchman who knew the way, he bicycled into the city. Dusk was falling, but the streets were still crowded with armed and mounted Boers. It occurred to him that once again he was behind enemy lines, but this time he was a British officer holding a commission and disguised in plain clothes. If caught he could be tried and shot as a spy. Preoccupied by these thoughts, and pushing his bike up a steep incline, he suddenly became aware of being slowly overtaken by an armed Boer on horseback. Looking as casual and unconcerned as possible, and talking French to his companion, he steadily met the Boer's curious gaze. It seemed like an eternity as the three of them climbed the hill, then the horseman finally galloped off. Churchill was not, after all, to be unmasked as a spy. Four days later Pretoria capitulated and he personally helped liberate his old prison at the State Model School. Two weeks later he left South Africa to fight a General Election.[14]

He left behind a protracted campaign that was to drag on for two more years. For Churchill, the war simply confirmed the lessons of Cuba and the North-West Frontier. Armed guerrillas fighting with the support of the people could thwart the ambitions of even a great and powerful empire. The conviction had a lifelong effect on his strategic thinking. Some forty years later, when creating the Special Operations Executive, images of heroic Boer resistance helped animate his vision. And in personally meeting its secret agents, he relived his adventures behind enemy lines in the golden days of his youth.

Queen Victoria died at Windsor Castle in January 1901. Several thousand miles away Churchill heard the news in Winnipeg, on the last leg of a North American tour lecturing on his wartime adventures. He had met President McKinley in Washington and Theodore Roosevelt, the soon-to-be President, in the governor's mansion in Albany, New York. Mark Twain and his American namesake, the novelist Winston Churchill, had chaired meetings in New York City and Boston. Christmas he spent in Ottawa with the Governor-General of Canada and his wife, Lord and Lady Minto. He had already been elected as Conservative Member of Parliament for Oldham and he left New York for London on the day of the Queen's funeral. At 26 he was a celebrity, eager to embark on the political career of which he had long dreamed.

Churchill's rapid climb to the top of British politics over the next decade left observers breathless. G. W. Steevens, war correspondent of the *Daily Mail* who had sailed with him back to England from the

Sudan, dashed off a character sketch describing him as 'the youngest man in Europe'. At the rate Churchill was advancing, he predicted, 'there will hardly be room for him in Parliament at thirty or in England at forty'.[15] This was not far from the mark. Four years after entering Parliament Churchill deserted the Conservatives for the Liberals. Their election victory in 1906 saw him appointed Under-Secretary for the Colonies. Two years later, aged 33, he entered the Cabinet as President of the Board of Trade. Within two years he was Home Secretary, the youngest to hold the position since Sir Robert Peel some eighty years before.

How did his contemporaries see him? J. B. Atkins of the *Manchester Guardian*, who sailed with him to South Africa, caught his physique well: 'slim, slightly reddish-haired, pale, lively, frequently plunging along the deck . . .'[16] Added to that was a slight lisp and stammer, as well as a physical awkwardness, that made for an unprepossessing figure. His open admiration for Napoleon, his palpable ambition and his father's reputation all made him deeply suspect. Controversy accompanied his meteoric rise and opinions ran deep and divided. For his desertion of the Conservative Party Tories excoriated him as 'the Blenheim rat'. Leo Maxse of the *National Review* styled him as 'a violent and reckless political adventurer'. The *Spectator* denounced him as 'weak and rhetorical, a true demagogue'. Even Liberals distrusted him. Asquith thought he had no real convictions, although he admired him as 'a wonderful creature, with a curious dash of schoolboy simplicity . . . and, what someone said of genius – "a zigzag of lightning on the brain"'. But Margot Asquith, his wife, complained of Churchill's 'noisy mind'. Nearly all critics believed he was too much in love with the limelight, unstable, lacking in judgement, with an excessive yearning for excitement, action and melodrama.[17] An emblematic moment that helped seal this image came with the siege of Sidney Street.

Late in 1910 the police surprised a gang of burglars attempting to break into a jeweller's shop in the East End of London. Three policemen were shot and two badly wounded. One of the criminals was killed and it emerged that he was a member of a gang led by one 'Peter the Painter', a Latvian. Two of its members were traced to a house at Sidney Street in Stepney, who began to fire wildly at the police.

Churchill received the news in his bath and within an hour was at the scene dressed in silk hat and astrakhan coat. Eager for a direct view he took shelter from the shooting in a doorway. One bullet pierced the coat of Patrick Quinn, head of the police Special Branch. Seven hundred police and Scots Guards armed with rifles surrounded the house joined by a horde of journalists, photographers, newsreel cameramen and curious bystanders. One report described Churchill 'moving restlessly hither and thither among the rather nervous and distraught police, a professional soldier among civilians, talking, questioning, advising . . .' The image was caught in countless newspaper photographs and cinema newsreels.

Eventually the house caught fire. Churchill, alarmed for the safety of the fire brigade, instructed it to hold back until the shooting had stopped. When police finally kicked their way into the burned-out interior they found two bodies, one asphyxiated by smoke, the other shot by a police bullet. They were identified as Fritz Svaars, a Latvian, and William Sokolow, a Russian.

The Tory Opposition poured scorn on Churchill's appearance at the scene and his search for headlines. He later accepted he should have stayed away, but this affair exposed more than his impetuosity. It also revealed his fascination for the mysterious world of anarchists and revolutionaries, the darkness that lurked beneath the surface of Edwardian society. He termed the Sidney Street gang 'a germ cell of murder, anarchy, and revolution . . . pursuing their predatory schemes and dark conspiracies'. Peter the Painter was 'one of those wild beasts who, in later years . . . were to devour and ravage the Russian state and people'. Again, this is typical Churchillian language, but also not so far from the truth. Peter the Painter – or Peter Piatkow, a Latvian painter of street signs – was never caught and was probably far less significant than legend affords. But the larger group comprised mostly Latvian Bolsheviks carrying out 'expropriations' to finance their crusade against Tsarist Russia. Fritz Svaars, one of the Sidney Street dead, was a proven activist, while the man who in fact shot the police at Houndsditch – and who miraculously escaped imprisonment – was Jacob Peters. He was another Latvian Bolshevik who after 1917 became known as the 'Robespierre of the Revolution' as right-hand man to Felix Dzerzhinsky, head of Lenin's secret police the Cheka, where he indulged in an orgy of killing and executions of enemies of the regime before himself falling victim to Stalin's purges.[18]

The Sidney Street siege guaranteed there was no ignoring Churchill. The first biography, written as early as 1905 by Alexander

MacCallum Scott, predicted greatness based on his will, courage, originality and magnetism. Discerning men, wrote Scott, predicted that 'he will make history for the nation. The youth of thirty is confidently spoken of by his admirers as a future Prime Minister . . . he is of the race of Giants. In the tempestuous gambols and soaring ambitions of his youth, we read the promise of a mighty manhood.'[19]

As a minister Churchill demonstrated dynamism and concentration, refused to be browbeaten by civil servants, was a powerhouse of original ideas and successfully pushed his legislation through Parliament. He took risks, showed considerable moral and political courage, and deferred to few. On the eve of the First World War Alfred Gardiner, the influential editor of the Liberal newspaper the *Daily News*, drew a complex portrait.

> He is always unconsciously playing a part, in that fervid and picturesque imagination there are always great deeds afoot . . . He flashes through life taking impressions, swift, searching, detached . . . his mind once seized with an idea works with enormous velocity round it, intensifies it, enlarges it, makes it shadow the whole sky. In the theatre of his mind it is always the hour of fate and the crack of doom . . . [He was] the man of action simply, the soldier of fortune who lives for adventure, loves the fight more than the cause, more even than his ambition or life.

None the less, Gardiner was deeply impressed by Churchill's uncontestable assets. Here was 'a singularly daring and far-sighted man — a mind that sweeps the field with the eye of the strategist, weighs the forces, estimates the position, and when the hour has come strikes with deadly sureness at the vulnerable place'.[20] This also captures his approach to secret service.

2

Secret Service

'The parishes of Fermanagh and Tyrone faded back into the mists and squalls of Ireland, and a strange light began immediately, but by perceptible gradations, to fall and grow upon the map of Europe.' So Churchill remembered the fateful Cabinet meeting on the afternoon of Friday 24 July 1914 when he first caught a glimpse of the approaching Armageddon. A long and inconclusive debate about Ireland had come to its end. Ministers were about to disperse when Sir Edward Grey, the Foreign Secretary, quietly but dramatically announced the news of Austria-Hungary's ultimatum to Serbia. As the implications of a possible European war sank in, Churchill left 10 Downing Street by the garden door and cut across Horse Guards Parade to his office at the Admiralty. On a small piece of headed stationery he wrote out a checklist in preparation for war. Most points involved the disposition of Britain's ships around the world, and questions of supply, ammunition and fuel. But one stood out as different: item 14 was marked, simply, 'K. Espionage'.[1]

Churchill had been a Cabinet member in Asquith's Liberal government for six years. As President of the Board of Trade, Home Secretary and now First Lord of the Admiralty he had been in the forefront of its political and constitutional battles. As Chairman of the Budget League he led the fight, along with his 'terrible twin' and fellow radical, Chancellor of the Exchequer David Lloyd George, for the 1909 People's Budget against the bitter opposition of the House of Lords. During major strikes he ordered troops into coalfields and principal cities and was (wrongly) accused of having ordered soldiers to fire on strikers in South Wales. Suffragettes blamed him for the force-feeding of hunger strikers, and Sidney Street had brought more headlines. Publicity followed him to the Admiralty. Determined to strengthen the Royal Navy he dismissed feisty and resistant admirals, established a Naval War Staff and began construction of the 'Queen Elizabeth'-class battleships with their powerful fifteen-inch guns and oil-driven engines. To guarantee oil supplies he nationalised the Anglo-Persian oil company.

Throughout, he deployed his energies well beyond his departmental responsibilities. For all his youth – at 33 he had become the youngest Cabinet minister for almost fifty years – he was a senior member of the government and a major party strategist. He rarely shrank from confronting an issue, however difficult. Undoubtedly the most intractable was what he called 'the haggard, squalid, tragic Irish quarrel'. The long-expected Irish Home Rule Bill of 1912 opened a Pandora's box. Ulster Unionists threatened resistance, Sir Edward Carson placed himself at the head of the Ulster Volunteers, and in Belfast Churchill had to be protected by troops from an angry crowd. All this had made news headlines.

Behind the scenes, however, he had been deeply involved in virtually unnoticed developments in the realm of national security. Item 14 on his list provided the clue. 'K. Espionage' referred to Vernon Kell and the work of Britain's Secret Service Bureau. Since its foundation in 1909, Churchill had enthusiastically supported its work and given it the weapons it demanded. Most were covert, introduced without parliamentary or public knowledge. Churchill, as well as his biographers, remained largely silent on the subject. But during the five years of peace before 1914 he established a relationship with Britain's intelligence service that was to last for the rest of his political life.

Britain's modern intelligence community was born out of the débâcle of the Boer War and the Anglo-German rivalry of the succeeding years. All the major powers had been hostile to its South African venture, and with the regular army thousands of miles away Britain had been swept by an invasion scare. The nightmare continued to haunt Edwardians. When Anglo-German naval rivalry began in earnest it became acute. The author and civil servant Erskine Childers captured the beginnings of popular unease in 1903 with his surprise bestseller about plans for a German invasion of Britain, *The Riddle of the Sands*. William Le Queux, reputedly Queen Alexandra's favourite novelist, graphically depicted the horrors of German boots on British soil with his 1906 bestseller, *The Invasion of 1910*, which was followed soon after by *Spies of the Kaiser*.

Le Queux's fiction reflected fears emanating from the highest quarters. Lord Roberts of Kandahar, Britain's greatest living military hero, spoke darkly of thousands of German spies paving the way for attack, while Campbell-Bannerman, the Liberal Prime Minister, instructed the Committee of Imperial Defence to examine the invasion threat. Secretly it reported that if Britain ever lost command of the seas the subjection of the country was inevitable. This was designed to reassure, on the grounds that the Royal Navy formed an impenetrable shield around the British Isles. But when his successor, Herbert Asquith, announced the committee's conclusions to the Commons in July 1909 they merely fuelled fears of some sudden catastrophic attack.

Spymania flourished in this climate. Inevitably, like other national-security phobias, it found its way to the Committee of Imperial Defence. In March 1909 Asquith asked Richard Burdon Haldane, the Secretary of State for War, to examine the threat from foreign espionage and recommend ways to counter it.

Haldane was a shrewd Scots lawyer. A portly bachelor, he relished good food and wine and, as he once confessed to Lord Edward Gleichen of War Office intelligence, enjoyed twelve 'super-excellent' cigars a day. But he also had a great capacity for work and the rare ability, for a civilian, to persuade colonels to do his bidding. He had already implemented a major restructuring and modernisation of the Army including the creation of an Expeditionary Force. He believed that most of the spy stories appearing in the press were fantasy. As for those that reached his desk, he astutely guessed that some at least had been concocted by the French in order, as he said, 'to wake us up'. In agreeing to head the espionage inquiry he hoped to reassure public opinion. Instead, within a matter of weeks, both he and his committee had become convinced that the threat was real.

A key figure in the proceedings was Lieutenant-Colonel John Spencer Ewart, Director of Military Operations and Intelligence at the War Office. A veteran of Tel-el-Kebir, Omdurman and the Boer War, since 1906 he had been in charge of strategic planning and intelligence. A sociable and well-connected Scot, he enjoyed a close relationship with Haldane and they frequently lunched or dined together to talk over War Office business. Ewart was obsessed with espionage, both lamenting the lack of British spies abroad and deploring the presence of German spies in Britain. For much of the previous six months he had been laying plans for a new organisation that would handle all its aspects. After Haldane admitted that there was little doubt the German General Staff was systematically collecting information, he seized his chance and suggested the creation of a Secret Service Bureau whose very existence would be kept hidden. In this way, no direct evidence of official dealings with spies could ever come to light. Over that spring and summer, while Churchill and the Liberal government waged war with the Lords over the Budget, a small working group thrashed out the details.

Their work was given a dramatic boost in July 1909 when Sir William Curzon Wylie, political aide-de-camp to Lord Morley, the Secretary of State for India, was assassinated by a Punjabi student after attending an evening event at the Imperial Institute in South Kensington organised by the National Indian Association. There was a public outcry against aliens and demands for the stronger surveillance of political suspects. The Home Secretary, Herbert Gladstone, quietly authorised the Post Office to open telegrams between Britain and India. When Asquith chaired the Committee of Imperial Defence barely three weeks later it quickly approved the formation of the Secret Service Bureau.[2]

Churchill had frequently talked of joining the Intelligence Department while he was in the Army and since leaving South Africa had often spoken publicly about Britain's intelligence weaknesses. During his first three years in Parliament he made his mark with vigorous criticisms of the conduct of the Boer War, aspects of War Office reorganisation, and a plan by St John Brodrick, the Secretary of State for War, to reorganise the Army. A major theme of his attacks was that the Army had failed to capitalise on its intelligence resources both before and during the fight against the Boers, and that more should be done to strengthen intelligence staff.

Churchill was right. The Army's Intelligence Department had been well informed about the Boer Republic's capabilities and plans but had frequently been ignored by High Command. General Sir Redvers Buller, the first Commander-in-Chief of the South African expeditionary force, had curtly returned a copy of the department's manual on South Africa with the comment that he already knew everything there was to know. Predictably, the Royal Commission set up to examine the war concluded that while intelligence had achieved valuable successes it had been considerably undermanned and undervalued.

Long before its conclusions Churchill was pressing the case for reform. As the Boer guerrillas continued to harry British troops on the veld, he urged far greater use of local South Africans (meaning white colonists) who had lived all their lives there and knew the country far better than intelligence officers sent from Britain. 'The whole Intelligence service', he complained in October 1901, 'is starved for want of both money and brains.' He wanted a complete reorganisation of the Intelligence Department headed by someone, soldier or civilian, 'of profound mind and proved business capacity' with a free hand to secure by any means possible the greatest amount of information in regard to the enemy. Six months later he returned to the charge. Vigorously attacking Brodrick's Army estimates in the Commons, he stressed that value for money could best be guaranteed by a first-rate Intelligence Department. By this time he had at least one good source within the department: Captain Aylmer Haldane, his former fellow prison inmate in Pretoria, who was also a cousin of Richard Burdon Haldane. It was probably Haldane, whom he continued to meet privately, who informed him that the British Intelligence Department had only twenty or so officers in contrast to Germany's two hundred. This, Churchill told the Commons, was unacceptable.

> If there was one Department on which money could be spent with advantage it was the Intelligence Department . . . We wanted an Army based on economy; it should be an Army of efficiency, and it should be an Army of elasticity, so that comparatively small regular units in time of peace might be expanded into a great and powerful Army in time of war. For that expansion nothing was more needed than an efficient and well-staffed Intelligence Department.

Churchill's plea fell on deaf ears. As he later complained, expenditure on the department had in fact fallen. Yet his own experience of war had taught him 'on what tiny trifles the fortune of battles depended'. The battle of Spion Kop was a case in point. Had there been dependable maps the troops could have taken up a near-impregnable position. Turning to the larger strategic picture, he also lamented that despite Britain's new alliance with Japan no British officers were being posted there on military fact-finding missions.[3]

By 1909, War Office intelligence had considerably improved, and it was John Spencer Ewart, as Director of Military Intelligence, who was instructed by Haldane to get the new Secret Service Bureau up and running. In August he found space in a small office in Victoria Street, close to Parliament Square. Initially it consisted of two divisions, military and naval; within a year they had been redesignated as 'home' and 'foreign' respectively. Eventually they became more generally known as MI5, or the Security Service, and MI6, or the Secret Intelligence Service (SIS).* In charge of the military division was Captain Vernon Kell, the 36-year-old son of an army officer, who had been a contemporary of Churchill's at Sandhurst. He was to remain head of MI5 for the next thirty years. His opposite number in the naval section was 50-year-old Commander Mansfield Smith-Cumming, usually known as Cumming, or 'C'. Born in India, he was a graduate of the Royal Naval College at Dartmouth and had already carried out occasional intelligence missions for the Navy.

Churchill quickly made contact with the new secret service. As President of the Board of Trade he played no part in the spring or summer discussions, but that September he travelled to Wurzburg at the invitation of the Kaiser to observe the annual German Army manoeuvres. He was overawed. 'This army is a terrible engine', he told his wife Clementine. He returned to Britain with a heightened sense of German power and sombrely told his Cabinet colleagues that Imperial Germany was fast approaching an internal crisis. 'Will the tension be released by moderation', he wondered, 'or snapped by calculated violence?' From then on concern about war steadily began to overshadow his interest in social and domestic affairs.[4]

Haldane seized upon the change in his radical young colleague to mend political fences. In Cabinet he had already fought a hard-won battle against attempts by Churchill and Lloyd George to reduce the Army estimates, and he appreciated the potential significance of Churchill's figures on German finance for the secret service he had fathered. Early in November 1909 he instructed Ewart to meet Churchill to find out more. Six days later the War Office intelligence chief was closeted in Churchill's private office at the Board of Trade.

It was a curious meeting. The Board of Trade was housed in a former private mansion in Whitehall Gardens close to the Committee of Imperial Defence. Churchill occupied the former drawing room, one of the grandest offices he was to occupy in his long political career. On the writing desk between the two men stood the small bronze bust of Napoleon that Churchill took with him from ministry to ministry. Hostile critics took it as a sign of megalomania; to Ewart it might have confirmed his worst fears. Despite his

---

* To avoid confusion by using their ever-changing bureaucratic designations, these will be the terms used throughout this book.

personal respect for Haldane, Ewart detested the Liberal government as a harbinger of socialist revolution. 'I do not see how any patriotic men can continue to support a party which is kept in power by the unnatural combination of Little Englandism, disloyal Fenian Roman Catholics, Welsh and English non-conformists, Temperance fanatics, miscellaneous cranks, and traitors of the Keir Hardie type', he had confided in his diary just the month before. In particular, he entertained a special loathing for 'the terrible twins' of Liberal radicalism: 'It is dreadful to think that we have such men in the Cabinet as Winston Churchill and Lloyd George. The one a half-bred American politician, the other a silly sentimental Celt . . .' Elsewhere, he dismissed Churchill as 'a fussy interfering gasbag'.

He can only have been agreeably surprised by Churchill's sudden concern for national security and the German threat. As for Churchill, notoriously blind to the effect he had on others, he probably saw little further than the uniform in front of him, a fellow veteran of the Sudan and South African campaigns whom he could dazzle with his impressions of the Kaiser's Germany and pump for information about the state of the nation's intelligence. It proved to be a long and productive meeting. Churchill passed on a copy of his secret memorandum to the Cabinet on Germany's finances, and Ewart stressed how useful the Board of Trade could be in helping with intelligence assessments of German strength and intentions. What in particular, Ewart wondered, were its commercial interests and vulnerabilities? Would Germany be likely to respect the neutrality of Belgium and Holland? Would the Board of Trade receive advance notice of abnormal purchases of preserved foods, boots, clothing, horses, medical supplies, and so on, that might signal war? Did they know how many foreigners were resident in Britain? Before he left Whitehall Gardens later that afternoon Ewart had extracted a promise: if he sent a comprehensive list of questions, Churchill would do his best to answer them. Two weeks later Ewart submitted his list and Churchill kept his promise. Summarised by the War Office, the Board of Trade's reply stretched to more than sixty pages. Disappointingly to Ewart, on the all-important question of whether the Board of Trade could guarantee advance notice of war through its economic data, Churchill gave a negative reply. Consular officials in Germany would be particularly useless, he noted, because nearly all were unpaid nationals of the countries concerned.[5]

Shortly after the first meeting of this ill-matched pair the House of Lords threw out Lloyd George's Budget and Asquith called a

General Election. The campaign only deepened Ewart's loathing. 'Torrents of scurrilous and socialist oratory are being poured out upon the country by Lloyd George, Winston Churchill . . . and other demagogues', he wrote in his diary. 'There is an ugly rumour that if the Radicals return to power Winston will come to the War Office. God Forbid . . .'[6] Although the Liberals were returned, Churchill did not go to the War Office. But this did not save Ewart from further contact with him on intelligence matters.

Haldane saw the Secret Service Bureau as merely one component in a far larger national-security package. He also demanded a new Official Secrets Act, closer surveillance of the mail to unmask spies and yield useful intelligence, tighter press censorship to prevent the leakage of sensitive information, and the firm control of aliens. The government, its attention distracted by its fight with the Lords and an election campaign, finally got round to dealing with these issues early in 1910. Then a Cabinet reshuffle saw Churchill promoted to the Home Office. It was a broad portfolio, but at its heart lay responsibility for internal security, the Metropolitan Police and Britain's political police, the Special Branch. It was therefore a logical choice when Asquith appointed him chairman of two separate Committee of Imperial Defence subcommittees to follow up on Haldane's proposals.[7]

To help Churchill in his work was a team of top Whitehall mandarins. Several had served on the espionage committee, including the Director of Naval Intelligence, Rear-Admiral Bethell, and two representatives of the General Staff: Major-General Archibald Murray and Lieutenant-Colonel George Macdonogh. Murray had been an intelligence officer in the Boer War and was to become Chief of Staff of the British Expeditionary Force to France. Macdonogh, an intelligence officer of encyclopaedic knowledge, was to go as Director of Intelligence at GHQ France in 1914 and return as Director of Military Intelligence supervising MI5. Churchill later described him as 'the best Intelligence officer in Europe'.

To brief himself for the work ahead, Churchill not surprisingly turned to Ewart. This time the two men met in Churchill's private room at the House of Commons. Ewart explained some of the basics about Kell's operation. The Secret Service Bureau, Churchill learned, had no executive powers of its own and enjoyed a minimal staff. For that reason it needed the closest possible co-operation of the police to identify, track and if necessary arrest the large number of suspected spies nationwide. This could be done only with Churchill's full support because the Home Office was in regular touch with Chief Constables across the country. Again, Churchill listened carefully and responded generously. He would do anything, he promised, to help.[8]

Ewart's revelations opened Churchill's eyes to secret-service fears about German espionage, but he needed no private lessons on the murky world of secret agents. Scarcely had Kell and Cumming begun their work than a series of revelations about secret operations some twenty years before caused a massive political row. As Home Secretary, Churchill found himself in the eye of the storm.

The furore began with Sir Robert Anderson, a former spymaster in the Home Office. An Anglo-Irishman of passionate Unionist views, he had run undercover operations against Irish Fenians for the Home Office and only eight years before had retired as head of Scotland Yard's Criminal Investigation Department. He had personally run the most successful 'mole' of the Victorian age, secret agent 'Henri Le Caron' who for twenty years was Britain's single most important source of intelligence on Fenian affairs across the Atlantic. Anderson skilfully exploited this remarkable intelligence asset to enhance his career at the Home Office, but all was exposed in 1889 when Le Caron emerged from the shadows to testify as a witness against Parnell. This terminated his career as a spy. Shortly afterwards his autobiography, *Twenty-Five Years in the Secret Service: The Recollections of a Spy*, became a bestseller.

Irish terrorism had cast its shadow over Churchill's early life and Dublin furnished his most powerful childhood memories. In 1876 his family moved there when his father, Lord Randolph, had gone as secretary to his own father, the Duke of Marlborough, the Lord-Lieutenant. The next three years living adjacent to the Viceregal Lodge stamped powerful images on Churchill's impressionable young mind: morning walks in Phoenix Park; the looming presence of Dublin Castle, the seat of British rule in Ireland; tales of Oliver Cromwell's conquest of the Irish two centuries before; the fears of his nurse, Mrs Everest, of the Fenians, 'wicked people' who would stop at nothing if they got their way; and Mr Burke, who lived in a house surrounded by trees in Phoenix Park and kindly gave him a drum, and who was murdered in the park two years after Churchill left. Ireland and its problems accompanied him back to London. His father bitterly fought Gladstone's 1886 Home Rule Bill and three years later the Parnell scandal broke. Since then Irish issues had simmered beneath the surface of British politics. They were about to erupt with a vengeance.

Liberals had been horrified by Le Caron's revelations of dirty tricks and Irish Nationalists had always suspected government complicity in the campaign to destroy Parnell. So in October 1909, when extracts from Anderson's memoirs began to appear in the monthly *Blackwood's Magazine*, he reopened deep and bitter wounds. Provocatively, he strongly defended Le Caron as a man of great personal charm and sterling integrity. This was bad enough in Nationalist eyes. Worse came when he confessed that he himself had written some of the articles in the 'Parnellism and Crime' series. An outcry followed. High on the outrage list were demands for the cancellation of his Home Office pension. Nationalists made hay of official complicity in Parnell's destruction. Liberals recoiled, once again, at revelations about underhand methods. Conservatives were horrified that he had spilled the beans about his secret-service work.

The storm reached its peak in April 1910 with a long and heated debate in the House of Commons. The Irish Nationalist T. P. O'Connor passionately concluded a long rehearsal of Irish griev-ances over the Parnell affair by appealing to what he called 'the racial instinct' of the British people against the spy and the informer. The choice for the future, he declared, was 'between Le Caron and Anderson or Gladstone and Parnell, between the policy of the spy and the informer and the forger and . . . giving to Ireland equal rights with England.' Backbench MP Edward Pickersgill captured the Liberal temper when he denounced the affair as a sordid business. 'I suppose secret service work is necessary', he conceded. 'But it is dirty work, and when a man has been at the business for twenty years . . . [his hand] is imbued with that dirty work as is the dyer's hand.'

As Home Secretary Churchill bore the brunt of the anger. He rejected all suggestions that Anderson's pension should be cancelled. The spymaster's undoubted abuse of secret intelligence had hap-pened too long ago, he declared, and his present revelations were 'trivial and unimportant'. But, carefully protecting his Liberal cre-dentials, he strongly dissociated himself from Anderson's behaviour, showed sympathy for the grievances of the Nationalists, and took several partisan swipes at the Tories. The *Blackwood's* articles he described as the garrulous inaccuracies and indiscretions of old age. 'They are written', he caustically observed, 'in the style of "How Bill Adams Won the Battle of Waterloo"'. None the less there was an important issue at stake, even if he refused to apply it in this particular case. The Police Superannuation Act of 1906 permitted a pension to be forfeited if its recipient revealed 'in an improper or discreditable manner' confidential information obtained during employment with the police. Churchill strongly asserted the state's right to veto the publication of memoirs by public servants: 'It would be absolutely intolerable if ex-police officers and ex-agents of the secret service were to be allowed, after they retired, without fear of consequence to publish secrets.' This was particularly true, he believed, in the case of secret-service agents. They could inflict grave harm as much by fabricating secrets as by revealing truths. 'It is far easier', he told the Commons, 'for them to invent . . . fairy tales in many cases than to give authentic facts.'[9]

The Anderson affair taught Churchill two useful lessons. It was a potent reminder of the power of undercover work to affect the course of politics, and the parliamentary furore raised a warning flag for the future. The Liberals' natural supporters regarded the secret world with loathing and suspicion. Any expansion of its work would have to be handled with great political sensitivity.

As Home Secretary Churchill was a sincere and humane reformer. He pushed hard to eliminate Dickensian remnants in the penal system, was the principal force behind the Shops Act which improved the hours and conditions of shop assistants, and introduced safer working practices in the coal mines, including pithead baths. But he was also a paternalist wedded strongly to law and order and the authority of the state. Threats to national security from foreign espionage, in the form of strikes and riots, demanded their own stern response. By the time he left the Home Office he was even convinced they were connected. Over the next few months, against the backdrop of the constitutional crisis caused by the Lords' rejection of the Budget and a second General Election campaign, he received a crash course on secret-service fears about German spies in Britain. His imagination in overdrive, he quickly forgot his warnings of 'fairy tales' to embrace the grim scenarios painted by MI5. Once convinced, he readily promoted counter-measures that extended and enhanced the secret state. By the time he left the Home Office for the Admiralty in October 1911 he had helped to extend significantly its boundaries and strengthen the covert powers of Whitehall. Most of this had been accomplished behind the scenes with minimal or no parliamentary scrutiny.

When Churchill and his group of Whitehall mandarins finally got to work he quickly discovered that the General Staff wanted to take drastic wartime measures equivalent to those imposed during the Napoleonic Wars, which had given the government dictatorial powers over the movement of foreigners. Their principal aim, said Macdonogh, was 'to guard against spies and ill-disposed persons'.

Churchill readily agreed. His committee approved the draft Aliens Restriction Bill that empowered the government by Orders-in-Council to remove enemy aliens from sensitive areas such as naval bases, dockyards, and large areas of coastline that could be used for enemy landings or British naval and military operations. They would be forced to register with the police, severely restricted in their movements, and forbidden to possess explosives, firearms, motor cars and cycles, 'telegraphic or signalling apparatus and carrier pigeons'. Dangerous aliens could be deported or forced to live in specified areas. All aliens entering or leaving the British Isles would have to do so through carefully delimited ports.

Churchill's eagerness was tempered only by his continuing concern about Parliament, so it was agreed that the Bill should be held back until its unimpeded passage could be guaranteed by events. The moment came in 1914, the day after Britain's formal declaration of war, when it quickly passed through and received Royal Assent that same evening. The government now had a virtual free hand: all known German spies were arrested and there was a massive round-up of German and Austrian nationals. Over the next twelve weeks the Special Branch conducted over 100,000 enquiries and there were 6,000 house searches.

Macdonogh and Murray also wanted immediate peacetime measures. Like Haldane, specifically they demanded an effective press and postal censorship system, and an immediate strengthening of the Official Secrets Act. Churchill supported the idea of a new Act and the proposal was passed easily at a meeting he chaired at the Committee of Imperial Defence offices in July 1910. But with memories fresh from the Anderson affair, he again worried how best to present the Bill to Parliament, especially as parliamentary protest had sabotaged a previous official secrets bill only two years before. The new Act eroded some long-standing principles of British law. It not only reinforced the law against espionage, but also clamped down heavily on the unauthorised release of official information. Section 1 made it a felony for anyone, 'for a purpose that could be prejudicial to the safety or the interests of the state', to communicate any plan, drawing or other piece of official information that could be useful to an enemy. The hypothetical language meant there was no need to prove that actual harm had taken place. Guilt could be inferred from the circumstances of a person's behaviour or character. It would be enough, for example, for a person simply to be caught in certain restricted places: the onus would be on the accused to prove innocence, not the prosecution guilt. Section 2 of the Act made both the unauthorised communication *and* receipt of any official information an offence. It was, in short, a highly illiberal and draconian measure.

Churchill decided on a strategic sleight of hand to get the Bill through Parliament. Rather than introduce it himself as Home Secretary, it would be presented at some appropriate time by the Secretary of State for War, dressed up as an urgent national defence issue. The opportunity came at the height of the war scare generated by the Agadir crisis in the summer of 1911. Haldane, now elevated to the peerage, presented it in the House of Lords as a nothing more than a small change of procedure to the 1889 Act. Only two members of the Lords responded, both in favour, and it passed its third reading sandwiched between the Lunacy Bill and a question on the Asylum Officers' Superannuation Bill. It was then sent to the Commons. Blandly, the Under-Secretary for War, Churchill's close friend Colonel Jack Seely, announced that 'in no way would the powers be used to infringe any of the liberties of His Majesty's subjects'. The Attorney-General, Sir Rufus Isaacs, promised that there was nothing novel in the principle of the Bill and that innocent people had nothing to fear.

Both ministers were being more than economical with the truth, but few protested; although one member objected that it upset Magna Carta, he and others were easily outvoted. The Bill was rushed through its second and third readings in half an hour on a Friday afternoon when the House was virtually empty. Churchill was amongst the handful of those present and he deliberately kept quiet. No bill, Seeley later observed with satisfaction, had ever before passed through all its stages in one day without a word of explanation from the minister concerned. According to Maurice Hankey, Whitehall *éminence grise* and long-serving Secretary to the Cabinet, the whole affair was 'a masterly example of Parliamentary strategy'.[10]

Churchill moved with his customary energy to establish a register of foreigners and improved postal censorship. Distinct echoes of

Ewart's briefings could be heard in his confession that he believed the kind of alien who was a danger to the country was one 'who established himself in trade in a place like Portsmouth and got in touch with the residents with a view to acquiring secret information'. Special Branch had in fact already sent one of their officers to Portsmouth to look out for suspicious-looking Germans. But, again with one eye on Parliament and public opinion, he rejected methods proposed by Macdonogh, who had demanded a system compelling aliens to self-register, and landlords and hotel owners to keep registers of all visitors. In the first place, Churchill observed, spies would simply provide false information and thus defeat the purpose. More importantly, a compulsory system could not be kept secret and would provoke widespread opposition. Instead, he floated Ewart's idea of an informal one, where the best results would be obtained by the police who 'had ramifications everywhere and knew what was going on in the country. They would take great interest in this work and if any foreigner were suspected of being a spy he could be shadowed.'[11]

Shortly afterwards Kell provided the Home Office with an aliens registration form for the police to complete. Churchill personally approved it and passed it on to Chief Constables around the country. 'A very good form', he declared after scrutinising Kell's handiwork, 'and quite suitable.'[12] The only change made to Kell's original was an explicit warning, in red, that police investigations should be kept strictly secret. Churchill was determined to avoid any risk of unfavourable publicity. Once completed the forms were returned to Kell, who assigned every file a serial number. Thus was born MI5's famous registry, 'the most important and controversial weapon in the British counter-intelligence armoury'. Too often, as history was to reveal, it would become packed with unsubstantiated allegations, rumour and innuendo. By the end of the First World War it contained thousands of names.

This was still not enough for Macdonogh and Murray, as the informal system remained geographically incomplete. Churchill had agreed to contact only the county police forces; major towns and cities were left out of the scheme. Many of these, with their Navy and Army installations, were prime espionage targets. In March 1911 the War Office men returned to the idea of a compulsory registration system, this time confined to specified locations of military or naval sensitivity. They also suggested a more drastic step. Foreign army or naval officers would be required to obtain prior permission from the relevant authority to visit these restricted areas, and if they were staying for more than 48 hours would also require advance police permission. These conditions, Macdonogh argued, were identical to those in force in many parts of Germany.

Churchill was sympathetic. He had, after all, himself conjured up the spectre of the foreign spy nosing around the naval installations at Portsmouth, and he brushed aside Admiral Bethell's observation that these people were likely to be occasional visitors who would avoid such a net. The problem, again, was publicity. To push a bill through Parliament would be impossible; even to extend the informal system from the counties to borough police forces would be dangerous. Chief Constables in the counties exercised a great deal of personal discretion and were able to act without much publicity. Borough police forces were far more closely scrutinised by their elected Borough Watch Committees. Once these heard of the scheme there would be uproar.

Churchill decided to wait. A year later the Agadir crisis dramatically changed the climate and Kell compiled a list of thirteen towns that he considered vital for surveillance. One of Churchill's last acts as Home Secretary was to approve it. He also signed a letter recommending Kell and his work to Chief Constables.[13] Fears of adverse publicity proved unfounded, and the entire country – with the exception of London, where the sheer number of aliens made comprehensive registration impossible – was soon covered by the scheme. By July 1913 Kell's list contained over 29,000 names. Kell himself, armed with Churchill's personal letter of introduction, embarked on a country-wide tour to introduce himself to Chief Constables.

In drawing up their lists the police were helped by the Post Office. Churchill quickly found out that as Home Secretary he already enjoyed extensive powers over the mails and could issue a warrant at any time, at the request of the War Office or Admiralty, to open a suspect's letters. Once again his concern was to avoid inflaming either Parliament or public opinion, while amassing as much information as possible using powers that already existed or that could be extended without legislation. He believed that 'The Police, working with the War Office [i.e., Kell], should have lists of individuals who might be suspected of sending information to foreign governments'. Once these lists were compiled, he speculated, 'a warrant might be issued in time of emergency authorising the correspondence of these individuals being censored'.[14]

Churchill, in short, was proposing a significant extension in the clandestine surveillance of the mails. Up to then, a separate warrant had been required for the opening of each individual letter. General warrants would permit the opening of all the mail of a named individual or even organisation. Before he left the Home Office Churchill, on his own admission and without reference to Parliament, began to issue such warrants giving Kell and MI5 greatly increased powers to detect German spies. Hankey again expressed the satisfaction of Whitehall mandarins with Churchill's work. It had, he recorded, 'laid the first slender foundations of a structure whose scientific foundations [were] tinged with something of romance and mystery'.[15] It gave Kell's men greatly expanded powers to spy on not only suspected aliens but also domestic dissenters. Already, on at least one occasion, Churchill had received a copy of a resolution passed at a branch meeting of the Independent Labour Party protesting at police espionage. One of the first acts of his successor as Home Secretary, Reginald McKenna, was to authorise a general warrant for the interception of all telegrams to and from the Women's Social and Political Union – the suffragettes. Secret state surveillance was spreading from espionage to political subversion.

Publicity was harder to avoid over the issue of press censorship. The General Staff wanted a powerful Act to control the press even before a declaration of war, and complained bitterly about sensitive defence information appearing in newspapers. Foreigners, they argued, handled the matter far better. The Japanese, Ewart pointed out, even declined to publish casualty lists. Churchill suggested a more subtle management of news, proposing that an officer of literary ability 'could supply the public press with accurate information which would be both more ample and more readable than that contained in official despatches'.[16] Eventually a consensus emerged that voluntary rather than legislative co-option of the press would work better. Talk began of a Press Bureau that would exert control through advice.

Once again the Agadir crisis produced results. Churchill moved to the Admiralty in October 1911 and adopted the more hostile viewpoint towards press freedom of Macdonogh and Murray. He was helped on his way by an interview he gave to Archibald Hurd, the defence correspondent of the *Daily Telegraph*. When Hurd revealed that he was familiar with some inside gossip, Churchill demanded to know the source. With admirable journalistic instincts Hurd refused, although he assured Churchill that it was not within the Admiralty. This did not end the matter. That December Churchill wrote to Hurd personally, regretting his refusal to help. 'The lack of secrecy which prevails in this country in regard to naval matters, and the levity with which disclosures are regarded, appear to me to amount to a very considerable national evil', he complained. And he threatened that legislation could be prevented only if newspapers voluntarily co-operated with the Admiralty. The legislation, of course, was already in place in the form of the Official Secrets Act, with its wideranging provisions for the receipt of official information.[17]

In June 1912 a Joint Standing Committee of the Admiralty and War Office and five major newspaper organisations was secretly established to exercise a system of voluntary and informal press censorship. In the Commons Churchill was strictly economical with the truth. 'It is believed in cases where information is recognised as secret and directly affecting the defence of the country, the government may rely on the cordial co-operation of the newspaper press in preventing its publication.' Thus was born the 'D-notice' system for the vetting of national-security stories in the media. It lasted as an effective self-censorship system for the next seventy years.

By 1912 Churchill had actively helped build Britain's secret service. MI5 and MI6 had been born, the Official Secrets Act governed discussions of national security, and the press had been tamed. A secret register of resident aliens had been created and German spies could be identified, located, and if necessary prosecuted. Clandestine examination of the mails had become a regular affair and domestic dissenters could be kept under careful surveillance. But what did Churchill think the German spies were doing and how were they a threat to national security? More importantly, did his fears have any foundation in fact?

3

Spy Fever

In late July 1911 Churchill joined a throng of ambassadors, civil servants, members of parliament and figures from the literary and artistic world at the last garden party of the season at 10 Downing Street. It had been a hot, dry summer and drought was beginning to affect parts of the country. But it was the threat of war, not water shortages, that preoccupied Churchill. Earlier that month the German government had triggered a major international crisis by sending a gunboat, the *Panther*, to the Moroccan port of Agadir. Sir Edward Grey, the Foreign Secretary, feared an imminent naval attack and a war scare followed when contact was lost with the German fleet. Only the day before, John Spencer Ewart, now Adjutant-General at the War Office, had met with Haldane and the General Staff to review mobilisation plans, and the Committee of Imperial Defence warned of the risk of sabotage to naval cordite stores.

Churchill had been briefed by Ewart on secret-service fears about German spies. 'War might be preceded', he said, 'by the arrival of a number of men charged with the execution of demolitions.' As the Secret Service Bureau began its work a Home Ports Defence sub-committee of the Committee of Imperial Defence recommended that the railways, Nobel's explosive works and the Admiralty's oil reserves be given special protection against attacks by enemy agents or sympathisers. This involved the guarding of ammunition dumps, factories producing war material, wireless stations, vital railway communications and coal mines. Contingency plans were also laid for the Army to occupy London and build an intelligence network amongst subversives.[1]

Amongst those present at the garden party was Sir Edward Henry, the Commissioner of the Metropolitan Police. Soon he and Churchill were deep in conversation and the subject of sabotage was raised. Did Churchill know, Henry asked, that the Home Office and the Metropolitan Police were responsible for guarding the reserves of naval cordite stored at Chattenden and Lodge Hill? And that for years the job had been carried out by a mere handful of unarmed police constables? Churchill did not, and he asked with alarm, 'What would happen if twenty determined Germans in two or three motor cars arrived well armed upon the scene one night?' 'They could do what they liked', Henry ominously replied. Churchill immediately left the garden party and, after failing to reach Admiralty officials by telephone, won Haldane's consent to the dispatch of troops. Four days later, five hundred men were ordered to guard the naval magazines and oil reserves. To avoid creating war panic, the official reason given was the hot weather and the danger of fire. In Churchill's mind, however, the threat was clear:

> All around flowed the busy life of peaceful, unsuspecting, easy-going Britain. The streets were thronged with men and women utterly devoid of any sense of danger from abroad ... Most of them would have been incredulous ... if they had been told that we might be near a tremendous war, and that perhaps within the City of London ... resolute foreigners might be aiming a deadly blow at the strength of the one great weapon and shield in which we trusted ...[2]

His obsession that German saboteurs would exploit the crisis, which coincided with the first ever national rail strike, was reinforced by others. Sir Guy Granet, the General Manager of the Midland Railway, informed him of allegations that railway union leaders were receiving payments from a German agent. 'I cannot help believing there is some truth in it', he confessed. Granet was not easy to dismiss. He had a reputation for strong opinions and had frequently appeared as a persuasive expert witness before parliamentary committees. He encountered a receptive imagination. Three days later Sir Almeric Fitzroy, the clerk of the Privy Council, noted in his diary: 'Winston Churchill is said to be convinced that the whole trouble is fomented by German gold, and claims to have proof of it, which others regard as midsummer madness.'[3] Madness it may have been, but the climate affected many others. It was on that very day that the House of Commons passed the Official Secrets Act.

Churchill's fears now turned to another crucial Admiralty resource – South Wales coal used by the Royal Navy. After consulting Ewart and General Nevil Macready, responsible at the War

Office for military assistance to the civil power, he ordered Lieutenant-Colonel Freeth, the officer commanding troops in South Wales, to protect Admiralty supplies from agents of a foreign power. Now thoroughly alarmed, and wise to the potential of the motor car (he and Clementine had just purchased their first), he painted for Macready a dramatic scenario of likely German action: 'A party of three or four skilled and armed men, who would arrive in a motor car without warning [could] hold up the men working, and smash up the machinery of a power house.'[4]

Freeth was Kell's brother-in-law and his report to Churchill certainly had the Kell touch. Many of the electricity plants powering the South Wales collieries, he pointed out, were of German manufacture. It would therefore be easy for a handful of knowledgeable Germans to put them out of action. Moreover, sticks of dynamite placed in the tunnels or underneath the viaducts of the Taff Vale and Barry Railway Company could paralyse Admiralty supplies. In November Colonel Andrew Pearson, Inspector of Mines, told Kell that 'apparently systematised acts of espionage of certain German subjects' had been brought to his attention by the South Wales Coal-Owners Association. Four Germans had been spotted in the Rhondda Valley – 'intelligent men, and quite likely to be officers' – marking collieries on a six-inch-to-the-mile Ordnance Survey map.

All this convinced Churchill of the need for effective surveillance of the railways. Kell and his Secret Service Bureau were brought into the discussions and Churchill closely followed progress when he moved from the Home Office to the Admiralty. 'Press this forward constantly', he urged when discussions dragged. Eventually, after endless bureaucratic wrangling over who would pick up the bills, Kell took the train to Cardiff to instruct personally two specially employed men on their secret surveillance work. The date was 1 July 1913 – two years to the day after the 'leap of the Panther'.[5]

The Agadir crisis, fears of sabotage, the passing of the Official Secrets Act and events real or imagined in the South Wales coalfield threw Churchill firmly into the arms of Kell, and images of subversion from some inner Fifth Column began to haunt him. He also revealed what was to become only too familiar to those who worked with him in later life: an appetite for raw intelligence reports.

War-scare feelings were still running high in September. Henry Wilson, Ewart's successor at War Office intelligence, sent an officer to gather information about German troop movements from the

Malmedy region in Belgium while Kell kept an eye open for commercial indicators suggesting a German attack. Soon he reported
that they were making heavy wheat purchases, and Wilson received
intelligence that manoeuvres close to the Belgian border could
provide cover for a surprise attack. Churchill warned Lloyd George:
'Captain Kell of the WO secret service has reported to us this afternoon that the price of flour has risen today by 6/- on large German
purchases in "floating bottoms" otherwise destined for this country.
He reported two days ago that one small firm of the name of Schulz
purchased as much as 30,000 bags and refused to sell at a higher
price. I send you this for what it is worth.'

But what was it worth? The answer, it transpired, was not much.
The next day Churchill confessed to the Chancellor that 'the flour
news was all wrong' and the price rise could be simply explained by
the bad European harvest. Ewart's 'sentimental Celt' – in reality a
shrewd and hard-headed realist – had in any case already drawn a
quite different conclusion than Churchill from Kell's facts. Even if
the Germans were not planning an attack, he pointed out, they could
reasonably be expected to take precautions of their own.[6]

Churchill was undeterred. A few weeks later he forwarded a
bundle of Kell's reports to Sir Edward Grey. 'They are well worth
looking through', he urged, 'because they show that we are the
subject of a minute and scientific study by the German military and
naval authorities, and that no other nation in the world pays us such
attention.' Kell, he added, was extremely well informed, and thanks
to Churchill's own system of general warrants possessed records of
the names and addresses of all the spies involved. He also implored
Grey to pass the reports on to Lloyd George, with whom he knew
Grey was dining that night. But the Foreign Secretary was apparently
as unimpressed as the Chancellor and returned Kell's bundle of
reports with two lines of crisp comment: 'I hadn't time to look at this
till today and Lloyd George has gone to Bath so I send it back to
you.' Churchill believed he was the only member of the Cabinet alert
to the menace of German spies.[7]

The Agadir crisis also precipitated Churchill's transfer to the
Admiralty. The spectre of a European war revealed wide dis-
crepancies between War Office and Admiralty planning, and Asquith
decided on an immediate change at the top to create a Naval War
Staff along the lines of the Army's General Staff – a reform long
resisted by the Admirals. The two contenders were Haldane and

Churchill. In Haldane's favour stood his reforming record at the War Office. Churchill brought his energy, ambition and new-found enthusiasm for matters strategic. The die was cast over a game of golf on the private links at Archerfield, an Adam house overlooking Asquith's Fife constituency where he spent his summers. Here he offered the job to Churchill. Asquith's daughter Violet met him as he returned to the house: 'I saw in Winston's face a radiance like the sun.' The two walked down to the sea, where the Fidra lighthouse was already flashing out its signal. 'The fading light of evening', wrote Churchill in *The World Crisis*, 'disclosed in the distance the silhouette of two battleships steaming slowly out of the Firth of Forth. They seemed invested with a new significance to me.' Over the next three years Churchill threw his energies into preparing the Admiralty for war. His reforms, as Asquith anticipated, caused friction and controversy. So far as intelligence was concerned, Churchill was now in the front line.[8]

German spies in Britain were controlled by a former naval officer and ex-Pinkerton detective called Gustav Steinhauer. Over six feet tall and of massive build, he prided himself on his large collection of menu cards from Simpson's in the Strand. His selection of agents was less impressive. Most were of poor calibre, recruited from German nationals living in towns and cities with naval installations, and tasked to report on the movements of warships and work in progress in dockyards and arsenals. Kell had little difficulty in penetrating their efforts. Armed with the new Official Secrets Act the government prosecuted several of them in some highly publicised pre-war cases. All involved Admiralty secrets.

The first case made headlines a month after Churchill became First Lord, when a Dr Max Schultz appeared in court at Plymouth. He had set himself up in a houseboat where he threw parties, met local dignitaries and propositioned a local solicitor with an offer of £1,000 a year to provide him with naval information. His recruit immediately informed on him and he was sentenced to twenty-one months in jail. Hardly had he been imprisoned than Heinrich Grosse appeared before the Winchester Assizes. A convicted forger, he recruited a naval pensioner to supply information about the Portsmouth naval barracks and coal supplies. He, too, chose badly. After the pensioner informed the police, Kell fed Grosse with false intelligence which in turn sparked further demands from Berlin about naval guns, range-finding devices and other Admiralty secrets. For this Grosse received three years. Then Armgaard Karl Graves was arrested in Glasgow. His mission was to investigate the Rosyth naval base and the Glasgow arms manufacturer Beardmore and Sons, which had recently won a contract for the new 13.5-inch guns for Dreadnoughts. A globe-trotting fantasist, Graves posed as an Australian medical student, but so clumsy were his efforts that Kell was soon intercepting his mail. When arrested he was carrying a map of Rosyth, a code book and forged notepaper. Described as a 'dark-skinned man . . . [with] a double-breasted suit with silk lapels', he was sentenced at the High Court in Edinburgh to eighteen months' imprisonment.

More sensational was the case of George Charles Parrott, a naval gunner arrested in November 1912. The only Englishman to be tried for espionage in this period, he had fallen into a honey trap set by a German agent. Arrested in possession of a letter from his controller in Berlin ordering him to the Firth of Forth, he was sentenced at the Old Bailey to four years' hard labour. Two more cases came before the courts prior to August 1914, the escalating sentences reflecting increasing concern about espionage. Wilhelm Klauer, alias William Clare, worked as a dentist in Portsmouth and offered his services to the German Admiralty which asked him to report on recent torpedo trials. Soon he was trapped by an *agent provocateur* and received five years' hard labour in March 1913. Barely a year later Frederick Adolphus Schroeder, alias Gould, received six years' hard labour. Half-English, he had settled in Rochester on the Medway, where he ran a public house and sent to Berlin useful gossip he gleaned from personnel working in the nearby Chatham naval dockyards. He, too, had been kept under close watch by Kell.[9]

As Home Secretary Churchill scrupulously read files on individual prisoners and those condemned to death. At the Admiralty he followed spy cases with similarly close attention, reading either the intercepted reports of the spies themselves or detailed summaries provided by Kell. Briefly he wondered what harm espionage was doing to Anglo-German relations and complained to Sir Edward Grey that espionage on both sides was a continual cause of suspicion and ill-will; he proposed instead a full and open mutual inspection of dockyards by naval attachés. But mostly he found espionage prosecutions helpful in mobilising public support behind his naval rearmament programme. It also proved a useful political weapon in

Cabinet battles. During his 1912 campaign to improve conditions and pay in the Navy he told the Cabinet that German agents' reports dwelt continually upon the discontent of sailors with their wages, and that there was no doubt that German opinion on this point was well founded. 'We have had great mutinies in the past in the British Navy', he threatened, 'and we ought not to continue to bear the responsibility of refusing all redress to grievances so obvious and so hard.'[10] More importantly, these highly public spy cases and secret reports sent by Kell reinforced all his fears about invasion.

Although the Committee of Imperial Defence had officially discounted the idea, Churchill imagined the worst. What, after all, *were* the plans of the German Navy? Was it secretly preparing a bolt from the blue that would see German troops landing without warning on British soil? Kell and the Secret Service Bureau were wrong in their assessment of the German spy threat. Admiral von Tirpitz, head of the German Navy, regarded invasion talk in Britain as 'wholly stupid and impossible to understand'. As early as 1900 the Germans had abandoned the idea and their spies in Britain were not involved in sabotage. Their task was simply to gather intelligence, but Churchill, along with most others in Whitehall, accepted Kell's version. Admiralty manoeuvres in the summers of 1912 and 1913 explored the problem of intercepting the German Fleet before it could cover the landing of troops on the east coast.

The results were far from encouraging. In the 1913 manoeuvres Admiral Jellicoe, leading the Red (German) fleet, succeeded in landing some 48,000 men on shore, while the Blue (British) Commander lost a considerable part of his fleet – notionally – to submarine attack. Concerned that the Germans might discover this, Churchill called a halt after only five days.[11] By this time Asquith had established yet another official inquiry into the invasion threat. Churchill energetically prepared a number of studies and organised war games at the Naval War College which demonstrated, as he put it, 'the kind of mental picture I was able to summon up in imagination of the tremendous period which was soon to rush upon us'. It was a dramatic vision. British defences against invasion or raids from across the North Sea were much weaker than those that had previously occupied planners against a French attack across the Channel. The east coast was flat and undefended, with the vital Scottish bases not yet completed or fully defended. By contrast, the Germans, sheltered behind the strong defences of the Heligoland Bight, would be able to assemble a large attacking force unobserved and send some 20,000 men to land in Britain.[12]

Such fears, reminiscent of *The Riddle of the Sands*, remained firmly lodged in Churchill's mind until the outbreak of war and beyond. On 1 August 1914 he received an intelligence report containing a list of armed mercantile vessels moored at Hamburg and Bremen, with a note attached that some were being fitted as transports. He minuted on this '24 [ships] carry 15,000 men' and sent it over to the War Office. In September he promoted the idea of capturing the island of Sylt by arguing that a British base there would give advance warning of invasion, and when the General Staff identified invasion as a German strategic objective the following month he asked anxiously, 'How are we going to get early intelligence?' Secret agents at Emden and Hamburg, he was assured, had received their instructions. As late as December he ordered that any enemy troop transports spotted at sea should be immediately sunk even if they raised a white flag on the grounds that this would merely be a ruse by the invasion fleet to fool the Royal Navy. His anxiety lingered well into the second year of the war, keeping the secret service alert both at home and abroad.[13]

Invasion scenarios always led back, one way or another, to espionage. But what light could British spies throw on German intentions, and specifically on plans to invade or carry out raids? What was the naval, or foreign, section of the new Secret Service Bureau under Mansfield Smith-Cumming doing in the interests of national security?

Churchill had to admit that the answer was 'not much'. In March 1913 he confessed that British intelligence was not well equipped to detect such preparations. 'The rigour with which [British] agents suspected of sending information have [*sic*] been pursued during the last five or six years has made it difficult to arrange for the transmission of intelligence.' No doubt he had in mind the embarrassing case of Lieutenant Brandon and Captain Trench. Three years before they had been sent by the Admiralty's intelligence branch to reconnoitre German North Sea defences and had been quickly arrested exploring the coastline made famous by *The Riddle of the Sands*. In court, Brandon even admitted that he had read Childers' book three times and they were sentenced to four years' imprisonment. Cumming worked hard to do better, with some success. He recruited his agents from the world of business, men with good and natural covers and regular incomes. Many provided excellent technical information that supplemented what could be gleaned from open publications. These included details about U-boat trials and battleship construction, the accuracy of long-range naval guns, and the high priority given by the German Navy to mines, aircraft, torpedoes and submarines. But Cumming's spies were far less effective in reading naval intentions and failed to challenge the Whitehall consensus or Churchill's belief that German spies were paving the way for invasion.[14]

Although Churchill's move to the Admiralty deepened his links with Kell, he was content to rely exclusively on neither him nor Cumming. Startling new evidence from his personal archive reveals that he also employed at least one agent of his own to report on German espionage.

In October 1912 Churchill passed on to Rear-Admiral Bethell, his Director of Naval Intelligence, a letter from a man he called 'Captain' Tupper containing details about German spies at work in ports around the country. Churchill told Bethell that Tupper was an Indian Army veteran who had come to his notice during the 1911 strikes in persuading strikers to return to work, and since then he had kept in friendly touch with him. At one point Tupper had looked after one of his wife's uncles when he became mentally disturbed.

Tupper had prepared his list of spies at Churchill's request. 'I have always treated him on the basis that he is to be trusted in any emergency affecting the country', Churchill told Bethell, 'he is a very able man in his way.' He then instructed the DNI to contact Tupper at his home address to arrange a meeting. But he added an astonishing cautionary note: 'Don't hand him over to Commr Cumming, as he might not know the circumstances as I have explained them to you and would perhaps treat him roughly ... I want him carefully handled and well treated.' There might be future crises, Churchill added, when Tupper's services could be extremely useful.[15]

Cumming would certainly have dealt with Tupper harshly had he known about him. It was bad enough that the First Lord of the Admiralty was using an agent behind the back of the head of the Secret Intelligence Service. Far worse was the individual concerned, for on the face of it Churchill's relationship with the union militant was extraordinary.

Edward Tupper stands out as one of the more bizarre and colourful figures in British labour history, a man who left an intriguing but shadowy trace in its records.[16] A burly seventeen-stone firebrand sporting a drooping black moustache, he burst on to the national scene in 1911 as the organiser of the National Seamen's and Firemen's

Union, and general hatchet man to its founder and president, Havelock Wilson. For years Wilson had led bitter fights against the Shipping Federation, the owners' association. In June, at the height of that summer's industrial crisis, he had called out the seamen.

Tupper spearheaded the strike at Cardiff and for his success in wringing concessions from local shipowners along the South Wales coast emerged in union mythology as 'the Hero of the Bristol Channel Ports'. This was Tupper's finest hour, and he duly matched it with a personal legend that rose to the occasion. He claimed that he had been born in Canada and after briefly training for the priesthood had attended Harrow, Sandhurst and the Indian Army Staff College. He had first seen action during the Nile Expedition for the relief of General Gordon, and his subsequent Army career as Captain had seen him in the service of the Nizam of Hyderabad, in Burma and in charge of Indian forces on the Malakand Pass on the North-West Frontier. He also claimed to have been attached as an observer with the Greek Army during the Graeco-Turkish war of the 1890s, and in the Boer War was wounded twice outside Mafeking fighting with irregular forces. It was thanks to the secret service, he said, that he was now involved with the Seamen's Union. It had employed him to investigate its affairs, but he had since become convinced of the justice of its cause.

Most of this was the Walter Mitty fantasy of a discharged bankrupt and ex-company promoter. The truth was more prosaic. Tupper was born in Worthing, Sussex, the son of a coachman turned publican who ran local meetings for the Conservative Primrose League. His first call to duty had been as an errand boy delivering groceries in his home town where he was remembered by locals as a high-spirited lad who liked nothing better than to pretend he owned the shop. Precisely what he had done between then and joining the Seamen's Union remains obscure, although there was a brief spell as a music-hall entertainer. He claimed to have declined an invitation to stand as a Liberal candidate for Parliament and to have led a campaign to expose profiteers during the Boer War; he is unlikely to have spent time as a soldier in India, Burma and Greece as he never held a commission, nor even visited India or South Africa. When he first met Havelock Wilson he was working for a private-detective agency in London. Wilson had hired him to help in a bankruptcy fight against the shipowners. From then on his loyalties became firmly attached to the autocratic union leader.

Teller of tales though he was, there was no mistaking Tupper's effectiveness as troubleshooter for Wilson in his endless battles with the shipowners and local militants who challenged his leadership. He was a born leader who ruthlessly strong-armed opponents of the union and anyone else who got in his way. 'I went into battle asking no quarter and giving none', he fondly recalled. 'Men walking on two legs were divided into two species – friends of the seamen, or foes to be jumped on tooth and nail.' He was no socialist or syndicalist either, and focused his attack on low wages and foreign – especially Chinese – blackleg labour. Dirty tricks were his speciality. When Cardiff shipowners attempted to bypass Tupper's pickets by housing strike-breakers in an old windjammer hulk moored offshore, he waylaid them, sunk the pinnace that was to take them out to the hulk, and then tied the hapless men together by cord and marched them eight miles into Cardiff. 'I suppose', he wrote cheerily in later life, 'that I was born for trouble as the sparks fly upwards.'[17] Charged with unlawful assembly for his role in the Cardiff strike, he made a flamboyant appearance before the Quarter Sessions wearing a frock coat and silk top hat. To local cheers he was acquitted on all charges.

Trouble and headlines followed him. After Cardiff he was in Liverpool supporting the dockers, where he witnessed riots that left two people dead. Then he travelled to Glasgow to help the seamen's strike on Clydeside. It was here that Emanuel Shinwell – later Minister of Defence in the post-1945 Labour government, but then a union militant on Clydeside – first met him. Wilson's interfering lieutenant quickly alienated him after introducing himself as 'Captain Tupper, VC', and before long enmity between the two men degenerated into a court case in which Havelock Wilson and Tupper succeeded in getting Shinwell thrown out of his Glasgow office. But Tupper's most famous claim to notoriety came in 1917. By then the fate of seamen killed and drowned by U-boats had turned him into a strident anti-pacifist crusader. Denouncing 'Cranks and Bolshies', he spent his wartime energy breaking up anti-war meetings. In June 1917, learning that the Labour leader Ramsay MacDonald planned to take part in a peace conference in Petrograd, he rushed to Aberdeen, alerted the ship's crew and personally blocked MacDonald's path to the ship. Despite appeals to London, MacDonald was forced to abandon his visit. It was, he confessed in his diary, a humiliating setback, and the ship's crew had been 'worked up and doped with lies'.[18]

Tupper first came to Churchill's notice during the 1911 Tonypandy riots when word reached the police that a huge crowd of miners planned to march on Cardiff. Terrified of a rampaging mob, they prevailed on Tupper to calm it down. This he did by a masterful display of oratory and by the end of the day the miners were marching around the local football field singing Welsh hymns. This so impressed Churchill that during the dockers' strike in Glasgow he turned to Tupper for help. According to Tupper's highly coloured account, after a long conversation the two men walked from their hotel to the heavily guarded railway station. As Churchill boarded the train he turned and spoke loudly so that all those around could hear: 'Goodbye, Tupper. See that this strike is settled tonight.'[19]

Churchill's faith in Tupper was amply repaid by his patriotic response to evidence of German espionage in the seamen's ranks. 'Men came to us', Tupper recalled, 'with yarns of folk lavishly supplied with beer-money who were very affable in such places as the carriages of Portsmouth trains and any bar that was handy . . . they were "a sight too bloomin nosey" about Navy vessels and guns – particularly guns.' It was after hearing of suspicious activity in the Hull dockyards that Tupper, calling on the relationship that had developed between them, gave his list to Churchill. Again according to Tupper, the two men met personally at the Admiralty before Churchill passed him on to Bethell. Ironically, Tupper thought he had been given the brush-off. He remained in the dark about Churchill's enthusiastic endorsement of his abilities to the Director of Naval Intelligence.[20]

What became of Tupper's spy allegation, or Bethell's instructions, remains obscure. What is clear is that Churchill found Tupper's service in neutralising militant labour invaluable and later, as Minister of Munitions, turned to him to intervene in a strike of munitions workers at Coventry. Tupper marched a column of seamen who had survived torpedo attacks into the city, threatened to cut off its food supplies and brought the strikers to heel. Alexander MacCallum Scott, Churchill's parliamentary secretary (and his first biographer), left a vigorous contemporary description of Tupper: 'a rollicking adventurer, a soldier of fortune, an irresistible bounder, a happy reckless freelance. He is quite without scruples and is tied to no formulae, and in pursuit of his aim he is quite reckless of consequence. If his aim is roast pork he is quite willing to burn the house down to get it.'[21]

A more sinister side to Tupper's wartime ultra-patriotism emerged in the witch-hunt against German-born residents in Britain that climaxed after the sinking of the *Lusitania* in the spring of 1915. Two of the most prominent victims were Sir Edgar and Lady Speyer.

Speyer was a successful financier and patron of the arts. Born in New York, he was the second son of Gustav Speyer, a Jewish banker from Frankfurt. After settling in Britain he became a director of Speyer Brothers, the family merchant-banking firm that financed the Metropolitan District Railway Company, of which Speyer became chairman. By 1906 he was a naturalised British subject, active in Liberal politics and a friend of the Asquiths. Knighted that same year, three years later he was appointed a Privy Counsellor. Through his wife, a professional violinist, he became an influential patron of Sir Henry Wood's Promenade Concerts, subsidised the Queen's Hall, and organised concerts at his home where artists including Strauss and Debussy conducted their own works. None of this protected the Speyers against the violent xenophobia of 1914. Indeed, their very prominence made them vulnerable targets. Tupper proudly recounted how he had joined the campaign against 'spies in high places' and singled out Speyer for particular denunciation. 'He was a very dangerous man if he was a spy', declared Tupper piously, citing the defence of his seamen. The idea of enemy agents giving information that led to the sinking of ships, he claimed, was a perpetual nightmare.[22]

It was as nothing compared to the hardships inflicted by spymania on Speyer and his wife. He was forced to resign from various charitable boards, and he and his house were placed under police protection. That his brother James, who ran the New York branch of the business, was suspected of being the tool, if not an actual spy, of Count Bernstorff, the German ambassador in the United States, did not help. Although Asquith rejected his offer to renounce his baronetcy and resign from the Privy Council, after the *Lusitania* went down Speyer and his family fled to the United States. In 1921 his naturalisation was shamefully revoked and he was struck from the Privy Council list.[23]

Although Churchill rejected Tupper's extremism, by July 1914 he was certainly infected by spy fever. After noting Kell's initial on his emergency checklist following the Cabinet meeting of 24 July, the pace of events rapidly gathered speed. He spent that Sunday with his family at fashionable Overstrand, near Cromer on the Norfolk coast, where they had rented Pear Tree Cottage for the summer. But on hearing further news about European events he returned early that evening to the Admiralty and drafted a communiqué announcing that the First Fleet had been ordered not to disperse. The next day he posted soldiers at naval magazines and oil tanks to protect them against air attack and sabotage. He then ordered a complete clamp-down on all news about Admiralty preparations. 'The moment had come', he wrote in *The World Crisis*, 'to draw down the curtain.' That same afternoon the Fleet was ordered to its war station. Later that night Churchill told the King about the measures taken.

Still later, at midnight from his room at the Admiralty, Churchill wrote to Clementine about the impending catastrophe. 'I am interested, geared up, and happy . . . the preparations have a hideous fascination for me . . .' So, too, did the spectre of spies, for he ended by urging his wife to be discreet on the telephone. 'My darling one', he admonished, 'this is a vy good plan of ours on the telephone . . . Ring me up at fixed times. But talk in parables – for they all listen.'[24]

Who did Churchill fear was listening in? The servants? Or spies tapping the phone? That he might have had other ears in mind altogether is suggested by an intriguing fact. Pear Tree Cottage possessed no telephone of its own, but kind neighbours who had also rented a house for the summer had offered Clementine the use of theirs. Regularly she would walk the few yards to their house each evening and here, waiting for the connection in the study, admire a lovely Madonna over the mantelpiece as it gazed out over piles of business books scattered on the writing table. But the Churchills' neighbours were no ordinary summer tourists: they were Sir Edgar and Lady Speyer.

No evidence links Churchill with Tupper's witch-hunting crusade against Speyer, and he would certainly have urged Clementine to be discreet on any telephone. But even in retrospect, during the years of post-war peace, Churchill defended many aspects of 1914 spymania. Writing in 1932 (coincidentally the year of Speyer's death in Berlin), he noted how amateur spy-catchers had often inflicted unmerited sufferings on individuals. None the less, he asserted, their efforts had constituted an important additional element of security.

Sharp eyes followed everybody's movements; long ears awaited every incautious expression in the streets, in the public conveyances, on the railways, in the theatre, in the restaurant or tavern; tireless industry unravelled to the third and fourth generations the genealogy of all who bore non-British names or who had married foreign wives . . . Thus did whole communities protect themselves against the subtle peril which dwelt privily in their midst.[25]

Was this, perhaps, a measure of self-justification for some acts of commission or omission of his own in 1914? On the evidence available it is impossible to know and nowhere in his voluminous writings does he even refer to Speyer. But he may have harboured private reservations about him. Men close to him certainly did. Sir David Beatty, whom he personally sought out as his Naval Secretary, was by 1914 Commander of the First Battle Cruiser Squadron and privately denounced 'that German Jew Sir Edgar Speyer' and his wife as probable German spies who should be locked up. One of the more ludicrous accusations against Speyer was that he had been signalling to German submarines from his Norfolk home.[26]

Whatever Churchill's attitude to Speyer, there was no mistaking his determination to round up all German spies known to the Secret Service Bureau. When at the end of July the final steps before official mobilisation were taken, Kell alerted police forces around the country to be ready to arrest those who had deliberately been left at large in order to monitor their correspondence with Berlin. That same day he also began to live in his office around the clock, surrounded by telephones. He kept in constant touch with Churchill and on 3 August, the day before the declaration of war, Churchill ordered him to send out the pre-arranged coded telegrams to Chief Constables. The next day all but one of the suspected German spies were arrested, thereby foiling any sabotage plans. But Churchill remained nervous about his family's safety. A letter from Clementine, full of wild rumours about spies, only fanned the flames. She had heard that a neighbour had seen two men walking along the cliffs speaking in a foreign language and giving her 'evil glances'. Suspicious, the neighbour had followed and seen them release four carrier pigeons concealed beneath their jackets. She had immediately alerted the police, who arrested the men, retrieved one of the pigeons and found it was carrying a coded message. Clementine's elderly mother, who had joined the family at Pear Tree Cottage, was convinced that the message revealed a plan to kidnap Clemmie and fly her to Berlin where she would be ransomed for several of Britain's Dreadnoughts. 'If I *am* kidnapped', Clementine wrote, 'I beg of you not to sacrifice the smallest or cheapest submarine or even the oldest ship ... I could not face the subsequent unpopularity whereas I should be quite a heroine and you a Spartan if I died bravely and unransomed.' He replied by urging her to get their broken-down car repaired and ready for the road. The Cromer beach was an excellent landing area, he pointed out. 'Keep it', he urged, 'so you can whisk away at the first sign of trouble.' But the car was 'a lame duck', she replied, until a replacement cylinder could be fitted. She could only hope that the Germans wouldn't arrive before then.

Summer visitors to Cromer were hurriedly packing their bags and leaving. So concerned were the local authorities that they arranged for the nearby cinema to flash a special announcement on the screen pointing out that if Cromer was safe for Mrs Winston Churchill then it was certainly so for everyone else. One night, returning from the Speyers after a telephone call, Clementine was challenged by a startled territorial soldier patrolling for suspected spies. And 'Goonie' – Churchill's sister-in-law – arrived one day for lunch in a highly excited state after having vainly joined in the chase of a 'foreign-looking man' by two territorials. The man, she declared, was obviously a spy.[27]

Spymania was not confined to the Churchills and Beatty. Rear-Admiral Sir Henry Francis Oliver, the Director of Naval Intelligence, was also afflicted. Universally known as 'Dummy' because of his taciturnity, and greatly admired by Churchill, he worked closely with Cumming to whose office he was linked by private telephone. He was alert to spies and on the morning war was declared recommended the arrest of Friedrich von Bülow, the London representative of the Krupp armament firm, whom he believed was involved with espionage. The next day von Bülow was detained while attempting to leave Britain with departing German diplomats and appealed personally to Churchill. But when Churchill asked Oliver for guidance he was told firmly that Kell's advice was to hold him on the grounds that his knowledge of local conditions in Britain would be useful to the Germans, that he would be a valuable hostage for the good treatment of Britons held in Germany, and that his release would be 'a bad precedent for other applications'. Across Oliver's minute, in red ink, Churchill boldly scrawled 'Hold him'.[28]

The most extraordinary manifestation of Churchill's 1914 spy fever was a bizarre affair involving a searchlight and a retired Tory MP. To avoid detection and attack by German submarines, the

Grand Fleet spent the early months of the war sailing from one anchorage to another, a wearying routine that stretched the nerves of admirals and sailors alike. In mid-September it was moored in Loch Ewe, off the Scottish north-west coast. Churchill decided a visit would be useful. With him went Oliver, Admiral Hood, the Naval Secretary, and Commodores Keyes and Tyrwhitt. Travelling over-night by train to Inverness, the next morning they drove sixty miles across the moors to the west-coast anchorage. It was a clear autumn day and the group – perhaps under Oliver's influence – remained largely silent. Just outside the village of Achnasheen, Tyrwhitt spotted a searchlight installed on the roof of a baronial mansion close by the road. But before the others had time to see it the car had rounded a corner and the house was lost to view.

Shortly afterwards they arrived at Loch Ewe and Churchill saw spread before him the twenty or so Dreadnoughts on which depended Britain's command of the seas. Turning to his colleagues he asked, 'What would the German Emperor give to see this?' Soon, fuelled by Oliver, his imagination was racing. Suppose a submarine flotilla were lurking close by and a German spy was at loose in the neighbourhood? And that there was a Zeppelin? And a spy on shore had signalled to the Zeppelin and that the Zeppelin signalled to the submarines? 'Suppose', added Oliver, 'someone had a *searchlight* . . . ?' Once aboard the battleship *Iron Duke*, Jellicoe's flagship, their atten-tion turned to other matters. But over lunch Churchill reverted to the house and its mystery searchlight. Jellicoe's response shocked him. 'There might be something in it', ruminated the Admiral. 'We have heard several bad rumours about the place.' One was that the house was full of foreigners, another that a mysterious and untraceable aeroplane had been seen in its vicinity.

Convinced that the mix of foreigners, the Grand Fleet, a search-light and some mystery aeroplane signalled a German spy ring, Churchill decided to investigate on their return. Preparing for the worst, and reminding himself of the hostile reception that had greeted the police at Sidney Street, he ordered the group to arm themselves. Jellicoe provided service revolvers from the *Iron Duke*'s armoury, but Churchill managed to borrow a Belgian automatic pistol from the Coast Guard commander who took them back to shore. It made his companions distinctly unhappy. 'It was a very wet night', Oliver recalled, 'and I sat by the driver in front of Churchill and wondered when I would be shot as he spent a long time investigating the mechanism of the foreign pistol.' Towards midnight, after their headlights had startled a deer that leaped across the bonnet of the car, they reached their destination.

Loch Rosque castle was one of the many homes of Sir Arthur Bignold, a wealthy former Tory MP, member of the Carlton Club, and a founder of the Kennel Club. There are two accounts of what happened next. The more dramatic is Churchill's.

Pistols at the ready, the group walked up to the front door, rang the bell and were greeted by a portly butler who told them that Sir Arthur was at dinner entertaining guests. They demanded to see him, and soon there appeared a bewildered ruddy-faced old man with grey hair. Oliver, with his customary lack of charm, came to the point: Was there a searchlight on the roof? Bignold's frank and ready admission that there was briefly disarmed Churchill, but his suspicions rapidly returned when the still-bemused owner of Loch Rosque castle continued, 'We use it to locate the game on the hillsides', explaining that at night the searchlight lit up the eyes of the deer so they could be quickly found by stalkers the next morning. Besides, he added, with this light they could distinguish the eyes of cattle, which were white, and deer, which were green.

To Churchill this 'farrago of improbabilities and impossibilities' only confirmed his suspicions and he demanded to see the searchlight. With Bignold as hostage leading the way, and Hood standing guard below, they climbed up a long spiral stairway to the top of the tower. There, on the battlements, was a searchlight. Churchill again asked for an explanation. Once more Bignold repeated the story of the deer. Churchill then said there would have to be a full inquiry and that in the meantime the light would have to be dismantled. After removing various spare parts and bidding Sir Arthur 'sullen adieux' the group returned to their car, to Inverness, and London.

Oliver's account differs in one crucial respect. On arriving at the castle, he remembered, Churchill had remained in the car – perhaps with memories of the roasting he had received at the hands of the press during the Sidney Street siege for placing himself recklessly in the front line. There he stayed until the others had climbed the tower, and it was only after the main drama was over that he had impatiently appeared at the front door demanding to know what was going on.

Whatever the truth, Churchill took the affair seriously. No sooner had he reached London than he instructed Oliver to prepare a full report on how and when the searchlight had been installed, on Sir Arthur Bignold, his guests, friends and servants, and on the aeroplane rumours. It turned out to be one of the wilder spy scares of 1914. Sir Arthur Bignold and friends were free of all pro-German suspicion, the searchlight had not even been used since the war had begun, and the rumours about strange aeroplanes in the neighbourhood turned out to be without substance. But Churchill remained unrepentant. Bignold, he said, could comfort himself that others in much less suspicious circumstances had been far more inconvenienced. 'And for myself', he recorded later, 'I say without hesitation that in similar circumstances I should do the same again.'[29]

It is easy to laugh at this episode, and indeed it might be classed – especially if we accept Churchill's account – as in the same histrionic vein as the siege of Sidney Street. But anxieties about German espionage had long pervaded all levels of the Navy. During the 1913 invasion exercises Churchill had drafted a discussion paper entitled 'A Time Table of a Nightmare' and sent it for comment to Vice-Admiral Lewis Bayly, one of the few senior naval officers whom he admired. Bayly replied with a hypothetical scenario of his own in which he imagined he was Germany's spymaster. 'I would have an agent in New York', he told Churchill, 'and one at every principal port in the UK. These agents would telegraph to New York, to be transferred to Berlin, in the kind of code here enclosed – allowing four hours for transmission and re-transmission, there would be ample time.' He ended with a reminder of Napoleon's network of spies in Britain.[30] Bayly's fears were matched by Beatty. Not long after the Bignold scare he told Churchill that if 'we ever use Scapa anchorage again I trust that some steps be taken to deal with the spies that exist there, which are a very serious danger.' He also told his wife that 'all over Scotland anywhere there is a possibility of there being a naval base, the postmistress (not postmaster) is a German.'[31] Churchill was sympathetic. Later that month he had the Admiralty assume control of censorship throughout the north and west coast of Scotland and the north coast of Ireland. Then, in early November, after high-level Admiralty consultations, he declared most of northern Scotland a prohibited area. 'The exclusion of all alien-born postal servants', he added, 'must be undertaken forthwith.'[32]

4

SIGINT: 'The Intelligence that Never Fails'

By the time Churchill was taking radical security steps, the safety of the Grand Fleet was being transformed by a revolutionary new source of intelligence. This was SIGINT, or signals intelligence. Churchill was fascinated by it. 'Our Intelligence service', he boasted in *The World Crisis*, 'has won and deserved world-wide fame. More than perhaps any other Power, we were successful in the war in penetrating the intentions of the enemy.'[1]

The day after war was declared he received an early-afternoon visit from Sir Henry Oliver and Sir Alfred Ewing, the Director of Naval Education. A meticulous dresser with a penchant for striped waistcoats and bow ties, one of Ewing's interests was radio telegraphy. Another, cryptography, had led him to design a cipher machine that had been seriously considered by the Admiralty only two months before. This explained his arrival with Oliver, for as soon as war broke out Oliver found his desk swamped with intercepts of German wireless messages but with no means or expertise to decipher them. He turned to Ewing for help, and Ewing agreed to create an Admiralty decoding centre.

Churchill's knowledge and understanding of intercepts and their intelligence value reflected orthodox thinking. During the South African conflict the British had successfully broken Boer ciphers and over the following few years the War Office carefully planned how to exploit cryptography in the next war. But the emphasis was on cable traffic, where intercepts were limited in number and restricted in value. Wireless was a new technology, and the vulnerability of messages sent over the airwaves – and hence the rich harvest of intelligence they yielded – was severely underestimated. The 1914 *Naval Annual* declared that interception posed no threat to naval radio transmissions.

Churchill accepted this view. During his exchanges with Vice Admiral Bayly on 'A Time Table of a Nightmare' he had even queried Bayly's frequent references to the hypothetical German interception of British radio signals. 'How is this possible?' he asked. 'Surely our wireless orders will be in cipher, and we ought not to assume that they can be instantly intercepted and decoded.'[2] Events quickly revealed his error and, as with other forms of new technology, he was eager to learn. On hearing Oliver's account of the intercept bounty that lay on his desk, and of Ewing's interest in cryptography, he readily agreed to their proposal. Thus was born what became known as 'Room 40', named after the room in the Admiralty Old Building that eventually became its home.[3]

Room 40's early targets were German ciphers containing strategic intelligence. But this priority changed with the arrival of the first significant intercepts relating to a quite different source: German naval tactical traffic. This promised to open the door to the mysteries of their High Seas Fleet.

In the early hours of 26 August there occurred what has been described as 'the most fateful accident in the history of cryptography'.[4] The *Magdeburg,* a German light cruiser, was carrying out a reconnaissance mission in the Gulf of Finland when she ran aground off the coast of Estonia. Amidst reports of approaching Russian warships the captain decided to blow her up, but before the crew could abandon ship in good order the fuses were prematurely lit and confusion followed. Then, Churchill wrote, 'The body of a drowned German under-officer was picked up by the Russians . . . and clasped in his bosom by arms rigid in death, were the cypher and signals books of the German Navy.'[5] It was a striking image. What the Russians in fact recovered were copies of the Imperial German Navy code book and cipher key hurriedly flung overboard as well as left behind in the Captain's cabin. But Churchill can be forgiven the poetic licence, for this was an intelligence coup. The Russians immediately offered the Captain's undamaged copy to the British and it was carried to Scapa Flow, heavily weighted with lead in case of capture, on board a British ship, HMS *Theseus.* Sir George Buchanan, the British ambassador in St Petersburg, kept Churchill and Sir Edward Grey informed, and by the time the precious cargo reached Britain the King and Asquith were also in on the story. Captain Wolkoff, the Russian Naval Attaché, delivered it personally to Churchill in London – 'a gift more precious than a dozen Fabergé eggs'.[6]

It was also as priceless as the reconstructed version of the German Enigma machine presented to the British by the Poles in 1939. Shortly afterwards, as the result of a coup by the Royal Australian Navy, the Admiralty also received a copy of the *Handelsverkehrsbuch* (HVB), used by the German Admiralty and warships for communicating with their merchantmen and within the High Seas Fleet itself. Then, in late November, the Admiralty notched up its final triumph when a British trawler dredged up off the Dutch coast a copy of the *Verkehrsbuch* (VB) jettisoned from a German destroyer sunk in an earlier encounter with British warships. This was the last of the Imperial German Navy's three vital code books, and with its capture virtually any of their radio signals could now be read. Before long, Room 40 was also breaking German diplomatic ciphers.

Churchill rapidly appreciated that such high-grade intelligence needed special treatment to safeguard its secrecy. Already information gleaned from the SKM cipher had been passed to the French Naval Attaché and sent on to Paris by conventional and insecure channels; the secrets of Room 40 could soon be known in Berlin. Urgency was heightened with the first successful decrypt of a cipher sent by the German Commander of the High Seas Fleet, Admiral von Ingenohl, to U-boats on patrol in the Irish Sea and English Channel. Here was operational intelligence of the highest importance, able to decide the fates of the two great battle fleets that faced each other across the North Sea.

Yet guarding such important information was only one aspect of the challenge that now faced the Admiralty. Individual intercepts themselves meant little – or worse, could be entirely misleading – unless they were properly assessed by experts familiar with the larger intelligence picture. Churchill's natural instincts resisted this conclusion. Always a 'hands-on' minister, he found the temptation to involve himself in the details of operational matters irresistible. Here he met his match in the newly appointed Director of Naval Intelligence, Captain Reginald 'Blinker' Hall.

Hall's greatest wartime intelligence triumph was his handling of the 1917 Zimmerman Telegram affair that helped bring the United States into the war and won him a knighthood. Walter Hines Page, the Anglophile American ambassador in London, described him to President Woodrow Wilson as a clear case of genius, and Admiral Sims, the Commander of US naval forces in Europe, spoke in awe of 'the uncanny ability of this great Sherlock Holmes'. The son of Britain's first Director of Naval Intelligence, Hall earned his nickname from the habit of screwing up his eyes and blinking furiously as he talked. Appointed DNI on Oliver's promotion to naval Chief of Staff shortly after war broke out, he also embraced with gusto the cloak-and-dagger world of deception, double agents, censorship, disinformation, bribery and blackmail, and quickly became one of the most powerful men in Whitehall.

He soon learned how to cope with Churchill, leaving an indelible image of him at work that would be instantly familiar to his Chiefs of Staff in the Second World War. A great admirer of Churchill, he praised his 'dash' and genius, and noted in awe his 'almost frightening' energy and capacity for work. Even in highly technical matters Churchill would insist on the elaborate presentation of his own views, often arguing with such persuasiveness that Admiralty officials, through sheer exhaustion, would capitulate against their better judgement. Hall vividly recalled one occasion when he himself managed successfully, but only just, to resist such treatment.

> Once, I remember, I was sent for by Mr Churchill very late at night. He wished to discuss some point or other with me – at once. To be candid, I have not the slightest recollection what it was: I only know that his views and mine were diametrically opposed. We argued at some length. I *know* I was right, but Mr Churchill was determined to bring me round to his point of view, and he continued his argument in the most brilliant fashion. It was long after midnight, and I was dreadfully tired, but nothing seemed to tire the First Lord. He continued to talk, and I distinctly recall that although it would be wholly against my will, I should in a very short while be agreeing with everything that he said. But a bit of me still rebelled, and . . . I began to mutter to myself: 'My name is Hall, my name is Hall . . .'
>
> Suddenly he broke off to look frowningly at me. 'What's that you're muttering to yourself?' he demanded.
>
> 'I'm saying', I told him, 'that my name is Hall because if I listen to you much longer I shall be convinced that it's Brown.'
>
> 'Then you don't agree with what I've been saying?' He was laughing heartily.
>
> 'First Lord', said I, 'I don't agree with one word of it, but I can't argue with you; I've not had the training.'
>
> So the matter was dropped, and I went to bed.[7]

Churchill followed Room 40's work with minute attention, not only to consume its product but also to follow its production.

Although Room 40 possessed the German code books, the key to read them was changeable. On one memorable occasion a German change of key precipitated a major crisis for the code-breakers. All the staff were mobilised and the cryptographers who had gone home for the evening were summoned back by telephone. Work continued frantically all night until, to everyone's relief, the new key was obtained in the early hours of the next morning. The first to thank them was Churchill. Striding into Room 40 first thing that day he congratulated the experts who had done such a splendid job. But there was a price to pay. His enthusiasm for the details of intelligence created tensions that came to a head shortly after Hall took over as DNI. Out of this crisis came a decision that marks a milestone in the history of British intelligence.

Churchill, still obsessed by fears of German invasion, regarded the occupied Belgian ports as dangerous staging posts. He ordered that all intelligence reports from Belgium, 'as and when they arrived', should be sent directly to him. In the first week of November Hall received intelligence from an agent at Zeebrugge reporting that the Germans had rushed two or three hundred 'submarines' there. From previous reports Hall knew that this particular agent used the word to indicate any object below the sea's surface and that what he meant were mines, not submarines, of which the Germans were known to have only about two dozen. But dutifully as instructed he sent the raw report, exactly as received, to Churchill.

The result was an explosion. Churchill instantly rebuked Hall for giving credence to the report. Was he aware how many officers and men would be needed for such a huge flotilla of submarines? Was there any evidence that Germany had trained such numbers? 'The function of the Intelligence Division', he chided, 'is not merely to collect and pass on the Munchausen tales of spies and untrustworthy agents, but carefully to sift and scrutinise the intelligence they receive, and in putting it forward to indicate the degree of probability which attaches to it . . .' The incident graphically illustrates a temptation into which Churchill was only too prone to fall: he wanted to be his *own* intelligence officer and make instant assessments of the material in front of him. But why expend such time and energy, Hall demanded, when responsibility for acting on the report lay elsewhere? Was Churchill, the Minister, to spend his valuable time deciding what to do about German mines in Zeebrugge? That was the nub of the issue. Churchill, Hall confessed, 'had the defects of his great qualities: he was essentially a "one-man" show. It was not in his nature to allow anybody except himself to be the executive authority when any action of importance had to be taken.'[8]

Churchill quickly learned from experience, however. The day after this row with Hall he wrote out in longhand a 'Charter' for Room 40 headed 'Exclusively Secret' – a unique designation he concocted himself:

> An officer of the War Staff, preferably from the ID [Intelligence Division] should be selected to study all the decoded intercepts, not only current but past, and to compare them continually with what actually took place in order to penetrate the German mind and movements and make reports. All these intercepts are to be written in a locked book with their decodes, and all other copies are to be collected and burnt. All new messages are to be entered in the book, and the book is only to be handled under direction from COS [Chief of Staff – Oliver]. The officer selected is for the present to do no other work. I shall be obliged if Sir Alfred Ewing will associate himself continuously with this work.[9]

Churchill initialled the order in red ink. Fisher, now the First Sea Lord, signed in green.

With this charter, Churchill did three things. First, he recognised the prime importance of Room 40's work and the need to give it special and top-secret priority. Second, he acknowledged that intelligence needed to be interpreted by an expert if 'Munchausen tales' were not to be given credibility. Finally, by drafting the order himself, he indicated his intention to keep a close eye on Room 40's work. Ewing's code-breakers now focused their energies on tactical naval traffic revealing the movements of the German High Seas Fleet and enemy submarines.

At the same time Hall appointed a qualified naval officer to analyse and produce appreciations of the intercepts. This was Commander Herbert Hope, who had been working in the Admiralty Chart Room. His job was to 'extract the juice' from the raw intercepts and to provide naval expertise to Ewing's collection of cryptographers and linguists. It was he who now decided which intercepts should be circulated and which merely logged, and he compiled a detailed order of battle for the German fleet.

What was extraordinary was who did, and did not, receive the intercepts. In a second order – this time classified 'Most Secret' and dated 29 November 1914[10] – Churchill decreed that only one copy should be made of each intercept and it was to go, 'direct and exclusively', to Oliver as Chief of Staff, who would then pass it on to the First Sea Lord. This meant it was seen within the Admiralty by a handful of people. Apart from the cryptographers themselves, the regular recipients were Churchill, Oliver, the First and Second Sea Lords, the Naval Secretary, 'Blinker' Hall, Sir Arthur Wilson (the retired First Sea Lord brought back on the declaration of war to help the Admiralty), the Director and Assistant Director of the Operations Division, and the Duty Captains.

Remarkably absent from the list were any members of the Cabinet or War Council, the supreme body created by Asquith to run the war. Outside the Admiralty the Prime Minister alone was routinely informed of Britain's great intelligence triumph and even then he received the information only by courtesy of Churchill. 'Mr Churchill', wrote Oliver, 'would not allow anyone to know about the decyphering . . . without his permission.'[11] Asquith confided as much to Venetia Stanley, his close confidante to whom he frequently scribbled notes of endearment during Cabinet meetings. In one he referred to an item of Room 40 intelligence and added that 'Winston revealed to me as a *profound secret*, wh. he is not going even to breathe to Grey [the Foreign Secretary], that tomorrow (Tues) the Germans are contemplating a new naval adventure against us. So keep your eyes open, as I shall. I shall say nothing to any other human being . . .'[12] Asquith also told his daughter Violet about the work of Room 40. She found the secret difficult to keep and wished she had not been told. 'So much depended on it that the knowledge tortured me', she wrote years later. 'I was sometimes haunted by the insane fear which grips one on the giddy edge of cliffs and tempts one to jump over – the fear that I might go mad and shriek it from the housetops.'[13]

Given the measures that Churchill took to guard Room 40's secret, it seems bizarre that Asquith should have been so careless with his confidences. But he was by no means alone. Security in general remained lax and gossip was rampant. Walter Hines Page considered that the social contacts of his American Embassy staff provided him with the best secret service that any neutral power could expect. Churchill himself was sometimes no better than Asquith, despite his special order to the Navy stressing the need for 'secrecy, silence, and suddenness' and an extraordinary request to the King to be careful in what he said. Clementine regularly burned secret documents Churchill sent her to read at Pear Tree Cottage that summer, and Violet Asquith's burden of knowledge owed as much to him as to her father, for he told her in advance about plans for the Dardanelles as well as the secret of the intercepts. Churchill regularly showed off the War Room, with its charts pinpointing the positions of British ships, to journalists and other visitors whom he sought to impress. Oliver's first task after visiting Churchill each morning was to shift the flags showing any important movements to incorrect places. After all, the MPs, Cabinet members, editors, bishops and other dignitaries didn't know the difference.

Churchill had seized upon a vital source of intelligence and instinctively realised its power. He had yet to appreciate how complex a matter it would become. As the trickle of daily intercepts became a flood, his notion that one officer could handle them all had to be modified. But he was determined to restrict knowledge to the smallest possible number of people in the Admiralty, and created a system that was over-centralised and inefficient.

For one thing, Commander Hope at first found himself completely isolated from Room 40 and only after pleading with Fisher was he allowed to meet the producers of the reports he was expected to analyse. As for Ewing, he continued to operate independently of Hall, and while the latter personally knew about the intercepts other members of his staff did not. This damaging separation of the cryptographers from intelligence was rectified only after Churchill had left the Admiralty. More harmful still, Churchill's system excluded the commanders at sea. This was not Ewing's original intent. He prepared one hundred copies of the HVB code book and key for circulation to every ship in the British fleet, but Churchill firmly stamped on the plan and insisted that intercepts were to remain within the Admiralty. It alone would decide what intelligence should be passed to ships at sea. This, as events were soon to prove, was a mistake.

Ewing was soon so confident about his victory over German ciphers that five days before Christmas he told Fisher that Room 40 could confidently and accurately read all German naval signals. What this meant in practice had been revealed to Churchill just four days previously.

Shortly after eight o'clock on the morning of Wednesday 16 December 1914 two German battle cruisers loomed out of the mist off Scarborough, on the North Yorkshire coast. Approaching to within a mile of the shore they indiscriminately shelled the town before disappearing back into the fog. Half an hour later they inflicted similar treatment on Whitby. Further north three other cruisers shelled Hartlepool. In all, the attacks killed or injured some five hundred civilians and left behind an angry public demanding to know how the most powerful Navy in the world had failed to prevent the attack. 'Where was the Navy?' asked the Scarborough coroner, a question that echoed around the country. Churchill, who bore the brunt of the public anger, was unable to tell the whole story. 'We had to bear in silence the censures of our countrymen', he lamented. 'We could never admit for fear of compromising our secret information where our squadrons were, or how near the German raiding cruisers had been to their destruction.'[14] How near is revealed by the events that had begun on the Monday.

At seven in the evening Sir Arthur Wilson informed Churchill that intercepts revealed German battle cruisers to be on the move in a possible raid on the east coast. The intelligence did not reveal their destination, but did give their time of departure and return to Germany. Churchill and his advisers decided to catch the Germans as they returned home, and Jellicoe was ordered to ensure that battle and light cruisers were in place to intercept the returning enemy ships. He duly dispatched the Second Battle Squadron to meet them off the south-east coast of Dogger Bank.

There followed a tense thirty-six hours. Was the intelligence correct? Was this an opportunity to strike a great naval victory by catching the Germans unawares? After alerting Asquith to be prepared for dramatic events, Churchill waited for the news with mounting impatience. The tension broke while he was still enjoying his morning bath. The door opened and an officer hurried in with a naval signal. Churchill took the note with a dripping hand and read: 'German battle cruisers bombarding Hartlepool.'

Jumping out of the bath and pulling on clothes over his damp body, Churchill ran downstairs to the War Room. Here he found that Fisher had already arrived, and Oliver, who regularly slept in the War Room, was methodically plotting positions on the map. They showed the German battle cruisers off the Yorkshire coast; 150 miles to the east, cutting off their line of retreat, were the ships of the Second Battle Squadron. As the three men ate a hurried breakfast, it seemed as though the trap was about to be sprung. But the opportunity was missed. By mid-afternoon it had become dismally apparent that the Germans had escaped. North Sea mists descended and the British ships lost sight of their prey. In addition, human error played a part, with mistakes made in signalling at a crucial moment.

The episode also highlighted deeper problems with the system for handling Room 40's intelligence. Incomplete deductions had been drawn from the initial intercept alerting the Admiralty to the raid. From the absence of any reference to battleships, Oliver had concluded that the High Seas Fleet itself was taking no part in the engagement. He was wrong. Von Ingenohl had ordered his battle fleet out to lend support to Admiral Hipper's raiding force. So when a subsequent intercept, in the early afternoon, revealed its presence in the North Sea, the War Room mistakenly jumped to the conclusion that it had just appeared and was advancing towards the British ships. Fearing an unequal encounter the War Room ordered its ships not to advance too far east. The reality was that von Ingenohl, far from advancing, had decided to retreat on *his* mistaken assumption that he was about to encounter the British Grand Fleet. The Admiralty error, compounded by a two-hour delay in transmitting a crucial intercept revealing Hipper's exact position, allowed the Germans to escape.

The Navy lamented that a golden opportunity had been lost. Fisher believed that everyone involved had made a hash of it, Jellicoe was 'intensely unhappy' and Beatty confessed that 'there never was a more bitterly disappointing day'. Churchill was also dismayed. The only comfort he could draw – and it was a major one – was that the intercepts, a new and untested source, had proved reliable. As long as Room 40 continued to decipher German signals any major enemy move into the North Sea would be detected. The Grand Fleet could now rest more secure than in the past. No longer did it have to carry out endless reconnaissance sweeps of the North Sea or remain in a constant and anxious state of alert. That was worth a great deal. 'While the priceless information lasts', he reassured Jellicoe early in the New Year, 'we ought to rest our fleets and flotillas to the utmost.'[15]

There remained concern that the intercepts might dry up. Moreover, the crucial meeting in the war room on the morning of the 16th had dealt with information that, as Churchill candidly admitted, was 'obscure and uncertain'. Intelligence rarely presents a picture that is complete, but the gaps and misreadings were not helped by the rigid system Churchill had devised. Neither Room 40 itself in the shape of Ewing, nor the Intelligence Division represented by Hall or Commander Hope, were asked to comment on the intercept. Instead, the assessment was made by four people: Churchill, Sir Arthur Wilson, Sir Henry Oliver and Admiral Fisher. Nor did the system permit Jellicoe and those who would have to act on the information to receive it directly. The major actors at sea were dependent on the Admiralty. As Jellicoe pointed out forcefully to Fisher, if there were delays in Whitehall vital intelligence was denied to the admirals. Churchill apparently took this to heart and agreed that in the event of another German raid Jellicoe would be given complete control of the operation and that all information received by the Admiralty would be sent simultaneously to both him and Beatty.

Tension once more began to mount as Churchill waited for the next German sortie. It came just before midday on 23 January 1915 when Sir Arthur Wilson, followed by Oliver carrying charts and compasses, burst into his office and announced, 'First Lord, these fellows are coming out again.' 'When?' demanded Churchill. 'Tonight', replied Wilson. 'We have just time to get Beatty there.'[16]

Room 40 had intercepted a signal from von Ingenohl to Hipper ordering him to reconnoitre Dogger Bank. Hipper's battle and light cruisers would leave the Jade River that evening after dark and return twenty-four hours later. The Admiralty triumvirate ordered Beatty's force of two squadrons to rendezvous with Tyrwhitt's force from Harwich early the next morning thirty miles north of Dogger Bank and intercept Hipper's force. Later that day, the Grand Fleet left Scapa Flow for a general sweep of the North Sea with orders 'to act as you feel best to intercept the enemy'. All ships were ordered to maintain radio silence wherever possible.

That evening Churchill attended a dinner for Alexandre Millerand, the French Minister of War. He found it difficult to concentrate, 'separated . . . by a film of isolated knowledge and overwhelming inward preoccupation . . . Only one thought could reign – battle at dawn! Battle for the first time in history between mighty super-Dreadnought ships! And there was added a thrilling sense of a Beast of Prey moving stealthily hour by hour towards the Trap.'[17]

Before dawn he was awake and waiting in the Admiralty War Room. At eight Admiral Goodenough's 1st Light Cruiser squadron broke radio silence to report an initial sighting of Hipper's force. Churchill recalled the scene with palpable excitement:

There can be few purely mental experiences more charged with cold excitement than to follow, almost from minute to minute, the phases of a great naval action from the silent rooms of the Admiralty. Out on blue . . . there is the wrath of battle . . . But in Whitehall only the clock ticks, and quiet men enter with quick steps laying slips of pencilled paper before other men equally silent who draw lines and scribble calculations, and point with the finger or make brief subdued comments. Telegram succeeds telegram at a few minutes interval as they are picked up and decoded, often in the wrong sequence, frequently of dubious import; and out of these a picture always flickering and changing rises in the mind, and imagination strikes out around it at every stage flashes of hope or fear.[18]

Out in the North Sea the water was calm and visibility perfect. Soon after nine o'clock the leading British ships opened fire on the *Blücher*, the rearmost ship of Hipper's squadron which was now retreating rapidly to the east. It seemed as though Churchill's hopes of a great naval victory might be realised, but once again human error and misunderstanding intervened. Beatty, in his flagship the *Lion*, received reports of submarines. Believing he was being lured into a trap, and himself sighting what he thought was a periscope, he ordered his ships to turn sharply to port, putting them astern of the enemy. Then, as he desperately tried to signal his ships to continue hot pursuit, a signalling error led them to concentrate all their fire on the *Blücher*. The other German ships escaped and by that evening were safely back in the shelter of the Jade estuary.

The Dogger Bank incident remained just that – an incident. Technically it was a British victory – the *Blücher* sunk with the loss of 951 German lives as against the *Lion* damaged and 10 British sailors killed. The press and public were elated. Scarborough was avenged. But those in the know believed that another opportunity presented by Room 40's intelligence had been lost. 'The disappointment of that day is more than I can bear to think of', wrote Beatty, 'everyone thinks it was a great success, when in reality it was a terrible failure.'[19] Churchill resisted all demands for an internal inquiry. He was glad to bask in the public praise after several months of bad publicity for the Navy.

Once again, events at sea had exposed serious flaws in the intelligence system. Despite the promise to Jellicoe, the Admiralty still kept a tight hold on intelligence. The Churchill, Wilson and Oliver triumvirate had determined the place and time for Beatty to intercept Hipper's forces in the North Sea, yet conditions there were notoriously unpredictable – fog could descend without warning – and in reality Beatty made the deadline only by traversing a German minefield. Nor did the War Room provide him with prior information about the whereabouts of German submarines. Had he known they were some forty miles to the south – information sent to him only after he made his crucial turn to port – the results of the encounter would have been rather different.

Beatty's reaction to the U-boat rumour revealed how deeply the submarine was feared, a new weapon of war whose potential was slow to be understood. Conventional opinion judged it as principally defensive, useful only for operating close to its own shores. The Admiralty was quickly undeceived when U-boats began to appear as far north as Scapa Flow, and the nation was shocked by the torpedoing of three cruisers off the Dutch coast with the loss of almost 1,500 officers and men. By early 1915 U-boats were penetrating the Irish Sea and threatening transatlantic shipping. Merchant ships carrying war supplies from the United States now became a target for the Germans. Early in February Berlin announced it would no longer abide by the conventions of international law by which enemy merchant ships could be sunk only after they had been stopped and searched, and provision made for the safety of crew and passengers. The waters surrounding the British Isles, the Germans added, were now a war zone and all ships would be destroyed regardless.

Churchill closely followed the U-boat sorties. In January 1915 Hope began to submit a daily return, based on Room 40's intercepts, of the strength and general location of the German U-boat fleet. Its recipients remained restricted to Churchill, Fisher, Wilson and Oliver. On a piece of graph paper Hope carefully listed the number of each U-boat and the flotilla to which it belonged in the left-hand column. Next to it he added a comment on its known location and any information about its movements. He frequently included some general comment.

Churchill would scrutinise these reports, making comments or asking questions. Little escaped his attention and he often suggested a suitable response. In late February 1915, for example, when Hope noted that U-33 was at Emden 'preparing for a distant undertaking', later reporting that it had gone to Wilhelmshaven where engine trouble meant it would not be ready for action until mid-March, Churchill drew Hope's attention to the first with its ominous phrase about preparing for action. 'Watch this carefully', he instructed.[20]

Even when he had no comment or query he carefully initialled Hope's reports to indicate that he had read them. This he did on 1 May when he received Hope's sheet, compiled the day before, that noted against U-20 'At sea since Apl 30: gone NW: under orders for Irish Sea'. Neither he nor Hope were to know that thirteen days later U-20 was to fire a single torpedo into the Cunard liner *Lusitania* and send it to the bottom of the sea with the loss of some 1,200 lives.

U-20 was commanded by Captain Walter Schwieger, a tall, blond and blue-eyed 30-year-old veteran of Germany's submarine war. As Hope's intelligence accurately reported, his orders were to take U-20 into the Irish Sea then head for the busy waters at the mouth of the Mersey River near Liverpool. The day after he left Emden, the *Lusitania* sailed from New York for Liverpool. The fastest and most luxurious liner in the world, her passengers including almost two hundred Americans. By midday on 7 May she was off the Old Head of Kinsale, a prominent landmark for ships approaching St George's Channel. The weather was fine, the visibility excellent, the sea calm. U-20 fired its torpedos striking her on the starboard side just behind the bridge. She sank in eighteen minutes. In the panic and confusion most passengers never made it to the lifeboats. A macabre twist was the discovery, much later, that three suspected German spies had gone down with the ship. Caught on board with cameras shortly after leaving New York, they had been locked and unwittingly entombed in the ship's cell.

Conspiracy theories have ever since swirled around the *Lusitania* tragedy.[21] There was no doubt who sunk the ship – the German government admitted it and the German press lauded it as a victory for the U-boat war – but was the *Lusitania* quite the victim portrayed by British and American propaganda? Was there a conspiracy deliberately to send her into the path of the U-20 and thus swing American opinion irrevocably to the British cause? If the British had cracked the German codes and were able to track their U-boats, why did they not warn the ship and save the lives of 1,200 innocent people? And if there was a conspiracy, which British figure had spoken most forcefully about the need to 'embroil' the Americans with the Germans? Moreover, who had the means to direct such a sinister enterprise? None other than the man who commanded the Admiralty: Winston Churchill.

The *Lusitania* was certainly a less innocent ship than British propaganda claimed. Cunard had built her in the first place with the help of a massive government loan, and when war broke out its cargo space was placed at the government's disposal and the master made subject to Admiralty control when at sea. Thus, while to all outward appearances a simple commercial passenger liner, it was also a merchant ship under government instructions carrying war supplies from the neutral United States to a belligerent Britain. On its fateful journey it was carrying several million cartridges and other war material.

Churchill knew this, as did the Germans. He also knew how important it was to win wholehearted American support for the British war effort if the vital chain of supplies from North America was to hold. This was not guaranteed. Important segments of American society were either actively anti-British or simply isolationist, and President Woodrow Wilson strongly protested against the British blockade of Germany that interfered with the freedom of the seas and America's right to trade with Europe. In February 1915, eight days after the Germans announced their submarine blockade of the British Isles, Churchill told Walter Runciman, President of the Board of Trade, that it was vital to attract neutral shipping to British shores in the hope 'of embroiling the US with Germany'. The more neutral the shipping the better, 'and if some of it gets into trouble, better still'.[22]

Conspiracy theorists have identified this as the smoking gun that proves Churchill wished to provoke a war between the United States and Germany. The opportunity was allegedly provided by secret intelligence revealing that U-20 was in the Irish Sea and that the *Lusitania* was a major target. Churchill's sudden departure for Paris two days before the U-20 attack compounds the allegations, implying that he set the conspiracy in motion and then absented himself to let matters take their course. Once the ship was sunk he supported a cover-up that pointed the finger of blame at the *Lusitania*'s captain.

Little of this stands up to close examination. If the ship was packed with vital war supplies, it is extremely unlikely that Churchill would have arranged for it to be sent to the bottom of the ocean. It would have made far more sense if less important supplies had been on board rather than precious shells and cartridges. Second, when Churchill talked of 'embroiling' the United States with Germany he did not mean war. On the contrary, it was in British interests not to have the United States enter the conflict at this time: as a belligerent, the US would need to equip its own armed forces and supplies, and the transatlantic pipeline would diminish. What Churchill intended was a souring of Washington–Berlin relations that would benefit Britain by turning American opinion decisively against the Germans. For this he did not need the deaths of 1,200 civilian passengers on a British ship, even if many of them were American. As Britain's ambassador in Washington, Sir Cecil Spring-Rice, forcefully pointed out the day following the disaster, Britain's main interest in the United States was as a source of supplies.

As for intelligence, Room 40 did not stretch to locating German submarines all or even most of the time. Hope's lists were compiled from intercepts of the position reports that U-boats usually made to their home base for the first two or three days of their journey. They gave accurate information about their course and speed of advance, but once out of radio range the intercepts ceased. After that, knowledge of their whereabouts came from surface sightings and sinkings.

U-boat reports were regularly sent on to local commanders and then to ships that appeared threatened. U-20's departure, for example, led Oliver to alert a number of warships and some – including the battleship *Orion*, due to proceed from Devonport to Scapa Flow – delayed their sailing or were given destroyer escorts. Further news of U-20, apart from some early intercepts picked up in the North Sea, came after the first sinking. Queenstown immediately sent an *en clair* message to all merchant ships that a U-boat was active off southern Ireland and after midnight a similar warning was broadcast to all homeward-bound British merchant ships. The next day, after U-20's further sinkings, Queenstown warned all British ships that U-boats were active in the southern part of the Irish Channel and had been last heard of twenty miles south of the Conigbeg lightship. There were plenty of warnings for the *Lusitania* to pick up. More might conceivably have been done, but the cause was not conspiracy, rather an Admiralty mindset slow to wake up to the ruthless nature of modern war at sea and still convinced that merchant ships should be treated differently from warships. Oliver was quite prepared to order warships to stay in port, or give them escorts, at the news of U-20's sortie. He could have done something similar for the *Lusitania*; instead, he left her to take her own chances. This was more foolish in retrospect than at the time. A previous attempt to provide her with an escort had failed and the liner had still reached port safely. She was a fast ship with every chance of evading a submarine by zigzagging or even passing unnoticed altogether.

Churchill was not the mainspring of a conspiracy to sink the *Lusitania* because none existed. Ironically, he himself thought there might be one. His immediate response was to initiate a damage-control exercise to absolve himself and the Admiralty of blame. Five days after the tragedy the Admiralty's Trade Division, responsible for merchant shipping, suggested that German spies or sympathisers might have penetrated Cunard's New York office and learned of the *Lusitania*'s route. The manager was an anti-British American and other officials were German nationals. The man in charge of the Cunard dock in New York was an Irishman and, according to Sir Cecil Spring-Rice, was 'intimate with German agents'. The report also hinted that Captain Turner of the *Lusitania* was either utterly incompetent or, more sinister, had 'been got at by the Germans'. The impetuous and increasingly unstable Fisher endorsed the suggestion with gusto, declared that Turner had obviously been bribed, and demanded that he be arrested whatever the result of the official inquiry.

When these suggestions reached Churchill he seemed to grasp at the conspiracy notion. His own position at stake, he agreed that Turner should be pursued 'without check'.[23] He also embraced the suspicions that spies had been at work, ordered that security in New York should immediately be tightened up, and agreed that Room 40 intelligence should be concealed from any inquiry. This was not to cover up a conspiracy, but to safeguard the secret that Britain was reading German ciphers.

In any case Churchill had far more pressing things on his mind than concocting some spurious conspiracy around the *Lusitania*. The Dardanelles campaign was reaching its disastrous climax and he had only ten days left in charge of the Admiralty. While the public howled for revenge against the Hun and the scapegoat-hunting season began, Churchill was fighting for political survival.

The disastrous Dardanelles campaign caused the death or injury of over half a million men and inflicted a political wound on Churchill that left a permanent scar. The seductive vision of forcing the Dardanelles and compelling Turkey to quit the war captivated the War Council in January 1915 as a way of breaking the stalemate on the Western Front and relieving a hard-pressed Russia. An Anglo-French naval attack on Turkish forts and batteries was launched in March and quickly encountered disaster when six of the nine battle-ships engaged were either sunk or crippled. Six weeks later 30,000 troops under the command of General Sir Ian Hamilton landed on the Gallipoli peninsula in an effort to accomplish what the Navy had failed to do. This effort was also in vain. Soon they and the thousands who followed were bogged down in a campaign of butchery that ended only with their withdrawal in January 1916.[24]

Responsibility for the disaster was widely shared and many factors explained Churchill's enthusiasm. Intelligence helped to fuel it throughout. Reports in October 1914 of Turkish plans to invade Egypt and diplomatic intercepts revealing promises to Vienna of an early entry into the war strengthened his belligerence. After Turkey entered the war in November, and especially following the January 1915 War Council decision, he seized on any evidence that would buttress his case.

He was particularly fired up by a Room 40 intercept that reached him a week before the March naval attack. It was a message radioed from the Nauen transmitter outside Berlin to Admiral von Usedom, the German Inspector-General of Coast Defences and Mines in the Dardanelles, reporting that the Kaiser was doing everything possible to arrange for ammunition supplies to be sent and that von Usedom should maintain a confident tone with the Turks. Berlin was also considering sending out a German or Austrian submarine. Hall immediately took the intercept to Fisher, whom he found standing by the fireplace in Churchill's office. Fisher read it aloud and waved it over his head. 'By God', he shouted, 'I'll go through tomorrow', meaning he would order Carden, the Admiral in charge of the operation, to proceed with the naval assault the next day. Churchill was equally excited. After carefully reading the message he cried, 'That means they've come to the end of the ammunition.' Fisher repeated 'Tomorrow' and Churchill nodded and said, 'Then get the orders out.' Up until this point he had advised Carden to proceed cautiously. Now, disguising the source as an agent, he told Carden that the enemy was harassed and anxious, and that he should press forward 'resolutely day and night the unavoidable losses being accepted'. The severe naval setback of the first day's attack did little to dent his enthusiasm. The next morning, as the War Council digested the news, he again used intelligence about the Turkish ammunition crisis to argue that the operation should continue. As with Carden (who collapsed under the strain and was replaced by Admiral de Robeck), he did not reveal the source. Only the combined resistance of Fisher, Wilson and Jackson prevented him from ordering de Robeck to renew the attack, but it did not deter him from instructing Hall to launch a subversive operation to stop war material passing through Romania and Bulgaria to Turkey. Churchill told him to recruit Bulgarian and Romanian agents to watch the railways and canals. 'Money should be spent freely', he suggested, to bribe railway employees to provide intelligence about ammunition transiting the Balkans bound for Turkey. 'Not a day should be lost in instituting this necessary service.'[25]

The encounter in Churchill's office also revealed another secret operation lubricated by sovereigns, one of the most extraordinary episodes of the whole war. While Fisher sat down to draft the orders to Carden, Churchill turned to Hall and asked him what the latest news was from his agents in Turkey. He was referring to George Griffin Eady and Edward Whittall. Their secret mission, in an operation suggested by Hankey, one-time Intelligence Officer of the Mediterranean Fleet, was to bribe the Turks to leave the war. Eady was a civil engineer with much experience of Constantinople and close contacts with Turkey's leaders. Whittall was a veteran member of one of the old British merchant houses in Constantinople who had lived there all his life and knew almost everyone of political importance. Early in 1915 Hall recruited Eady and Whittall and authorised them to commit the British government to up to £4 million. Using as their principal intermediary the Grand Rabbi of Turkey, their main contact was Talaat Bey, the acting Minister of Finance and Minister of the Interior. In February news filtered back to London that certain Turks were willing to talk peace, intelligence that spurred Churchill's enthusiasm for continuing to force a collapse. By early March things had progressed to the point where the Turks had agreed to meet Eady and Whittall. At the very moment Churchill was asking questions of Hall, they were on their way to the Turkish town of Dedeagach and a meeting with Talaat.

Hall took the opportunity to brief Churchill more fully on the operation and for the first time revealed the huge sum of money involved. Churchill was clearly taken aback: 'Who authorised this? The Cabinet surely knows nothing about it?' Hall replied that he had acted on his own initiative. 'I imagine they'd be glad enough to pay', he added. Flabbergasted, Churchill turned to Fisher. 'Do you hear what this man has done? He's told his people they can go up to four million to buy a peaceful passage! On his own!' Then, before he could say more, Fisher interrupted. 'No, no, I'm going through tomorrow or as soon as the preparations can be completed.' While Churchill was still recovering from Hall's confession the First Sea Lord ordered Hall to break off all negotiations immediately. 'There was nothing to be done', recorded the Director of Naval Intelligence sadly, 'but obey orders.'[26] In fact, they made little difference. Eady and Whittall were unable to promise Talaat what was vital to his political – and physical – survival: that Constantinople would remain in Turkish hands after the war was over. Behind the scenes, the city had already been promised to the Russians. After twenty-four hours Talaat broke off negotiations, and Eady and Whittall returned to Salonica. That same day de Robeck's ships launched their assault.

Churchill still clung to the hope that divisions amongst the Turks might lead to their collapse or withdrawal from the war. Only a week before the Gallipoli landings he seized upon information from an agent on Corfu suggesting that Enver Pasha, the most pro-German minister in the Turkish government, was seriously isolated and that Talaat Bey remained open to the idea of an early peace. Success at the Dardanelles, he argued, would tear open the rift, and spark revolution and peace in Constantinople. Hankey, fully briefed on the background, dined with Churchill at Admiralty House and found him 'extremely optimistic'. Three days later, a Russian secret agent in Constantinople repeated the story about Turkish ammunition shortages and Sazonov, the Russian Foreign Minister, passed it on to Grey, who informed Churchill. Immediately he sent it to de Robeck, suggesting that he incite the Turkish forts to fire as much as possible. But de Robeck, too, resisted this Churchillian prod.

Following interception of the Kaiser's message to von Usedom, Churchill obsessively scrutinised Captain Hope's Room 40 U-boat reports for any signs that German submarines were being sent to the eastern Mediterranean. On 10 April he sent a 'Most Secret and Personal' message to de Robeck warning him to keep an eye out for German submarines and telling him that U-33 was reported to have left for an unknown destination. Again, he carefully disguised the source to suggest it came from 'a trustworthy agent'. At the end of the month Hope reported that U-21 had been at sea since 25 April, and a few days later that it was probably in the Mediterranean. He was right. It reached the Adriatic port of Kotor on 19 May. Six days later Churchill scribbled on Hope's report: 'Med or going there: U-40 perhaps, U-21 certain, U-27 perhaps.'[27] That same day, U-21 torpedoed the battleship HMS *Triumph* at anchor off Gallipoli and Churchill received the 'sinister' news early the next morning. It was his last day at the Admiralty. He was to see no more secret intelligence reports for some time.

Churchill's thirst for intercepts highlight the general intelligence drought elsewhere. A pre-war appreciation of a hypothetical Dardanelles operation, drawn up by naval intelligence and the Army General Staff, that highlighted the difficulty of the enterprise had been filed away and ignored. A similar fate befell an assessment drawn up in September 1914 by Lieutenant-Colonel Cunliffe-Owen, the British Military Attaché in Constantinople, that stressed how energetic German help given to the Turks was rapidly outdating all pre-war assessments of the Dardanelles' defences. The result was that the true nature of Turkish forts and minefields was never properly appreciated. Neither report was known to General Sir Ian Hamilton when he sailed to the Mediterranean to take up his command armed with maps based on fifty-year-old surveys and an almost total ignorance of Turkish troop dispositions. By contrast, non-existent British and allied security in Egypt meant that enemy agents delivered a full allied Order of Battle to Turkish intelligence. Hamilton compensated with bluff bravado and his General Staff appreciation largely consisted of guesswork. The Dardanelles Commission reported that the operations had been ill-conceived and ineptly executed, while a joint services inquest drily concluded that any operations should be based on 'a well-considered estimate' of the forces necessary to obtain the desired result. In short, intelligence, in almost all its meanings, was lamentably absent at the Dardanelles. It is scarce wonder that one of the greatest satirists of British intelligence, Sir Compton Mackenzie, author of *Water on the Brain*, received his baptism of fire as an intelligence officer at Gallipoli.

Four days before and half the globe distant from de Robeck's disastrous naval strike of March, another naval engagement threw revealing light on the intelligence war. On a sunlit Sunday morning in Cumberland Bay in the virtually deserted Juan Fernandez Islands four hundred miles off the coast of Chile, the German light cruiser *Dresden* blew herself up to avoid capture by British ships that had come upon her unawares at anchor. It was the final chapter in a saga that had begun late the previous year.

In November 1914 the German Far Eastern Fleet commanded by Admiral Graf von Spee inflicted a resounding defeat on British ships off Coronel. Shortly afterwards the humiliation was avenged at the Battle of the Falklands when von Spee went down with his flagship and his warships were sunk. Only one escaped: the *Dresden*. For the next three months she eluded her pursuers off the coast of Chile. Finally she was forced, through lack of coal, into Cumberland Bay. Here, as her captain signalled by radio using the German merchant-navy code, he planned to meet up with a collier organised by the German Naval Attaché in Chile. In contrast to Royal Navy ships in the North Sea, those based in the South Atlantic had been provided with details of the German merchant-vessel cipher. As a result the *Glasgow*, the principal pursuer of the *Dresden*, was able to intercept and decipher the captain's message, surprise her at anchor and open fire. After retaliating with a couple of rounds 'for the honour of the flag', the *Dresden* blew herself up.

The sinking of the *Dresden* again revealed how Churchill and the Admiralty regarded intercepts as almost private property. Churchill had responded to the news from the *Glasgow* by ordering an immediate attack. Learning of this from 'Blinker' Hall, Maurice Hankey sounded the alarm. Cumberland Bay was in Chilean waters and Chile was a neutral power; Churchill's order had serious political implications. Hankey informed Asquith who was completely in the dark about the whole affair. The next day he summoned a hastily convened meeting with Churchill and the Foreign Secretary, Sir Edward Grey. What transpired there may be guessed from events that followed. Asquith emerged from the encounter looking heated.[28] Nine days later, ignoring the niceties of international law and under direction from the Admiralty, the *Glasgow* opened fire and precipitated the *Dresden*'s self-destruction.

There is an intriguing footnote to this story. After the initial salvoes Captain Ludecke of the *Dresden* raised the white flag and sent a Lieutenant by pinnace to protest that his ship had already been officially interned by Chile, but this was a *ruse de guerre* while Ludecke prepared to scuttle the ship. The Lieutenant who boarded the *Glasgow* under the flag of truce, a taciturn fair-haired officer and Ludecke's most trusted aide, was named Wilhelm Canaris. In the Second World War, as an Admiral, he was to head the German *Abwehr* as one of the major players in the intelligence war.

Room 40's intelligence accompanied Churchill to the very end of his time at the Admiralty. The climax came after two exhausting days. First he defended the Admiralty over the *Lusitania* sinking in the

House of Commons, then had to cope with Fisher's angry resignation as First Sea Lord over violent disagreements about the Dardanelles. This, combined with a crisis over alleged shell shortages on the Western Front, precipitated Asquith's decision to form a coalition government with the Conservatives. Having solved the Admiralty crisis by replacing Fisher with Wilson, Churchill went to report to Asquith in the Prime Minister's office at the House of Commons. Here Asquith told him abruptly of his decision to form a new government and to replace Kitchener as Minister of War. 'And what are we to do for you?' he added.[29]

Barely had Churchill digested the fact that he had been fired than a secretary came in carrying an urgent telephone message from his parliamentary private secretary, Masterton-Smith. Intelligence 'of the kind that never fails' had just arrived and he was needed at once. Ten minutes later, sitting at his Admiralty desk, he learned from Room 40 that the entire German fleet was coming out and that a message from the German Commander-in-Chief contained the phrase 'Intend to attack by day'. Over the hours that followed Churchill took charge of preparing the Navy for action and ended the day by telling Jellicoe, 'tomorrow may be The Day. All good fortune attend you.' But luck had deserted Churchill. Later that evening a red dispatch box arrived at his office from Asquith requesting his resignation. Churchill made it clear that he would take no new office other than a military appointment; failing that, he would prefer employment 'in the field'.

His immediate and pressing concern remained the German Fleet. He rose before dawn the next day and watched events closely from the War Room, hoping desperately for a major victory that would keep him at the Admiralty. It was not to be. After a few hours in the North Sea the German High Seas Fleet returned to base, its sortie merely to cover the laying of a minefield on Dogger Bank. By mid-morning Churchill knew the game was up. He grabbed at the paltry bone flung to him by Asquith: Chancellor of the Duchy of Lancaster. One of his very last acts had been to approve the cutting of the Monrovia–Pernambuco cable used by the Germans for transatlantic communications.

After seven years at the centre of power, Churchill was out in the cold. He had no executive power, no ministerial responsibility, no army of bureaucrats and secretaries at his command. Nor did he have any access to secret intelligence, one of the more potent aphrodisiacs of power. Aged 40, the Dardanelles appeared to have sunk his political career for ever.

In his wartime months at the Admiralty Churchill had confronted most of the major issues that were to reappear during the Second World War in connection with signals intelligence: its distribution, assessment, security, operational use, and its strengths and limitations. He had made mistakes and learned lessons. He had also revealed himself as a ready user of other weapons in Britain's intelligence armoury. Horrified though he was by the sums involved, he was prepared to subvert the Turkish government through bribery and more than willing to spend money employing secret agents in the Balkans if it would help.

On all these fronts he had also learned the impressive power that control of intelligence conferred on 'Blinker' Hall. He was almost certainly aware, too, that Hall had played a part in his downfall. At the height of the crisis over the mid-May sortie of the High Seas Fleet, Fisher impetuously abandoned his post as First Sea Lord because of a row with Churchill over the Dardanelles. Deeply shocked by his behaviour and believing he was no longer fit to hold office, senior Admiralty officials asked Hall to approach Asquith. Instead, he consulted Lord Reading, the Lord Chief Justice. The Director of Naval Intelligence told Reading of the repeated friction between Churchill and Fisher, and of his blunt opinion that the latter was no longer up to the job. 'If either of them is to leave the Admiralty', Reading finally asked, 'which of them is it to be?' It was the question that Hall had been waiting for. 'Regretfully', he replied, 'I have to say both.'[30] Powerful political currents against Churchill were also at work, but it was clear that no future intelligence chief should be permitted such unbridled power.

Churchill eventually found solace in action on the Western Front. From January to May 1916 he commanded the 6th Royal Scots Fusiliers, an infantry battalion stationed at Ploegsteert in Belgium. Here he made friends who were to be vital in his future dealings with the secret world.

The most important was Major Desmond Morton, a professional artillery officer who had won the Military Cross and been appointed aide-de-camp to Field Marshal Haig, Commander of British forces in France, after suffering serious wounds at the battle of Arras. He first met Churchill painting a canvas at his headquarters in a farmhouse behind the trenches. The two quickly became firm friends and when Churchill returned two years later as Minister of Munitions to tour the front, Morton escorted him around the battlefields. After the war Morton entered SIS and in the 1930s ran the Industrial Intelligence Centre. He was to be Churchill's most important follower, adviser and contact with the secret world.[31]

Second only to Morton was Brigadier Edward Louis Spears, the intelligence officer who was to airlift General Charles de Gaulle to Britain in 1940, introduce him to Churchill and become his special liaison officer with the Free French leader. Loyal service to Churchill in the Second World War was built on foundations laid in the First. Born in Paris he was educated privately in France and Ireland. August 1914 found him in Paris working to develop a new military cipher system usable by both British and French armies. Shortly afterwards he was appointed liaison officer with the French Deuxième Bureau, under the direct orders of Colonel George Macdonogh. He performed brilliantly in the task, was a Brigadier by 1917, and at the armistice was senior British liaison officer with the French and head of the military mission in Paris. He had also won the Military Cross and was a Commander of the Legion of Honour. In that year he married Mary Borden, a well-known American novelist, and changed the spelling of his surname to Spears on the grounds that Spiers was too often mispronounced. It also looked German.

Churchill knew Spears well enough by 1916 to request – unsuccessfully – that he become his second-in-command on the Western Front. He was able, gregarious and charming. A great conversationalist and host, he also nourished violent likes and dislikes, and ruthlessly pursued vendettas. Sir John Colville, Churchill's private secretary during the Second World War, described him as 'a man of high intelligence who made enemies almost as easily as he made friends [with] a streak of metallic ruthlessness which was not difficult to discern'. Many people found him devious, in both business and politics. But to his friends – and Churchill was one of his closest – he was loyal and generous. Churchill reciprocated. He found him an invaluable interpreter of events on the Western Front and in the complexities and nuances of Anglo-French relations. He also respected Spears as a brave soldier and admired him as a fluent writer. In later life, when asked to recommend books on the Western Front, he would invariably recommend Spears' two volumes, *Liaison 1914* and *Prelude to Victory*.[32]

When Haig vetoed Spears as his second-in-command, Churchill plumped for Archibald Sinclair, the future leader of the Parliamentary Liberal Party (1935–45) and, during the Second World War, his Secretary of State for Air. Like Spears and Morton, and despite his different party affiliation, he became a partisan supporter of Churchill's campaign against appeasement and a bitter opponent of the Munich Agreement. So vitriolic were his attacks that MI5 tapped his telephone during the opening months of the Second World War believing he was receiving inside information about government policy. When Chamberlain confronted him with the transcripts, only Churchill's influence dissuaded a furious Sinclair from exposing the incident in the Commons.

With his fine features, black hair and dark complexion, Sinclair resembled, in Sir John Colville's words, 'a Spanish grandee rather than the Highland Chieftain he really was' (head of his clan, Sinclair later became Lord Thurso of Wick).[33] Churchill met him before the war when they were both learning to fly. Typically, Churchill fell for his dashing heroism. Uncanny similarities in their backgrounds strengthened the bonds. Sinclair's mother was American, he was mostly brought up by a devoted private nanny, and like Churchill had learned to control a bad childhood stammer. After Eton he had opted for Sandhurst, and when Churchill met him was a polo-playing officer in the fashionable 2nd Life Guards. Soon Churchill was manoeuvring to find his new young protégé a seat in the Commons, and helped him become ADC to his old friend Jack Seely, the former Secretary of State for War and Commander of the Canadian Cavalry Brigade in France. The two men kept in close touch. Churchill praised Sinclair for his gallantry, while the young Scot lent a sympathetic ear to his misfortunes over the Dardanelles.

At Ploegsteert their friendship deepened into a powerful bond and when Churchill returned to London he continued to advise Sinclair on his future in politics – although by now, married and with a child, and uncertain of the Liberal future, Sinclair was cautious. One of his own early contacts in the secret world was his close friend Stewart Menzies, a fellow officer in his regiment serving on the intelligence staff of GHQ in France and destined to become, as 'C', Churchill's 'spymaster' in the Second World War. When Sinclair introduced them, Menzies cryptically described Churchill as 'an entertainment'.[34] The next known contact between them came in the 1930s when they were recorded as shooting together on Sinclair's

Scottish estate. Menzies was undoubtedly suspicious of Churchill, as were most regular officers of the time. Sinclair, friend and confidant of both, proved a useful intermediary.

Such were the principal intelligence contacts that Churchill made on the Western Front. By mid-1916 he was back in London and a year later he was Minister of Munitions in the Coalition government headed by his old Liberal colleague, David Lloyd George. Here he was faced by a challenge that demanded a different form of secret service.

5

The Red Peril

In the wartime factories of Clydeside David Kirkwood was a force to be reckoned with. Chief shop steward at the huge Beardmore's Forge at Parkhead, Glasgow, he led the fight against the 1915 Munitions Act that introduced labour conscription and compulsory leaving certificates for workers. Following a strike at Beardmore's he was banished from Glasgow under the Defence of the Realm Act, and even after his deportation order was lifted Beardmore's refused to reinstate him. Churchill's appointment as Minister of Munitions galvanised Kirkwood into action. In Churchill he saw a swashbuckler afraid of no one: 'I felt that if I could win him over there was nothing he would not do.'

Kirkwood chose his moment well. Churchill arrived at the Ministry of Munitions at a critical time. By 1917 labour discontent was threatening his promise of 'masses of guns, mountains of shells, clouds of aeroplanes'. The Russian Revolution that toppled the Tsar boosted socialist hopes and stimulated a wave of strikes. The day before Churchill took office an official inquiry recommended a policy of labour appeasement through the introduction of food subsidies, and reforms in housing and education. He promptly abolished the hated leaving certificates and awarded wage increases.

He also met Kirkwood, surprising him with his conciliatory manner. 'How do you do, Mr Kirkwood? I have heard a great deal about you', he began. 'I dare say you have', replied Kirkwood. 'Yes, and I want you to know that, whatever happens, nothing is to be allowed to stand in the way of the production of the munitions of war', Churchill responded. 'Quite right', agreed Kirkwood. Then Churchill rang a bell, saying, 'Let's have a cup of tea and a bit of cake together.' With that small gesture, Churchill won a convert. Before Kirkwood's eyes flashed the tedious hours he had sat in outer rooms waiting to catch the attention of indifferent or hostile officials. Churchill had offered him the 'bread and salt of friendship'. Kirkwood left the meeting fuelled by tea and cakes, and a firm promise that Churchill would do his best to get him re-employed. He kept his word. Three days later Kirkwood became manager of Beardmore's Mile End Shell Factory in London where he remained until the end of the war. Within weeks the factory broke all production records.[1]

Churchill knew when and with whom to be conciliatory. But by now, under the impact of war, he had cast off his radical clothing and was moving steadily to the right. Millions of men were under arms, and labour at home was as vital as troops at the front. So when he suspected treachery or subversion, he was quick to deploy the full force of the state.

Subversion now competed with espionage as a concern of national security. To root it out in the munitions factories Churchill possessed an intelligence service specially geared to the task. Its origins lay in the ever-pervasive fears of German sabotage. Despite the round-up of spies Kell continued to worry that others remained at large and intent on sabotage. After the sinking of the *Lusitania* the Home Office instructed Chief Constables to report suspected arson by foreign agents at factories, in docks and on railways working on government contracts. An explosion at the Nobel Explosives Factory at Ardeer, Scotland, was enough to persuade the Minister of Munitions to set up a special intelligence unit early in 1916.

Staffed by MI5 officers fluent in German, it was known as the Ministry of Munitions Labour Intelligence Division, or MMLI. At first its mission was simple: to protect munitions factories from enemy sabotage and vet the background of alien employees. Before long it was investigating any factors that threatened production – including 'extremism' amongst the workers. In short, it added counter-subversion to its list of duties. It then evolved into an even more secretive organisation known by the cover name 'PMS 2', standing for Parliamentary Military Secretary Section 2.[2] Soon it was employing an army of private agents reporting on labour relations as well as strikes, stoppages and suspected sabotage. After its use of *agents provocateurs* became an embarrassment, its work was transferred to the flamboyant head of the Special Branch, Sir Basil Thomson. Three months before Churchill took over at Munitions Thomson was given exclusive control of all intelligence relating to subversion and strikes. Before the end of the year he was reporting regularly on subversion to Churchill and the War Cabinet.

By this time fears of revolution and German spies had coalesced to create a mood of near hysteria in the increasingly conservative War Cabinet. Lord Milner, arch-imperialist and natural autocrat, warned Lloyd George that drastic steps would have to be taken 'to stop the rot' and head off a Russian-style revolution in Britain. With the Independent Labour Party picking up on the call of Russian revolutionaries for a peace without annexations or indemnities, and the Labour Party decision to send delegates to Petrograd to confer with socialists from enemy as well as allied countries – the plan so neatly scuppered by Churchill's agent Tupper – the government acted. It established a National War Aims Committee 'to resist insidious influences of an unpatriotic character' under Churchill's polo-playing cousin and crony, Captain F. E. (Freddie) Guest, who as Chief Whip to the Liberal members of the Coalition also played a dubious role as 'evil genius' in raising funds for Lloyd George's notorious slush fund. The Committee received money from the secret-service vote and Guest breezily proclaimed that working-class unrest could best be solved by 'drugging their tea'. More practically, the Committee worked through patriotic organisations such as the British Worker's League and the British Empire Union to disseminate anti-socialist and anti-pacifist propaganda.[3]

The government also let loose the Special Branch. Through *agents provocateurs* it sabotaged attempts to create workers' councils and covertly supported counter-demonstrations by feeding Guest's Committee advance intelligence about pacifist rallies. Their main target was E. D. Morel, head of the anti-war Union of Democratic Control. MI5 tapped his telephone and opened his mail, and he was imprisoned under the Defence of the Realm Act on the flimsy pretext of having sent anti-war propaganda to the French pacifist Romain Rolland in Switzerland. The real reason for putting him away was fear of his influence over munition workers. Churchill roundly denounced him as a member of 'that band of degenerate international intellectuals who regard the greatness of Britain and the stability and prosperity of the British Empire as a fatal obstacle to their subversive sickness'.

After the Bolshevik Revolution, Special Branch searched frantically for evidence of their propaganda in the labour force while MI5 hunted Soviet subversion in Britain's munitions factories. Churchill took Thomson's reports so seriously that he financed his work outside London. He also complemented their efforts through an aggressive strategy of labour conciliation and propaganda. One tactic, to organise regular morale-boosting trips to the Western Front by munitions workers to see conditions for themselves, was developed through a special department of the Ministry of Information headed by the spy novelist John Buchan. The trick, Churchill told Lord Beaverbrook, Buchan's boss as Minister of Information, was to ensure that labour delegations to France always included the 'really controlling spirits' in any particular region. Inevitably Tupper made another cameo appearance visiting the front to demonstrate that the Merchant Marine was far from beaten. Churchill believed that active propaganda was a vital prophylactic against the deadly virus of Bolshevism. 'I am increasingly convinced', he confessed to Beaverbrook, 'that there can be no more valuable propaganda . . . than graphic accounts of the Bolshevik outrages and futility, of the treacheries they have committed, and what ruin they have brought upon their country and the harm they have done to us and our fighting men.'[4]

Churchill's response to the Bolshevik Revolution was immediate and negative. Lenin, he declared, wore 'hatreds tight as the hangman's noose'. The Bolsheviks, he assured the House of Commons, 'destroy wherever they exist [and] by rolling forward into fertile areas, like the vampire which sucks the blood from his victims . . . gain the means of prolonging their own baleful existence'.[5] As Minister of Munitions his power to act against them was limited, but in January 1919 Lloyd George made him Minister for War and Air. He was now able to lead an unrelenting crusade against Moscow and its disciples in Britain.

One of his first tasks was to prepare the Army to fight revolution in Britain. Basil Thomson, now promoted as supreme Director of Intelligence, considered that the first three months of 1919 saw Britain closer to revolution than at any time since the Chartist riots of the 1830s. Early in the New Year events in Glasgow seemed to confirm his fears. A general strike was declared, the red flag was raised over the city hall, and Kirkwood and Emanuel Shinwell were arrested when a mass demonstration by strikers in George Square turned into a riot. Nineteen battalions of troops and half a dozen tanks were called in, and the *Glasgow Herald* warned that the first steps had been taken towards Bolshevism. The Cabinet thought likewise, as did King George V. He was, reported the Chancellor of the Exchequer Andrew Bonar Law, 'in a funk . . . about revolution'.[6]

This set the scene for Churchill's order to GHQ to prepare a plan to help the civil authorities in the event of a revolutionary national strike. Its first move was to create an Army intelligence staff to liaise with Thomson's Special Branch and by September 1919 during the national railway strike Churchill, acting on their intelligence, moved over 20,000 troops to secure key points against sabotage or violence. Even after the Home Office resumed full responsibility for public order Churchill, anxious to ensure that the War Office was not deprived of its own secret intelligence weapon, approved the formation of the 'Silent Section', known officially as MO4(X). Headed by Major-General C. F. Romer, Haig's Chief of Staff who had been deeply involved in the security measures of the preceding twelve months, its mission was to study all matters relating to internal security and to co-ordinate with MI5 and Special Branch. So long as fears of domestic revolution lasted, it continued to collect intelligence about political activists, as well as the loyalty of local authorities and the general population.[7]

MO4(X) had also been tasked to monitor morale and subversion within the armed forces. This was a major worry. Churchill's immediate challenge was the demobilisation of some three and a half million soldiers still under arms. He inherited a volatile situation that threatened major disorder. 'Everywhere', he noted, 'the subversive elements were active.' The War Office had concocted a scheme that allowed only men who had secured civilian jobs to leave the Army, which meant that those who had served since 1914 often saw soldiers enlisted later leaving ahead of them. Riots broke out at demobilisation centres, troops mutinied at Calais and Folkestone, and in Luton a mob burned down the town hall. Churchill acted with typical speed. He immediately released those who had enlisted in the first two years of the war, and gave those who were retained for continuing duties – such as the occupation of Germany – increased pay and extra leave. Still, unrest in the Army continued to cause anxiety. Early in February 1919 Churchill watched from his War Office window while Grenadiers with fixed bayonets dispersed an angry crowd of soldiers on Horse Guards Parade. Here was a threat, he recorded, pointed at 'the physical heart of the State'.[8]

Spearheading discontent was the Soldiers', Sailors', and Airmen's Union (SSAU), which recruited from veterans and servicemen.

Crucially it gained support from the socialist newspaper the *Daily Herald*. Its editor was George Lansbury; he was to become a particular object of Churchill's loathing.

Born in a toll house on a Suffolk turnpike, Lansbury unloaded coal trucks for the Great Eastern Railway before entering municipal politics in London's East End and becoming known as the 'John Bull of Poplar'. A convinced Christian Socialist, he was also a lifelong pacifist who became leader of the Labour Party after the bitter split over Ramsay MacDonald's decision to form a National Government in 1931. His position became untenable faced with the rise of the European dictators and he was forced to resign.[9]

The *Herald* was largely his own creation. It enjoyed close contacts with the Labour Party and trade unions whose financial support meant they named half its board of directors. It staunchly supported the new Bolshevik regime and fixed the crusading Churchill firmly in its sights. With him at the War Office, it declared, Britain would become a conscript and militarised nation rent by repression and revolt, dispatching armies of imperialist aggression around the world. Listing a catalogue of Churchillian misdemeanours, beginning with his use of troops in the pre-war strikes, through the Dardanelles expedition and his campaign against the Bolsheviks, it laid the foundation stone of a left-wing indictment of Churchill that long endured. Three months later it added another charge. Under the headline 'Plots against Labour. War Office organises wide secret service', it denounced Churchill for the secret penetration of labour and the use of *agents provocateurs*.[10]

Thus began a vendetta between Churchill and Lansbury that saw Churchill mobilising MI5 in an attempt to marshal incriminating evidence to prosecute him. In the meantime Churchill denounced the *Herald* as subversive. The paper, he fulminated, deliberately sought 'to foment discontent in the Army and to encourage mutinies, strikes, and riots'.[11] The SSAU planned a campaign to climax on 11 May 1919, six months to the day after the Armistice, when men all over Britain and France would remove their buttons, shoulder straps and badges, and declare themselves discharged. Simultaneously, pamphlets distributed in the Navy urged sailors to seize ports and unite with the soldiers in a general strike. This, claimed the SSAU, would be legitimate, as the men's contracts of enlistment promised release six months after the termination of hostilities.

Churchill kept informed by reading Special Branch reports based on informers who had infiltrated the SSAU from its birth. He also ordered all commanding officers to provide secret weekly reports on the sentiments of their troops, particularly intelligence about the formation of soviets, and attitudes towards strike-breaking and service in Russia. To Churchill's fury, Lansbury promptly obtained a copy of the order and published it in the *Herald*. Three days before the promised self-demobilisation Churchill assured the Cabinet that all Army commanders had been alerted and would nip any trouble in the bud. As he spoke, Scotland Yard's Criminal Investigation Department was raiding the SSAU headquarters and seizing its records. The planned demonstration fizzled out. Gradually, order returned to the Army and fears of revolution temporarily subsided.

In the wider world, revolutionary and ethnic turmoil had followed the collapse of the Russian, Austro-Hungarian and Ottoman Empires. Nationalism threatened British rule in India, and Ireland had erupted in revolt and civil war. 'What a disappointment the Twentieth Century has been', read the notes for one of his post-war speeches. 'How terrible and melancholy its long series of disastrous events ... We have seen in ev part of globe one gt country after another wh had erected an orderly, a peaceful, society, relapsing in hideous succession into bankruptcy, barbarism or anarchy ... only intense, concerted & prolonged efforts among all nations can avert further & perhaps even greater calamities.'[12]

With the post-war world so dangerous and uncertain, and Britain's armed forces being drastically pruned, Churchill saw the intelligence services as a vital weapon, both sword and shield of the state. Society had to be protected against internal subversion, the nation against foreign danger. As a member of the Secret Service Committee chaired by the Foreign Secretary Lord Curzon, in 1919 he recommended that Sir Basil Thomson become Director of Civil Intelligence and was appalled when a year later Curzon caved in to Treasury demands for cuts to MI5 and MI6 budgets. While it took five to ten years to build up an effective secret service, he pointed out, it could all too easily be destroyed by the stroke of a pen. Such a move, he protested, would paralyse secret intelligence in Germany, Russia and China, and would effectively cripple MI5 at home. Instead he proposed the creation of a unified intelligence service to produce a more cost-effective service and better value for money. 'With the world in its present condition of extreme unrest and changing friendships and antagonisms', he told his Cabinet colleagues in March 1920, 'and with our greatly reduced and weak military forces, it is more than ever vital to us to have good and timely information.' He lost both arguments but other weapons were added to the national-security armoury. The 1920 Official Secrets Act gave the government the right to see all overseas cables and telegrams, and the Cabinet agreed with Churchill and the Secret Service Committee that Britain needed a peacetime successor to the code-breakers of Room 40. The Government Code and Cipher School (GC & CS) began its work in 1919, at first under Admiralty control and then under the Foreign Office and SIS. Over the next few years it enjoyed striking success in breaking the diplomatic ciphers of the United States, France, Turkey, Japan and other powers. Its most valuable harvest, however, was Bolshevik: intercepts of Moscow's secret communications soon began to land on ministers' desks.[13]

Churchill was one of their keenest readers. These intercepts opened an unprecedented window on Soviet activities in Britain and around the world, and he treasured them as highly as he had the work of Room 40. They provided compensation for intelligence cut-backs elsewhere. Barely eight weeks after the Cabinet's reduction of the secret-service budget they began to prove their worth.

On the last day of May 1920, flanked by senior colleagues, Prime Minister David Lloyd George shook hands with Leonid Krasin, head of a Soviet delegation recently arrived in London to negotiate a bilateral trade treaty. It was the first time a representative of the Soviet state had been received officially by the head of the government of a Great Power. The discussions represented a triumph for Lloyd George, who believed that European trade and economic recovery was the best antidote to revolution. Not all his colleagues were convinced. Curzon refused to take the hand proffered by Krasin and stared resolutely into the fireplace until Lloyd George shamed him by exclaiming, 'Curzon, be a gentleman!' Churchill solved the protocol problem by staying away from the meeting altogether. But Krasin was not so easily evaded. Thanks to the code-breakers, intercepts of Bolshevik messages soon revealed that he and his colleagues were up to subversive dirty tricks. It became Churchill's dominating obsession to see Krasin and his fellow Bolsheviks expelled from Britain.

It was to Leonid Krasin that Lenin made his famous promise that, under Bolshevism, electricity would replace God in the eyes of the

Russian peasant; when Lenin died in 1924, Krasin took charge of embalming his body. In short, he was a practical man, a person 'of immediate effects and instant results' in Trotsky's words. The son of a Tsarist police chief, he had trained as an electrical engineer and served as the Bolsheviks' chief financier and supplier of weapons. Hunted by the authorities he fled to Berlin, severed his links with the Party and by the time war broke out was back in Russia as the general manager of Siemens' Russian operations in St Petersburg. Twice he rejected personal appeals by Lenin to return to the Party. Only Trotsky's intervention persuaded him back, first to help with the peace negotiations at Brest-Litovsk, then as Commissar for Foreign Trade and Transport. From there it was a short step to lead the trade negotiations with Britain. Many in London perceived him as a 'good' Bolshevik determined to guide Russia towards normal democracy. Sir Basil Thomson happily noted his 'contempt for the official creed' and alone of the Soviet delegation Krasin was exempted from signing a declaration promising to stay out of Britain's internal affairs on the grounds that his personal word was enough. Unlike the Bolshevik of popular demonology, his courteous manners and impeccable Bond Street suits marked him as a gentleman. One British journalist described him as 'the best dressed Communist in the world'.[14]

Churchill would have none of this. To him, a Bolshevik was a Bolshevik, and he was convinced that the interests of Krasin and the delegation in London went beyond trade. GC & CS intercepts confirmed his fears. Combined with tumultuous events on the domestic front, they convinced him that Britain faced a revolutionary threat which called for a far-reaching response. So grave did he consider events that he was quite prepared to reveal Britain's most secret source of intelligence if it would save the country.

Affairs came to a climax in August 1920. War between the Bolsheviks and the newly independent Polish state under Marshal Pilsudski had deteriorated from minor border skirmishes to a full-scale attack by the Poles that took them as far as Kiev and the heart of Ukraine. It seemed for a moment as though the Poles might accomplish what the White Russians had failed to do and overthrow the Bolsheviks. Labour reacted promptly and dockers in London refused to load a munitions ship, the *Jolly Roger*, bound for Poland. Events became even more divisive on the home front when the Red Army launched a counter-attack, advanced to the gates of Warsaw, and Trotsky triumphantly promised that Poland would soon cease to exist. With the spectre of the Red Peril spreading westwards into Germany, Lloyd George declared that unless the Soviet advance was halted the British fleet would move to the Baltic. *The Times* warned that war was imminent and the *Daily Herald*'s headlines grimly announced: 'Britain plunging into war with Soviet Russia.'[15]

The *Herald* took the lead in Labour's bitter opposition to British intervention against the Bolsheviks. 'Not a man, not a gun, not a shilling!' shouted its banner headline on Sunday 8 August. The next day it declared: 'Workers! You will not be deceived! You know it is the same old gang at the same old game: seeking to shed your blood in capitalism's filthy quarrels: lying, intriguing, ruining the world. War is upon us! Down tools to stop it!' The same day the Trades Union Congress, the Labour Party National Executive and the Parliamentary Labour Party formed a Council of Action to organise a general strike against war, and around the country three hundred Councils of Action sprang into existence. Once again, Britain seemed poised for revolutionary upheaval. The sense of impending crisis deepened when the miners' union voted overwhelmingly to strike for higher wages and received the support of the railway and transport workers. The dreaded pre-war 'Triple Alliance', with its power to paralyse the country, had been reborn.

Amidst all this turmoil Churchill read with mounting alarm the GC & CS intercepts revealing links between Krasin's delegation and the Council of Action. He was particularly angry at evidence of Soviet duplicity and deception, and on one of the intercepts, a message from Lev Kamenev to Maxim Litvinov, he scored a vertical line down the side of a particularly incriminating passage and scribbled furiously: 'This is unmistakeable avowal of mala fides [bad faith].'[16]

Most provocative of all was evidence that the *Daily Herald* was being subsidised by Moscow. To Churchill this presented an irresistible opportunity to target Lansbury. The *Herald* had always hovered on the brink of insolvency and Lansbury had arranged for Soviet credits to purchase newsprint in Sweden and Finland. The intercepts revealed that Francis Meynell, one of the *Daily Herald*'s directors, had concocted a scheme with Maxim Litvinov, the Soviet Deputy Commissar for Foreign Affairs, to support secretly a variety of pro-Soviet causes in Britain including a direct subsidy to the *Herald*. Without it, Litvinov advised Lenin, the newspaper would cease to be of any use to the Bolsheviks. Krasin made a brief visit to Moscow that summer and when he returned was accompanied by Lev Kamenev, a member of the Politburo and brother-in-law to Trotsky. Hidden in their possessions were over £40,000 worth of diamonds and platinum that they sold on the London market. The proceeds, invested in Exchequer Bonds, provided a valuable subsidy for the *Herald* and also set the newly formed Communist Party of Great Britain on its feet.

The government, desperately anxious to discredit Lansbury and the *Herald*, leaked the intercepts to the Tory *Morning Post*. In the public row that followed Lansbury claimed he had known nothing of the deal, even though his son Edgar was one of Meynell's accomplices. The *Herald*'s board of directors took the same line and returned the money to the Soviet delegation. Meynell resigned from the board.[17]

For Churchill the temporary embarrassment of Lansbury was not enough. Since the *Herald*'s violent denunciations the year before it had continued to target him. It had followed its publication of his secret circular to local commanders about the political sentiments of the troops with revelations about yet another confidential War Office instruction ordering British commanders in the occupied Rhine district of Germany to seize and burn bundles of the *Daily Herald* arriving at the railheads. The reason, Lansbury swore, was obvious. The authorities 'dared not allow the soldiers know the truth' either about the goodwill of local Germans or the extent of British and allied intervention in Russia against the Bolsheviks. Again, Churchill denounced Lansbury and his newspaper for seeking to encourage 'mutinies, strikes, and riots'. Worse was to follow when Lansbury published a poem in the *Herald* written by the author and poet Osbert Sitwell. Entitled 'A Certain Statesman' it was bitter satire on Churchill and his 'nice new war' that savaged his support for Alexander Kolchak, the leader of the White Russian forces, denounced him for wasting 'a million lives' at Gallipoli, and painted him as a bloodthirsty warmonger for whom wars were nothing more than a form of sport like football or 'kiss-in-the-ring'.[18]

Churchill's opportunity to hit back came when Lansbury decided to visit to Soviet Russia to see things for himself. He departed early in 1920 an enthusiast for the Revolution and nothing in Moscow or Leningrad disappointed him. Meeting the top Bolsheviks, he waxed lyrical about 'the most astonishing freedom of discussion, and even of action' to be found in the new Jerusalem, and while initially suspicious of the Cheka, Lenin's secret police headed by the dreaded Felix Dzerzhinsky, he was persuaded that 'they were really saving life'. As for Lenin, Lansbury declared he was 'confident that he loves little children'. Amidst these startling conclusions he accidentally bumped into some British prisoners of war out on parole. Expecting to find them disillusioned with their capitalist leaders in London, he was dismayed to discover many were passionately pro-Tsarist. There followed a lively discussion about the merits of the Revolution. Rumours of what had been said quickly reached Britain.[19]

Lansbury had been under secret surveillance throughout his journey. He was shadowed day and night, he recalled, 'by all sorts of queer personages'. In Copenhagen spies followed him when he went to see Litvinov and sat patiently outside his hotel room when he stayed in. One night he even returned to find his room occupied by two Englishmen, 'obviously secret police', who at first begged an introduction to Litvinov and then went on to discuss the horrors of Bolshevism. In Stockholm a patent attempt was made to entrap him by a man – 'obviously a spy' – who talked at length about paper supplies, money and the future of the *Herald*. Lansbury may have exaggerated, but he was not being paranoid. Lefevre, the French Minister of War, admitted to Louis Spears that even French spies tracked him.[20]

No sooner had the fuss about Soviet diamonds died down than new rumours suggested that Lansbury had attempted to incite British soldiers in Russia to mutiny – a reference to his encounter with the prisoners of war in Moscow. This, if true, was a serious offence for which he could be prosecuted. Churchill seized the chance to put paid to his press tormentor.

Early in June 1920 Military Intelligence reported that, according to officers recently returned from Moscow, Lansbury had not contented himself with proselytising for Bolshevism amongst British prisoners but had also declared that the best way of forcing the British government to recognise Lenin's regime was to keep the men in prison. The news enraged Churchill who demanded a full compilation of the evidence. Lieutenant-General Sir William Thwaites, the Director of Military Intelligence, rustled up formal statements from the officers involved. 'My object', Churchill told him, 'is to secure in one document the complete statement of the case against Mr Lansbury.'[21] Two days later Thwaites instructed MI5 to take the matter in hand. The officer he chose for the job was one Major Joseph Ball (later Sir Joseph Ball), a lawyer and expert fly-fisher who had joined the service on the outbreak of war.

Ball enjoyed at least two lives. One, highly public, was as Director of Publicity for Conservative Central Office in the 1920s and a parti-san supporter of Neville Chamberlain in the 1930s. The other, behind the scenes, was as an officer and contact with MI5 and shadowy political fixer who devoted much of his energy in Conservative Central Office to running dirty-tricks campaigns against both the Labour Party and opponents of Chamberlain within the Conservative Party itself. J. C. C. Davidson, later Lord Davidson and Chairman of the Conservative Party, said that Ball had as much experience as anyone he knew in the seamy side of life and the handling of crooks.[22]

The Lansbury investigation furnished a useful apprenticeship. Ball's enquiries turned up mixed evidence. Five of the soldiers inter-viewed by MI5 flatly denied they had heard the alleged statements. Others corroborated and expanded them; Lansbury, they said, had even declared himself a Bolshevik who hoped to find a Bolshevik government on his return to London. Several men were reluctant to make any statement at all. The sum of evidence, Ball concluded, meant that it would be unwise to publish any government statement. Lansbury had already suffered serious damage from the *Daily Herald* revelations and a communiqué likely to be disputed by some of those interviewed would do little to increase it. Instead, why not arrange to publish interviews with the men prepared to vouch for the case against Lansbury? The journal Ball had in mind was *John Bull*, the right-wing ultra-patriotic paper owned by the notorious MP Horatio Bottomley.

Ball's suggestion, along with MI5's recognition that Lansbury's alleged statements were insufficient for prosecution, landed on Churchill's desk at the height of the war scare over the fate of Warsaw in August 1920. Thwaites supported Ball's line and added that any leak to the press should carefully disguise its War Office origin. Churchill concurred. 'It is likely', he noted, 'that the soldiers will carry their complaints to the newspapers. If so Mr Lansbury will be no gainer by the exposure.' Two months later Bottomley raised Lansbury's behaviour in the House of Commons and showed a familiarity with the facts that could only have come with help from

MI5. Lloyd George lamented that the evidence was insufficient to launch a prosecution. But, as Churchill had predicted, these further allegations about his behaviour further damaged Lansbury's already murky reputation as a fellow-travelling pro-Bolshevik.[23]

Churchill's campaign against Lansbury revealed the depth and fury of his anti-Bolshevism. The summer of 1920 also saw him come close to flirting with treason. Throughout that summer his alarm over Bolshevism at home was fuelled by Sir Henry Wilson, the robustly opinionated Ulster-born Chief of the Imperial General Staff who was so convinced of the gravity of the crisis facing the British Empire that he frequently fantasised about a *coup d'état* to get rid of Lloyd George on the grounds that his tolerance for Krasin and his misdeeds could have only a sinister interpretation. Churchill saw Wilson several times a day that month. On the evening of 17 August Wilson read a series of intercepts that demonstrated Kamenev's involvement in the revolutionary excitement sweeping the labour movements. Early the next morning he discussed the material with Thwaites, and to prepare for a possible war against the Council of Action they alerted military commanders around the country. Anxieties deepened when MI5 calculated that amongst the 'revolutionaries' were some 100,000 ex-servicemen. And when Sir Basil Thomson revealed that the Cabinet had decided to take no action against the Soviet delegation, despite being fully informed of its transgressions, Wilson erupted in fury against Lloyd George. Thomson agreed, claimed Wilson, that even he was 'seriously beginning to think L.G. was a traitor'.[24]

Wilson reported all this to Churchill and hinted ominously that he would have to take action if the Cabinet failed to act. Churchill promptly instructed him to put his fully documented case on paper and promised to circulate it to the Cabinet. This Wilson did, stressing the dangers to the country from revolutionary labour and the problems faced by the overstretched Army in preparing to defend the established order. On top of all this, he complained, he had been confronted by irrefutable evidence proving 'three amazing and disturbing facts': Krasin and Kamenev were engaged in a plot to create red revolution and ruin in Britain; Kamenev and the Soviets were seeking to drive a dangerous wedge between Britain and France; the Council for Action was collaborating with the Bolsheviks for the downfall of Britain. Drastic action against the Council and the Soviet delegation was thus urgently required. 'I await the decision of the

Government', concluded Wilson ominously. Meantime he claimed that Admiral Earl Beatty, the First Sea Lord, Rear-Admiral Hugh Sinclair, the Director of Naval Intelligence, and Air Chief Marshal Sir Hugh Trenchard, Chief of the Air Staff, all supported his demand for action.

What remained crucial was Churchill's position as Secretary of State for War. He was certainly in a highly excitable state about the intercepts. 'A veritable plot is being hatched against England and France', he told Lloyd George after he had talked to Wilson, and he sent him several damning intercepts including one where Kamenev talked of buying arms for the working class. But although he lent a sympathetic ear to Wilson's rantings, he drew back from any hint of joining in a military-inspired conspiracy. Wilson quickly sensed the change. The day after Ball's recommendations on how best to blacken Lansbury's name he confided in his diary that he had been forced to resort to extravagant exhortation: 'I told Winston it was the chance of his life to come out as an Englishman and that in one bound he would recover his lost position and be hailed as saviour by all that is best in England.' He also warned that if Churchill did not act, 'we soldiers' might have to, in which case Churchill's position would be impossible. 'He agreed', wrote Wilson, 'we have got him pretty well fixed.'[25]

Wilson was deluding himself. It took yet another day and a second appeal before Churchill finally sent a note to Lloyd George and it was significantly less than Wilson had hoped for. Churchill certainly reported how perturbed senior intelligence officers were by the evidence of conspiracy by Kamenev and Krasin, and warned the Prime Minister that some of them might resign if nothing were done. But he conspicuously failed to threaten resignation himself and concentrated instead on demanding the expulsion of the Russians. 'Are we really going to sit still', he asked, 'until we see the combination of money from Moscow, the Kameneff-Krassin propaganda, the Council of Action, and something very like a general strike, all acting and reacting on one another, while at the same time our military forces are at their very weakest?' He also enclosed a conciliatory cover note to his old political friend begging him to consider carefully the case for expulsion and think of the dangerous consequences of letting Krasin and Kamenev remain. 'I am quite clear', he stated, 'that [they] ought to be given their passports.' Their presence not only encouraged Labour, whom he saw as a growing political threat, but it also alienated the Conservatives, and as he and Lloyd George were National Liberals in a coalition government they could only worry about that. 'It is ever my desire', he concluded, 'to be a help not a hindrance to you.'[26]

Churchill's appeal fell on deaf ears. Lloyd George was in a far less alarmist mood. It was not just that he was committed to the trade negotiations and determined to keep moderate Liberal and Labour opinion behind his government. He also refused to take the intercepts at face value and believed they did more to discredit than to help the regime in Moscow. The British working class was manifestly resistant to revolution and the revival of the economy afforded the best protection against possible subversion. Dazzled by the material in front of him, Churchill leaped to conclusions about the effect of Soviet subversion from the expressed intentions of Moscow; Lloyd George was more sceptical. In any case he believed the expulsion of Krasin would have little effect – the *Daily Herald* could be subsidised by Moscow gold from abroad just as well as from London. Most important of all, it would have the damaging consequence of ending the intercepts and thus deprive the British government of a unique insight into Bolshevik thinking. This was intelligence, in his view, far too valuable to be thrown away in a fit of panic.

Yet Lloyd George threw a bone or two to keep Churchill and his rebellious intelligence chiefs happy. One was the release to the press of intercepts revealing Moscow's subsidies to the *Daily Herald*. But these were intercepts of *wireless*, not cable messages, and were all between Litvinov, in Copenhagen, and Chicherin, his boss in Moscow. None, therefore, revealed that *cables* between London and Moscow were also being read by British intelligence. A second was the expulsion of Kamenev, inevitable after the intercept of a message from Lenin instructing him to spread propaganda amongst the British masses. In September 1920 Lloyd George summoned Kamenev to 10 Downing Street and told him that he would not be welcome back after his impending visit to Moscow. Krasin, however, was spared.

These measures only partly appeased Churchill and his intelligence allies. They demanded a far more drastic move: the publication of the cable intercepts. Only this would fully expose Moscow's perfidy and the threat to Britain. And although it would instantly reveal the top-secret work of GC & CS, they felt it was fully warranted by the extreme gravity of the threat to national security.

Churchill took the lead. He instructed Wilson to convene a meeting with Sir Basil Thomson, General Thwaites and Admiral Sinclair (who as Director of Naval Intelligence was also responsible for GC & CS) to discuss how the intercepts could be published 'without undue damage to the permanent interests of the cipher school'. Against publication was the obvious fact that foreign powers (and not just the Soviets) would be alerted to GC & CS operations, leading them to adopt ciphers that might prove impossible to break. It would also make it more difficult for the government to get hold of copies of foreign cablegrams, the raw material of such intelligence, and might also threaten the relevant amendments to the Official Secrets Act then before Parliament. Arguments in favour of publication were that it would firmly convict the Russian delegation of improper behaviour, furnish irrefutable evidence to support their expulsion, and definitively break up Soviet intervention in Britain. At six o'clock on the evening of 31 August the two service intelligence chiefs, Sinclair and Thwaites, joined Thomson and Churchill in his room at the War Office. Here they agreed that the risks of publication were far outweighed by the grave national danger faced by the country. Sinclair, titular head of GC & CS and two years later Cumming's successor as head of SIS, took the most uncompromising position. He was concerned about Bolshevism in the Royal Navy, and for that reason alone was anxious to see the back of Krasin and Kamenev, but he also believed that publication of the intercepts would strike a death blow to the revolutionary movement in Britain. 'I will go so far as to say', he confessed in an extraordinary statement for an intelligence chief, 'that even if publication . . . was to result in not another message being decoded, then the present situation would fully justify it.' Churchill urged the Cabinet to take action. 'I am convinced', he told his colleagues, 'that the danger to the State which has been wrought by the intrigues of these revolutionaries and the disastrous effect which will be produced on their plans by the exposure of their methods outweigh all other considerations.'[27]

The Cabinet rejected his advice and decided *not* to publish the intercepts. So enraged was someone behind the scenes that there followed very quickly a deliberate leak of information and neither Kamenev's expulsion nor the arrest of prominent pro-Bolsheviks that autumn lessened Churchill's obsession with Krasin. Only a week after Kamenev left the country, after seeing an intercept implicating Krasin in the passing of money for political purposes Churchill instructed Thwaites to prepare a detailed note showing all the evidence available to convict him of complicity with 'the Kameneff misconduct'. 'As long as any portion of this nest of vipers is left intact', he declared, 'it will continue to breed and swarm.'[28]

Two months later the Cabinet reaffirmed its decision to negotiate with the Soviets. So upset was Churchill that he sat out the Cabinet meeting pale with anger. That night he delivered a vitriolic anti-Bolshevik speech at the Oxford Union. There would be no recovery in Russia or Eastern Europe, he told the assembled students, while 'these wicked men, this vile group of cosmopolitan fanatics, hold the Russian nation by the hair of its head and tyrannizes over its great population'. And when the novelist H. G. Wells returned from Moscow with glowing reports of the Bolsheviks' new social order, Churchill replied with a virulent and scornful attack: 'We see the Bolshevik cancer eating into the flesh of the wretched being; we see the monstrous growth swelling and thriving upon the emaciated body of its victim. And now Mr Wells, the philosophical romancer, comes forward with the proposition that the cancer is the only thing that can pull the body round.'[29] Three years later Wells retaliated with his thinly disguised portrait of 'Rupert Catskill' in his satirical novel *Men Like Gods,* 'a slow moving, intent, sandy-complexioned figure in a grey top hat', of whom Mr Cecil Burleigh, the Conservative leader, complains that he 'always had too much imagination . . . I sometimes think that it would have been better for both of us if Rupert had taken to writing romances – instead of living them.'[30] It was a view of Churchill that his dramatic reactions to secret intelligence and its revelations of Bolshevik behaviour had done much to create.

6

Bolsheviks

The virulence of Churchill's exchange with H. G. Wells was significant, for even as he delivered his Oxford polemic another British visitor to Russia was returning to write a glowing account of the new regime. Her name was Clare Sheridan, and she was none other than Churchill's first cousin. Her offence exceeded that of Wells. Not only had she returned from Moscow convinced of the Soviet Utopia. She had actually nestled in the Bolshevik 'vipers' den' in London, befriended Krasin and accompanied Kamenev back to Russia. The episode adds an intriguing dimension to the story of Churchill's duel with the Bolsheviks that summer. Not surprisingly he omitted all references to the affair in later accounts of this tempestuous period.

Clare Sheridan was the only daughter of Churchill's Aunt Clara and her husband Moreton Frewen, an Anglo-Irish merchant speculator known as 'Mortal Ruin'. A bridesmaid at Churchill's wedding, Clare developed an exuberant taste for silk gowns and glamorous jewellery. Henry James, a neighbour of the Frewens in Sussex, drily congratulated her father on 'so radiant and interesting a daughter'. After her husband William, a descendant of the playwright Richard Brinsley Sheridan, was killed at the battle of Loos in 1915 she launched on a picaresque career as society sculptress, journalist and travel writer. Amongst her many adventures she counted a drive across southern Russia on a motor bike nicknamed Satanella, six months carving on an Indian reservation in North America, and a narrow escape from an amorous pass made by Mussolini during a joint sculpting session. 'You will not leave till dawn', he promised, 'and then you will be broken in' – a quick knee to the groin put paid to that.[1]

Churchill described Clare as close to a sister. 'Our love is eternal', he once told her, and the tragic wartime loss of her husband only tightened the bond. The summer of 1920 saw them draw even closer. Churchill spent much of his time at Templeton, Freddie Guest's Roehampton mansion, indulging in his new passion for painting. Clare was a frequent visitor and Guest conceived the bright idea of advancing her career by commissioning her to sculpt the heads of his political friends and exhibit them at Agnew's Gallery in London's West End. Churchill's was one of the first, followed by Lord Birkenhead, also a frequent visitor. Clare, Churchill and Birkenhead became an inseparable trio, and society was soon buzzing with gossip about an affair between Clare and Birkenhead. Churchill indulgently refused to be scandalised: both were special people and whatever they did was fine by him. Clare particularly, after her wartime suffering, could do no wrong.

Not, that is, until 1920. Clare led an active social life and one of her closest friends, Sidney Russell Cooke, suggested it would be a feather in her cap to include busts of Krasin and Kamenev in her exhibition. Thrilled, she asked him to arrange it. Shortly afterwards she went to the New Bond Street offices of the Soviet trade delegation. It was August 1920, at the height of the Polish-Soviet war scare, Churchill's attempted prosecution of George Lansbury, and Sir Henry Wilson's mutterings about the need for a coup against Lloyd George. Kamenev proved surprisingly obliging. Like Krasin he failed to fit the Bolshevik stereotype, although *The Times* and the rest of the anti-Bolshevik press invariably stressed his Jewishness by referring to him as Kamenev-Rozenfeld. Just two years older than Clare, he was a self-assured man with amiable manners.

Three days later he arrived at her studio in St John's Wood and sat for three hours. After he had left Clare rushed off to a lunch with her cousin Winston. Here she listened, starry-eyed, while he expounded on Bolshevism. Nobody hated it more than he, and he would like to shoot every one he saw. But, he added with a grin, Bolsheviks were like crocodiles: sometimes they became simply too expensive to hunt.[2]

The next morning Krasin arrived at the studio. He, too, stayed for the whole morning. 'He has a beautiful head', Clare noted in her diary, 'and he sat almost sphinx-like, severe and expression-less . . . his piercing eyes looked at me impassively while I worked.' Later she noted how delightful he was, 'calm, sincere, dignified, proud, without self-consciousness and without vanity and scientific in his analysis of things and people. Eyes that are unflinching and bewilderingly direct, nostrils that dilate with sensitiveness, a mouth that looks hard till it smiles, and a chin full of determination.'[3] Ironically, even as she worked to capture Krasin's features, an outraged Sir Henry Wilson was meeting with Sir Basil Thomson and General Thwaites at the War Office to pour over the intercepts of Krasin's communications with Moscow and demand his expulsion from a sympathetic Churchill.

By this time Clare had fallen heavily for Kamenev and he for her. He sent her roses and they dined at the Café Royal. The next day they lunched at Claridges and strolled around the Tate Gallery. Walking to Trafalgar Square they found themselves in a 'Hands Off Russia' demonstration organised by the Council of Action. The speaker was George Lansbury who soon noticed them in the crowd. 'Gangway please for Comrade Kamenev' went up the cry and they were wildly cheered, but prudently, aware of the risk of expulsion, he declined to speak. Then the couple visited Hampton Court and rowed on the Thames with Kamenev humming Volga boat songs. Clare arrived back home at midnight. 'Twelve hours with Kamenev', she noted ecstatically.[4]

There followed more studio sessions, dinners and visits, culminating in an idyllic weekend as guests of Sidney Cooke at his summer cottage on the Isle of Wight. Lying together in the grass, Kamenev entranced them in his halting French with stories of the Revolution. He and Cooke composed an ode to Clare on a five-pound note, taking it in turn to compose lines.

Infatuated with the dangerous romance, and tempted by Kamenev's promise of sittings with Lenin and Trotsky that would bring her international acclaim, Clare decided to return to Russia with him. Birkenhead was forgotten, as was a projected summer cruise on his yacht with Winston, and Agnew's exhibition which opened without her. She contemptuously dismissed warnings from the Foreign Office that she could be shot as a spy or taken as a hostage for Churchill. The day after Lloyd George told Kamenev he was *persona non grata*, she threw her possessions into two small suitcases, handed her jewellery to Cooke and left London with him. Krasin saw them off at St Pancras station. His parting gift was a large box of chocolates tied with red ribbon.

It was red tape that greeted Clare in Moscow. Kamenev's wife was less than thrilled to meet her, and an embarrassed Kamenev soon made himself too busy to look after her. Endless days passed in her spartan quarters at the official Soviet guest house on the Sofiskaya Embankment. Requests for sculpting sessions went unanswered. She suspected that this was because she was Churchill's cousin. 'My God, how they hate him', she wrote in a letter home. Speaking no Russian, left on her own, and making do with cold water, black bread and salt herring she grew restless. John Reed, the American Communist and author of *Ten Days that Shook the World*, told her to stop complaining and fend for herself. Nor was her temper improved when she bumped into H. G. Wells, whom she had last met during the war when he and Winston had eagerly discussed the exciting new idea of tank warfare over lunch in her studio.

The novelist was in a bad temper. He had had an unsatisfactory interview with Lenin, complained bitterly about the shuttered shops and bad food, and was scornful of her hopes to sculpt the Soviet leader. 'You'll find he has no time for the likes of you', he sneered.[5] He was wrong. Patience and persistence paid off and in October, in a makeshift studio in the Kremlin, she sculpted the leading personalities of the Soviet state – Lenin, Zinoviev, Dzerzhinsky and Trotsky, with whom she teetered on the edge of yet another passion. Of Dzerzhinsky, head of the Terror, she sympathetically observed 'his eyes bathed in tears of eternal sorrow' and noted how 'his mouth smiled an indulgent kindness'. Lenin was mostly taciturn, but told her that Churchill was Russia's greatest enemy: 'All the force of your Court and your Army lie behind him.' By contrast Trotsky was flirtatious, kissing her hand. 'Even when your teeth are clenched', he whispered as she worked, '*vous êtes encore femme.*' 'I will tell them in England how nice you are', she replied. 'Tell them', he murmured back, 'that when Trotsky kisses he does not bite.'[6]

Clare returned to London, a press sensation, in November 1920. *The Times*, under the heading WITH LENIN AND TROTSKY, published extracts from her diary every day for a week. 'There is a certain piquancy in the mere event', it noted in an editorial, 'which is not lessened by the fact that Mr Churchill's cousin is a lady, and that her sympathies appear to be rather with her Russian hosts than with her kinsmen.'[7] Not everyone appreciated the irony. Society, not to mention her horrified family, was scandalised by her dallyings with the Bolsheviks. Ostracised, she soon left for the United States while tempers at home cooled down.

Outwardly Churchill was furious at his cousin's defection to the enemy. At a family gathering he exploded in rage: 'Clare's in Russia with those filthy communists. She's mad, I tell you. Mad! It's absolutely typical of Clare, but this time she's really gone too far. I'll not forgive her.'[8] When she returned two months later he refused to see her, but in the end he was able to forgive. Before he left the War Office he wrote her a gracious letter, signing it 'Your affectionate cousin, Winston'. 'No one has felt more sympathy or admiration for your gifts than I have', he wrote, 'and I should be very sorry if you did not feel that I would do my best to help you in any way possible or that you did not count on my friendship and kinship.' He also wished her well in America, and hoped that when she returned there would be a healthy gap between her and 'an episode which may then have faded and to which we need neither of us ever refer'. Discreetly, he also asked his friend Bernard Baruch, the wartime chairman of the United States' War Industries Board, to keep an eye on her. 'She's brave', he wrote, 'but has no judgement and might get in trouble.' Twenty years later, completely forgiven, Clare spent a wartime morning sculpting her cousin at 10 Downing Street. As was customary, he was in bed, insisting on his cigar and restlessly stroking his black Persian cat. But he finally agreed to sit still. 'I want it to be a success', he grunted. 'We'll call it Prime Minister by Obstreperous Anarchist.'[9]

Yet despite genuine anger at Clare's flight to Moscow, Churchill knew a great deal more about the affair than he was willing to admit to the family then or to history later. Clare was astute enough not to tell him of the Kamenev sculpting sessions and confided her Moscow plans only to a handful of trusted friends. One was their cousin Shane Leslie, who through Francis Meynell, of the *Daily Herald* diamonds scandal, learned that there were 'spies in the Bolshevik HQ' and feared that Churchill would discover everything.[10] He was right to be worried. Special Branch was keeping a close watch on the Soviet delegation and could hardly have failed to learn the name of Kamenev's glamorous companion. But what Leslie did not know, and what documentary evidence now clearly suggests, is that she was used by British intelligence, with Churchill's knowledge, to get closer to the Soviet delegation.

The key to the affair was her friend Sidney Russell Cooke. Clare revealed little about him except to say that he was intelligent and good-looking, and a frequent dining and dancing partner. In reality he was more. A former private secretary to Herbert Asquith, and co-author of a well-informed book about oil trusts and Anglo-American relations based on excellent contacts in Whitehall, it was he who suggested that she sculpt Krasin and Kamenev, and he seemed inordinately interested in all that concerned the Russians. He particularly wanted to know whether Kamenev had accepted Lansbury's invitation to speak at the Trafalgar Square demonstration.

One day Clare accused Cooke of spying on her. He readily admitted that he had once been in touch with the Intelligence Department and that he was 'just a little in touch with that Department now'. He confessed that he had, in fact, been making daily reports on Kamenev's movements based on what Clare had told him. 'Winston', he told her, 'had emphatically demanded that those Soviet emissaries be watched . . . and that someone must be got into the Soviet office.' He also said that he had told his intelligence masters of her plans to visit Moscow.

Clare, rarely an entirely reliable source, later claimed that she was not sure if she believed any of this. 'To me', she recalled, 'it sounded rather like a penny novelette.'[11] No doubt it did, but so did much real-world spying and for once her vivid imagination had not misled her. Conclusive evidence from War Office files confirms that Cooke was an MI5 officer. More significantly, he had been personal assistant to its Director, Vernon Kell. War Office lists reveal that in 1915 and 1916 'Lieutenant S. R. Cooke' was attached to Kell and shared Room 326 with him at the War Office, later being transferred to another military intelligence department, MI5 (G), headed by Major J. F. C. Fuller who would earn later fame and notoriety as a fascist sympathiser and writer on military affairs. Significantly, in civilian life Cooke also worked for the City stockbroking firm of Rowe and Pitman, a well-known home for intelligence recruits, including the wartime personal assistant to 'Blinker' Hall, Claud Serocold, and in the 1930s Ian Fleming. The best man at his wedding, Sir Campbell Stuart, was director of wartime propaganda to enemy countries and had many intelligence contacts, and his sister was married to Brigadier 'Jasper' Harker, a leading MI5 officer who temporarily took over as Acting Director after Kell's departure in 1940.[12]

Cooke's connections with MI5 make Clare's adventure with Kamenev even more astonishing, for it was at Cooke's house that she and Kamenev had passed their idyllic weekend on the Isle of Wight, and when she left London Cooke saw her through port formalities at Newcastle and waved her off at the quayside. He was the first to greet her when she arrived back in London, then borrowed her diary for several days before returning it without comment. He also arranged her press conferences and carefully edited the diary before selling extracts to *The Times*. It was he, too, who arranged her visa and passport when she left for the United States. Shane Leslie, accused by the family that he had recklessly let her go to Moscow, defended himself by saying that she had been 'accompanied by the Secret Service'. He was right: Sidney Cooke was her MI5 minder.

Her Moscow hosts suspected or knew as much. Litvinov grilled her thoroughly about Cooke. All Clare admitted was that he might have been in British intelligence during the war. Litvinov drew heavily on his cigarette and stared at her in silence until she felt 'like the author of a murder'. Kamenev made her feel even less comfortable. Her nationality and her relations were unimportant, he declared. The only thing the Bolsheviks could not stand was – *l'espionnage!*[13]

Did Clare know she was being used by British intelligence? She alleged in her memoirs that Birkenhead had told her about the intercepts. 'We have discovered the secret of Krasin's code and are deciphering all the telegrams he is sending to the Soviet government!' he supposedly confessed. So when Kamenev revealed he intended to ask Moscow for permission to take her with him, she begged him not to mention her name, fearing Winston and Birkenhead who might prevent her departure. Kamenev assured her that he would telegraph in cipher. 'Are you sure your code is not understood?' she asked. But Kamenev shrugged off the idea. If they knew that, he said, then they knew many more important secrets.[14]

Cabinet members did, of course, know the secrets of the intercepts, and Churchill was their most avid consumer. So he could not have missed Kamenev's 'Most Secret' telegram to Chicherin of 29 August 1920. After complaining about a campaign by 'the Churchillites' against his contacts with the Council of Action, he reported that H. G. Wells 'and an acquaintance of his, an English sculptress' wanted to visit Russia and recommended the idea as useful for Soviet propaganda in British artistic and literary circles. He did not give the name of the sculptress but declared that she hoped to sculpt both Lenin and Trotsky and that her work was 'very good'.[15] Did Churchill guess that this was Clare? Given Cooke's reports and Churchill's own insistent demands for incriminating evidence against the Bolsheviks in London, it seems certain that he did. If so, then he did nothing to stop her going, and his shock in front of the family was feigned. Oswald Frewen, Clare's brother, who was also in on the secret, recorded in his diary a meeting in which Churchill's stepfather reported Churchill as saying calmly on hearing of the news, 'How enterprising, good luck to her.'[16] Whatever the intelligence benefit, and however deeply implicated he was, Churchill chose to forget the affair once it was over. No references to it appear in any of his many published volumes. This, clearly, was a family secret best kept quiet.

Clare's sympathies for the new Russian regime did not diminish her respect for her cousin. 'Winston is the only man I know in England who is made of the stuff that Bolsheviks are made of', she wrote in *Russian Portraits*, 'he has fight, force, and fanaticism.'[17] As Secretary of State for War he more than proved her point by spearheading efforts for the overthrow of the Moscow regime.

After Lenin took Russia out of the war in the spring of 1918 the Western allies supported anti-Bolshevik forces in the hope they would continue resistance to the Central Powers and block allied supplies from falling into German or Bolshevik hands. Additionally, Britain sought to protect the periphery of its Indian Empire now threatened from the north. Intelligence experts in the War Office, long accustomed to the Great Game against the Tsars, renewed the battle against their Communist heirs and hoped that indigenous guerrillas, sparked by professional soldiers, could be harnessed to the pursuit of British goals. In March 1918 Lloyd George sent British forces to Murmansk and Archangel. Other powers followed and soon almost 200,000 foreign troops were embroiled in the civil war. The armistice of November 1918 removed the original *raison d'être* of allied intervention. But the troops stayed on for months while the allies bickered and dithered about whether to withdraw them.

On New Year's Eve 1918 the British Cabinet decided against overthrowing the Bolsheviks by force, but what to do with the men in Russia was left unclear and Churchill exploited their presence in a vain and desperate attempt to change Cabinet policy. Frustrated by Cabinet disagreement and allied opposition – especially from President Wilson – he grasped at every stratagem he could to undermine the Bolsheviks. Even when the Cabinet decided to withdraw British forces he planned their retreat so as best to assist the White

Army. Throughout he waxed enthusiastic about their struggle against Moscow.

As British forces withdrew, his anti-Communist rhetoric reached an apocalyptic pitch. 'Bolshevism', he declared in June 1919, 'means in every country a civil war of the most merciless kind between the discontented, criminal, and mutinous classes on the one hand and the contented or law abiding on the other . . . it means . . . the slaughter of men, women and children, the burning of homes, and the inviting in of tyranny, pestilence, and famine.'[18] In practice, he sought a military defeat of the Red Army and hoped politically for a broad anti-Bolshevik coalition that would include the Left. Hence, when the prominent socialist Gregor Alexinsky fled from Petrograd to Paris, he arranged for Vernon Kell and military intelligence to bring him to London and provided introductions to radical and labour newspaper editors, as well as leading figures from the Left such as J. R. Clynes. He even spoke of finding him financial support through the military intelligence budget.[19] In short, war against Lenin was to be fought on a political as well as a military front. This also meant mobilising underground conspirators and secret warriors.

Churchill was an enthusiastic partisan of subversion, sabotage and special operations. His fascination for terrorists often sat uncomfortably with his conservative beliefs. The Fenians of his youth and the 'anarchists' of Sidney Street had left their mark. Kell's alarmist reports about the subversive influence of German agents in Britain had seriously disturbed him. Now, faced with a captive Russia, he believed that it could be set alight by daring men taking the battle behind enemy lines.

He pinned his hopes on Boris Savinkov, a former anti-Tsarist revolutionary and now anti-Bolshevik conspirator. As a member of the Social Revolutionary Party he had planned the murder of V. K. Plehve, Russian Minister of the Interior, and the 1905 assassination of Grand Duke Sergei, uncle of the Tsar and Governor of Moscow. Forced into a Parisian exile he indulged a taste for stylish clothes, expensive restaurants and exotic brothels. He also became a morphine addict, mixed with poets and artists such as Apollinaire, Modigliani and Diego Rivera, and found time to write a novel, *The Pale Horse*, a thinly disguised fictional account of the assassination of the Grand Duke. The First World War transformed him into an ardent patriot and bitter opponent of the Bolsheviks. After the February Revolution he became Deputy Minister of War under

Alexander Kerensky; after the Bolshevik Revolution he formed the Union for the Defence of the Motherland and Liberty, and joined the underground. The British secret agent Robert Bruce Lockhart, who was visited by Savinkov disguised in a pair of huge horn-rimmed dark glasses, summed him up as a talented schemer more adept at spinning late-night schemes over brandy than following them through. 'He had mingled so much with spies and *agents provocateurs*', noted Lockhart, 'that . . . he hardly knew whether he was deceiving himself or those whom he meant to deceive.'[20] This did not prevent Lockhart from providing him with several million roubles for his anti-Bolshevik plots.

These were unmasked by the Cheka early in 1919. Savinkov fled to Paris and it was here that Churchill first met him lobbying for allied intervention to help the White Army. He was immediately mesmerised. Savinkov exuded a powerful sexual magnetism – he had a string of mistresses to his name – and he possessed a flair for the melodramatic that placed him firmly centre stage in the drama of his own life. He often wore disguises and invariably carried a Browning pistol that he would ostentatiously place on the table beside him to impress his visitors. Churchill, reading *The Pale Horse,* was impressed by its graphic description of the assassination, and its brutal candour about the adventures and group dynamics of the small cell of conspirators.

'I had never seen a Russian Nihilist except on the stage', Churchill confessed, 'and . . . he was singularly well cast for the part. Small in stature; moving as little as possible, and that noiselessly and with deliberation; remarkable grey-green eyes in a face of almost deathly pallor; speaking in a calm, low, even voice, almost a monotone; innumerable cigarettes . . . a frozen but not a freezing composure; and through all the sense of an unusual personality, of veiled power in strong restraint.'[21] Savinkov was also a great admirer of Napoleon and as a young man had even written a play about the Emperor's escape from Elba where he starred in the central role. In Savinkov's version Napoleon won the battle of Waterloo.

Churchill provided an admiring audience. Savinkov needed all the help he could muster to destroy the Bolsheviks and saw Churchill as his best British bet. For his part Churchill saw in Savinkov a comrade-in-arms against Lenin, the last best hope for an effective leader of a new Russia. A terrorist he may have been, but in Churchill's eyes he was 'that extraordinary product – a Terrorist for moderate aims'; or, as he quaintly put it in the final volume of *The*

World Crisis, 'the essence of practicality and good sense expressed in terms of nitro-glycerine'.[22] So impressed did he remain that he included Savinkov with twenty other leading personalities – including Lawrence of Arabia, George Bernard Shaw and Adolf Hitler – in his 1937 collection of biographical sketches, *Great Contemporaries*.

Churchill embraced him as the saviour of Russia. Militarily, all depended on the White Army under Anton Denikin. But Denikin was reactionary in his domestic views, an old-fashioned Russian imperialist hostile to the Poles and the newly independent Baltic states. Churchill saw Savinkov as a moderating influence and, virtually alone among Western statesmen, gave him enthusiastic and unwavering support. Late in 1919 he met him at the War Office, along with official Finnish representatives, to discuss Finnish help for a projected attack on Petrograd. After the Finns had left, Churchill bluntly told Savinkov that unless Denikin adopted more democratic policies he could count on no official British support. It was up to Savinkov to see that this happened. He did his best, urging Denikin to give land to the peasants, halt anti-Jewish pogroms, and treat the Poles and Finns as equals. Churchill backed this up with his own message to Denikin stressing how much he was impressed by Savinkov.

It was all in vain and by 1920 the White Army was defeated. Savinkov won Pilsudski's support for an anti-Soviet force and a shadow Russian government in Warsaw. Following the Bolshevik defeat at the gates of Warsaw he grandly predicted that the Red Army was on the verge of collapse and that what was needed to bring down the Bolsheviks was to kindle the flame of revolution, so he sent his Russian Volunteer Army across the frontier. It would, he said, 'produce a snowball effect and pick up irresistible strength as it rolled towards Moscow'.[23] Instead, it rapidly melted when confronted by Soviet forces and streamed back to Warsaw. Savinkov reorganised his men for cross-border raids and re-established his old Union for the Defence of the Motherland and Liberty, with an 'Information Bureau' controlling a network of agents for propaganda, espionage and sabotage. Over the next two years these guerrillas, known as 'the Greens' to distinguish them from the Reds and the Whites, carried out attacks on Soviet territory, blowing up trains, assassinating Bolsheviks and ambushing Red Army patrols.

The climax of his efforts came with an All-Russian Anti-Bolshevik Congress held in Warsaw in June 1921. Dressed in a British-style uniform and adopting his best Napoleonic stance, he again predicted the imminent collapse of Bolshevism when Red commissars would descend on the villages to requisition food. Revolt, he said, 'would roll from one province to the next like a tidal wave sweeping the commissars to their destruction'. Outwardly, there was much to support his optimism as catastrophic famine forced Lenin to make a radical U-turn with his New Economic Policy (NEP). The Kronstadt mutiny and a peasant revolt in Tambov province also indicated widespread dissent. But Savinkov, like many others, underestimated the Cheka. Not only did it ruthlessly quash opposition in Russia, it also penetrated his own organisation. Alexander Opperput, his propaganda chief, was one of Dzerzhinsky's most resourceful agents.

Despite these setbacks Churchill remained deeply impressed, met Savinkov whenever he came to London and ensured he saw Lloyd George. Comparing Savinkov's guerrilla force to Sinn Fein in its ability to win over the peasantry, he romantically described it as waging 'a sort of Robin Hood warfare'. When official British policy prevented him from diverting supplies to the rebel leader he complained bitterly about having had 'to put a spoke in Savinkov's wheel'. He was powerless to help Savinkov financially in Poland, but he did hold out the prospect that £8 million in the pipeline for Denikin could be diverted to him and toyed with funding him from secret-service funds.[24]

Lloyd George showed enough interest to keep their hopes alive – but not too much to provoke the anti-interventionist Left. But Churchill told a sceptical Lord Curzon, the Foreign Secretary, that Lloyd George was firmly on board. 'We have had several long confabulations and lunches at 10 Downing Street', he told him and claimed that Lloyd George thought more highly of Savinkov than of any other anti-Bolshevik Russian. Savinkov effusively returned Churchill's compliments. 'In your person', he avowed 'the Bolsheviks have an implacable enemy and we Russian patriots a sure friend.'[25]

Churchill was particularly helpful when Savinkov's welcome ran out in Poland and he was forced to relocate to Prague. By this time Britain and France were moving towards recognition of the Bolshevik regime, a step that Churchill was determined to prevent. Savinkov had convinced himself that the NEP meant that the Bolsheviks were desperate to widen their base of support. Perhaps this was an opportunity for a 'political' NEP that would include concessions to opponents of the regime? Perhaps even a new leadership with room for Savinkov himself? With such thoughts in his mind, early in December 1921 Savinkov headed for London.

Churchill also believed he faced a historic opportunity. The West needed to place stringent conditions on any aid to the desperate Bolsheviks in order to bring about a fundamental reform of the regime: the Cheka should be abolished, private-property rights reinstated – but with the important proviso that peasants should keep the land they had won since the Revolution – and free elections to the soviets held. If these principles were accepted, then peace and prosperity would eventually return to Russia. If not, then Churchill remained adamantly opposed to any deal with Moscow. Preliminary Anglo-French talks on these issues were scheduled in London just before Christmas and Churchill urged Savinkov to put his case personally to Lloyd George. More than ever he was convinced that Savinkov was the man of the hour.

Churchill's enthusiasm for Savinkov was encouraged by one of his closest friends. Archie Sinclair was now officially his personal military secretary in the War Office, but this title was deceptive. The future Liberal leader played a more active if covert role in Churchill's anti-Bolshevik war than has been previously known. It was to Sinclair that the overstretched Churchill delegated his Russian interests, relying heavily on him to communicate with the major players, take care of numerous Russian supplicants, and collect and assess intelligence about the Bolsheviks and their enemies. This, in Churchill's own words inscribed on the newly released files of Russian material in his personal archive, was all 'Archie's work'.[26]

No relation to Admiral Sinclair, the DNI and future 'C', Archie Sinclair enjoyed intimate links with the secret intelligence world. In February 1921 a dinner was thrown at the Army and Navy Club by military intelligence officers for three men who were formally leaving its service: Sinclair, Major George Hill and Captain Malcolm Woollcombe. Hill was one of Cumming's most important intelligence officers in Russia, later wrote a bestseller about his adventures entitled *Go Spy the Land*, and in the Second World War ran the Special Operations Executive's Moscow office. Woollcombe had served in military intelligence in the First World War and from 1921 to 1940 was the SIS principal liaison officer with the Foreign Office. In addition to Hill and Woollcombe, Sinclair's close friend Stewart Menzies was now the official War Office liaison with SIS and frequently added useful interpretive notes of his own to material handled by Sinclair.

'Archie' filtered the material to Churchill, a mixture of human and technical (intercept) intelligence from a wide variety of sources, prepared his own evaluations, and followed up Churchill's responses with requests to 'C' and others for information. When Churchill was too busy to look at the extensive raw material himself, Sinclair would summarize it – as he did with much of the intercept material on Krasin and the Soviets. But he also had important personal contacts.

Of these Sinclair thought most highly of Savinkov. It was through Sinclair that Savinkov dealt with Churchill on his frequent visits to London, and when Sinclair received reports from the Foreign Office in late 1921 of an uprising in Karelia promoted by Savinkov's supporters, he told Churchill that the former nihilist had 'won for himself the foremost place in Russian opinion among the opponents of Bolshevism'. Churchill immediately sent the report to Lloyd George. 'See Sinclair's note about Savinkov', he minuted the Prime Minister in red ink. 'He is the only man who counts.'[27]

Not surprisingly Churchill worked hard to bring Savinkov to London in late 1921. It was not easy. Foreign Office officials regarded him as unreliable, even crooked, and refused him a visa. SIS chief Mansfield Cumming also declined to help, but Churchill leaned on his intelligence contacts in France. Before the Foreign Office had woken up, the British Passport Office in Paris had issued a visa and Savinkov was in London.

There then took place an extraordinary clandestine meeting on whose outcome Churchill believed the future of Russia could turn. Two days after his arrival in London Savinkov met secretly with Leonid Krasin. They had briefly co-operated during the Social Revolutionary terrorist campaign before the war and Krasin was one of the few Bolsheviks he respected. If the slightest chance existed that the Bolsheviks were prepared to bring in moderate leftists to join their government, then Krasin was the person to help. The encounter took place over dinner at a private house in London. After the meal was over, the English host – whose name Savinkov never revealed – withdrew, leaving the two Russians in earnest tête-à-tête until two o'clock in the morning. What precisely they agreed remains a mystery. Savinkov later claimed that an eager Krasin initiated the meeting and offered him a post in the Bolshevik government. Instead, he countered with the three conditions for reform familiar to Churchill: abolition of the Cheka, property rights and free elections. Krasin promised to forward the proposals to Moscow. By contrast, SIS claimed that it was Savinkov who had initiated the meeting. This might have been right, for at least one SIS officer (possibly the mysterious host himself) attended the dinner but withdrew when serious discussion between the Russians began. Unfortunately his account of events has been carefully laundered from the archive.[28]

Hardly had Savinkov returned to his hotel than Churchill sent Archie Sinclair round to find out what had happened. The next day Sinclair invited Savinkov to his home for breakfast. When the Russian arrived he found Churchill sitting at the table eager for details. Having heard them he observed that the conditions Savinkov had laid before Krasin were quite acceptable to the British government but that he doubted the Bolsheviks would agree. Savinkov promised that in this case the Greens would continue their fight. Churchill then brought others into the discussion. The next day, this time over tea at Churchill's home, Savinkov met Birkenhead who agreed that recognition of the Soviets had to be wholly conditional on their acceptance of Savinkov's three points.

Churchill's efforts were designed to prepare Savinkov for a personal meeting with the Prime Minister. A week before Christmas 1921 the two men motored down to Chequers. They arrived to find Lloyd George surrounded by Free Church ministers and a band of Welsh singers. This, as Churchill drily admitted, was 'a novel experience for Savinkov'. For some time the two men listened politely to Welsh hymns before Savinkov put his case to Lloyd George. Any official dealings with Moscow, he pleaded, should be on the stringent political conditions agreed by him, Churchill and Birkenhead.

Lloyd George, ever the shrewd tactician, was sympathetic but non-committal. Privately he dismissed Savinkov as a 'seductive nihilist' and his response reflected his scepticism. For years, he told Savinkov, people had been predicting the imminent collapse of the Bolsheviks, but normalising relations was the best way of bringing peace and a strong economy to Europe. Revolutions, like diseases, ran their course. The Bolsheviks would either grow more responsible or fall out amongst themselves, as in the French Revolution, and thus open the way for moderate leaders. To this the ex-nihilist riposted that the fall of Rome had been followed by the Dark Ages.

Savinkov and Churchill left Chequers empty-handed. Later, from a secret source almost certainly acquired through Archie Sinclair,

Churchill received a copy of Savinkov's highly embellished account of the meeting. It featured not only Welsh hymns but also an imaginary scene featuring Lloyd George and his family singing 'God Save the Tsar'. Churchill sent it on to Lloyd George. 'This will amuse you', he added.[29]

This was Churchill's last known meeting with Savinkov, although he followed it up by sending Archie Sinclair to see Krasin for the other side of the story. His wry comment to Lloyd George suggested that he was already beginning to detach himself from the veteran terrorist. It was just as well. With hopes of Western support now dashed, a fruitless meeting with Krasin, money running short and his Green guerrilla movement going nowhere, the old nihilist was reverting to type. Even as he dealt with Churchill he was plotting the assassination of Bolshevik leaders. Financed by Gustav Nobel, the Baku oil magnate, he masterminded failed attempts in Berlin to kill Chicherin, Karl Radek, head of Moscow's mission there, and Nikolai Bukharin who was attempting to stir up revolution in Germany. Then he travelled to Genoa to have another try at Chicherin at the European summit of April 1922. Here he was arrested by the Italian police and unceremoniously deported back to France.

Effectively, this was the end for Savinkov. The Genoa conference granted Western *de facto* recognition to the Bolshevik regime; disheartened and disillusioned, he was tempted back to Moscow in 1924 with the promise of a role in the new government. Instead he was arrested, thrown into prison and sentenced to death. This was commuted to ten years, and he produced a subsequently all-too-familiar letter of recantation proclaiming the virtues of the Bolsheviks. He died, either voluntarily or otherwise, after exiting from a window of the notorious Lubyanka prison, in May 1925. His arrest, trial and death amidst accusations of treachery and double-dealing failed to tarnish Churchill's view of him. A vigorous exchange of letters in the Tory *Morning Post* saw Savinkov violently denounced for betrayal. 'By this event', thundered one correspondent, 'Savinkov has erased for ever his name from the scroll of honour of the anti-communist movement.' Churchill felt compelled to reply. 'I shall wait to hear the end of the story before changing my mind about Savinkov', he wrote. He never did alter his view. His final verdict in *Great Contemporaries*, published a decade later, was that Savinkov had 'displayed the wisdom of a statesman, the qualities of a commander, the courage of a hero, and the endurance of a martyr'.[30]

The exchange of views in the *Morning Post* was significant, for Churchill's bitter interlocutor was Britain's legendary master spy, Sidney Reilly. Here was irony indeed. Reilly would suffer a similar fate to that of Savinkov; he had also been the mainspring of Savinkov's efforts and the principal facilitator in his dealings with Churchill.

Sidney Reilly's life and career have been surrounded by sensational and romantic myths. The facts reveal a larger-than-life swashbuckler with a magnetic attraction for Churchill. His real name was Sigmund Georgevich Rosenblum, the son of a prosperous Jewish family from Russian Poland. By the late 1890s he had moved to London, adopted the name Reilly, and launched his career as international business adventurer, gambler, philanderer and spy. One recent biographer has described him as a man with seven languages and eleven passports – and a wife to go with each. Another has characterised him as 'part thug, part chameleon … [and] above all a skilled and ruthless manipulator of people'.[31]

On the eve of the First World War Reilly moved back to Russia to become a successful commission agent for several major companies – and to carry out occasional work for Cumming's Secret Intelligence Service. He then moved to New York as purchaser of supplies for the Russian government. Here he met Cumming's SIS station chief in New York, Sir William Wiseman, and his deputy Norman Thwaites, who were laying the early foundations of the British–American intelligence alliance. Approached by Reilly in 1917 to see if he could get him into the regular services, Thwaites described him as 'complexion swarthy, a long straight nose, piercing eyes, black hair brushed back from a forehead suggesting keen intelligence, a large mouth, figure slight, of medium height, always clothed immaculately'. Impressed, Thwaites sent Reilly to Toronto where he enrolled in the Royal Canadian Flying Corps. He also alerted Cumming to Reilly's forthcoming arrival in Britain.[32]

No sooner had he arrived than Cumming promptly sent Reilly back to Russia, where he soon met Savinkov. They were kindred spirits: both were flamboyant, shared a strong taste for good living, and identified with Napoleon – Reilly had become an ardent collector of Napoleana since a visit to Elba. To Reilly, Savinkov provided an entrée into anti-Bolshevik conspiracies. For Savinkov, Reilly was a useful source of outside help; from then on he became the principal source of Savinkov's funding.

Reilly's stay in Moscow ended in disaster. He joined a plot to overthrow Lenin that turned out to be heavily infiltrated by the Cheka, and when Dzerzhinsky's men rounded up the ringleaders after the failed assassination attempt on Lenin in August 1918, he only just escaped with his life. Later that year, back in London, he received the Military Cross for his SIS work.

Early in 1919 'C' sent him to Paris, along with his – and Archie Sinclair's – friend George Hill, to report on White Russian activities during the Paris Peace Conference. Cover was provided by 'Blinker' Hall at the British Naval Mission headquarters in the Majestic Hotel. It was here, according to one source, that Churchill first met him. The introduction was made by Sir William Bull, a Unionist MP and assistant to the ultra-Conservative Walter Long, First Lord of the Admiralty and a personal friend of Cumming, as well as a keen supporter of the secret service. The meeting appears to have come at the prompting of the Director of Military Intelligence and 'C'.[33]

It was the beginning of an important relationship. For the next five years Reilly was a major figure in Churchill's undying hopes for an anti-Bolshevik rising. In turn, Reilly considered Churchill to be the only useful British politician in the anti-Bolshevik cause, all the more valuable as not everyone in London – not even Cumming – was entirely sure of Reilly's true loyalties. Cumming was more than happy to listen to Reilly's opinion on Russian affairs and frequently invited him to his office in Whitehall Court, but he refused to place Reilly on the SIS's full-time books out of deference to Foreign Office suspicions – in one of its files he was even described as a former German spy.

Churchill's support was a valuable counterweight to such suspicions. The two men kept in constant touch by letter or telephone, and Archie Sinclair, who acted as the crucial intermediary, thought highly of the master spy's skill, once telling Churchill that he was 'the keenest and ablest of all the "anti-Bolo" [anti-Bolshevik] spade-workers in London'.[34] Sinclair was also a frequent dining companion and one of Reilly's handful of trusted contacts in London. All this led Reilly to confess to his old friend Commander Ernest Boyce, one-time SIS station chief in Petrograd and later head of its anti-Soviet operations in Helsinki, that Churchill had been a pillar of strength. In a letter from New York written early in 1925 he told Boyce that 'only one man is really important, and that is the irrepressible Marlborough [i.e., Churchill]. I have always remained on good terms with him . . . His ear would always be open to something sound.'[35]

He also revealed that Churchill had written him several private and confidential letters. These, along with much other Reilly material, have since disappeared; but strong traces of the Churchill–Reilly link remain in the evidence of 'Archie's work' in Churchill's papers.

Reilly's chief value to Churchill was as a link to Savinkov's plans for an anti-Bolshevik revolt. Despite reservations, Reilly considered the nihilist 'a man of courage, commanding personality, resolution, courage, optimism, shrewd, patient'. So keen was he on Savinkov's schemes that he even joined one of his raiding parties across the Polish border before being abruptly ordered back by Cumming. He took part in the anti-Bolshevik conference in Warsaw in June 1921 and a few weeks later drew up a lengthy assessment of the Russian situation that he passed to Churchill. The two met and Churchill spoke of taking him to meet Lloyd George.

Dated August 1921, Reilly's report echoed Savinkov's optimism in predicting a general uprising against the Bolsheviks that could produce a new and more moderate Russian government. This, he said, opened up avenues for Savinkov – especially if it created dissensions within the Bolshevik leadership and led to executive power passing into the hands of moderates – and, he added significantly, 'more especially a man like Krassin'.[36]

It was no surprise, therefore, that Churchill had pressured the British Passport Office in Paris to give Savinkov his visa. It was Reilly who did the footwork through his friend and SIS colleague in the Paris Passport Control Office, Captain Field Robinson, and he travelled with Savinkov to London, accompanied him to the meeting with Krasin, and then, following its failure, did his best to shore up Savinkov's flagging morale and finances. Eventually the two men drifted apart and Savinkov ignored Reilly's appeals not to return to Russia. Within a year Reilly fell victim to the same deception plot that had lured Savinkov back. Convinced that he was dealing with a genuine anti-Bolshevik resistance movement – the so-called Trust – Reilly agreed to help it in Moscow. In reality, the Trust was run by the Cheka. A few days after crossing the Finnish border in September 1925 he was arrested outside Moscow. Two months later he was shot.

Churchill quickly washed his hands of Reilly. Confirmation of his capture first reached the West in June 1927 following the assassination in Warsaw of the head of the Soviet mission, which the Soviets blamed on agents of the British. One Sidney George Riley (*sic*), they claimed, had been caught illegally crossing the Finnish frontier. He had subsequently confessed to coming to Russia 'for the special purpose of organising terrorist acts, arson and revolts, and that when coming from America he had seen Mr Churchill, Chancellor of the Exchequer, who personally instructed him as to the reorganisation of terrorist and other acts calculated to create a diversion'. Later Soviet press reports that year described Reilly as 'a confidential agent of Churchill'.[37]

Had Reilly indeed seen Churchill before leaving for Russia? No evidence exists apart from the Soviet allegations, but it is not implausible given Churchill's long-standing relationship with him. It could equally have been a complete fabrication. In any event, Reilly's widow soon found out that Churchill was denying everything. Desperate for news about her husband, she first approached the Foreign Office, using as intermediaries both the SIS officer (and Reilly's best man at their wedding) George Hill and his friend Archie Sinclair. The latter, she was convinced, 'had been closely connected with my husband's department'. Receiving little useful information, she turned directly to Churchill, raising the allegation that he had been responsible for Reilly's mission. All she received was an eleven-line reply signed by Eddie Marsh, Churchill's private secretary. Addressed 'Dear Madam', it claimed that her husband had not gone to Russia at the request of any British official, but on his own private affairs. 'Mr Churchill much regrets', the letter concluded, 'that he is unable to help you in regard to this matter, because according to the latest reports which have been made public Mr Reilly met his death in Moscow after his arrest there.'[38]

It was a classic letter of deniability, as though Churchill hardly knew who Reilly was, never mind had been a willing and active party to his anti-Bolshevik plans. Clearly he wished to keep this episode in his shadow life hidden. Reilly's name is also conspicuous by its absence in his essay on Savinkov in *Great Contemporaries* and is omitted, too, from his final volume of First World War memoirs. Like Clare Sheridan's adventures in Moscow, here was an episode of secret war that he wished to keep quiet.

There may have been another reason for Churchill's wish to distance himself from Reilly: the master spy's possible role in the notorious Zinoviev Letter affair.

Three days before the voters went to the polls in the October 1924 election the *Daily Mail* published what it claimed was the text of a letter to the Communist Party of Great Britain from Grigori

Zinoviev, head of the Comintern. Written in the full-blooded language of revolutionary Marxism, it urged the party to foment agitation in the armed forces and mobilise its supporters in the Labour Party, whose leader, Ramsay MacDonald, headed the government. Amidst anti-Red hysteria and unfounded charges that MacDonald had intended to suppress the letter, Labour lost the election and the Conservatives returned to power.

For many years it was accepted that the letter was a forgery. Recent evidence suggests this is unlikely.[39] But, authentic or not, the letter did reflect Comintern policy and there was undoubtedly a conspiracy to sabotage Labour's electoral chances. All the evidence points to a political time bomb detonated from within the intelligence services. The letter originated from someone in their midst and Conservative Party Central Office was also implicated.

How did the letter reach the intelligence services in the first place? Circumstantial evidence points to Sidney Reilly's involvement – a copy of the letter in Reilly's handwriting is to be found in the Foreign Office files. Certainly, by the time Churchill gave Reilly's widow the brush-off, this notion had entered popular folklore. Churchill relished the results of the affair and knew most of those involved. Thomas Marlowe, the *Daily Mail* editor at the heart of the scandal, certainly considered Churchill a sufficiently useful contact in the anti-Bolshevik front to send him a package of Zinoviev material two years later suggesting that he should make whatever use of it he liked.[40]

If Reilly was involved – or Churchill suspected he was – it was a murky affair best kept at arm's length. The Tory Party line was to quash any idea that government officials, including intelligence officers, had in any way been involved; the most they would admit was that the letter had been acquired, somehow, from the Communist Party of Great Britain by 'patriotic businessmen'. But rumours about Reilly abounded, and the Labour Party, stung by the feeling it had been tricked into losing the election, was eager to make political hay out of what they saw as a Tory/intelligence plot. In the circumstances, Churchill had every reason to conceal his links with Reilly.

One important Churchill link with Reilly was Edward Spears. As head of the British Military Mission in Paris he was a valuable asset. With his vast network of contacts, Spears became Churchill's personal private eye, passing on political gossip, providing his own spin on the changing currents of allied opinion, and alerting him to adverse political currents. He also provided an alternative source of intelligence from the Foreign Office. Churchill lobbied for months to have him appointed to the British Embassy in Paris and made a thorough nuisance of himself to the ambassador, Lord Derby, on one occasion even telling him that Spears gave him 'more valuable information about the political state of the country' than anyone else. The insult provoked Lord Derby to denounce Spears as Churchill's 'political spy'.[41]

Most importantly, Spears was a valuable ally on Russian affairs, a keen promoter of Savinkov, and a friend and business associate of Reilly. He described Savinkov as 'an extraordinarily interesting and disquieting character', and told Churchill, who had asked him to report discreetly on the Russians in Paris, that Savinkov was one of the most able and impressive of the anti-Bolshevik Russians. Churchill responded immediately. 'Get in touch with the Savinkoff group,' he ordered, 'and let me know more about them.'[42]

Spears was soon entangled with Savinkov's schemes. With full access to British intelligence reports from Europe and the Far East, as well as French intelligence material passed to him by old friends in the Deuxième Bureau, he was a valuable source for Savinkov as he tracked Red Army movements and the failing fortunes of the Whites.

Churchill's blatant lobbying for his friend only served to deepen mistrust of both men in the Foreign Office and London. After Spears resigned from the military mission his friendship with Savinkov opened up even more byzantine paths of scheming and intrigue. Spears was ambitious, keen to enter the world of business and eager to make a fortune. Savinkov dazzled him with his plans to open up Poland, the Ukraine and Romania to Western capital, which would also offer useful intelligence possibilities. But it was Reilly who became his real mentor in business affairs, especially after Spears, through his contacts in Prague, won an official government contract to handle Czech radium exports. Spears told Churchill that he found Reilly 'rather seedy but really quite nice' and over the next few months the two men swanned around Europe promoting their schemes. Spears opened useful political doors for Reilly, while also reporting on Reilly's schemes to the sceptical Cumming in London.

As well as keeping Churchill up to date about Reilly and Savinkov, Spears also played a crucial backstage role in the mysterious Savinkov–Krasin meeting in London of December 1921. The principal partner in his various East European financial ventures was a Finnish banker named Brunstrom, who knew Krasin from pre-revolutionary days and considered him an important figure to be cultivated. One of Brunstrom's reports on Krasin, bursting with wish-fulfilment about an imminent Bolshevik collapse, so impressed Churchill that, typically, he sent it on to Lloyd George, Bonar Law and Balfour. Then in November 1921, Brunstrom dined privately with Krasin in London and persuaded him to meet Savinkov. The next day, over lunch at the Savoy, Brunstrom told Spears news of the meeting and the two men went into conference with Reilly – ironically to chide him on 'the dangers of dealing with shady people and mixing politics with business'. Spears indeed may well have been the mysterious host for the Krasin–Savinkov meeting in London. It would explain both why Savinkov refused to divulge his name, and a (still withheld) report on the meeting ended up in the SIS archive.[43]

Spears remained mesmerised by the mirage of opportunities that would follow the Bolshevik collapse promised by Reilly. But eventually he wearied of this wild mixing of business and intelligence affairs, and in 1922 finally broke off contact. Later that year he successfully stood for Parliament as a National Liberal candidate and began to build himself a more orthodox business career. Defeated in the 1924 General Election he later returned to the Commons as a Conservative, where he kept his seat until the great Labour landslide of 1945. Throughout the 'wilderness years' of the 1930s he remained a staunch Churchill ally and kept his links with the secret world; in the late 1930s, in liaison with French military intelligence, he quietly trained linguists for the War Office. In later life, after his Second World War adventures and misadventures with General Charles de Gaulle, he passed over his curious adventures in the secret war against the Bolsheviks as though they had never happened. 'I did not know any of these people at all well', he claimed when asked about Reilly and Savinkov shortly before he died in 1974. Like Churchill, he was suffering from an acute attack of political and intelligence amnesia.[44]

7

Guerrillas

Revelations of Clare's encounters with Trotsky and Lenin were not the only headlines to confront Churchill when he opened his copy of *The Times* on Monday 22 November 1920. More serious was the news from Ireland. The day before, fourteen men had been hauled from their beds in Dublin and shot in cold blood. Some were still in their pyjamas or reading their newspapers. Others were shot in front of their wives. Most were British intelligence officers. This 'Bloody Sunday' slaughter brought to a climax months of mounting violence that had pitched the British Army and police against the Irish Republican Army (IRA) led by Michael Collins. The bitter conflict was to intensify Churchill's fascination for guerrilla warfare and demonstrate once more the value of good intelligence.

The descent into violence had already affected him. Two weeks before, Sir Basil Thomson had warned him that he was on an IRA hitlist uncovered in Glasgow and that he should stay away from Scotland. He also assigned Churchill a personal bodyguard, Detective Sergeant Thompson, a former Special Branch constable who, with only one short break, stayed by his side until the end of the Second World War. Thompson had been in the front line of the secret war for many years, taking part in the 1914 round-up of German spies and escorting foreign suspects detained at British ports for personal interrogation by Thomson. Once, like Churchill in the Sudan, his enthusiasm for spy-catching ran away with him and he detained a suspicious-looking Belgian woman until informed by MI5 that she was one of their agents. Thompson found Churchill an exacting mission made tolerable only by a growing affection for his ward. On their first meeting he found Churchill pacing up and down in his study. 'Had Walt Disney created Mickey Mouse in those days', he remembered, 'I might have been tempted to believe that Mr

Churchill's gait was the inspiration for his famous cartoons. His walk, there and back, up and down, hands behind him and head bowed in thought, always reminded me of Disney's famous creation.' He soon became used to Churchill's wild and unpredictable alternations between indifference and alarm about security. In Cairo, met by stone-throwing crowds, he was horrified when Churchill slipped out of their hotel for a stroll without telling him. On another occasion, while driving through Hyde Park during the Sinn Fein scare, Thompson noticed a man loitering by the side of the road. Churchill, gripping his Colt automatic, calmly suggested that they stop. 'If they want trouble they can have it', he growled. Thompson thought otherwise. 'Drive like the Devil!' he instructed the driver and the car emerged from the park unscathed.[1]

The IRA threat was real. A year later Sir Henry Wilson, by now an Ulster MP and security adviser to the Northern Ireland government, was assassinated on the steps of his London home. Before the news even reached the Cabinet Thompson was personally conducting a room-to-room search of Churchill's house and armed troops had been placed on duty outside. Churchill was immediately assigned the armoured Rolls-Royce used by General French in Ireland – a two-and-a-half-ton monster with half-inch steel plates and bullet-proof glass – and began to carry a loaded service revolver. A second car invariably followed with three detectives. Churchill regularly received death threats, some of them naming the actual time and manner of his death. 'I don't like it', he admitted. On the night of Wilson's murder he slept in his attic behind a door protected with a metal shield, his revolver by his side.

By IRA standards Churchill had earned his place on their hitlist. The election of 1919 saw most Irish seats captured by Sinn Fein, a party pledged to full independence, whose MPs boycotted Westminster and set up their own parliament, the Dáil, in Dublin. In London the government continued as though little had changed. Its Home Rule Bill, introduced into the Commons that February, allowed for separate northern and southern Irish parliaments and a Council of Ireland drawn from twenty members of each. To Sinn Fein and the IRA, bitterly opposed to partition and any compromise on independence, Churchill offered a mailed fist. His rhetoric matched in its imagery his bloodthirsty visions of Bolshevik terror. 'Surrender to a miserable gang of cowardly assassins, like the human leopards of West Africa', he warned his Dundee constituents, 'would be followed by a passionate repentance and a fearful atonement.' Only two weeks before Bloody Sunday he promised that Great Britain would not allow itself to be destroyed by a 'malevolent and subversive force, the rascals and rapscallions of the world who were now on the move against us'. As Minister of War he was responsible for the welfare of troops in Ireland. Terror, he believed, should be met by counter-terror and Michael Collins's brilliant successes in penetrating the British administration in Ireland should be matched by a ruthless stepping-up of the intelligence war.[2]

Churchill's most notorious contribution to events in Ireland was his enthusiastic support for the Black and Tans, a force of British ex-servicemen under the command of a wartime comrade-in-arms, Major-General Henry Hugh Tudor. But this was not his only response to the demands in May 1920 by Sir Nevil Macready, Commander of forces in Ireland, for more help. The military chief also asked for 600 wireless and telegraphic experts and 'a first rate intelligence officer ... to collate information and form by degrees a secret service or detective branch for the police forces in Ireland, which is now non-existent'. Maurice Hankey, the Cabinet Secretary, who was sceptical of most of Macready's proposals, saw value in this one. 'His Secret Service might be better', he noted grudgingly and a secret scheme was forwarded to the Directorate of Military Intelligence. Churchill strongly supported the initiative and believed that the 'rapier of good intelligence' and selective counter-terror would be even more effective than the bludgeon of brute force. This brought him into conflict with Sir Henry Wilson, his erstwhile ally on the anti-Bolshevik front, who wanted full-scale war against Sinn Fein. Over the long hot summer of 1920, as Wilson fantasised about a coup against Lloyd George, the two men argued over the use of reprisals. Wilson talked wildly of taking hostages and then shooting them by roster when violence broke out. Churchill disagreed. 'It is no use ... saying I should shoot without mercy. The question immediately arises "whom would you shoot". And shortly after that "where are they?" In other words, what was needed was an intensified intelligence war.[3]

Churchill's faith mirrored that of Michael Collins. The IRA was well informed about the British. 'There were spies everywhere', an intelligence inquest later drawn up by GHQ Ireland concluded, 'and a very large percentage of the population were ready to act as extra eyes and ears for Sinn Fein and for the IRA even if they were not prepared to fight for them.'[4] This was why Collins took care, often by taking brutal steps, to 'blind' the British by targeting their intelligence apparatus. 'Without her spies England is helpless', he pronounced, making his principal task the identification and elimination of British intelligence officers and their agents. Sinn Fein moles and informers inside Dublin Castle, the heart and symbol of British rule in Ireland, accomplished the first task; hand-picked squads of gunmen under Collins's orders the second. Their method was merciless in its simplicity. One hit man recalled, 'two or three of us would go out with an [IRA] Intelligence Officer walking in front of us . . . His job was to identify the man we were to shoot . . . He would take off his hat and greet the marked man . . . As soon as he did this we would shoot.'[5] Bloody Sunday was the death squad's most dramatic success.

To identify and locate the IRA, and to turn such methods against them, Churchill enthusiastically supported efforts to improve British intelligence. It badly needed an overhaul. Hampered by divisions between the police and the military, confused by differences between London and Dublin Castle, and fighting a frightened and often hostile population, it was clearly losing the secret war. Between 1914 and 1918 it had largely concentrated on the wrong target, mesmerised by fears of German intrigue and neglecting the inexorable rise in Irish nationalist sentiment after the 1916 Easter Uprising and the repression that followed. Peacetime cutbacks made things worse, and while intelligence officers operated at brigade and battalion level, as late as the autumn of 1920 the Army's central intelligence staff consisted merely of two staff officers, a records officer and four outstation officers. The Irish campaign was the British Army's least successful counter-intelligence campaign in the first forty years of the century.[6]

For the police the situation was little better. The Dublin Metropolitan Police was infiltrated by Sinn Fein. Its special intelligence section – 'G' Division – suffered special terror tactics by Collins's men and morale plummeted. Potentially more valuable was the Royal Irish Constabulary (RIC), but it lacked effective leadership, and was increasingly hampered by the alienation of the population and Republican threats to the families of its men. As IRA attacks on personnel and local police stations multiplied the RIC simply abandoned rural areas, giving free reign to Collins's flying squads of guerrillas. In desperation, Lord French asked Churchill to lend him Vernon Kell and MI5. 'We are suffering terribly', he confessed, 'for want of a proper Criminal Investigation Department.' But whatever help Kell gave – a secret still interred in MI5 archives – it made no immediate or obvious improvement. Macready complained bitterly that his efforts were like working in a thick fog.[7]

Churchill also supported Macready's request for a new Co-ordinator of Intelligence in Ireland. This was Brigadier-General Ormonde de l'Epée Winter. Despite a spirited military career in India and a legendary reputation for horse-racing, he had no obvious qualifications for the task – although he was rumoured to have been tried for murder for 'a little escapade' while doing secret-service work. Tudor thought he possessed great nerve and determination, which probably explains why Churchill placed such high hopes on him. He also looked the part with a monocle and black greased hair. He smoked endless cigarettes, could speak several languages, was a genius at cards and relished being known by the *nom de guerre* 'O'. Sir Mark Sturgis, a leading Dublin Castle official, thought him a 'most amazing original' and said he resembled 'a wicked little white snake'.[8]

Unfortunately, Winter failed to live up to expectations. He enjoyed an excessive taste for cloak-and-dagger operations. Sturgis once encountered him wearing a false moustache and wig, trench-coat, and bowler hat – 'looking *the* most complete swine I ever saw' – fresh from having secretly removed £4,000 from one of Collins's hidden IRA accounts at the Munster and Leinster Bank. 'Hardly his job', noted Sturgis, 'and bad make up at that!' Another problem was that while talking grandly of photographing the entire population of Ireland, he focused almost exclusively on Dublin. More importantly, he never effectively co-ordinated police and army intelligence. Macready eventually became exasperated with him. 'Winter has not got the right method', he complained. 'He is, I fancy, a "born sleuth", but I doubt his organising power.' None the less, Winter did succeed in narrowing the intelligence gap between the British and the IRA. He won MI5's co-operation for the training of agents who infiltrated Dublin disguised as shop assistants or garage hands and provided useful local intelligence. He set up a reward and resettlement scheme for informers and created a special office to organise raids on IRA hideouts. Over the next few months it organised several thousand raids, captured thousands of documents, and put considerable pressure on Collins, whose own hideout in Dublin was eventually discovered. Bloody Sunday might have been a victory for the IRA, but it paid Winter the compliment of calling him 'the Holy Terror', put £1,000 on his head, and even tried to kill him as he paid his first visit to the Viceregal Lodge. The Army, too, gradually adapted. At the

Curragh, its main base, it established a training school in guerrilla warfare and began to take the offensive against the IRA flying squads that had dominated the countryside.[9]

Over the summer and autumn of 1920 Churchill was a hawk on Irish policy. He enjoyed the support of Lloyd George and continued to back the Black and Tans. He even defended them over the sack of Balbriggan, a village some twenty miles north of Dublin, an event that quickly entered Irish legend as a classic British outrage.

Churchill was unmoved. On the contrary, he personally greeted Tudor at the War Office when he arrived in London with one of his staff officers, Captain Hamilton Shore. Tudor gave him details of the reprisal murders being carried out against Sinn Fein activists by the Black and Tans and the newly arrived intelligence officers, and told him that the local police in Balbriggan had identified Sinn Fein activists and shot them. Churchill, according to Wilson who was also present, 'saw very little harm in this'. As did Lloyd George. When the meeting was over Churchill took Tudor to Downing Street where the Prime Minister confirmed that he would back him through thick and thin. The next day Churchill met Captain Shore, again with Wilson present. Shore talked calmly of murdering Sinn Feiners, revealed that he possessed a list of members, and declared that at the slightest show of resistance they would be shot. Once again, when the meeting was over, Churchill proudly took his visitor to brief the Prime Minister.[10]

It was hardly surprising that within a month Tudor was warning Churchill that Sinn Fein assassins had crossed the Irish Sea to carry on their work in Britain or that Churchill was a main IRA target. By this time events were spiralling rapidly downwards towards Bloody Sunday. This in turn sparked its own inevitable retribution. Within forty-eight hours five hundred members of Sinn Fein were arrested, and seventeen British troops were murdered at Macroom. In December, in one of the worst Black and Tan outrages, over three hundred buildings were burned down in the city of Cork. Two weeks later the Cabinet agreed to impose martial law in four Irish counties.

As so often, the darkest hour came before the dawn. In Britain overwhelming opinion condemned the Black and Tans. In Ireland the general population was wearying of constant violence. Both Lloyd George and Churchill were prepared, at the right time, to negotiate. The Prime Minister had skilfully kept back channels open to Sinn Fein, while Churchill's private views on Ireland had never been as intransigent as his rhetoric. The nationalist struggle, if not its methods, had gradually won his grudging respect. He also had a family connection that sensitised him to Irish issues: John Randolph Leslie, the eldest son of his Aunt Leonie and her husband Colonel Sir John Leslie, a member of the Irish Protestant ascendancy with large estates in County Monaghan. His cousin 'defected' to Irish nationalism while a student at Cambridge, converted to Roman Catholicism, renounced his lands and took the Irish name Shane. Churchill – himself something of a renegade to his class and background – was sympathetic and introduced him to John Redmond, leader of the Irish nationalist parliamentary party. In the elections of 1910 Shane ran unsuccessfully for the nationalists. He then went to America, linked up with Churchill's old mentor Bourke Cochran in a campaign to swing Irish-American opinion behind the British war effort, married Cochran's sister-in-law, and moved to Washington to continue his work with Sir Cecil Spring-Rice, the British ambassador. It was after a discussion with Leslie that Churchill warned Clare against simplistically equating the Irish with the Bolsheviks. 'Don't confuse the Irish revolutionaries with Russian revolutionaries', he warned. 'The Irish all believe in God, uphold the family, and love their country.'[11]

In December the Archbishop of Perth, with Lloyd George's support, met Michael Collins and Arthur Griffith, the founder of Sinn Fein and acting President of the Dàil, in Dublin. But at a special conference later that month the Cabinet drew back, convinced that they had the IRA on the run. Churchill was almost a lone voice proposing a truce. Most likely he was influenced by optimistic reports from those on the ground. General Strickland, Commander of the four southern Irish counties recently placed under martial law, promised that there would be 'definite and decisive results within four months'. Macready announced that the general military situation was improving and Tudor confirmed the same for the police; morale, he announced, had made a marked advance. Sturgis in Dublin noted that the arrest of IRA officers had greatly increased the flow of intelligence and strengthened the hand of the pro-peace faction in Sinn Fein. For the rest of the Cabinet this was a reason to continue the fight. For Churchill it was a compelling opportunity to negotiate from a position of strength.[12]

By the time a truce was eventually signed in June 1921 Churchill had been shifted to the Colonial Office. This gave him an even more direct role to play. Lloyd George chose him as one of a handful of ministers to negotiate with Sinn Fein, with special responsibility for air and naval issues. Once the treaty was signed, he took the lead in steering it through the Commons. The Sinn Fein delegation arrived for talks at Downing Street in October 1921. Its leader was Arthur Griffith, but the eyes of most British ministers were focused on the man by his side who had been the most wanted man in the British Empire: Michael Collins, Director of Intelligence of the IRA. Over the next twelve months Churchill was to establish a relationship with Collins almost as bizarre as that with Boris Savinkov.

Collins has been described as the founder of modern guerrilla warfare and the first urban terrorist. To many Irish nationalists he remains a hero and freedom fighter, a saint of national iconography, 'the man they couldn't catch' and 'Ireland's lost leader'. When he arrived in London he was still only 29 years old, a handsome, athletic, man with a fair complexion and ready smile. At just under six feet tall, he was known in Dublin as 'the Big Fellow'. He was also restless, impulsive and energetic, a man of action and rapidly changing moods who could both charm and bully. To his enemies he appeared a ruthless if smiling terrorist. Brought up in the republican tradition in County Cork, one of his boyhood heroes was the Boer guerrilla leader Christian de Wet, and he himself later became known as 'the Irish de Wet'. Aged 16 he crossed the Irish Sea to London, where he took a job in the Post Office Savings Bank. In 1909, as Churchill was learning about the workings of the Secret Service Bureau, Collins secretly joined the Irish Republican Brotherhood. Shortly before passing the civil-service exams he enrolled in the Irish Volunteers, drilling clandestinely at night in a gymnasium near King's Cross railway station.[13]

Early in 1916 he returned to Ireland to take part in the Easter Uprising. Amongst those who seized the city's general post office, epicentre of the abortive uprising, he was lucky to escape execution and spent several months in a British prison. Back in Dublin he threw himself into rebuilding the shattered republicans. By 1919, when the Dàil declared itself an independent parliament, he was Minister of Finance in the government, and Adjutant-General and Director of Intelligence of the IRA.

Collins's genius was to adapt his heavily outnumbered and locally organised forces to fighting a hit-and-run war and to devise, by hard-fought experience, the tactics of guerrilla war. His principal target was political and psychological: the destruction of British mastery over the Irish population. The route to this lay through paralysing Britain's intelligence system, much of which was due to Collins's own personal skill and daring. Dressed respectably in suit and tie, he moved openly around Dublin, often on a bicycle, fooling the police with his smile and ready charm, and encouraging his men. On one memorable occasion, with the help of a 'mole', he was smuggled into Dublin Police headquarters and spent the night reading its top-secret files. Even allowing for republican hyperbole, Collins and his guerrillas swam in a friendly sea. His assassination squad, known because of their number as the 'Twelve Apostles', was disciplined, dedicated and effective. Collins had no qualms about its work. Speaking of the murdered British officers after Bloody Sunday, he declared: 'By their destruction the very air is made sweeter. For myself, my conscience is clear. There is no crime in detecting and destroying in wartime the spy and the informer. They have destroyed without trial. I have paid them back in their own coin.'

Lloyd George described Collins as 'a wild animal, a mustang'. Churchill's first encounter with him was tense. Across the Cabinet table he saw the leader of what he had long denounced as 'the Murder Gang'. Collins, on his side, saw the progenitor and apologist of the Black and Tans that had wreaked havoc across his country. Churchill described it as 'a confrontation not without its shock'.[14]

At first Collins was deeply suspicious of Churchill's overtures, disliking his 'ex-officer jingo' and wondering whether he would prove 'a crafty enemy in friendship'. Yet the IRA possessed its own intelligence files, and his secret briefing on Churchill hinted at something more positive. Describing him as the dark horse of English politics, too adventurous and independent for ordinary party ties and labels, it astutely went on to say that despite his reputed militarism and dictatorial air he had 'more real idea of freedom and care for it than other politicians, and a better understanding of its political framework . . .' Churchill 'can look ahead to necessary and desirable developments'. This was remarkably prescient, a tribute to careful IRA research. Churchill in his turn would look back on Collins as an heroic figure: 'Successor to a sinister inheritance, reared among fierce conditions and moving through ferocious times, he supplied those qualities of action and personality without which the foundation of Irish nationhood would not have been re-established.'[15]

The two men soon established a rapport. Churchill was helped by memories of his earlier dealings with the Boers, bitter opponents whom he had come to respect. This, he admitted later, was his greatest source of comfort during the long and difficult weeks of negotiations over the issues of Dominion status, the boundary with Northern Ireland and British access to Irish ports. On this last point Churchill felt particularly strongly, linking it closely with his adamant refusal to accept an Irish Republic. Such a state, by definition outside the Empire, its citizens owing no allegiance to the Crown, would be a direct threat to Britain. 'If war broke out between the British Empire and the Irish Republic', he declared, 'every Irishman in the British Empire would become an alien enemy, and would be in exactly the same position as the unfortunate Germans who were in this country during the great war.' Besides eliminating this threat, Dominion status would also cement control of Irish defences, and hence those of Britain itself. No British minister, and certainly not Churchill, could forget that U-boats had turned the Irish Sea into a graveyard, and that Ireland straddled Britain's vital maritime links with North America and the wider world.

Yet Dominion status and continued allegiance to the Crown were hard for the Irish to accept. The impasse was broken only by long off-the-record meetings between the leaders of both sides. Churchill played a key role with Collins. One evening he invited Lloyd George and Lord Birkenhead to join him, Griffiths and Collins for dinner at his home in Sussex Gardens. After the five men had eaten, Lloyd George went upstairs for a long tête-à-tête with Griffiths. Collins remained with Churchill and Birkenhead. Later Churchill dramatically recalled the scene. Collins, he said, was 'in his most difficult mood, full or reproaches and defiance'.

> 'You hunted me night and day', he [Collins] exclaimed. 'You put a price on my head.'
>
> 'Wait a minute', I said. 'You are not the only one.' And I took from my wall the framed copy of the reward offered for my recapture by the Boers. 'At any rate it was a good price – £5,000 – . Look at me – £25 dead or alive. How would you like that?' He read the paper, and as he took it he broke into a hearty laugh. All his irritation vanished. We had a really serviceable conversation.[16]

It was a major step in reducing Collins's suspicion of Churchill. Combined with Lloyd George's negotiating skills it meant that early in December the Irish treaty was finally signed.

This was not the end of Churchill's dealings with Collins. On the contrary, it marked a new and more intensive phase. Collins became

Prime Minister of the provisional Irish Free State government and Churchill, as Colonial Secretary, was responsible for relations with Dublin. These involved the difficult and explosive issues of the transfer of power, the withdrawal of troops, and relations between the Free State and Northern Ireland. Collins also faced a crisis of his own: the Irish split over the treaty, with a minority faction led by Éamon De Valera refusing to accept partition.

Over the next six months Collins fought to establish his government's authority against republican opponents. Churchill now found himself supporting the former terrorist with rifles and armoured cars, as well as urging him to establish peaceful cross-border relations with Northern Ireland led by Sir James Craig. Using his considerable persuasive powers and exploiting his rapport with Collins, on at least two occasions Churchill brought the two opponents together in his office in London for crucial face-to-face private talks. But Collins was playing a clever double game. Outwardly he agreed with Churchill. Secretly he did his best to support a bloody IRA offensive in the north and establish an intelligence system in Ulster. Churchill was not uninformed about this. The British Army had not yet withdrawn from the south and British intelligence agents continued to operate. From the north Craig sent him captured IRA documents that conclusively proved Collins's hand in the terrorist campaign to destabilise the new state. Exasperated by Collins's duplicity over border issues, Churchill cursed him roundly as a 'corner boy [ruffian] in excelsis'. But political needs demanded continued support for Collins against the republicans to ensure the survival of the Irish Free State and the treaty. Craig's information about Collins, however accurate, was politically unwelcome. Intelligence that Churchill had once so eagerly deployed against the IRA leader he now deliberately ignored to save him.[17]

Collins's struggle with the republicans came to a climax in April 1922 when they seized the Law Courts in Dublin and Collins narrowly escaped an attack on his life. Churchill sent more guns and urged him to crush the republicans and establish the stamp of 'strong, bold, romantic personalities' on his government. The next month Collins met Churchill alone in his room at the Colonial Office. 'I shall not last long', he confessed, 'my life is forfeit, but I shall do my best.' Moved, Churchill replied with the words of the old Boer leader Johannes Brand, '*Alles zal legt kom*' – all will turn out well.[18]

It was Collins who was proved right. Provided by Churchill with eighteen pounder guns and high-explosive shells, he and his government soon recaptured the Law Courts. But De Valera went underground and civil war began. 'I hope you are taking good care of yourself and your colleagues', Churchill told Collins, 'the times are very dangerous.' Indeed they were. Sir Henry Wilson was assassinated in June, and six weeks after his own grim prediction Collins was killed in a republican ambush in County Cork. Only a few days before he had told a friend, 'Tell Winston we could never have done anything without him.' Thousands filed past his body as it lay in state and a three-mile cortege followed his coffin from the cathedral to Glasnevin cemetery. Seven years later Churchill paid homage to Collins:

> He was an Irish patriot, true and fearless. His narrow upbringing and his whole life had filled him with hatred for England. His hands had touched directly the springs of terrible deeds. We hunted him for his life, and he had slipped half a dozen times through steel claws. But now he had no hatred of England.[19]

Churchill's dealings with Collins deepened his respect for guerrilla warfare, strengthened his belief in the value of intelligence, and reinforced lessons learned from Cuba and the Boer War about the power of popular resistance to undermine the strength of an occupying force. It also nourished deep apprehensions about future security. The IRA, with its republican agenda and bitter opposition to partition, stood high on Special Branch and MI5 priority lists over the coming decades. Churchill can only have been alarmed by secret reports in 1920 that up to 30,000 armed Sinn Fein sympathisers in Scotland were ready to launch a guerrilla war in support of Collins's campaign in Ireland. The role that the Irish might play as an internal subversive force continued to worry him. After De Valera came to power in 1932 and began to undermine the treaty, Churchill reverted to seeing the Irish as potentially dangerous aliens. De Valera's declaration of neutrality in September 1939 only deepened his perception of threat. Here, Churchill believed, was a breeding ground for spies.

Several army officers destined later to cross Churchill's path earned their spurs fighting the IRA. Amongst them was the future Field Marshal Sir Bernard Montgomery, who set up a special intelligence unit in Cork; General Percival, who surrendered Singapore to the Japanese having earned a reputation in Ireland for 'interrogation in depth'; and Brigadier Kenneth Strong, chief intelligence officer to General Dwight D. Eisenhower at D-Day, who learned his trade running agents in rural Ireland. The most innovative, however, was the Major in the Royal Artillery who handed over his guns to Collins for the attack on the Law Courts. A few weeks later he had the melancholy task of providing the gun carriage and six black horses that carried Collins to his last resting place.

Colin Gubbins had arrived in Ireland with the British Army two years earlier. With him he brought recent experience of fighting with the anti-Bolshevik forces in Murmansk, where he had served as ADC to the commander of British forces, General Ironside. In Ireland he found himself 'being shot at from behind hedges by men in trilbys and mackintoshes and not allowed to shoot back!' A short course in guerrilla warfare briefed him on basic techniques, and the rest he learned from experience. Sixteen years later it proved invaluable. In 1938, working in GS(R), a research unit of the War Office created to examine subversive war, he helped draft a handbook on guerrilla warfare and a companion booklet entitled *Partisan Leaders' Handbook*, full of practical details such as how to organise an ambush and what to do with enemy informers (kill them). By the time war broke out in September 1939, GS(R) had concluded that 'if guerrilla warfare is co-ordinated and also related to main operations, it should, in favourable circumstances, cause such a diversion of enemy strength as eventually to present decisive opportunities to the main forces'. In 1940, when Churchill created the Special Operations Executive, Gubbins was the natural choice to be its director of training. Three years later he was in charge of the entire operation. By this time SOE was supporting guerrilla and underground forces around the world. Knowingly or not, they were often following techniques that had been pioneered in Ireland by Michael Collins.[20]

In joining GS(R) Gubbins had been assigned to work with a chain-smoking major in the engineers, J. C. F. (Joe) Holland. He, too, had served in Ireland. Like Gubbins he was impressed by what guerrillas could achieve and determined that in a future war they would be used to support rather than attack Britain. But it was not only Ireland that had influenced him. As an airman in the First World War he had won the Distinguished Flying Cross at Salonika and worked in the desert with a man whose name had already become legendary for his work with Arab guerrillas in the war against the Turks –

T. E. Lawrence. Amongst those most captivated by Lawrence of Arabia was Churchill.

Churchill first met Lawrence during the Paris Peace Conference. This encounter was not a success, but a few weeks later Lawrence appeared in Arab robes looking, in Churchill's glowing words, like 'one of Nature's greatest princes'. He became one of his most fervent supporters and placed him, along with Savinkov, in his pantheon of Great Contemporaries. When the Great War had faded in memory, he wrote, Lawrence's work with the Arab guerrillas – especially as told in *Revolt in the Desert* and *Seven Pillars of Wisdom* – would 'gleam with immortal fire'. In 1936, at the unveiling of a memorial to Lawrence at the Oxford School for Boys, he noted how 'the world looks with some awe upon a man who appears unconcernedly indifferent to home, money, comfort, rank, or even power and fame', and went on to speak of Lawrence as 'strangely enfranchised, untamed, untrammelled by convention, moving independently of the ordinary currents of human action'. [21]

Lawrence truly won his place in Churchill's heart because of his desert campaign. The story, as Churchill saw it, was simple and stirring. The Turkish armies attacking Egypt depended on a single-track railway across the desert. If this were cut, then they would perish and Turkey would be ruined. From this would follow the collapse of Turkey's ally in Europe: Germany. 'Here was the Achilles' Heel', noted Churchill, 'against which Lawrence directed his audacious and romantic assaults.'[22] Once again Churchill had been drawn unerringly to the romance and power of the secret war. Lawrence began his military career as an intelligence officer working at GHQ Cairo under the command of Colonel Gilbert Clayton, its brilliant Director of Intelligence with a long experience of the Middle East. He also advised the Governor-General of the Sudan, Sir Reginald Wingate, who as Director of Intelligence in the 1890s had received Churchill's fulsome praises for his assistance at the time of the River War.

Lawrence soon graduated to guerrilla warfare. In 1916 the British decided to launch a major offensive in Palestine and Syria, and to prepare the way for regular troops mobilised Bedouin raids for a guerrilla campaign. Lawrence led several daring raids against the Damascus–Medina railway line that crossed the Arabian desert. Here the Turks deployed almost 30,000 troops, a threat to the eastern flank of British forces advancing north from Cairo. A war of attrition, Lawrence believed, could hurt Turkey where it was most vulnerable. His campaign never achieved the promised results and the Turks succeeded in quickly repairing the railway whenever it was blown up. But the guerrillas were kept happy, thousands of Turkish troops were pinned down and Lawrence became famous. The campaign also gave a misleading boost to the claims of guerrilla-war enthusiasts. The Turks had lacked aircraft and vehicles to patrol the desert, and diverted few of their troops to fight the guerrillas. Had they done so, guerrilla successes might have been far less impressive.[23]

However, the facts could not displace the legend. By the summer of 1919 Lawrence of Arabia was a household name. Lowell Thomas, an American propagandist, had seen the potential in Lawrence as a modern Arab liberator for boosting Anglo-American relations in the post-war world. Sponsored by the English-Speaking Union, of which Churchill was an ardent supporter, a Thomas-inspired film replete with lecture and symphony orchestra began a six-month run at the Royal Albert Hall and was seen by over a million people. Lawrence as chivalrous hero also met the need of the times. Here was a warrior as free agent, in welcome contrast to the hapless soldier in the mechanised carnage of the Western Front. Here, too, was a man who used his brains to save rather than sacrifice the lives of his men. A civilian by temperament, a poet and writer contemptuous of the orthodox, Lawrence embodied Victorian ideals of heroism while appealing to a younger generation in revolt against the mass slaughter of the Somme and Paschendale.

He was a natural magnet, therefore, for Churchill, and when the latter found himself responsible in 1921 for settling Middle East affairs he quickly brought Lawrence on to his staff as a special adviser. Sir Henry Wilson, already in dispute with Churchill over Ireland, was predictably disgusted and described Lawrence as 'a dangerous little fellow', but, he added resignedly, 'if you have poor Winston at the top he naturally surrounds himself with men of like kidney'. This only served to spur Churchill on. Lawrence travelled with him to the Cairo Conference of 1922 and impressed him deeply. The admiration was reciprocated. In Churchill Lawrence saw a larger-than-life man of courage who also defied the conventions. He became a frequent visitor to Chartwell and remained close to Churchill until he was killed on his motorbike in 1935.[24]

Throughout the 1920s and 1930s Lawrence's ideas on guerrilla warfare received close attention from military theorists. The most influential was Basil Liddell Hart, military correspondent of the *Daily Telegraph* and later *The Times*. Liddell Hart's name became indelibly attached to his notion of 'the strategy of the indirect approach', an attempt to circumvent the frontal clash of massed armies that had created the slaughter of the Western Front. Significantly, Liddell Hart was one of the first biographers of Lawrence, whom he described in 1934 as 'a strategist of genius who had the vision to anticipate the guerrilla trend of civilised warfare that arises from the growing dependence of nations on industrial resources'. As military adviser to the *Encyclopaedia Britannica*, Liddell Hart drew directly from Lawrence's own notes in writing its entry on guerrilla warfare for its 1927 edition, and in one of his earliest works on strategy stressed how vital it was for modern armies 'to discover and exploit the Achilles' Heel of the enemy nation' – the very phrase used later by Churchill in his essay on Lawrence.[25]

Liddell Hart turned into a savage critic of Churchill during the Second World War, denouncing him for rejecting a compromise peace and waging total war. Lawrence, he believed, would have been a moderating influence. Ironically, he singled out for particular criticism Churchill's call for popular resistance by the occupied peoples of Europe, a war cry directly inspired by Lawrentian visions. The costs in reprisals, Liddell Hart argued, far outweighed the benefits and bred a generation addicted to violence. As for guerrillas, they were effective only to the extent that they were combined with operations of the regular forces. Debates about the costs and benefits of supporting the resistance and the likely value of guerrilla war were to form a bone of contention with Churchill's generals in his conduct of the Second World War.

8

Private Networks

Churchill remained bitterly anti-Bolshevik throughout the 1920s. As Chancellor of the Exchequer from November 1924 he found a ready ally in the Home Secretary, Sir William Joynson-Hicks, a diehard Tory known as 'Jix'. Through MI5 and Special Branch he amassed overwhelming evidence implicating leaders of the British Communist Party with attempts by Zinoviev and the Comintern to subvert the armed forces. Along with the rest of the Cabinet Churchill agreed that they should be prosecuted for sedition and in November 1925, after only twenty minutes' deliberation, an Old Bailey jury found them guilty. The next year, during the General Strike, Jix brought Churchill on to the Supply and Transport Committee, which worked closely with MI5. Again Jix circulated secret intelligence reports to underpin the charge of a Communist conspiracy. Churchill was also fired up by Birkenhead, now Secretary of State for India, who was regularly briefed on Communism in the Raj by intelligence reports from Delhi. Churchill remained convinced that Moscow posed the greatest threat to Britain and vowed to resist it by every means possible.[1]

How far he was prepared to go emerged graphically in February 1927 when the Cabinet told the Foreign Secretary Austen Chamberlain that unless the Soviet Union changed course a breach in relations with Moscow was inevitable. Two weeks later a GC & CS intercept revealed the existence of a 'new' Zinoviev letter referring to espionage in Britain while other intelligence suggested that an employee of Arcos – the All-Russian Co-operative Society, a company operating in London – had obtained a copy of the British Army's signals training manual. But a raid by Special Branch on the Arcos office and the Soviet trade delegation failed to produce incriminating documents and presented the Cabinet with a serious dilemma. It had already decided to break diplomatic relations with Moscow. What evidence could it now produce to justify such a radical step? There remained only one solution: publication of the secret intercepts.

After what has been described as 'an orgy of governmental indiscretion about secret intelligence' when Baldwin quoted extensively in the House of Commons from a plethora of intercepted messages between Moscow and the Soviet legation in London, the Soviet chargé d'affaires was sent packing. The expulsion was a triumph for Jix, Birkenhead and Churchill, but it represented a disaster for British intelligence. The Soviet Union adapted the virtually unbreakable one-time pad system and immediately blinded GC & CS in its quest to read their intercepts. Alastair Denniston, its head, bitterly condemned the Cabinet's decision.[2]

Churchill had been deprived of access to Soviet intercepts since 1924. Three years before, when leaving the War Office for the Colonial Office, he had successfully ensured they continued to reach him. 'As you know', he told Lord Curzon, 'I have for years made a very close study of all these documents, and I regard them as essential to forming an instructed view. It is only necessary that you should direct that the Colonial Office should be placed on the list of those who are served by the "C" organisation.' Curzon obliged. As did Walter Long, the First Lord of the Admiralty, when he requested continuing access to intercepted naval telegrams.[3]

When Churchill returned to office in the Baldwin government he encountered strong resistance from Austen Chamberlain. Security procedures in Whitehall had been tightened, and intercepts and Special Branch reports were no longer circulated automatically to the Cabinet. Churchill was outraged. 'I have studied this information over a longer period and more attentively than probably any other minister has done', he protested furiously to Baldwin. 'In the years I have been in office since [Room 40] began in the autumn of 1914 I have read every one of these flimsies and I attach more importance to them as a means of forming a true judgement of public policy in these spheres than to any other source of knowledge at the disposal of the State.' Even if the Foreign Office kept its intercepts to itself, he argued, he should see exactly what the War Office and Admiralty saw. Chamberlain refused to budge, citing security. But this was only a pretext. He knew that intercepts would allow Churchill to attack foreign policy with which he disagreed.

Chamberlain was right about Churchill's likely use of intercepts, as Churchill's old naval ally Lord Beatty, now First Lord of the Admiralty, found out. The Navy was pressing for a substantial budget increase to launch a new programme of shipbuilding and to develop Hong Kong and Singapore as major bases in the Far East. Not only did the estimates strike at the heart of Churchill's campaign to rein in government expenditure; he also believed they reflected a false appreciation of the strategic threat. 'A war with Japan! . . . I do not believe there is the slightest chance of it in our lifetime', he protested. Early in 1925 he sat down with Beatty to thrash out the issue but they failed to agree, and Churchill was mortified because in promoting his case Beatty quoted from intercepts between the Japanese Embassy in London and Tokyo that Churchill had not seen. He protested to Baldwin that while he received financial intercepts from GC & CS, none to do with War Office or Admiralty matters reached his desk. Yet these were directly related to his work, for if Beatty had quoted them correctly they revealed important details about Japanese shipbuilding and rearmament. 'How can I conduct the controversies on which the management of our finances depends', he asked, 'unless I have the same knowledge of secret state affairs freely accessible to the officials of the Admiralty? The words "monstrous" & "intolerable" leap readily to my mind. I prefer to bury them in the cooler word "absurd".' Baldwin capitulated and soon Churchill was seeing intercepts relating to Japan. They made no difference at all to his view on naval rearmament or the Japanese strategic threat, but they did enable him to fight with Beatty on more equal terms and score a minor victory over the Navy estimates. Once again secret intelligence had revealed itself as a useful weapon in a domestic political battle.[4]

Electoral defeat in 1929 threw the Conservatives out of office and Churchill was not to return to a British Cabinet for the next decade. The 1930s were his famous 'wilderness years'. As he dramatically told the story, he was out of office and out of favour, a lone voice crying prophetically of the Nazi menace and denouncing appeasement that so shamefully climaxed in the 1938 Munich Agreement. Only when Britain declared war on Germany did he return to high office as First Lord of the Admiralty – the very position he had held on the outbreak of the First World War. Eight months later, as Hitler's attack on the Low Countries and France finally discredited the men of Munich, he assumed the burden of supreme office to become his nation's wartime leader. 'I felt as if I were walking with Destiny', he wrote, 'and that all my past life had been but a preparation for this hour and this trial.'[5]

Cast as an essentially heroic and moral tale, Churchill's account has frequently been challenged – appeasement seen as a rational response to Britain's limited resources, his political exile a largely self-inflicted wound, and his resistance to the dictators less firm and consistent than he claimed. There is much truth in this. Yet he grasped more quickly and clearly than did Ramsay MacDonald, Stanley Baldwin or Neville Chamberlain the moral nihilism, ruthless dynamics, and grasping territorial ambitions of Hitler and Nazism. What has also become clear is that if the decade was a wilderness, it was a brilliantly illuminated one in which he enjoyed impressive sources of information. Out of office he may have been, but he was frequently better informed about both British and Nazi rearmament than many Cabinet ministers.

His principal source was Major Desmond Morton, who after the war had worked for the Secret Intelligence Service on Soviet and German affairs. In 1931, as the Depression took hold and disarmament headed the international agenda, he became Director of the Industrial Intelligence Centre, formed by the Committee of Imperial Defence to report on industrial development and arms manufacturing in Europe. Funded by the secret-service vote and briefly sharing premises with SIS, it enjoyed extraordinary access to a wide range of economic and arms-related data. Morton continued to rely heavily on his SIS contacts and also counted leading figures in MI5 amongst his sources.

He also renewed contact with Churchill, their growing friendship facilitated by close proximity as neighbours. He lived less than a mile away from Chartwell and would frequently stroll over in the evenings, a bundle of intelligence reports – sometimes even raw diplomatic intercepts – under his arm. Shrewd and imaginative, he became a trusted intimate who knew Churchill's mind almost as well as its owner. The Oxford historian Bill Deakin, later to parachute into wartime Yugoslavia, worked as a research assistant to Churchill in the 1930s and frequently observed them together. Morton, he remembered, had Churchill's absolute trust, and his loyalty was 'without limits or reserve'.[6]

Yet Churchill enjoyed many other secret sources and Chartwell became a virtual private intelligence centre as well as alternative government-in-waiting. The contrast with Chequers, the official country retreat of the Prime Minister, could not have been greater. When Harold Macmillan arrived for lunch with Churchill the day Italian forces attacked Albania he witnessed a scene of frantic action: 'Maps were brought out; secretaries were marshalled; telephones began to ring.' By contrast at Chequers, the solitary telephone was kept hidden in the butler's pantry where it would least disturb the occupants.

Amongst Churchill's army of informants were civil servants, politicians and serving officers in the armed forces, all of whom disagreed with appeasement and supported his rearmament campaign.[7] One, whose existence Churchill kept secret to his dying day, was Squadron Leader Torr Anderson, a First World War hero and winner of the Distinguished Flying Cross who by the mid-1930s was Director of Training at the Air Ministry. One evening he turned up at Churchill's London flat carrying a seventeen-page memorandum and fourteen pages of statistical information revealing serious shortfalls in RAF preparations for war. He, too, became a frequent visitor to Chartwell, often staying overnight after discussions that went on until the early hours.

He also acted as a conduit for reports from Group Captain Lachlan MacLean, Senior Staff Officer at Bomber Group HQ. Taken by Anderson to meet Churchill in London, he provided information on pilot training, aircraft maintenance and long-distance navigation. He also he gave Churchill details of setbacks in bomber training and after the Munich Agreement was invited down to Chartwell. Churchill greeted him by growling that the British Empire was finished and that Britain should have gone to war. Surprised, MacLean remarked that the detailed information he had provided indicated how unprepared and unable Britain was to fight. Churchill simply ignored the point and complained that Munich had deprived Britain of numerous first-class Czech divisions as well as the Skoda armaments factories. His reaction provided a revealing glimpse of how he tailored his intelligence to suit the policy he was advocating.

Ralph Follet Wigram, head of the Foreign Office's Central Department responsible for German affairs, was another source. In March 1935, after Hitler introduced conscription, he gave Churchill secret Foreign Office material on German rearmament. One typical Wigram package consisted of dispatches written by Sir Eric Phipps,

Britain's ambassador in Berlin, warning of Hitler's rearmament ambitions. Another was a paper based on Air Ministry intelligence figures revealing the rapid pace of *Luftwaffe* rearmament. A year later one of Wigram's former assistants and the then Foreign Office expert on Austria gave Churchill details of the German Army's most recent mechanised equipment. Shortly after, Group Captain Frank Don, former British air attaché to Berlin, turned up with the most recent data on German air strength and production capacity.

An even more senior Foreign Office source was Sir Robert Vansittart, its Permanent Under-Secretary from 1930 to 1937 and convinced Germanophobe mesmerised by German air power. Not only did he share Churchill's view of the German threat, but he was also a kindred spirit highly tuned to the value of intelligence as both knowledge and power who used his access to secret sources with calculation and skill. One source was SIS Director Sir Hugh ('Quex') Sinclair, with whom he dined regularly. When financial stringency hindered SIS expansion, Vansittart encouraged Sinclair to build up a parallel private network known as the 'Z' organisation, and himself developed a web of informants on German rearmament focused on Group Captain Malcolm Christie, a First World War pilot and later air attaché to Berlin who had entered the business world. Owning a house on the Dutch-German border, Christie enjoyed excellent contacts that kept him informed about *Luftwaffe* affairs. Other Vansittart informants included Carl Goerdeler, the anti-Nazi mayor of Leipzig, and Theodore Kordt, counsellor at the German embassy in London. Dick White, who enjoyed the rare distinction of later heading both MI5 and SIS, worked at the time for MI5 on German affairs and was another of Vansittart's sources. In turn Vansittart kept in touch with Churchill, feeding as well as shaping his campaign against appeasement. When he was replaced at the end of 1937 by Chamberlain, shunted aside to become 'Chief Diplomatic Advisor' to the government, Churchill was devastated.

Yet, for all his inside sources and access to secret intelligence of the most sensitive kind, Churchill remained curiously blind to some important aspects of the darkening international scene. His use of intelligence as a weapon against appeasement paid off politically and made him the inevitable Prime Minister in 1940. But the intelligence he sought and exploited was as much a tool of his political crusade as one of objective and dispassionate analysis.

'Wars come very suddenly', he declared in the House of Commons in February 1934, reminding a packed chamber of July 1914 when minor trouble in the Balkans seemed a harmless ripple on the surface of European tranquillity. A visit from an ambassador followed by an ultimatum had brought catastrophe within days. Then, at least, island Britain had been protected by its Navy. Now, however, air power had revolutionised events and 'the crash of bombs exploding in London and cataracts of masonry and fire and smoke' would apprise the nation of any inadequacies in its air defences. Britain was vulnerable as never before in its history. London, he warned a few weeks later, was the greatest target in the world, a 'tremendous, fat, valuable cow tied up to attract beasts of prey'.[8]

Thus Churchill fired the opening salvo in his tireless campaign to ensure that Britain's Air Force rapidly acquired parity with Germany. As early as 1930 he had begun to warn of Hitler's aggressive instincts, and after the Nazi leader became German Chancellor in January 1933 he stepped up his warnings. Ten months later the German dictator withdrew Germany from the Disarmament Conference and the League of Nations. Churchill reacted by telling his cousin Clare, now completely forgiven for her Moscow adventures, that against Hitler he would even enter into an alliance with the Bolsheviks – a remarkable conversion for the one-time fan of Savinkov and Reilly. In over thirty major speeches during the next three years he hammered home his demand for rapid rearmament helped by inside information on the RAF and *Luftwaffe* from his army of informants.

His apocalyptic vision of aerial warfare was not unique. Nightmares of a 'knock-out blow' causing tens of thousands of casualties and a total breakdown of public order in London within the first few days of war were widely shared. George Orwell caught the fear well in *Coming Up for Air*, written shortly after Munich. 'War is coming', muses his protagonist, 'and there'll be plenty of broken crockery and little houses ripped open like packing cases and the guts of the chartered accountant's clerk plastered over the piano he's been buying on the never-never.' Such images also haunted government ministers. Baldwin declared ominously that 'the bomber will always get through' and the rearmament debate focused almost obsessively on the air. Chamberlain, flying back from Munich and approaching London over the River Thames, imagined a German bomber on the same course and decided that the country could not risk war. Even as he landed, thousands of people were scurrying to dig air-raid shelters and fill sandbags.[9]

Churchill and the government were not wildly out of step, but he was convinced it was moving neither fast nor far enough. In 1934 the Cabinet agreed to create a Home Defence Force of fifty-two air squadrons in the belief that Germany would have some 500 first-line aircraft by 1935 and double that figure by 1939. Churchill challenged the figures, and within months it became clear that German plans were for some 1,300 front-line aircraft by October 1936. Churchill's figures were again even higher, and in November 1935 he claimed that German front-line strength was already 1,500 compared to Britain's 960. Three months later, on the basis of French intelligence reports, he put the German figure at over 2,300. For all its efforts Britain was failing to achieve parity.

Churchill's figures were more accurate than those of the Air Ministry. Yet what exactly 'parity' meant was never clear. Numbers of aircraft, frequently a matter of dispute, meant little in themselves; most conspicuously they failed to address the vital question of German capabilities and doctrine. Was the *Luftwaffe* planning such a knock-out blow so dreaded by Churchill? We know now that it was not. 'There is no possibility of launching successful air operations against the British Isles', noted the *Luftwaffe* staff during the Munich crisis. *Luftwaffe* expansion was directed at creating air support for a major land campaign by the German Army, not a massive independent bomber force. Churchill, for all his access to inside sources, shared the government's mistaken premise about German intentions in the air.[10]

Nor was he a complete outsider. In 1935 he accepted an invitation from Baldwin to join a specialised sub-committee of the Committee of Imperial Defence on Air Defence, where he pressed for accelerated research on all anti-aircraft devices. Even when he was allowed in on the first successful radar experiments he complained that being on the committee was like watching 'a slow-motion picture'. The secret information, he claimed, had told him little that he did not know or could have guessed.

His claim to familiarity with scientific and technical secrets rested on yet another member of his Chartwell entourage, the controversial Frederick Lindemann – Professor of Experimental Philosophy (Physics) at Oxford University, known universally as 'the Prof' and later to become Lord Cherwell. Lindemann's loyalty to Churchill was absolute. After the death of Birkenhead he became Churchill's closest friend and virtual family member at Chartwell, welcomed even by the normally cautious Clementine. Born of parents who fled Alsace when it was taken over by the Germans in 1871, he had worked on quantum physics in Berlin and flown as a test pilot in Britain during the First World War. Later he turned the Clarendon Laboratory in Oxford into a world-class centre for low-temperature physics. On the face of it he and Churchill were polar opposites. To his forbidding high-domed head and iron-grey moustache he added the austere virtues of abstinence from alcohol, tobacco and meat. But he was bold and imaginative, and had little patience with academic caution and pedantry. He was also a Germanophobe. Churchill found in him a soulmate able to illuminate the mysteries of science, share his humour and indulge his fascination for intellectual adventure. Lindemann became Churchill's personal scientific think-tank and, once he became Prime Minister, his official scientific adviser. He could also be arrogant, intolerant, conceited, snobbish and spiteful. R. V. Jones, the brilliant young wartime scientist who became Churchill's scientific adviser in the 1950s, noted that Lindemann disliked opposition and was 'prone to ignore facts'. This was another bond with Churchill, whose historical method was not dissimilar. The Oxford historian Maurice Ashley, employed in the 1930s to help Churchill in the writing of his massive biography of the first Duke of Marlborough, never forgot his startling directive: 'Give me the facts, Ashley, and I will twist them the way I want to suit my argument.'[11]

If Churchill's inside intelligence was mistaken about *Luftwaffe* doctrines and plans, it also failed to identify crucial weaknesses in British naval rearmament. He too readily accepted the assurances by Lord Chatfield, the First Sea Lord, that the Royal Navy was highly efficient, and after witnessing a display of the new top-secret sonar-detection system, was mistakenly convinced that this 'Sacred Treasure' had fully mastered the submarine threat. Likewise he dismissed or ignored the threat of air power to Britain's ageing fleet of battleships. So long as they steamed together, he believed, aircraft could do them little harm: the Royal Navy was virtually immune from destruction.

Regarding land forces, like most other observers he placed inordinate faith in the French Army to hold a German attack and provide a shield while Britain mobilised its strength. After attending French Army manoeuvres in 1936 he came away convinced that therein lay France's strength, and his old friend Spears provided him with information culled from French intelligence that reinforced his views. Interestingly, this infuriated Desmond Morton, whose own intelligence suggested that the equipment of the French Army and Air Force was 'utterly rotten', and whose prediction that France would be overrun within a month made Churchill 'froth with rage'. The French could never be surprised, Churchill declared after inspecting the Maginot Line. Only two years before Hitler's blitzkrieg he doubted that tanks would ever again relive their glory days of 1918. Armies in the next war, he predicted, would advance as moles and use their spades more than their bayonets. As a result, he failed to press for an expanded British Expeditionary Force.

Churchill's blindest spot, however, was the Far East. He was convinced that Japan would never attack unless Britain had been decisively beaten, and even then Singapore could easily hold its own. 'Do not . . . let us worry about this bugbear', he pronounced. His inability to take Japanese rearmament seriously and his underestimation of Japanese capabilities was widely shared by official intelligence. As for the Soviet Union, his conversion to its value as an anti-German ally blinded him to its military weaknesses and made him overly susceptible to the skilful blandishments of its ambassador in London, the urbane ex-Menshevik Ivan Maisky. He was briefly shaken by Stalin's purge of the Soviet High Command in 1937 but soon resumed his belief in the strength of the Red Army.[12]

In March 1936 Hitler's troops marched into the Rhineland in clear defiance of the Treaty of Versailles. Shortly afterwards nationalist rebels plunged Spain into a three-year civil war and in 1938 Hitler triumphantly annexed Austria, the land of his birth. Then, in September 1938, after frantic diplomatic manoeuvres that culminated in the Munich conference, Britain and France caved into his demand for the Czech Sudetenland. Churchill loudly deplored events and demanded a grand coalition to resist Hitler. Munich he denounced as 'a total and unmitigated disaster'.

Six months later Hitler marched his troops into Prague and swallowed the remnants of the Czech state. Only five days before, Sir Samuel Hoare, the Home Secretary (and one-time intelligence officer in Russia), had spoken glowingly of a five-year peace plan that would produce a Golden Age. 'One could hardly believe', noted Churchill, 'that with all their secret information [the government] could be so far adrift.' On Good Friday 1939 Italian forces attacked Albania and Churchill again seized the opportunity to condemn the government's blindness. There had been a clear failure of intelligence, he told the Commons. How was it that only days before Hitler had moved his forces into Prague, British ministers had talked of a new age of tranquillity dawning in Europe? And how was it that as Mussolini's forces massed for their Albanian invasion, holiday routines were being maintained in Whitehall? With a quarter-century's experience of high politics he believed that the British secret service was the finest in the world. The fault could not lie there. Was there not, he wondered, 'some hand which intervenes and filters down or withholds intelligence from Ministers?' There was a tremendous risk if they permitted good and timely intelligence to be sifted and coloured, and accepted only that which accorded with their desire for peace.

It was not the first time that Churchill had blamed the government for its failure to accept unwelcome intelligence. Speaking in the defence debate in 1936 he had taken it to task for having ignored the early-warning signs coming from Germany: 'I cannot believe that the very admirable Intelligence Service of this country, which in the Great War was considered to be the best in the world, did not give its warnings . . .' He used identical words two years later to attack the government's failure to absorb intelligence about the *Luftwaffe*.[13]

Yet Churchill misunderstood the contribution of intelligence to British policy in the 1930s. It was not that the intelligence community was producing accurate assessments that were filtered away from ministers by some hidden hand. On the contrary, the intelligence services themselves were often badly informed or even appeasement-minded. Despite a 1935 Cabinet agreement to increase intelligence spending, SIS remained short of money, starved of talent and ill-equipped to provide technical expertise on rearmament estimates. The code-breakers at GC & CS had been deprived of Soviet intercepts since 1927 as the result of the Cabinet decision – Churchill included – to publish them; throughout the 1930s high-grade German military and diplomatic ciphers remained beyond it. The service intelligence directorates alternated between underestimating and exaggerating German strength. No effective central body existed to co-ordinate their assessments. In the crucial years between Hitler's march into the Rhineland and the Munich Agreement, 'The label *blindness* seems appropriate to the way in which the intelligence authorities failed to provide a balanced reading of German strengths and weaknesses . . .' There followed, in the last year of peace, a heady sense of military self-confidence in which analysts considered that

Britain, having survived the initial German assault, would go on to victory using the weapon of economic warfare.[14]

These varying assessments tended to move in tandem with changes in government policy: first underpinning appeasement, then encouraging the bolder commitments to Poland and others it gave in 1939. This was true for SIS as well as the service intelligence directorates. In addition, SIS fell victim more than once to deliberate German misinformation. In May 1938 it swallowed reports planted by Hitler's German opponents that he planned an imminent offensive against Czechoslovakia. Chamberlain issued a diplomatic warning and was convinced it had worked when no attack took place. Vansittart, a principal Churchill source, was also taken in. The scare fulfilled the hopes of the German opposition who wanted a stronger British stand against Hitler and also enhanced SIS prestige in Chamberlain's mind. Soon afterwards Sir Hugh Sinclair, SIS Director, produced an intelligence assessment entitled 'What Should We Do?' that explicitly urged an accommodation with Hitler. A few months later reports of Nazi-Soviet talks were dismissed as mere rumour designed to influence British discussions with Moscow. In short, the major impact of intelligence reporting was to confirm the government in what it had already decided to do. Churchill was not only wrong in his assessments of German strategy. He also held too high an opinion of the independence and originality of British intelligence itself.[15]

It has been widely claimed that Morton had the written permission of three successive Prime Ministers – MacDonald, Baldwin and Chamberlain – to provide Churchill with secret intelligence. This would be an extraordinary story if true, for it handed him the weapons he deployed so effectively against them. Churchill laid its foundation when he claimed in his war memoirs that Morton had received MacDonald's permission to keep him informed. Later writers extended this into written permission from Baldwin and Chamberlain, but Churchill's official biographer has turned up no such evidence.[16] This does not necessarily disprove the claim, but suggests a more credible explanation. When Churchill was writing his memoirs in the 1940s, Morton was still a senior civil servant. While keen to associate himself with Churchill's crusade in the 'wilderness', he also desired to protect himself from allegations of the unauthorised communication of secret information that could have threatened his career, his pension and his reputation. To claim prime ministerial written permission to pass on secret information was to protect himself against the Official Secrets Act.

Churchill, not to mention other informants, blatantly defied the Official Secrets Act throughout the 1930s. Convinced of the rightness of his cause, he tried to reassure his informants about the propriety of their acts. When Torr Anderson passed on one highly secret document, he confessed that he had never been so frightened in his life. Churchill's response that loyalty to the state overrode loyalty to the RAF would have cut no ice in law. Anderson was still demonstrably nervous when, some thirty years later, he met Churchill's official biographer to discuss his secret dealings, and at least one of Churchill's sources remained angry and bitter over his indiscretions. Wigram, who shared similar fears, asked Churchill to burn the documents he provided once he had read them. Dangerously for Wigram, although fortunately for historians, Churchill failed to do so. High officials in Whitehall knew what was going on. But Hankey, the long-serving Cabinet Secretary, was shocked to learn the true extent of the amount of sensitive material ending up with Churchill, especially from service sources. He denounced it as wrong, 'infectious' and subversive of service discipline. He also pointed out that if he had gone to Churchill before the First World War with comparable inside intelligence he would certainly have been severely chastised.

Hankey's reaction was a straw in the wind. After Chamberlain became Prime Minister in 1937 official tolerance for Churchill's freelance secret service markedly diminished. Churchill himself was too powerful to touch, but warning shots were fired across allied bows. Shortly before Munich the Official Secrets Act was waved threateningly at a close family member and ally in his anti-government crusade, the Conservative backbencher Duncan Sandys who had married Diana, Churchill's eldest daughter. He asked a pointed question in Parliament about London's air defences that suggested inside information and quickly found himself threatened by the Attorney-General with prosecution under the Act unless he revealed his source – almost certainly his father-in-law. He refused and successfully demanded a parliamentary select committee to decide whether the Act applied to Members of Parliament in the discharge of their official duties.

Churchill leaped to Sandys' defence. The Act had never been intended, he asserted, to shield ministers who had neglected national defence. Writing anonymously in the London *Evening Standard* he declared that the Act had been intended only for 'spies, crooks, traitors and traffickers in official information' and should never be used unless there was a strong prima-facie case on these specific grounds. Again he was wrong in law. The Act did not confine prosecution to cases of 'trafficking' in information (i.e., selling documents) but covered *any* unauthorised communication of an official document, however important or trivial. Churchill himself had approved the clause as a minister of the Crown. Nor did his pre-First World War initiation of MI5 general warrants prevent him, early in 1939, from lauding British freedoms in an interview with Kingsley Martin in the *New Statesman*. Were it not for Magna Carta, habeas corpus and the Petition of Right, he asserted, the individual citizen would be at the mercy of officials and liable to be spied upon in his own home. Ironically, if any such spying were taking place, Churchill bore a heavy part of the responsibility.[17]

The Sandys case went no further after the select committee found in favour of MPs' immunity. But Chamberlain's tolerance for Churchill became even more strained after the launch of a press campaign to bring him into the government in the early summer of 1939. In desperation he reverted to 'dirty tricks', and turned to the sinister Sir Joseph Ball who twenty years before had helped Churchill in his campaign against George Lansbury.

Since leaving MI5 Ball had run intelligence for Conservative Central Office and become one of Chamberlain's closest friends – the two were on a fly-fishing holiday together when Hitler occupied Prague. Ball served his master well by tapping the phones of his opponents, acting as an intermediary in shadowy contacts with Mussolini and manipulating the press. In 1936 he secretly gained control of the weekly magazine *Truth* and turned it into a weapon of rumour and innuendo against Chamberlain's critics. Throughout the summer of 1939 it ridiculed the notion of Churchill in office, and even after he returned to the Admiralty it warned sarcastically against 'pseudo-Napoleonic' antics. Again, however, it was a Churchill ally who presented an easier target. This time the victim was Archie Sinclair.[18]

Although now leading the Liberals, Sinclair was an impassioned loyalist in Churchill's crusade against Chamberlain. In December 1939 he delivered a powerful speech in the Commons that, like Sandys' question, revealed inside information. MI5 began to tap Sinclair's telephone, probably at the instigation of Ball, explaining that as his residence in Scotland lay in a prohibited military area it was a purely routine affair. Sinclair found out, protested to Chamberlain, and a full-scale public row was prevented only by Churchill's personal intervention and the crisis caused by Hitler's blitzkrieg in the West that drove Chamberlain from office. Ironically, at the height of this potentially lethal phone-tapping scandal, George Lansbury hit the headlines by dying – deriving wry satisfaction, perhaps, from the fact that Churchill and Sinclair were now recipients of the treatment they had once so willingly administered to him.

9

In the Dark

By the end of 1939 Churchill was back in office. Since 3 September, when he returned to the Admiralty, he had renewed official contact with the intelligence world. He was overwhelmed by a sense of *déjà vu*, his old desk in place, many of the same charts still in use. The first person he asked to see was his Director of Naval Intelligence, Rear-Admiral John Godfrey, and within weeks he had visited the fleet in Scottish waters, as he had in September 1914, confidently noting the battleships at anchor in Loch Ewe. Then, motoring back to Inverness across the Highlands, he retraced the route past the site of his adventure with the phantom German agent and the searchlight on the roof. His first instruction to Godfrey was to provide figures on German U-boats, an order that also recalled his intense examination of Captain Hope's secret intercepts some twenty-five years before. And to assist in the vital task of intelligence there now existed an updated version of Room 40, the Operational Intelligence Centre (OIC). Learning from past mistakes, it brought together intelligence and operations.

There was one crucial difference between 1939 and the First World War. This time it was the Germans, not the British, who were breaking enemy codes. In 1935 the B-Dienst, Germany's naval codebreaking service, broke the manual British naval cipher giving Admiral Raeder, Commander-in-Chief of Hitler's Navy, an almost open window on Royal Navy operations. By contrast British codebreakers failed to crack the German Navy's high-grade Enigma cipher until the spring of 1941. They were unable to provide advance warning of the U-boat mission that sank the *Royal Oak* inside the supposedly secure Orkney base of Scapa Flow, or headline-making sorties by German battle cruisers. In short, the OIC began its life mostly unable to help the Navy in its current operations. Churchill, geared for offensive action, found this deeply frustrating. When it appeared – falsely – that a U-boat had been sunk in the Clyde, he urgently demanded that divers be sent down to investigate and search for code books. Memories of the *Magdeburg* code-book coup remained fresh in his mind.[1]

Frustration over intelligence blindness did not help his relations with Godfrey, connected by marriage to the Chamberlain family. A tall man with an unflinching gaze and misleadingly soft voice, Godfrey had patrolled the Yangtse in a gunboat, served as a staff officer at the Dardanelles, sabotaged munition dumps at Sebastopol, and commanded the battle cruiser *Repulse* in the Mediterranean during the Spanish Civil War. Appointed DNI in January 1939, one of his first visitors was the still-energetic 'Blinker' Hall. The veteran intelligence genius was generous with his advice, warning Godfrey particularly of the political pitfalls in intelligence work, and when Godfrey found his official wartime quarters in the Admiralty uncongenial he moved into Hall's Curzon Street flat. Confronted with tricky problems, Godfrey would ask himself what Hall would have done. It was on Hall's advice, too, that he looked to the City of London to recruit his personal assistant and found him in Ian Fleming, the subsequent creator of James Bond. An admiring Fleming described Godfrey as having 'the mind and character of a Bohemian mathematician'. By the time war broke out Godfrey had built a formidable network of intelligence contacts in Whitehall.

This did not save him from running foul of Churchill on an intelligence-related episode omitted from Churchill's account of the Second World War. It began in November 1939 following heavy shipping losses. In a radio broadcast to the nation Churchill boasted that Britain was already causing a heavy toll to U-boats, a claim that he escalated in a major broadcast in January 1940 by declaring that they were being conquered: 'I do not doubt that we shall break their strength and their purpose.' Half the U-boats with which Germany began the war had been sunk and new construction had fallen far behind. But statistics from naval intelligence based on conclusions of the Submarine Assessment Committee contradicted this. Churchill promptly ordered that they should be shown only to himself, the First Sea Lord and the Deputy Chief of the Naval Staff, and that other sets of figures for broader circulation should be specially prepared and vetted by him before release.

Behind the rhetorical bravura lay a skilful massaging of the intelligence data. Churchill had counted probable sinkings or damage in his public total, and had presented a correction of early estimates of U-boat construction as a slow-down in the rate of building. For all that he insisted that Admiralty bulletins should establish an impeccable record of truthfulness, he regarded public statements about U-boat losses as matters of high policy. Early in 1940, as the phoney land war dragged on, shipping losses mounted and Finland succumbed to Russia in the Winter War, politics – not to mention Churchill's reputation as an effective minister – demanded morale-boosting news.

From the beginning Churchill's eye for publicity brought him into conflict with Godfrey. Almost as soon as war broke out he began to preside over weekly press briefings – 'more as an old journalist than as a First Lord', one observer noted – and he made a number of broadcasts to the nation emphasising the good news. Then, in December 1939, taking umbrage with figures released to the London *Evening Standard* that failed to highlight 'the mastery of the U-boat campaign', he abruptly transferred the head of the Admiralty's press section to sea. When Allied forces faced defeat in Norway in April 1940 a similar fate befell Captain Talbot, Director of the Anti-Submarine Warfare Division. An officer who rigorously abstained from wishful thinking, he had already encountered Churchill's temper. Returning to his office one day he had met Churchill who cheerfully gave him an upbeat version of the U-boat score. Talbot began to correct him. 'No sir, it's—' when he was furiously interrupted. 'Stop grinning at me, you bloody ape', Churchill shouted, and stormed off to his room. After documents captured from a German submarine sunk during the Norwegian campaign revealed conclusively that U-boat losses had been substantially lower than claimed by Churchill, Talbot incorporated them into an official report circulated within the Admiralty. Churchill exploded in rage. 'It might be a good thing if Captain Talbot went to sea as soon as possible', he acidly noted. The hapless Talbot, later to redeem himself as naval commander of the eastern assault force at D-Day, was relieved of his office with ten minutes' notice.

Godfrey observed all this with increasing anger. Finally, and recklessly, he disputed Churchill's claims in a detailed riposte. Intelligence estimates, he argued, were produced not to convey good or bad news but to state the truth as fully as possible. It was foolish to base policy on wishful thinking. Fortunately for Godfrey, the First Sea Lord

Admiral Dudley Pound made sure his comments did not reach Churchill, but two years later Godfrey was removed because other members of the Joint Intelligence Committee found him difficult. At the end of the war, alone of colleagues of his rank, he received no special decoration. Bitter over his treatment he welcomed Labour's victory and the end of the 'Churchill dictatorship'. His influence on naval strategy, Godfrey declared, had been malignant. Twenty years later, he also delivered a backhanded compliment to Churchill. 'He did not hesitate not to tell [the public] the truth or to paint a rosy picture that had no connection with reality', he wrote. 'He applied a most comfortable balm to their wounds and earned their gratitude and devotion.' 'Blinker' Hall's warnings to Godfrey about the political pitfalls of intelligence had not been without their point.[2]

On two important intelligence items, however, Churchill and Godfrey did see eye to eye: the problem of Ireland and the importance of locating the German fleet. Barely had Churchill taken possession of his Admiralty office than the passenger liner *Athenia* was torpedoed off the north-west coast of Ireland. Echoes of the *Lusitania* immediately resounded with predictable German claims of a Churchill conspiracy to gain American sympathy. Churchill certainly grasped the propaganda value but he was far more concerned about the implications of Irish neutrality proclaimed by President Éamon de Valera. Would U-boats seek shelter off the coast of Eire? Were German spies at work in the Emerald Isle? Was vital intelligence about the Royal Navy leaking out to Germany from Irish sympathisers hostile to Britain and the Crown?

Ghosts of the Phoenix Park murders hovered over Churchill's views of Ireland, not to mention distant but potent historical precedents of French and Spanish armies landing there on their way to attack England, and the more recent landing by Sir Roger Casement from a German U-boat before the Easter Uprising. Moreover, de Valera had opposed Michael Collins in the Irish Civil War and was a sworn enemy of Britain. In negotiating the 1922 Irish Treaty Churchill had insisted on continued British control of the naval bases of Queenstown, Berehaven and Lough Swilly, vital in his view for the protection of the western approaches to the British Isles. Deeply angered when the cost-cutting Chamberlain government had signed them away in the 1938 treaty with de Valera, he had denounced the decision as 'an improvident example of appeasement' and a feckless injury to national security. The launch of a major IRA bombing offensive against the mainland early in 1939 did not help his mood. The German legation in Dublin remained open, as did the border between Northern Ireland and the Republic, and travel across the Irish Sea. Here was a massive security gap that he filled with his brooding imagination. If the IRA could throw bombs in London, he remarked, they could surely provide fuel to enemy submarines. SIS should employ agents to keep a vigilant watch.

British intelligence, as so often, was divided in its view. SIS believed that Eire was only one amongst many possible sources of leakage; MI5, on the other hand, focused its suspicions on Ireland and particularly on Dr Eduard Hempel, the German minister in Dublin – although in reality Hempel was far too cautious to indulge in espionage that might jeopardise his more vital task of keeping alive a German presence in Ireland. Alarmed by MI5 reports, Churchill persuaded the War Cabinet to approve a special investigation into communications with Ireland, and simultaneously demanded the immediate removal of enemy aliens from all ports and bases. Although the War Cabinet rejected this, it did agree to declare five major ports 'Protected Areas' under the Aliens Order, a decision that in early 1940 permitted enemy aliens to be forcibly removed from them.

Churchill's concerns about Ireland were both shared and fuelled by Godfrey. Deeply worried about U-boat activity on the Irish west coast in October 1939, certainly with Churchill's knowledge he secretly authorised the HMS *Tamara* – an armed merchant ship disguised as a trawler and crewed by the Navy – to search the bays and inlets. Any lurking U-boats they would report to an accompanying British submarine. Such furtive missions continued for months.

Churchill and Godfrey were further reassured by an official Cabinet decision that November. All Irish cables would be routed through London, and machines would be loaned to the Irish government to help identify illicit (i.e., agent-controlled) W/T transmissions. De Valera was only too anxious to help. The IRA was its enemy too, already in clandestine touch with the *Abwehr* about arms and ammunition supplies. Moreover, dependent as Ireland was on Britain for its economic well-being, basic security and intelligence co-operation with Britain was merely prudent. Indeed, on the very day that Hitler's forces had attacked Poland in August, De Valera's Minister of Foreign Affairs had met secretly with a senior MI5 officer to discuss such mutual protection. A British naval attaché was dispatched to the Irish capital and Colonel Liam Archer, Dublin's *de facto* Director of Intelligence, was briefed by the Admiralty and MI5 on setting up an effective coastal-watching service provided with British radios to send in its reports. Postal censorship was upgraded using British equipment, and wide-scale telephone tapping began early in 1940. Just to be sure, Godfrey arranged for a reconnaissance overflight of the west coast, a mission that revealed no sign of German activity. To most intents and purposes Ireland had become an integral part of the United Kingdom security system. Churchill's U-boat anxieties finally died down.[3]

Elsewhere they remained high. Early in 1940 Bomber Command photo-interpreters thought they detected a concentration of U-boats at Emden. Naval intelligence was sceptical and decided to check the report with the Photographic Development Unit (PDU), virtually a one-man operation run by a buccaneering Australian named Sidney Cotton who had initiated the work with SIS before the war flying a Lockheed aircraft equipped with hidden cameras. Although the RAF had taken him under its wing on the outbreak of war, Cotton had continued to use the private Wembley-based Aircraft Operating Company (AOC) to process his photographs, a job they did better and with more advanced technology than the Air Force itself. Godfrey had been impressed by early photographs taken by Cotton of the German fleet at Wilhelmshaven and had sent one of his officers, Commander Charles Drake, to liaise with him.

One day in February 1940, Cotton telephoned Drake to say that he had completed an overflight of Emden using a specially stripped-down Spitfire, that the photographs were being rushed to the AOC for development and interpretation and should be ready the next morning. At this point the Air Ministry, jealous of its control over the PDU, forbade Cotton to communicate directly with Naval Intelligence. All next morning Drake waited impatiently for a call from Cotton while the Admiralty scrambled frantically for an alternative to gather intelligence about Emden. Finally, late that afternoon, after the maverick Cotton broke his orders and got in touch direct with Drake, an expert from the Operational Intelligence Centre rushed to Wembley to examine the results. To his relief, the suspected U-boats turned out to be river barges, their 'conning towers' nothing more sinister than washing hanging on the line. But the delay caused by Air Ministry obstruction infuriated Godfrey. He informed Pound, who mobilised Churchill. Within hours he had brought the Air Ministry to heel and forced it to take over AOC photo-intelligence work. Despite this, Kiel was photographed only in April, and then too late for any useful intelligence about the heavy concentration of shipping and aircraft revealed by the overflights. Two days later they formed part of the invasion force bound for Norway and Denmark. The surprise attack marked another failure for British intelligence.[4]

In November 1939 SIS Director Admiral Sinclair finally succumbed to cancer, precipitating a struggle for succession that shaped the future of British intelligence into the 1950s. The two main contenders were both insiders: Stewart Menzies, Sinclair's deputy, and Claude Dansey who ran the quasi-independent 'Z' organisation. Although Sinclair had designated Menzies as his chosen successor, Churchill challenged the choice when it came to the Cabinet.

Most sources have claimed Churchill had his own candidate in Godfrey, while Menzies' biographer has speculated on some personal antagonism at work. Neither supposition stands up to scrutiny. Churchill certainly floated a candidate, but more to protect his own and the Admiralty's interests than personally to thwart Menzies, a friend of Archie Sinclair and an intelligence officer whom he had met but hardly knew. As he told Sir Alexander Cadogan, Vansittart's successor as head of the Foreign Office, recent SIS intelligence had not served the Admiralty well and he had been shocked to learn that Godfrey had little original intelligence of his own except that passed on to him via the Foreign Office. Cryptography was a blank, and intelligence about U-boats and German capital ships was 'lamentably meagre'. Who took over from Sinclair was thus a matter of deep Admiralty concern. Nor could it be overlooked that by tradition 'C' was a Navy man. Churchill's own candidate, produced after talking with the First Sea Lord, was Captain Gerald Muirhead-Gould, then commanding the cruiser HMS *Devonshire*. After meeting him Churchill declared that he possessed many of the attributes of Cumming, the original 'C'.

Even on the most generous interpretation Muirhead-Gould possessed no obvious qualifications for the top job in British intelligence. But as British naval attaché in Berlin from 1933 to 1936 he had caught Churchill's eye and congratulated him on a barnstorming Commons speech on German rearmament. 'Magnificent', he had written, '. . . the Germans fear, and I hope, you will be 1st Lord – or

Minister of Defence!' The prospect of such an obvious Churchill protégé in command of SIS quickly united Cadogan, Halifax and Chamberlain behind Menzies – even though Cadogan, for one, had reservations about his suitability. At the end of November Halifax told Menzies officially of his appointment and he was to head SIS into Churchill's second premiership in 1951. Most crucially, he was to be 'C' to Churchill throughout the Second World War, controlling Ultra intelligence.[5]

In the midst of this struggle Churchill found himself enmeshed in even more contentious SIS business: the notorious Venlo affair. Five days after Sinclair's death Major Richard Stevens, SIS station chief in The Hague, and Captain Sigismund Payne Best, a monocled member of Dansey's 'Z' network, were kidnapped at Venlo on the Dutch-German border and carried into Germany. Fooled into thinking they were in touch with German conspirators plotting against Hitler, in reality they had been duped by a skilful 'sting' operation headed by Major Walter Schellenburg of Himmler's *Sicherheitsdienst*. Their abduction was a disaster for SIS. Not only had it been made a fool of, but under interrogation Stevens and Best revealed extensive details of SIS networks throughout Western Europe that enabled the Germans to roll them up when they occupied France and the Low Countries.

Responsibility for the débâcle reached deep into Downing Street. Lord Halifax and Chamberlain were convinced of serious internal divisions in Hitler's regime and had approved the operation in the hope of securing a bloodless victory over Germany. Halifax told the Cabinet that there existed significant military opposition to Hitler, and Chamberlain had personally ordered SIS to explore and exploit such divisions.

Churchill, like other Cabinet members, learned of the operation only when Chamberlain and Halifax finally informed them of what was going on. Scenting appeasement, his reaction was hostile. It was not enough to demand that Hitler simply be removed from a position where he could influence German policy. Even a ceremonial position should be completely ruled out. More importantly, the secret negotiations themselves presented a considerable danger. It would be too easy for the Germans to leak them to the French and undermine relations between London and Paris. By contrast, in standing completely firm there was a chance that the Germans themselves could disintegrate.

So strong was this reaction that neither Chamberlain nor Halifax dared give a reply to the so-called conspirators until after Churchill had agreed to one that explicitly demanded Hitler's complete removal from power as the *sine qua non* of any negotiations. Fortified with this response, Stevens and Best then made their fateful rendezvous at Venlo. Two weeks later, as discussions over Sinclair's succession dragged on, Schellenburg mockingly revealed to SIS by radio how they had been duped. For Churchill the episode reinforced his adamant opposition to any dealings with Germans, a reluctance that endured for the rest of the war. It also deepened his growing suspicion about the performance of British intelligence. At last he was beginning to revise his rosy picture of its performance.[6]

To the failure of GC & CS code-breakers and the blunders of SIS were added delinquencies of MI5. As in 1914, Churchill turned to Vernon Kell as soon as he took command at the Admiralty. The veteran spy-catcher was now a firmly entrenched fixture who had served five Prime Ministers. Chauffeured around London in an automobile flying a pennant that boldly proclaimed 'Safe but Sure', he was widely respected despite his growing infirmity. Churchill still regarded him as the cornerstone of national security. MI5 helped to identify potential traitors and spies in the Navy. Kell himself could also personally carry out missions of an especially delicate kind.

Thus, only four weeks after taking office, Churchill summoned Kell to his office in the Admiralty. Already worrying about a German attack on the Low Countries he was about to dispatch officers to investigate Dutch and Belgian sea defences. Now an opportunity had presented itself to strengthen the stance of neutral Belgium. Top-secret contact had been made with King Leopold via an intermediary named Walter Johannes Stein, an Austrian Jew. The King found himself in a highly sensitive position. He feared an imminent German invasion but his hands were tied by a government determined to maintain strict neutrality. So he was considering secretly approaching his army generals to see if they would quietly step up war preparations, and he had already talked to the Commander-in-Chief along these lines. He now wanted to know if the British would enter into military conversations about contingency plans against a German attack.

Churchill was keen and had met secretly with Stein the night before. Now he wanted Kell to dispatch an envoy to Brussels to test Stein's bona fides. If satisfactory, the way would be open for talks along the lines of Leopold's proposal, and British and Belgian officers could meet secretly aboard some British ship. Kell set about his task and Churchill informed the War Cabinet. Six days later the MI5 envoy returned to London, his mission accomplished; in the meantime events had overtaken him. The Belgian government had got wind of the plan and publicly vetoed the idea of staff conversations as totally incompatible with the country's neutrality. From then until May 1940 the Belgians comforted themselves with the fatal illusion that they could hold out against a German attack until France and Britain came to the rescue.[7]

Kell could hardly be blamed for this, but far less satisfactory for Churchill was his handling of the Revesz affair. In April 1933 Nazi stormtroopers, in an orgy of looting and destruction of Jewish-owned shops and offices, had wrecked the Berlin premises of a small news-distribution service. Its owner, a 29-year-old Hungarian Jew named Imre Revesz, fled the country with only the clothes he stood in and set up a new bureau in Paris syndicating articles by prominent figures in newspapers around the world. Churchill became one of his most important and bestselling clients. Shortly after war broke out Churchill thought he would be a useful channel for disseminating pro-Allied propaganda in the neutral press. Revesz was also keen to obtain British nationality and Churchill spoke to Sir John Anderson, the Home Secretary, to support his case. But a problem emerged. The MI5 files contained a negative report from French intelligence about Revesz. Churchill asked his friend Paul Reynaud, the then French Minister of Finance, to check him out with the French Sûreté. Simultaneously he asked Kell to do the same with the Deuxième Bureau.

Churchill was not pleased, therefore, when Kell told him that his sources in Paris regarded Revesz as a 'very suspect pro-Nazi propagandist'. The evidence amounted to little more than that Revesz's secretary and partner was the sister of the editor of *L'Humanité*, the French Communist Party newspaper. Churchill was scornful at the arrant nonsense sent to him by Kell. Whatever their other opinions, he reprimanded the MI5 Director, the Communists had been vehemently anti-Nazi. And the notion that Revesz was a Nazi propagandist flew in the face of common sense. His outburst had its effect. Six days later MI5 gave the green light for Revesz to enter Britain. Kell then further blotted his copybook by failing to inform MI5 officers at Heston airport so that Revesz flew in from Paris to have his papers confiscated and only after phone calls between Chartwell and MI5 was the muddle cleared up. Shortly afterwards, Revesz was granted British nationality, changed his name to Emery Reves, and arrived in New York to help with British propaganda. He also became a highly successful literary agent, helped negotiate US rights for Churchill's war memoirs, and purchased the foreign-language rights to Churchill's *History of the English-Speaking Peoples*. In the late 1950s Churchill was an appreciative guest of Reves and his wife at their villa in the South of France.[8]

Kell's clumsy handling of Revesz can have done him little good with Churchill. Neither did continuing security problems. Two days before Christmas, entombed in MI5's dismal wartime quarters at Wormwood Scrubs prison in London, Kell noted gloomily in his diary 'long interview with Winston Churchill at Admiralty re-leakages'.[9] Things would get much worse and their long relationship was to end abruptly less than six months later.

The break was precipitated by the issue of German spies and enemy aliens in Britain. In the darkening climate of the 1930s the idea of a knock-out aerial attack had largely filled the gap enjoyed before the First World War by invasion and spy scares. But Churchill adapted to the new age without abandoning the old. Vintage nightmares continued to haunt him. From September 1939 to May 1940 fears of German spies and invasion provided both script and subtext for many of his decisions, reinforced by his lifelong links with the professionally suspicious Kell. It was Kell's botching of the job of correctly identifying agents and aliens after the fall of France that prompted Churchill to dismiss him after thirty years at the MI5 helm.

In August 1939 Churchill firmly believed – against all the evidence – that 20,000 organised German agents were stationed in Britain. As in 1914, he was also convinced that war would stimulate an immediate outbreak of sabotage. Assassination, too, could not be ruled out. One of his first steps was to summon his faithful Inspector Thompson. Since saving Churchill from putative IRA plots in the 1920s and bravely hurling himself in front of a suspected Indian assassin during his 1932 visit to Chicago, the former Special Branch policeman had retired. But as Hitler's forces smashed Poland he returned, pistol in pocket as instructed by his master. Churchill got out his own weapons too. From then on, as he romantically put it, 'while one slept, the other watched'.[10]

Churchill was determined not to be taken by surprise. The approaching winter with its long dark nights heightened his worry and he spoke anxiously to Admiral Pound about a sudden descent of 20,000 Germans on the east coast of England. There was a good moon and fine weather, he pointed out, and the next two weeks could be a time of particular danger. Then, in late October, his anxiety reached fever pitch. Early that day Sir Ronald Campbell, the British ambassador in Belgrade, reported that Yugoslav military intelligence had learned of an impending German invasion of Britain using some 5,000 aircraft and a fleet of merchant ships. On Day One 12,000 men were to be parachuted along the east coast, British airfields and the Royal Navy would be neutralised, and 23,000 men would land by ship. Day Two would see a further 45,000 men landed, making for an overall force of 80,000. Diversionary attacks would simultaneously take place against the Maginot Line.

Lord Chatfield, the Minister for the Co-ordination of Defence, immediately summoned Churchill and a handful of others to assess the report. Churchill declared that the position was now far worse than it had been in 1914, when the Royal Navy had many of its ships stationed at various points along the east coast. Now they were dispersed, leaving the coast vulnerable. Desperate though the German plan sounded, the threat should be taken seriously. Sir Dudley Pound for the Navy, Sir Cyril Newall for the Air Force and Sir Walter Kirke for the Army detailed their plans for contingency counter-measures and Churchill added that they should think of bringing back an Army division from France. Only towards the end of the discussion did Leslie Hore-Belisha, the Minister for War, confess that the source of the report was highly unreliable and that it was probably a deliberate ploy to cause confusion, or a red herring designed to distract attention from an attack elsewhere.[11]

Deliberate plant or not, the invasion scare lingered for days. To Churchill it caused yet another historic nightmare that coalesced with his fears about Ireland. As part of his naval preparations Admiral Pound had planned to remove all capital ships from the east coast to protect them from German aircraft. Instead, they would take shelter in the Clyde. Churchill, as he brooded on matters, took a growing dislike to the idea. It was not just that the Forth was a better armed base with many more anti-aircraft guns. The Clyde itself was a positive threat. Glasgow housed a large Irish and Catholic population. Echoing Special Branch reports of significant IRA Scottish contingents dating from the 1920s, Churchill envisioned thousands of hostile eyes gazing on the Fleet. 'There are plenty of traitors in the Glasgow area', he informed Pound, adding that it would only take a single telephone call to alert the German ambassador in Dublin and his superiors in Berlin that British ships had abandoned the North Sea.

Meanwhile the Cabinet had again considered the invasion threat and Churchill's powerful imagination again came into play. He told the Cabinet that German parachutists could easily descend on London's parks, and ordered officers and able-bodied Admiralty employees to be provided with a rifle, bayonet and ammunition. Ten days later he was still sufficiently worried to urge the Cabinet to establish military pickets and patrols in Whitehall and Downing Street.

It was the last such alarm for several months. The invasion scare soon dissipated and concerns about Ireland diminished, but Churchill kept an eagle eye on MI5 investigations and one report in particular revealed his worries. While the Venlo drama was causing turmoil in SIS, Kell completed an investigation into companies in Britain that were either controlled by persons of German origin or had strong German connections. One, the Concrete Pump Company run by Karl Heinrich Markmann, a former Hitler Youth member who had been naturalised as a British subject earlier that year, had installed concrete works at several naval bases including Invergordon and Scapa Flow. Another, the Mercedes Group, supplied business machines to government departments including the War Office, Admiralty and Air Ministry. Its principal figure, Martin Herbert Simon, also a naturalised subject, was identified by Kell as 'probably head of the German intelligence system'. MI5 believed that both companies were integral parts of an active German espionage ring.

Kell sent his report to Admiral Godfrey who immediately showed it to Churchill. It prompted a typical and forthright response. He contacted Sir John Anderson, the Home Secretary, to demand that both firms be seized and Markmann and Simon interned. As bureaucrats hesitated over the legalities, Kell returned to the charge by demanding prompt action against Markmann. As the circumstantial evidence accumulated in his suspicious mind – Markmann used Irish mechanics, for example – and as the Home Office did nothing, Kell appealed directly to Churchill. Once again Churchill took it up directly with Anderson. Nothing less than internment would prevent this 'intolerable activity'. To his relief, the next day the Home Secretary assured him personally that he had ordered Markmann interned and his company taken over by the Board of Trade. Temporarily, Churchill was assured.[12] But his anxieties about some German Fifth Column in Britain, as well as dissatisfaction with the progress of the secret war, lingered on. Dunkirk, the collapse of France and the imminent prospect of invasion were to bring them dramatically to a head.

A bungled attempt to sabotage Swedish iron-ore exports to Germany, Britain's first clandestine operation of the war, completed the dismal list of intelligence failures experienced by Churchill at the Admiralty. Germany's annual pre-war imports of iron ore was 20 million tons. The outbreak of war halved this with the loss of the Lorraine ore fields in France, and making Germany crucially dependent on Swedish supplies. Most came from Gallivare in northern Sweden, to be shipped out of the Baltic port of Lulea in summer and, after the winter ice formed, by train across the mountains to the port of Narvik in Norway. The remainder, from southern Sweden, was shipped from Oxelosund, the main ice-free port on the Baltic. Eager to strike against Hitler, ever keen to find some Achilles' heel that would bring rapid and bloodless victory, and fortified by Desmond Morton's optimistic industrial intelligence about German vulnerability over ore requirements, Churchill seized on the idea of bringing the German economy to its knees. A decisive blow at the ore fields of neutral Sweden, he told the War Cabinet in December 1939, could be the equivalent of a first-class victory in the field or from the air. Mining neutral Norwegian waters, or sending Allied forces into Sweden and Norway to support Finland in its war against the Soviet Union, provided possible ways of doing this, but raised strategic and diplomatic problems that paralysed action for months. There existed a third alternative: the sabotage of one or all of the ports in a clandestine cloak-and-dagger operation.

SIS had been toying with this idea since 1938 and Stewart Menzies' first official call on Churchill in December 1939 had been to discuss the scheme. Following the *Anschluss* SIS had set up a special unit, Section D (for Destruction), under a flamboyant army officer named Major Laurence Grand, to plan dirty tricks targeted at Germany's economy. One aimed to blow up the Romanian oilfields, another to block the Danube at the Iron Gates. Swedish iron ore stood high on the list. Section D's man in Stockholm, a businessman named Alfred Rickman, operated under the cover of an import machinery company, and in best spy-novel fashion communicated with London using invisible ink in ostensibly private or business letters. Attempts at smuggling in explosives disguised as chocolate, biscuits or rubber through Norway having failed, Section D finally shipped them direct to Stockholm labelled as military and technical books. The military attaché who collected them disguised as a French chauffeur described the operation as 'real Edgar Wallace stuff, in a dark dirty wood at midnight'. Rickman's cellar was soon packed with several hundred pounds of explosives. By January 1940 the operation was ready to go. All that remained, he told London, was 'to press the button'.

No more eager a finger hovered than Churchill's. The 'Blinker' Hall tradition of Admiralty involvement in wartime dirty tricks survived and he was happy to leave the details of liaison with SIS to Admiral Godfrey. 'So proceed', he instructed Godfrey early in January after the DNI had met with him and Menzies and asked for £300,000 to back the Swedish scheme. He was also the operation's enthusiastic advocate in the War Cabinet. It was an uphill struggle, but once he had convinced the Chiefs of Staff of its importance he gave Section D the green light for Operation Lumps, a sabotage attack aimed at Oxelosund. But, as with his other Scandinavian plans, 'the tremendous array of negative arguments' came dismally into play. Hardly had he approved it than Chamberlain vetoed the operation as too dangerous for Anglo-Swedish relations. None the less he agreed that Section D should continue to develop its plans.

By this time two more players had entered the scene. One was the head of Section D's Scandinavian section, an ex-advertising executive named Ingram Fraser. The other was William Stephenson, a Canadian millionaire tycoon with extensive European business connections who in 1940 became Director of the New York-based British Security Co-ordination. An unobtrusive man with a legendary capacity for dry Martinis, Stephenson was adept at opening doors in important places and had worked for Dansey's 'Z' network reporting on German industrial production and contracts. Using Stephenson's contacts in Stockholm, Section D developed a plan to sabotage the bridge cranes at Oxelosund used to load the ore on to waiting German ships. One of Rickman's agents would drive from Stockholm in a car using Norwegian plates and leave it close to the port. Here Rickman would collect it, obscure the plates with mud or snow, and pick up two more of his agents who would plant the explosives at the base of the cranes. Their mission accomplished, he would drive them to the Malmo–Stockholm railway line where he would abandon the car which in the meantime would be reported stolen by his Norwegian agent.

This Stephenson–Fraser–Rickman plan hung fire throughout February. After months of hesitation the Anglo-French Supreme War Council had finally agreed to seize the Swedish ore fields with a target date of 20 March. But Chamberlain and the Cabinet still dragged their heels and twice vetoed the plan. Finally Churchill lost patience. Early in March 1940 he summoned Grand to his Admiralty office. What, he demanded, had happened? Grand's reply blaming the War Cabinet failed to mollify an exasperated Churchill. Why had he not tried harder to convince them? Typically slashing through the red tape, he confronted Chamberlain who finally lifted the veto. Hankey, ever the man of secrets, telephoned Grand with the news.

Anticlimax followed. The button pressed, nothing happened. That very same day Rickman's principal agent, a refugee German Social Democrat in Stockholm, suddenly backed out of the operation. Churchill and Section D fulminated but Rickman was unable to find a replacement. The German invasion of Denmark and Norway four weeks later finally stung Section D into direct action. The second-in-command of its Scandinavian section, a Royal Navy reserve yachtsman named Gerald Holdsworth, flew immediately to Stockholm to take charge. Fearing an imminent German invasion, he decided that Rickman's incriminating collection of explosives should be immediately dispersed to safer hiding places. But while Rickman was loading the explosives into his car the Swedish police who had had him under surveillance for months arrested him. Tried in camera he was sentenced to eight years' hard labour. He had failed, disastrously, to keep his agents unaware of each other's identities and had refused to believe that he was being watched.[13]

Such amateurish bungling reflected badly on Grand, Section D and SIS, not to mention prevaricating ministers in London. Churchill absorbed the lesson: SIS control of special operations did not survive the first two months of his premiership. Instead he created a separate new agency with its own enthusiastic minister – the Special Operations Executive under Hugh Dalton.

Even more momentous for the future of British intelligence was a barely remarked item slipped into a Cabinet discussion by Churchill after it had approved his proposal to use MI5 in contacts with King Leopold of the Belgians the previous October. He had just received a personal letter, he told his colleagues, from President Roosevelt of the United States. It was very friendly and said that the President, a former assistant secretary of the US Navy, would be glad at any time to receive a personal message on any matter that Churchill desired to bring to his notice. The Cabinet approved Churchill's ready reply. Thus began a momentous relationship. Out of it grew the most powerful and extraordinary intelligence alliance in history involving co-operation in practically every aspect of the secret war from code-breaking to dirty tricks.

Interestingly, Roosevelt had concluded his note by congratulating Churchill on the completion of his four-volume life of the Duke of Marlborough and saying how much he had enjoyed it. Perhaps he was being polite. But had he indeed read it, he could not have failed to note how significantly Churchill's ancestor had relied on intelligence, still less how emphatically Churchill had stressed the fact. In his famous march across Europe from the Rhine to the triumphant Bavarian battlefield of Blenheim, Marlborough had learned much of French campaign plans from deciphered and stolen documents, lavished extensive funds on his secret service, and deployed elaborate deception to convince the French into believing that his ally, Prince Eugene of Savoy, was moving elsewhere. Once positioned at Blenheim he had carefully planted false deserters who deceived the French into believing he planned to withdraw his forces the next day. Instead he attacked and gained the advantage of surprise. The accuracy of intelligence about the enemy and surprise created by deception, Churchill stressed, had been key factors in Marlborough's triumph. 'No war', the Duke himself had declared, 'can ever be conducted without early and good intelligence.' Lessons from history reinforced those of the present and guaranteed that intelligence would rank highly on Churchill's agenda when he took command.[14]

10

Fifth Columns

Churchill became Prime Minister on 10 May 1940 and faced an immediate crisis. At dawn Hitler's *Wehrmacht* launched their onslaught on the Low Countries and France. Four days later the Dutch surrendered and panzer divisions broke French defences at Sedan. It took them less than a week to reach the English Channel. The French Army was broken. That same day, Churchill began planning for the possible evacuation of British forces from France and northern Norway. He also sent a message to Roosevelt declaring that Britain would never surrender. Finally, he turned to the nightmare that had haunted him since before the First World War: an invasion of Britain assisted by enemy agents. With German troops poised across the Channel he anticipated parachute drops like those on Belgium and Holland. The War Cabinet ordered airports to be placed on alert and emergency rifle-training for local volunteers. Whitehall itself was prepared for attack. 'Good', noted Churchill with satisfaction after examining a plan to install Bren guns and road blocks around Downing Street and Admiralty Arch.[1]

His bunker mentality was fuelled by rampant rumours of European 'Fifth Columnists' who had opened doors for the Nazis. This was an old idea with a new name. General Emilio Mola had coined the phrase during his advance on Republican-held Madrid during the Spanish Civil War when he boasted of a fifth column inside the city supporting his four columns of troops. The term was picked up again by journalists following Vidkun Quisling's collaboration with the Nazis during the invasion of Norway. Even before Hitler's attack on France the Joint Intelligence Committee concluded that sabotage could play a dangerous part in a pre-arranged enemy plan. By mid-May almost two hundred IRA supporters had been expelled from Britain, and the day before

Churchill became Prime Minister a Treachery Bill was introduced into Parliament.

Concern turned to near-hysteria after 10 May. Reports from the Low Countries spoke of Nazi agents and sympathisers signalling from clandestine radios, and female saboteurs cunningly disguised as nuns flashing lights for parachute drops. Such fantasies caught on in Britain. 'Fifth Column reports coming in from everywhere', noted General 'Tiny' Ironside, the former intelligence officer and Chief of the Imperial General Staff, who was now Commander-in-Chief of the Home Forces. 'Important telegraph poles marked, suspicious men moving at night all over the country . . . Perhaps we will catch some swine.' A classic version was produced by Sir Neville Bland, Britain's ambassador to the Netherlands. 'It is clear', he warned, 'that the paltriest kitchen maid with [German or Austrian] origins . . . is . . . a menace to the safety of the country.' Sir Charles Tegart also expected a stab in the back from across the Irish Sea. An ex-Calcutta Chief of Police who was admired by Churchill, he had masterminded the 'Tegart Wall', a barbed-wire barrier strung along the Palestine–Syria border to keep out Arab rebels. Sent by MI5 to Ireland, he reported in June that German gauleiters were already in place to seize control when Britain was invaded. Desmond Morton forwarded the report to Churchill predicting that there would be revolution in Ireland as soon as German troops came ashore. Churchill found this too much to believe and asked for confirmation.[2]

'No Fifth Column existed in Britain' declared Churchill in his post-war history, but at the time his imagination was in overdrive and MI5 had his ready ear. For months Kell had been reporting cases of illicit signalling and his files on the subject formed a five-foot pile. As France collapsed, British forces struggled home from the Dunkirk beaches, and Mussolini threw in his lot with Hitler, Churchill sided decisively with MI5 and his Chiefs of Staff against a foot-dragging Home Office in demanding drastic action against what he assumed would provide the hard core of Britain's Fifth Column: the 70,000 enemy aliens in the country. These ranged from long-standing residents to thousands of recent refugees from Central Europe, many of them Jewish. They had already been classified into three major categories, from 'A' – known pro-Fascists or enemy agents who were to be interned – to 'C' – harmless refugees and anti-Nazis to be left at liberty (and, at 64,000, the largest category). Promises had been made that there would be no repeat of the indiscriminate mass detentions of the First World War and that only the handful of known enemy agents would be detained or expelled. These assurances were now swept away.

Churchill had robustly challenged the official moderate line even while at the Admiralty. On his first full day as Prime Minister he chaired a War Cabinet meeting that decided to detain at once all enemy aliens in coastal areas, and he personally suggested that the police be armed. That day, too, Hankey completed a top-secret report that referred ominously to 'the traitors within our gates'. The day that French Prime Minister Paul Reynaud confessed despairingly that the road to Paris was open, Churchill demanded a 'very large' round-up of aliens. To the 3,000 interned from coastal areas were now added thousands more men and women who already lived under curfew and travel restraints. In parts of the country a pogrom-type mood began to take hold. Newspapers demanded general internment, employers fired foreigners, and detainees committed suicide.

The images haunting Churchill were clearly etched. In his first message to Roosevelt as Prime Minister he anticipated attacks by parachute and airborne troops, and remarked how many reports had come in of possible such descents in Ireland. 'We must expect to be attacked on the Dutch model', he signalled. Roosevelt shared the nightmare, warning Congress of a fifth-column danger, and in one of his famous radio 'fireside chats' to the American people spoke darkly of the new methods of war involving spies, saboteurs and traitors.[3]

As the crisis rapidly worsened in France Churchill's suspicious gaze extended to British Fascists, Communists and other defeatists. 'Very considerable numbers' should be detained, he urged. By the time German troops reached the Channel on 20 May he was in a hawkish mood. Events in London were to enable him to move in for the kill.

That morning Captain Maxwell Knight, the head of Section B5(b) of MI5, knocked at the front door of 47 Gloucester Place in Marylebone. Knight, a jazz-playing eccentric who as 'Uncle Max' later became a popular BBC children's broadcaster, had been recruited by Kell at the time of the Zinoviev Letter affair. One of MI5's stars, he ran a network of informers in the Communist Party and British Fascist groups. He was also a friend of and security adviser to Desmond Morton.

The tenant at Gloucester Place was Tyler Kent, a cipher clerk in the American Embassy. A gifted linguist and Ivy League wastrel of isolationist and anti-Semitic views, he had arrived in London two years before from the American Embassy in Moscow where his conspicuous lifestyle and NKVD (Soviet secret police) mistress later had the FBI classify him as a possible Soviet spy. Joseph P. Kennedy, the Democratic but anti-interventionist American ambassador in London, had already waived his diplomatic immunity. Armed with a search warrant, Knight found a hidden suitcase containing some 1,500 documents and keys to the embassy's code and file rooms. Amongst the papers were copies of telegrams from Churchill–Roosevelt correspondence. Kent was immediately arrested, as was his chief accomplice, a White Russian exile living in London named Anna Wolkoff. She was the daughter of a former Russian naval attaché in London who ran the Russian Tea Rooms in South Kensington, and the secretary of the Right Club founded by Captain Archibald Ramsay MC, the elegant Eton-and-Sandhurst-educated Conservative Member of Parliament. She had introduced a sympathetic Kent to the club's work and together they planned to change the course of history and produce a negotiated peace with Hitler.

In their naive and conspiratorial minds it would be simple. The Churchill–Roosevelt correspondence revealed – so they believed – a plot to drag a reluctant United States into the war. Exposed to the right people at the right time – for example, by an MP such as Ramsay using his parliamentary privilege – it would be a bombshell that would destroy its protagonists. Conservatives would revolt against Churchill and replace him with a leader truly committed to talks with Hitler. Isolationists in the United States would be handed a weapon to drive Roosevelt from the White House in the coming election. Instead they found themselves tried in camera at the Old Bailey under the Official Secrets Act. The guilty verdicts were withheld until after Roosevelt's return to power.

Kent's treachery was unprecedented in the history of American diplomacy. More serious for Britain were the implications of Wolkoff's complicity. Her contacts included Captain Francesco Maringliano, an assistant military attaché at the Italian Embassy. GC & CS decrypts indicated that the German ambassador in Rome had been reading Churchill's correspondence with Roosevelt, and Maringliano seemed the obvious source. Here was a direct link

3. Vernon Kell, first head of MI5, who reinforced Churchill's belief in the German spy menace

4. Sir Alfred Ewing, appointed by Churchill as head of British naval code-breaking in 1914

5. 'The little white snake' – Colonel Ormonde de Winter,
who headed British intelligence efforts against the IRA in Ireland

6. Sir Basil Thomson, approved by Churchill in 1919 as Director of Intelligence to fight domestic subversion

7. Seen here with Mussolini, Leonid Krasin (*right*), head of the first Soviet trade delegation to London in 1920

8. Lev Kamenev, brother-in-law to Trotsky and Krasin's right-hand man in London

9. Clare Sheridan, Churchill's cousin, whose entanglement with Kamenev and friendship with an MI5 officer caused family ructions

10. Boris Savinkov, 'handled' by Archibald Sinclair, whose anti-Bolshevik guerrilla forces were supported by Churchill

11. Sidney Reilly, British secret agent, who plotted with
Savinkov supported by Churchill

12. 'Archie' Sinclair, Churchill's close friend and liaison with anti-Bolshevik conspirators in the 1920s

13. Edward Spears, professional intelligence officer, ally of Savinkov and trusted adviser of Churchill

14. Intriguingly caught on camera together, Churchill's *bête noire* and MI5 target George Lansbury (*second from left*) with 'Captain' Edward Tupper (*second from right*), Churchill's private agent

15. Sir Joseph Ball, MI5 officer on the Lansbury case and mastermind of Conservative 'dirty tricks' in the 1930s

16. Sir Stewart Menzies, head of the Secret Intelligence Service ('C'), Churchill's wartime spymaster

17. Ralph Wigram, secret informant for Churchill against appeasement, seen here (*right*) with him in the garden at Chartwell

23. Alan Hillgarth, British wartime intelligence officer and
secret post-war adviser to Churchill

21. Lord Swinton, appointed by Churchill in 1940 to fight 'the Fifth Column'

22. Admiral Darlan (*left*) with General Franco (*centre*) and Marshal Pétain (*right*). His assassination in Algiers removed a problem for Churchill

19. Churchill's first 'minister for ungentlemanly war', Hugh Dalton, instructed 'to set Europe ablaze'

20. Lord Selborne, Dalton's successor and trusted friend of Churchill

18. The man behind the scenes, Churchill's intelligence adviser Desmond Morton, seen here (*middle*) with Churchill and Admiral Sir Andrew Cunningham, First Sea Lord (*second from right*)

between a British organisation and the enemy – proof positive, it appeared, of a dangerous Fifth Column penetrating the heart of the Establishment.

Kell and MI5 had long been pushing for the wholescale detention of Fifth Column suspects but had been thwarted by the Home Secretary, Sir John Anderson (later Viscount Waverley), a Scot who had spent years as a tough-minded functionary repressing troublesome parts of the Empire, including Ireland and Bengal. Ironically, his punctilious passion for procedure now ranged him on the side of civil liberties. Talk of internment was all very well, he warned the War Cabinet, but there was simply no evidence that Fascists such as Oswald Mosley, leader of the British Union of Fascists, were likely to help the enemy. The Tyler Kent affair fatally wounded his position.

Only hours after Kent's arrest, Kell found in Anthony Eden, the Secretary of State for War, a sympathetic minister who confessed he was sick of lectures from Anderson on the rights of the subject. Within forty-eight hours the War Cabinet approved a huge round-up of British Fascists. 'If any doubt existed the persons in question should be detained without delay', Churchill instructed. Hours later the round-up began under Regulation 18B of the Emergency Powers Act.

Predictably, Ramsay was one of the first to be detained. Also on the list were Harold St John Philby, the pro-Fascist Arabist and father of Kim, later the most notorious British KGB traitor, and Admiral Sir Barry Domvile, a former Director of Naval Intelligence who was convinced that behind world affairs moved the mysterious hand of what he called 'Judmas' – his shorthand for a Judeo-Masonic conspiracy. But the most prominent detainee was Sir Oswald Mosley, long feared by Churchill as the most likely British Quisling. No evidence existed linking him with Ramsay or any other plot lurking behind the Kent–Wolkoff affair, but Churchill accepted MI5's argument that if an invasion occurred Mosley would either join the enemy or attempt a *coup d'état* in the pursuit of peace.

Speculation has lingered around the Tyler Kent affair, especially as regards its timing. MI5 had kept Kent and Wolkoff under surveillance for months, so why did they wait until this particular moment to swoop? The obvious explanation is that MI5 exploited the invasion panic to break the deadlock over internment with the Home Office. More provocative is the suggestion that the whole affair was a classic 'sting' operation by Churchill himself to discredit the defeatist Kennedy whose security would be revealed as lax, to provide a lever to use against the American President, and to produce proof of a Fifth Column, thereby swaying Cabinet waverers and doubters. But Roosevelt needed no additional prompting against Kennedy, and Churchill had no interest at all in weakening Roosevelt whose re-election was the best chance he had of drawing the United States into the war. More plausible is the notion that Churchill might have had a personal hand in the Kent affair. He was undoubtedly a hawk prepared to scatter Home Office doves and had not in the past been averse to using MI5 for political purposes – as the Lansbury affair revealed. Through Desmond Morton he also had a link to Maxwell Knight. Churchill may well have known what was going on and ordered the trap closed at a moment that suited him.[4]

In the weeks that followed Churchill was the driving force behind a massive round-up of aliens and British subjects in the name of national security.[5] MI5 happily obliged with a continuing flow of alarmist intelligence. His ferocity on this front went hand in hand with a ruthless determination to fight on against Hitler. With British forces triumphantly evacuated from Dunkirk, he delivered his historic speech promising that Britons would fight on the beaches, on the landing grounds, in the fields and in the streets, and in the hills. He also justified the wide-ranging internment measures that, as he spoke, were sweeping thousands of British subjects and foreigners into detention camps. Many, he acknowledged, were passionate enemies of Hitler, but events were so critical that distinctions could no longer be drawn. No sympathy, however, should be extended to Fifth Columnists. Parliament had given the government drastic powers to crush their activities until 'the malignancy in our midst' had been stamped out. 'When we see the originality of malice, the ingenuity of aggression, which our enemy displays', Churchill told the Commons, 'we may certainly prepare ourselves for every kind of novel stratagem and every kind of brutal and treacherous manoeuvre.'

It was in this mood that he ordered the immediate round-up of Italians when Mussolini declared war on 10 June, following this up after France's armistice with Hitler by the detention of all category 'C' aliens. Numbers peaked in late July 1940 with some 27,000 – most were harmless, many were active anti-Nazis. But having read the transcript of an MI5 interview with the former head of the Dutch security police arguing 'once a German always a German', Desmond Morton prevailed on Churchill to issue a warning against 'dangerous laxity' in their treatment. Revealing a high level of anxiety, Churchill told him to see that all car radios were removed to prevent signalling with the enemy.

So vivid was Churchill's Fifth Column nightmare that he feared the detention camps themselves could become focal points of unrest or even dropping zones for German parachutists. Instead, he demanded the internees be shipped overseas to Newfoundland or St Helena. The Canadian government had already been approached but its hesitant Prime Minister stalled for time. Churchill's enquiry prompted a reminder that stressed the danger to British national security posed by the 2,500 pro-Nazi aliens in the event of invasion or parachute drops. Mackenzie King capitulated and the shipment began.

Barely two weeks later the *Arandora Star*, a former luxury cruiser, sailed from Liverpool carrying some 1,200 Germans and Italians bound for Canadian internment camps. Within twenty-four hours she was torpedoed off the coast of Ireland. Over six hundred internees were drowned, many of them haphazardly caught up in MI5's desperate search for Fifth Columnists.

Their deaths provoked a public backlash, and early in August Churchill began to retreat. MI5 interrogations of detainees had failed to support conspiracy theories and he felt more relaxed. Two weeks later, as the Battle of Britain approached its climax, he told the House of Commons with an impressive display of amnesia that he had always thought the Fifth Column danger exaggerated. That autumn at Chequers, entertaining two of the Coldstream Guards officers who helped guard the house, he declared how intensely he disliked the suspension of habeas corpus and locking people up. In any case, he added, the 'filthy Communists' were more dangerous than the Fascists. He also began to demand better conditions for the detainees, such as permitting married couples to live together (prompted by Clementine, he particularly had the Mosleys in mind), and by early 1941 he was denouncing the 'witch-finding' activities of MI5. By late 1943, with the tide of war safely turned, he firmly backed the decision by Herbert Morrison, the Home Secretary, to release Sir Oswald Mosley. MI5 was unhappy, as were the Minister of Labour Ernest Bevin and large sections of the Labour movement. From Cairo, where he was preparing for the Tehran Conference, Churchill stiffened Morrison's resolve. The power of the Executive to cast a suspect into jail without legal charge or trial by jury was, he said, 'in the highest degree odious and ... the foundation of all totalitarian government whether Nazi or Communist'. The great emergency was over and he now believed internment should be abolished. But he was the captive of coalition politics, and Labour hostility kept the handful of remaining British Fascists in detention without trial until the end of the war. The day after VE Day, at his personal insistence, Regulation 18B was finally abolished.[6]

The other great casualty of the Fifth Column panic was Vernon Kell. MI5's mishandling of the affair was the last in a long series of mishaps. After the chairman of the Home Office advisory committee on internment condemned MI5 for 'gross mistakes and pathological stupidities' in its reports on individual aliens, Churchill had Kell fired by Sir Horace Wilson, head of the civil service. It was the end of a thirty-year relationship that had finally soured.

The writing had been on the wall for some time. The War Cabinet had already created an extraordinary body called the Home Defence (Security) Executive, later known simply as the Security Executive, and Churchill had entrusted Lord Swinton, Chamberlain's pre-war Minister of Air, with the special mission of finding out 'whether there is a fifth column ... and if so to eliminate it'. Swinton spearheaded all security measures and increasingly subordinated MI5 to his control. 'There were overlaps and underlaps', Churchill later explained to the Commons, 'and I felt that this side of the business of national defence needed pulling together.' He also appointed Morton as his personal representative. Some MPs were alarmed by Swinton's draconian powers, and the Labour MP Richard Stokes denounced the Executive as 'this rather odd secret Gestapo'. Ironically, Swinton's deputy, as well as Chamberlain's personal representative, was none other than Sir Joseph Ball.

In July Churchill gave Swinton executive control of MI5 as well as operational control of SIS activities in Great Britain and Eire. Swinton became Churchill's eyes on the intelligence services as they scrambled to adjust to the new regime in Downing Street. 'Press on and keep me informed, especially if you encounter obstacles', Churchill ordered. Kell's sacking was deeply unpopular amongst MI5's old guard. His successor, Acting Director Brigadier Jasper Harker, was ineffectual, and as Swinton met stubborn resistance in his attempts at reform, military intelligence became alarmed at MI5's disorganisation.

The ensuing crisis landed on Churchill's desk in late November

1940 thanks to an old political ally from battles over the India Bill a decade before, the robustly patriotic Baron Croft of Bournemouth, joint Parliamentary Under-Secretary for War in the House of Lords. From his Knightsbridge home, Croft sent him a cryptic handwritten letter warning that all was not well 'in certain quarters' and urging him to call for a Major Lennox of MI5 and ask him to speak freely. 'Do not consult *anyone*', he added conspiratorially. Lennox was the liaison officer between MI5 and Military Intelligence, and Churchill immediately handed the affair over to Morton. Lennox told him that MI5 was in a serious state, riven by internal jealousy, and that the blame rested squarely on Harker's shoulders. On Churchill's orders Morton interviewed the service directors of intelligence who insisted that MI5 urgently needed a forceful new director. Early in 1941 Churchill approved the appointment of Sir David Petrie, a former director of the Indian Police Intelligence Bureau.[7] Under Petrie MI5 finally sorted itself out, improved relations with SIS, and by the end of the war could claim some impressive counter-intelligence victories. The most dramatic was undoubtedly the 'Double-Cross system' – the manipulation of double agents that helped to deceive the Germans about Allied strategy.

Close to midnight on 19 September 1940 an *Abwehr* agent parachuted from a Heinkel bomber into a field close to Cambridge. His mission was to provide intelligence for the coming invaders. Early the next morning he bought *The Times* at the local newsagent and was proceeding to recover his wireless set when he was challenged by a vigilant member of the local Home Guard. Within twenty-four hours he was under MI5 interrogation in London. Two weeks later, faced with the prospect of the gallows, he agreed to work as a double agent. This was a turning point. The new arrival, code-named Tate, was the first of a wartime batch that eventually formed an impressive double-cross system that fooled the Germans into thinking they controlled a powerful espionage network in Britain. Insatiably curious as ever, Churchill was sent detailed reports of the interrogations from military intelligence and Swinton sent him equally lengthy reports marked 'Very Secret and Personal' on more batches of German agents who had landed in Scotland. At first his natural belligerence threatened the very creation of the Double-Cross system. Why had none of the spies yet been shot? he asked. MI5 was aghast. Intelligence, it argued, should have priority over 'blood-letting'. Churchill was quickly persuaded.[8]

At first MI5 used Tate and the others to find out as much as they could about German intelligence. Gradually it dawned that they could also be used more actively to deceive the Germans about British resources and plans. This raised difficult issues. To maintain credibility with their German controllers the double agents had to transmit true information with the false. Who was to determine what could safely be given away? More importantly, what was the larger deception message to be sent? MI5 looked after the handling of the agents; broader direction was need for policy guidance and control.

So sensitive was the problem that not even the Joint Intelligence Committee was consulted. Instead, in January 1941, Whitehall mandarins created the W Board (W stood for Wireless), consisting of the service directors of intelligence, top-level MI5 and SIS figures (including Menzies), and Sir Findlater Stewart, Chairman of the Home Defence Executive. It was responsible to no one, operated in total secrecy and had no written mandate, but what it dealt with was momentous. The Germans were instructing Tate and others to report on the location of food and other supplies, and on the effect of German bombing. The answers transmitted, true or false, could decisively affect German bombing policy, turning some towns and factories into targets. For that, the W Board – and the subordinate Twenty Committee that actually ran the operation (called after the Roman numerals that also form a double cross) – needed the highest level of approval. Sir John Anderson, appointed Lord President of the Council following the death of Neville Chamberlain, took the issue directly to Churchill. What transpired between them was never committed to paper or even Cabinet discussion, but Churchill made it clear that if there was a double-cross system to run then the W Board should get on with it. It could count on his support – although if events came to light and there was a public row it could not claim official authorisation. Until the end of the war the Twenty Committee met weekly while MI5 carried out the tricky daily task of handling the double agents. Their efforts climaxed in June 1944 with the successful deception masking the D-Day landings. Churchill approved the plan with his famous words, borrowed from Stalin: 'In wartime, truth is so precious that she should always be attended by a bodyguard of lies.'[9]

Desmond Morton's seat on the Security Executive was only one of many positions that placed him at the heart of Churchill's dealings with the secret world. To use the words of Sir John Colville, he descended on 10 Downing Street in May 1940 as one of three Churchill advisers who arrived 'like Horsemen of the Apocalypse' – the others were Lindemann and Brendan Bracken. Established civil servants regarded his drive and energy with alarm. 'For them', remembered Morton's then assistant, 'he was a cuckoo in the nest' – almost literally so, as he occupied space adjacent to the Cabinet Room with direct access to Churchill. Here he controlled relations with the secret services, channelled his dealings with the Free French and watched over the affairs of the exiled governments in London. He was also fully briefed on Ultra. His influence peaked in the early months of Churchill's premiership, when his long-standing peace-time contacts with SIS and MI5 provided both compass and anchor during the stormy summer and autumn months of 1940. From then on his influence gradually diminished as the Foreign Office appointed ambassadors to the governments-in-exile and Stewart Menzies built his own direct relationship with Churchill. Yet to the end of the war Morton remained officially in place, a target of suspicion by those who considered him a hostile gatekeeper favouring rival factions in Whitehall infighting. However by 1945 he was in only distant orbit round Churchill, and emerged a disappointed and marginalised figure. A still-friendly Churchill ensured him a knighthood and lunched with him from time to time, but the Chartwell days were over and Morton eventually felt used. 'I do not care if I never see him again', he confessed in 1960, 'and certainly would not wish to attend his funeral.'[10]

Churchill had promised to fight on the beaches and in the hills. The summer of 1940 saw the hastily improvised creation of a secret British underground movement. Its nucleus comprised small, locally raised Auxiliary Units, based on a cadre of intelligence officers, that would harass the enemy before melting away to carefully prepared hideouts in woods, cellars and fields.

To run the operation, General Ironside turned to a former member of his anti-Bolshevik force in northern Russia and expert in subversion, Colonel Colin Gubbins. Since fighting against Michael Collins's guerrillas, Gubbins had joined MI(R), the irregular warfare research unit in the War Office. The outbreak of the war found him in Poland and he later headed the Independent Companies – forerunner of the Commandos – in Norway. He undertook his unorthodox task to organise British resistance with energy and enthusiasm, and by September, when the invasion scare reached its peak, some three thousand men were poised for action. Churchill eagerly followed his progress, seeing the clandestine counterpoint to his beloved Home Guard. 'From what I hear', he told Anthony Eden, 'these units are being organised with thoroughness and imagination ... keep me informed.'[11] Eden did, but after Hitler postponed Operation Sealion the units had outlived their purpose. Soon Gubbins had other tasks involving sabotage and subversion. In November, promoted to Brigadier, he joined the newly created Special Operations Executive. This was one of the more momentous of Churchill's secret-service brainstorms generated that summer.

The War Cabinet meeting that placed Swinton in charge of fighting the Fifth Column also confronted the appalling prospect of a French collapse. Without the French Army to fight in Europe, how could the Nazis be defeated? True, there remained Britain's sea power, the promise of strategic bombing, and British and Dominion forces, but none could realistically remove the German armies from occupied Europe. Clutching at straws, and propelled by Churchill's aggressive instincts, the War Cabinet endorsed a proposal by the Chiefs of Staff to create a top-secret organisation to stimulate and supply sabotage and subversion behind enemy lines that would spark a European revolt and shake off the yoke of German oppression. At the Admiralty Churchill had thrown his support behind Section D. Now – his historical memory shaped by Victorian images of heroic national struggles against tyranny; his youthful experience of war forged in behind-the-lines action in Cuba and South Africa – he dreamed of a democratic Fifth Column that would pay the Germans back in their own subversive coin. Thus was born the Special Operations Executive (SOE).

To run it, Churchill finally settled for the forceful Labour politician Hugh Dalton, the Minister of Economic Warfare. This decision was prompted by coalition politics, not personal choice. Determined to balance Conservative control of the Foreign Office and Home Security, the Labour leader Clement Attlee threw his weight behind Dalton's intensive lobbying for the job. An old Etonian whose father had tutored the infant King George V, Dalton had graduated through the Fabian Society at Cambridge and a lecturer's post at the London School of Economics and Political Science to become a Labour MP in 1924. Five years later he was Under-Secretary of State in the Foreign Office and a keen consumer of GC & CS intercepts.

He held decided views about what was needed: 'Regular soldiers are not men to stir up revolution, to create social chaos or to use all those ungentlemanly means of winning the war which come so easily to the Nazis.' A vigorous opponent of appeasement throughout the 1930s, Dalton was a great admirer of Churchill and had high expectations of his appointment. He was to be bitterly disappointed. 'Keep that man away from me', Churchill once said, 'I can't stand his booming voice and shifty eyes.' None the less, at a late-night meeting on 16 July – a busy day in which he had already appointed his old friend Sir Roger Keyes as Director of Combined Operations (the Commandos), had an audience with the King at Buckingham Palace, discussed with SIS Director Stewart Menzies how to extract intelligence from Nazi-occupied Europe, and fielded complaints from Desmond Morton about the lack of publicity for General de Gaulle as leader of the Free French – Churchill reluctantly gave Dalton the job he so coveted. 'Now, set Europe ablaze!' he told him.[12]

SOE was in no position to set anything alight in 1940. Cobbled together from Section D, MI(R) and EH (a semi-secret Foreign Office propaganda agency), it had virtually no resources, communications, transport or trained agents. Its principal weapons were rhetoric and enthusiasm. Yet Dalton shared Churchill's grandiose vision. SOE would organise movements in occupied Europe comparable to Sinn Fein in Ireland, the Chinese guerrillas fighting against the Japanese, and the Spanish irregulars who had fought in Wellington's peninsular campaign against Napoleon – even, he admitted, akin to the Fifth Column organisations operated by the Nazis. 'We must use many different methods', he declared, 'including industrial and military sabotage, labour agitation and strikes, continuous propaganda, terrorist acts against traitors and German leaders, boycotts and riots.' Churchill lended Dalton his support: on the first anniversary of the outbreak of war he promised the Commons that the British Empire's continued survival would 'kindle again the spark of hope in the breasts of hundreds of millions of downtrodden or despairing men and women throughout Europe, and far beyond its bounds, and that from these sparks there will presently come cleansing and devouring flame'.

This was magnificent, but it was not a strategy. SOE wasn't effectively operational until early 1941, when it made its first parachute drop behind enemy lines into Poland. Even then it had to wage continual warfare with the service chiefs and the Foreign Office for a share in resources such as aircraft and weaponry, as well as proper recognition of its role. Only with Churchill's support did it survive. For if he was at times critical, SOE and the warfare it waged embodied the lifelong appeal that unorthodox and unconventional war held for him. Even those who admire his wartime strategy have argued that his youthful admiration for the Boer guerrillas caused him to misjudge the possibilities against a ruthless Nazi occupier in Europe. The result was hopeless resistance and insurrections that produced little but bloodshed, defeat and savage reprisals. As one British military historian has argued, it was all 'a costly and misguided failure'.[13]

This, however, is to attribute too much importance to Churchill's rhetoric, to ignore what SOE in fact achieved, and to deny agency to the occupied. The people of Europe well knew the risks of resistance, and while at first stunned by defeat into passivity, their revolts and uprisings owed little to efforts in London. Indeed, for much of the war SOE worked hard to dampen down the flame of revolt in order to preserve resistance for major sabotage campaigns around D-Day. In reality, the 1944 risings in Warsaw, Slovakia and the Vercors ran counter to SOE's strategy. Churchill's support for SOE and his faith in European resistance provided a beacon of hope, not a mirror of self-delusion, for those who lived in the darkness of Hitler's rule.

One of SOE's greatest handicaps was the hostility of SIS. Menzies had lost control of Section D, and Churchill did not even consult him about appointing Dalton. This was deliberate. SOE was a new and unorthodox secret service wedded to a doctrine of subversion whose job was to cause mayhem and disorder. SIS was charged with the quiet collection of secret intelligence. These were often contradictory missions and Churchill judged that SOE required a different sort of leader. Besides, Menzies had an even more vital role to play in the secret war: to provide Churchill with top-grade 'Ultra' intelligence now coming on stream from the code-breakers.

I I

Ultra

Two days after the raid on Tyler Kent, as Churchill discussed strategy with the French High Command in Vincennes, code-breakers at Bletchley Park sixty miles north-west of London made a historic breakthrough. Thanks to the Poles and French they had for months been attacking radio messages enciphered on the Enigma machine used by the German armed forces and the *Abwehr*, SS and railways. On 22 May 1940 they broke the main *Luftwaffe* operational key; from then on they read it daily until the end of the war. While they wrestled continuously with changing keys and new German techniques, Ultra firmly established itself as the single most important source of secret intelligence about the enemy.

Ultra dazzled Churchill. 'The magic and the mystery', writes Ronald Lewin, 'had an irresistible appeal for the schoolboy working inside a great man.'[1] Here was the authentic voice of the enemy unaware he was being overheard. Churchill had delighted in SIGINT since writing Room 40's charter in 1914. Now, a World War later, he described the Ultra transcripts as his 'Golden Eggs'. Remaining true to a lifetime's habit, he demanded deliveries of the raw intercepts direct from Bletchley Park. Only thus was he able to see, touch and feel the enemy, and act as his own intelligence officer. This way, too, he could be sure that no contemporary 'Blinker' Hall was manipulating affairs behind his back.

Ultra was a source of undreamed-of power; knowledge to use against the unsuspecting enemy, but also a trump card in his negotiations on strategy with his Chiefs of Staff and allies. For Churchill as war leader was instinctively a strategist: his entire being, his sense of history, not to mention his determination to avoid the disastrous military/civilian split of the First World War, demanded that he act as Britain's supreme strategic co-ordinator. To impose his own vision he made himself Minister of Defence, chaired the Defence Committee of the Cabinet, and set up his own military secretariat to liaise with the Chiefs of Staff.

One of his first demands was to order a thorough review of how intelligence related to operational and strategic decisions. In response the Chiefs of Staff made the Joint Intelligence Committee exclusively responsible for assessing operational and strategic intelligence, strengthened its secretariat, and ordered it to distribute its papers directly to Churchill, the War Cabinet and the Chiefs of Staff. By the end of the war the Committee had become the apex of the intelligence system. Progress was not always smooth and it was not always right. It was notably slow to foresee Hitler's attack on the Soviet Union, failed to predict the 1944 Ardennes offensive and consistently overestimated the impact of the strategic bombing offensive against Germany. But for all its faults it provided Britain with a more efficient and effective centralised intelligence system than Hitler's Germany, Stalin's Russia or Roosevelt's United States.[2]

This was largely due to Churchill's persistent demands for good intelligence, which sometimes took surprising and exasperating form. How was the Intelligence Service (Naval, Military and Air) organised, he asked his Chiefs of Staff in November 1940, and who was the person responsible for it? There was, of course, no single service intelligence directorate or supremo – a fact that Churchill well knew – but such provocative questions guaranteed the constant improvement of the intelligence machinery. One powerful reason the service chiefs worked harder to strengthen the Joint Intelligence Committee was to protect themselves against Churchill. Knowing the power of intelligence, Churchill wanted his own direct access to it. The Bletchley Park breakthrough on Ultra was a magnificent and fortuitous coincidence which he seized with alacrity. In August, as Ultra was providing the first detailed order of battle of the *Luftwaffe*, and the Battle of Britain was being fought over the fields of Kent and Sussex, Churchill demanded that all intelligence reports should be sent to him via his faithful Desmond Morton. 'I do not wish such reports ... to be sifted and digested by the various Intelligence authorities', he instructed his personal Chief of Staff. 'Major Morton will inspect them for me and submit what he considers of major importance. He is to be shown everything, and submit authentic documents to me in their original form.' A month later Menzies received a similar instruction about Ultra from Morton himself. He was to send daily all messages to Churchill in a locked box clearly labelled THIS BOX IS ONLY TO BE OPENED BY THE PRIME MINISTER IN PERSON. Once read, Churchill would send the reports back to Menzies who soon manoeuvred Morton aside.[3] 'As the web of Ultra started to extend', notes Lewin, 'Menzies was at its heart, like a rather elegant and inoffensive spider commanding every point of growth.' It was he who had received from French intelligence the Polish replica of the German Enigma machine that proved so crucial in the breakthrough. Thereafter he made himself the indispensable link between Ultra and Churchill, insisted on inter-service co-operation at Bletchley Park, and guarded Ultra's basic security.[4]

Thus began an extraordinary and unprecedented supply of intelligence that continued until victory. A secret revealed to the world only thirty years later, accounts of its use have focused almost exclusively on its military and strategic content. But the 1993 release of the intercept files passed to Churchill revealed that diplomatic material formed up to one-third of the total. Known as 'BJs' (for Blue Jackets, the colour of the file cover), they included the diplomatic traffic of enemies such as Italy, Japan and, after 1943, Germany itself; and neutrals like Ireland, Turkey, Spain, Portugal, Vichy France, most Balkan and South American countries, and (until December 1941) the United States. Allies, too, were targeted, including de Gaulle's Free French, the Dutch, the Czechs and other governments-in-exile. All, if not of immediate practical value, helped build up a complete picture of how friends, enemies and the uncommitted saw the unfolding of the war. Of particular value were the intercepts revealing the views of the Japanese ambassador in Berlin, a crony of von Ribbentrop who kept Tokyo fully informed of the state of the German armed forces and the thinking of its war chiefs. Churchill also pored over Turkish intercepts in his vain attempts to entice Turkey into the war. All the material he read with scrupulous care for the BJs helped illumine the wider geopolitical scene.[5]

Each daily batch Churchill received contained a cover note from Menzies highlighting some item or other that would in turn spark a response or query from Churchill. Frequently Menzies delivered the files personally to 10 Downing Street in a buff-coloured box that only Churchill could open with a key from his own key ring. When he travelled abroad, special measures existed to get the intercepts to him. He was demanding. 'Why have you not kept me properly supplied with news?' he complained to Menzies from his 1943

<u>MOST SECRET</u>.   September 27, 1940.

Dear C,

    In confirmation of my telephone message, I have
been personally directed by the Prime Minister to
inform you that he wishes you to send him daily all
the ENIGMA messages.

    These are to be sent in a locked box with a
clear notice stuck to it "THIS BOX IS ONLY TO BE
OPENED BY THE PRIME MINISTER IN PERSON".

    After seeing the messages he will return them
to you.

                Yours ever,

                Desmond Morton

P.S. As there will be no check possible here,
      would you please institute a check on receipt
C.   of returned documents to see that you have
      got them all back.

Churchill orders 'C', through Desmond Morton, to send him
Enigma (Ultra) messages daily.

Casablanca meeting with Roosevelt. 'Volume should be increased at least five-fold and important messages sent textually.' No doubt he wished to dazzle the President with an impressive clutch of eggs.

Churchill was rightfully obsessed with Ultra's security. To disguise its origin he first concocted the cover name 'Boniface' to suggest a human source such as a secret agent. As with Room 40's product a quarter of a century before, he also insisted that circulation be strictly limited to a tiny inner circle of those who really needed to know. 'The wild scattering of secret information must be curbed', he ordered. A list drawn up for his approval revealed thirty-one recipients, eleven of whom were Cabinet ministers including Labour members and the First Lord of the Admiralty, but not SOE minister Hugh Dalton. On at least one occasion he was so concerned about Ultra material appearing in an official document that he ordered its immediate withdrawal. 'The copies circulated are to be destroyed by fire under the supervision of the Defence Committee', he instructed. On another, when Ultra was sent to him at his Atlantic Charter meeting with Roosevelt off the Newfoundland coast, he specified – no doubt remembering the 1914 *Magdeburg* affair – that it should be sent in a weighted box so that if the aeroplane crashed it would immediately sink. Intercepts were withheld from military commanders until Special Liaison Units could ensure the tightest security at regional-command level. Some commanders at first discounted Ultra's value precisely because it was disguised as coming from a human source and hence unreliable. For that reason the designation 'Ultra', initially used only by the Royal Navy, eventually replaced 'Boniface'.[6]

One of the earliest Ultra pay-offs was the discovery of the *Knickebein* ('dog leg' or 'crooked leg'), a radio beam system to guide *Luftwaffe* bomber pilots precisely to their target. Churchill, as always, took a personal interest in the scientific Wizard War, as he termed it.

On 12 June, the day he listened to the French High Command dismally talk of abandoning Paris, R. V. Jones, a young scientist working with the SIS Air Intelligence staff, dropped in to visit the head of the RAF 'Y' (intercept) service and was handed an apparently meaningless Ultra message that referred to *Knickebein* and gave a map reference for Retford in Lincolnshire. To Jones it confirmed what he had already suspected; additional intelligence clinched the theory. Jones informed Lindemann (who had been Jones's tutor at Oxford), who immediately told Churchill. In turn the Prime Minister instructed

Archie Sinclair to explore further. The 28-year-old Jones found himself summoned to 10 Downing Street.

It was the day that the French were handed surrender terms and the mood around the Cabinet table was palpably grim. Churchill was present with his top scientific and Air Force advisers, but no secretaries were present and no minutes kept. Jones spoke succinctly for twenty minutes. When he finished, Churchill asked Jones what could be done. The first thing, he replied, would be to confirm the beams' existence by flying along them. Countermeasures ranging from 'bending' to jamming the beams could then be put into place. 'I gave all the necessary orders that very day in June', recorded Churchill, 'for the existence of the beam to be assumed.' That evening a British reconnaissance flight enabled work on countermeasures to begin. Contrary to widespread belief, the British did not 'bend' the beams. Instead, the RAF created a special unit, No. 80 Wing, to jam them – although on occasion this had the incidental effect of bending them and causing German bombers to release their bombs off-target. The purpose-built jamming machine was code-named Aspirin, and it caused a considerable headache for the *Knickebein* system.

The Germans then counter-attacked. Early in September Jones again confronted a mysterious Ultra intercept, this time referring both to beams and an 'X-Gerat' being fitted to bombers of Kampf Gruppe 100. This turned out to be an alternative system to *Knickebein*, and once more a jamming system, code-named Bromide, was devised. Late in October code-breakers finally deciphered Enigma messages revealing targets and beam frequencies. By this time KG 100 had become a pathfinder force, using the X beams to drop incendiaries to guide the following bomber formations. Coventry was one of their first targets.

Coventry remains the focus of a persistent story about Churchill's ruthless determination to protect the Ultra secret. The city was victim of a massive bombing raid on the night of 14 November 1940 when over 500 civilians were killed, the city centre flattened and the cathedral destroyed. Although Ultra had revealed the target, so this tale runs, Churchill refused to allow countermeasures for fear of revealing to the Germans that their ciphers had been broken. Coventry, in short, was deliberately sacrificed to preserve Ultra. This is a myth. Three days before the raid Ultra revealed *Luftwaffe* plans for a major operation code-named Moonlight Sonata, but gave no date or targets. On the basis of other intelligence, analysts – mistakenly –

concluded they would be in London or the Home Counties. It was only four hours before the raid, through interception of the beams, that Coventry was finally identified. Its defences had already been strengthened following previous raids, an alert immediately went out and the Germans were met with intensive anti-aircraft fire. It was the scale of the attack and shortcomings in defence, including incorrect settings of the Bromide jamming countermeasures, not some deliberate plan, that produced the heavy losses.

Churchill believed that the target for Moonlight Sonata was London. After lunch at 10 Downing Street he clambered into his car for the drive to Ditchley Park where he planned to spend the weekend. As he was leaving, one of his private secretaries handed him a top-secret message from Bletchley Park revealing that it was target day. He ordered the car to return to Downing Street and told members of his junior staff to take shelter in a nearby Underground station. 'You are too young to die', he said. He spent most of that evening on the Air Ministry roof waiting to watch the raid that never came. The intelligence identifying Coventry as the target failed to reach him, or if it did he assumed that London would also be hit. There is no convincing evidence to support the idea of a deliberate sacrifice; plenty exists to refute it.[7]

Churchill's insistence on seeing all intercepts soon proved impracticable. Over the winter of 1940/41, when the code-breakers had achieved mastery only over the *Luftwaffe* key, the daily number of intercepts climbed to about 250 and Menzies had to select the best of the 'Golden Eggs' to show him. By mid-1942 the total was at least 3,000 a day. This did not deter Churchill from using them to surprise or outflank his Chiefs of Staff, a habit which became a menace when not controlled. Raw intercepts required expert assessment and an appreciation of the total intelligence picture had to be built up not just from Ultra but also from photo-reconnaissance, prisoner-of-war interrogations, secret agents' reports, and so on.

Enhancing the power and assessment capacity of the Joint Intelligence Committee was the Chiefs of Staff best defence against Churchill's attempts to be his own intelligence officer. In the spring of 1941 they finally gave the Committee a fully adequate staff and the individual service intelligence branches began to provide the Chiefs with bulletins, often three or four times a day, based on the latest Ultra material. From then on the Chiefs were able to battle with Churchill on a level playing field.

If information was power, Ultra represented special potency and influence. Churchill rationed it carefully, and with calculation and deliberation. In the summer and autumn of 1940 this dictated his response to intelligence about Hitler's invasion plans.

Hitler signed his Führer Directive No. 16 ordering planning to begin for Operation Sealion, the invasion of Britain, on the same day that Churchill ordered Hugh Dalton to set Europe ablaze. Three days later, to members of the Reichstag assembled in Berlin's Kroll Opera House, he predicted that Churchill would shortly flee to Canada and made a final peace offer. This was firmly rejected by Lord Halifax on the BBC. The next night Hitler watched a performance of *Götterdämmerung* at Bayreuth.

Despite Ultra, intelligence about Hitler's plans was partial and opaque. That he was assembling an invasion fleet was apparent, but where and when – and indeed if – the attack would come was the subject of intense debate. The special unit set up in May 1940 to co-ordinate invasion-related intelligence, the Combined Intelligence Committee, offered mostly alarmist predictions. Fears subsided during the Battle of Britain but peaked again early in September when GHQ Home Forces issued its 'Cromwell' alert of imminent invasion and church bells rang out across the southern counties. Three days later Churchill warned on the BBC that invasion could come at any time. 'We must regard the next week or so as a very important period in our history', he stirringly told the nation. 'It ranks with the days when the Spanish Armada was approaching the Channel, and Drake was finishing his game of bowls; or when Nelson stood between us and Napoleon's Grand Army at Boulogne.'

Churchill's public rhetoric, however, contrasted with his inner conviction. The operational demands of a successful invasion made him sceptical, and his Fifth Column fears had abated. 'Those who knew most', he later admitted, 'were least scared.' The Royal Navy still enjoyed command of the seas and the Royal Air Force enjoyed air superiority. So while keeping an eagle eye on Britain's defences, lauding the Home Guard and scrutinising Ultra daily, he privately discounted the gloomiest intelligence predictions.

Once again, however, Churchill found it useful to manage the information. In July – before Hitler even issued his directive – he held a lively discussion at Chequers with his top military advisers where he bluntly admitted that anti-invasion preparations were serving a useful purpose. The creation of the Home Guard was relieving burdens on the Army's regular divisions and keeping up domestic morale. Invasion fears also helped to maintain his political health. He was still held suspect by many Tories, and not until Chamberlain's death did he take over leadership of the Tory Party. Who, at a time of supreme national danger, would dare rock the boat?

His attitude changed little even after photo-reconnaissance showed invasion barges dispersing and Ultra revealed the *Luftwaffe* disbanding a special unit attached to the invasion forces. Group-Captain Frederick Winterbotham, the SIS air liaison officer with Bletchley Park, captured the high excitement when Ultra revealed that Hitler had authorised the dismantling of invasion equipment at Dutch aerodromes. Both he and Menzies arrived at a meeting in Churchill's underground war room to find the Chiefs of Staff already fully briefed and relief on their faces. Then Churchill appeared and read out the signal. He smiled broadly, lit up a cigar and suggested they all take a little air. Above, a German air raid was in full force, fires lighting the sky, and the sound of exploding bombs and rattle of the AA guns filling the air. 'It was a moment in history to remember, and above the noise came the angry voice of Winston Churchill', recalled Winterbotham, ' "By God, we will get the B's for this".'[8]

Churchill was not about to let others in on the secret just yet. His strategic gaze was directed across the Atlantic. As he told the War Cabinet, 'If the picture was painted too darkly, elements in the United States would say that it was useless to help us, for such help would be wasted and thrown away. If too bright a picture was painted, then there might be a tendency to withhold assistance.' Even as analysts at the Combined Intelligence Committee were finally conceding that the invasion risk was reduced and Churchill informed the Defence Committee that it was relatively remote, he did not reveal this to Roosevelt. 'I cannot feel that the invasion danger is past', he told the President in late October. 'We are maintaining the utmost vigilance.' Two days after the crucial Ultra intercept he reminded Roosevelt yet again of the difficulty of defending Britain against sixty German divisions and a powerful air force. To Mackenzie King, his principal Dominion ally, he confessed that he did not intend to let the Americans view too complacently the prospect of a British collapse.[9]

This selective use of invasion intelligence was particularly apparent in his dealing with Roosevelt's personal envoy Harry Hopkins when he arrived in London early in January 1941 for a first-hand view of Britain's needs and morale. This frail Iowan had directed the New Deal Emergency Relief Administration and was Roosevelt's troubleshooter, a man so close to the President that he lived in the White House as part of the family household. He arrived in Britain with the self-defined mission of being the 'catalytic agent between two prima donnas'. His mission was a brilliant success and a milestone in the history of the Anglo-American special relationship.[10]

Churchill shrewdly treated him as visiting royalty, inviting him to Chequers for relaxing weekends, and introducing him to Britain's top military and political figures. He was also taken on gruelling tours to demonstrate the nation's war-winning grit. They surveyed the gun batteries at Dover and gazed across the Channel at Hitler's Fortress Europe; they visited the Blitz-ravaged streets of Southampton and Portsmouth, and toured the dockyards of Tyneside; and Churchill's own wartime crony Brendan Bracken drove Hopkins out to Blenheim Palace, Churchill's birthplace and seat of the Dukes of Marlborough. They even travelled in a blizzard to Orkney and the great naval base of Scapa Flow to see off Lord Halifax on his way to take up his post as ambassador in Washington aboard Britain's most recently launched battleship, the *King George V*.

Throughout, Churchill talked endlessly of the war, of Britain's needs and of the way ahead. Hopkins was powerfully impressed. Churchill, he reported to Roosevelt, was *the* government, the one and only person he needed to have a full meeting of minds. In turn his personal amiability swept away fears that Roosevelt was less than wholehearted about supporting Britain. 'We're only interested in seeing that that Goddam sonofabitch, Hitler, gets licked', he drawled after dinner one evening at Ditchley Park, Churchill's alternative wartime country retreat. Such sentiments quickly endeared him to Churchill. 'He is an indomitable spirit', Churchill told Roosevelt, 'I rate him high among the Paladins.' Genuinely moved by Hopkins's death in 1946, Churchill described him as 'a soul that flamed out of a frail and failing body . . . a crumbling lighthouse from which there shone the beams that led great fleets to harbour.'

Yet not all secrets are shared with friends. The day after the Ditchley Park dinner Churchill received an Ultra report that further confirmed the unlikelihood of invasion. German wireless stations linked with the headquarters responsible for *Luftwaffe* equipment in Belgium and Northern France would no longer be manned after

10 January. Churchill kept this carefully to himself. In Hopkins' company he continued to stimulate invasion talk, and at Chequers one evening enthralled him with an account of 'Victor', an anti-invasion exercise taking place on the south coast. If the Germans landed and he had to deliver a speech, Churchill joked, he would begin by saying that 'The hour has come: kill the Hun'. But later that night he privately confessed to Sir John Colville that he did not believe the Germans would invade.

Hopkins was convinced by the invasion talk. In his thirty-page cabled account to Roosevelt of his stay in Britain he declared that the single most important observation he had to make was that almost everyone thought invasion imminent. No matter how fierce the attack, Hopkins promised, the British, led by the defiant Churchill, would resist and defeat it. 'I cannot urge too strongly that any action you may take to meet the immediate needs here must be based on the assumption that invasion will come before May 1. If Germany fails to win this invasion then I believe her sun is set.'[11] Churchill had generously gifted Hopkins his rhetoric. He had obviously not shared Ultra with the President's confidant.

Ultra was one of the few valuable assets now left to Britain in its bargaining with the Americans. Payment for the war had already exhausted British assets and Roosevelt's Lend-Lease Bill had yet to pass through Congress. All the more valuable, therefore, were British scientific and cryptanalytical secrets which could be traded for American know-how. Churchill was no dupe of Roosevelt wantonly disposing of assets for the sake of a sentimental vision of the special Anglo-American relationship. His vision certainly sprang from deep personal roots and its realisation during the Second World War provided the cornerstone of Western defence during the Cold War. At its heart lay agreements about intelligence exchange and co-operation unique in the annals of the secret world. But while they were facilitated and burnished by personal diplomacy, they were built on the solid foundation of hard-nosed bargaining and mutual need. A small American mission that arrived in Britain just three days before Hopkins returned to Washington proved the point.[12]

The *King George V* arrived back at Scapa Flow in February 1941 in a snowstorm. On board were four wooden crates accompanied by four American officers who were transferred to a British cruiser which made its way to the port of London. Here they were met by car and driven north through the blacked-out capital. Eventually they reached a red-brick Victorian mansion where they were effusively welcomed before being whisked off to a nearby country estate for a good night's sleep.

The first American cryptanalysts had arrived at Bletchley Park. They had been greeted at the London docks by Commander Edward Travis, its second-in-command; their welcoming host was its Director and Room 40 veteran, Alastair Denniston. Carefully packed in the crates was a reconstruction of the Japanese diplomatic cipher machine, known as 'Purple'. In exchange for handing it over to the British the Americans were to be given the secrets of Ultra. Head of the American mission was Abraham Sinkov, a US Army reserve officer and mathematical cryptanalyst.

The path that led to Sinkov's mission had not been straight or smooth. Inter-war relations between Britain and the United States had often been difficult and intelligence co-operation was limited. It took the collapse of France and the London Blitz – captured dramatically in photographs, broadcasts and newsreels for American audiences – for US opinion to swing decisively Britain's way. Churchill had worked on Roosevelt assiduously, and in August 1940 London and Washington had agreed in principle to a 'free exchange of intelligence'. It was an unprecedented step that saw ambassador Joseph P. Kennedy receiving a regular bulletin based on the JIC's daily intelligence summary.

Shortly afterwards a British mission to Washington headed by Professor Henry Tizard saw the two nations exchanging top-level secrets on such items as submarine-detection devices and radar. In October the US naval observer in London met with the Director of Naval Intelligence and the SIS Director to begin proper cryptanalytic negotiations. Some time in December, shortly before Hopkins's arrival, the text was signed of a still-secret and unacknowledged Anglo-American pact on sharing cryptographic secrets that opened the way for Sinkov's mission.

Throughout, Churchill was positive but cautious. Early promises made by Roosevelt to provide London with State Department and consular intelligence produced little of value, and the Tizard mission exposed the weaknesses in American military technology. Churchill insisted that the process be an exchange, not a one-way street. 'Are we going to throw all our secrets into the American lap?' he asked. 'If so, I am against it. It would be very much better to go slow, as we have far more to give than they.' Generally speaking, he confessed, he was in no hurry to give up British secrets until the United States was much closer to coming into the war. 'I expect', he added, 'that anything given to the United States Services, in which there are necessarily so many Germans, goes pretty quickly to Germany in time of peace.'[13]

This directive, with its curious blend of hard-nosed *realpolitik* and Fifth Column paranoia, sometimes meant applying the brakes. In November 1940 Churchill instructed that the amount of intelligence passed to the American military attaché in London, including disguised Ultra material, should be cut back. Future reports, he ordered, should become less informative and 'padding should be used to maintain bulk'. This was partly a matter of security. It also reflected his desire not to give away secrets without exacting a price.

By the time Sinkov arrived at Bletchley Park the Americans finally had something serious and substantive to offer. This was MAGIC, the name given to intelligence derived from the Purple machine used to encipher Japanese diplomatic traffic, the breaking of which was the triumph of William F. Friedmann, the brilliant chief cryptanalyst of the US Army Signal Intelligence Service. The task was completed in October 1940 with the construction of a duplicate Purple machine. By the spring of 1941 the Americans had built four of them. One was in the Philippines, two were in Washington – and the fourth was the machine delivered by Sinkov to Bletchley Park.

Now Churchill could afford to be more generous. But only when the Bletchley Park experts and the Chiefs of Staff had fully satisfied themselves as to Purple's value – some three weeks into Sinkov's visit – did he finally agree to tell the Americans about the progress made in probing German armed forces cryptography.[14] The Americans departed having gained invaluable insights into the successful marriage of cryptanalysis and intelligence assessment, as well as interservice co-operation, that characterised Bletchley's work and contrasted so vividly with the grim Army–Navy rivalry causing endless roadblocks in Washington. They also visited intercept stations and the Admiralty's Operational Intelligence Centre in London, and reached agreement on the security procedures to be used for exchanges across the Atlantic. However, they did not receive an Enigma machine in exchange for Purple, were not told about the development of the British *bombes* (electromechanical deciphering machines), and when Bletchley Park finally broke into the German naval cipher in May the news was withheld. Exchanges were still on a need-to-know basis and the Americans were not yet full military partners. Churchill had set definite limits.

Highly though he regarded Ultra, Churchill did not lose his enthusiasm for more conventional 'humint' (human intelligence), or espionage. In the presence of General Sikorski, leader of the Polish government-in-exile, he ordered Desmond Morton to take Stewart Menzies to see Colonel Mitkievitch, who ran Polish Naval, Military and Air Intelligence networks in occupied Europe, and strike a deal on Polish–SIS collaboration that proved invaluable for wartime intelligence.[15] And as soon as Churchill became Prime Minister he had initiated an extraordinary intelligence operation in Spain involving a man who was to remain a trusted contact for the next decade.

Captain Alan Hillgarth was the swashbuckling type so attractive to Churchill. 'Adventure', Hillgarth once lamented, 'was once a noble appellation borne proudly by men such as Raleigh and Drake ... [but is now] reserved for the better-dressed members of the criminal classes.'[16] He did his best to compensate for the lapse. The son of a Harley Street surgeon, he entered Osborne Naval College aged 8, was wounded as a midshipman at the Dardanelles, got caught up in the 1920s Rif rebellion in North Africa, prospected for gold in Bolivia and had a successful stab at writing adventure novels. In 1933 he was appointed British Vice-Consul in Majorca, where Churchill met him on the eve of Franco's rebellion. In the Civil War Hillgarth's astute diplomacy won the admiration of Captain John Godfrey who as Director of Naval Intelligence made Hillgarth naval attaché in Madrid. Revelling in Iberian cat-and-mouse games with German intelligence and brilliantly tracking U-boats in Spanish waters, he was soon entrusted with the delicate mission of co-ordinating the clandestine activities in Spain of SOE, SIS and Naval Intelligence. Churchill was determined to keep Spain, guardian of the western Mediterranean, neutral, and sent Sir Samuel Hoare as ambassador to Madrid to ensure just that. But for judgements on Spain Churchill relied more on Hillgarth, a man who shared his wavelength and knew Spain from long experience. Meeting with Hillgarth at the end of May 1940, Churchill charged him with an urgent and top-secret mission: to keep Spain out of the war through a campaign of bribery and corruption. To finance it Churchill arranged with Stewart Menzies and the Treasury to deposit $10 million in an account of the Swiss Bank Corporation in New York.

The main target of Hillgarth's efforts was the Spanish Army.

Amongst its leading officers were key figures prepared to resist any move by General Franco to side with Hitler. The crucial intermediary was his trusted contact Juan March, a wealthy multimillionaire Majorcan banker and owner of oil and shipping companies who had financed Franco's 1936 rebellion. March had rendered services in Spain for British intelligence during the First World War and with Hillgarth's help resurfaced in London in 1939 with an offer secretly to buy up interned German shipping and provide munitions. Treasury officials regarded him as a self-serving scoundrel but Churchill was keen to use him. 'The fact that . . . he made money by devious means in no way affects his value to us at present', he curtly remarked.[17] March's role in the bribery scheme was to pay out the money in instalments to chosen officers prepared to resist any moves by Franco to enter the war. By late June 1940 the scheme was already showing results. Of the $10 million, at least $2 million went to General Antonio Aranda Mata, Commander of the Spanish War College who was expected to head the Spanish armed forces if Franco were toppled. Whether or not the 'Knights of St George' – British gold sovereigns – rode to war accomplishing anything more than enriching those who would have argued the neutrality case anyway remains a moot point. It may even be that as their pockets filled the Spanish generals lost any enthusiasm they had once possessed for provoking Franco's anger. But Churchill clearly thought the operation worth the vast expense and the handling of the affair deepened his trust in Hillgarth's judgement and skill. 'I am finding Hillgarth a great prop', he told Hoare. Sir Alexander Cadogan, the permanent under-secretary at the Foreign Office, thought Hillgarth a charlatan, but an effective one.[18] Churchill was to lean on him again when affairs in Spain took a turn for the worse.

Snagging the Americans into the secret war involved more than Ultra. Since the First World War American, British and Canadian authorities had co-operated closely on counter-intelligence about Communists and other subversives. During Hitler's blitzkrieg in the West, Roosevelt swallowed the Fifth Column idea as readily as Churchill. SIS seized on the chance to strengthen its links with the FBI and ensure security for the production and delivery of vital British war supplies. In May 1940 Menzies sent William Stephenson to New York to see what could be done.

It was an inspired choice that fully explained Stephenson's eventual knighthood and receipt of the American Medal for Merit.

Although in later life his self-promoted myth as 'Intrepid' did his reputation few favours, his personal charm and skill, backed by Churchill's support, opened important doors in Washington and New York. His mission was both to represent 'C' and to tighten British security in Canada, the Caribbean and South America. One of his first steps was to meet with FBI Director J. Edgar Hoover and ensure Roosevelt's approval for close SIS–FBI co-operation. A second was to form an alliance with William J. ('Wild Bill') Donovan, future head of the Office of Strategic Services (OSS), forerunner of the CIA.[19]

A First World War hero and wealthy self-made New York lawyer of Irish immigrant stock, Donovan has been described as America's last hero and its first director of central intelligence. In 1940, despite his 57 years, he was a man of indefatigable energy and fertile imagination whose enthusiasm for action and adventure was to place an indelible stamp on the American intelligence community. Donovan, mused movie director John Ford, who once worked for him, was 'the sort of guy who thought nothing of parachuting into France, blowing up a bridge, pissing in *Luftwaffe* gas tanks, then dancing on the roof of the St Regis hotel with a German spy'.[20] Although an anti-New Deal Republican, he was friendly with Roosevelt, a contemporary at Columbia Law School, and in the 1930s had carried out with his blessing a series of transatlantic intelligence missions. He was also a close friend of Frank Knox, Roosevelt's Republican Secretary of the Navy. Stephenson shrewdly saw that he could open a door to the White House. So when Roosevelt sent Donovan to London in the summer of 1940 to report on Britain's capacity to survive, Stephenson ensured he received red-carpet treatment. Churchill gave him time, he had an audience with the King and he met other top intelligence figures. A second visit in December 1940 went even better. Churchill gave him a generous lunch at Downing Street where he talked expansively about his strategy for defeating Germany and his concept of 'setting Europe ablaze' with the fires of sabotage and revolt.[21] Then he ensured the brilliant stage management of Donovan's fact-finding tour of the Middle East and the Balkans by having a British officer, disguised as a civilian, assigned to him and ensuring that practically everywhere he went British missions arranged his financing, travel and appointments. Back in London Donovan gave a personal briefing to the directors of service intelligence, a first for an American, and had another long meeting at Downing Street that prompted Churchill to cable Roosevelt, 'Magnificent work!' He returned to Washington determined to create a centralised American intelligence agency. In July 1941 Roosevelt appointed him Co-ordinator of Information. 'You can imagine', Stephenson cabled London, 'how relieved I am . . . that our man is in a position of such importance for our efforts.' Donovan's appointment and Stephenson's co-operation with the FBI created a euphoric mood in Downing Street jubilantly captured by Desmond Morton. Churchill knew, he recorded, that 'to all intents and purposes US security is being run for them at the President's request by the British'.[22] Five months before Pearl Harbor the still-neutral United States had joined in the building of a transatlantic intelligence alliance, the eventual dimensions of which were to surpass even Churchill's wildest dreams.

12

A Waiting Game

In his first official minute of 1941 Churchill told the Cabinet Secretary that greater secrecy should govern all matters relating to the war. The physical security of documents should be improved and the wide circulation of intelligence reports curtailed. When news reached him only hours later of what appeared to be a major security breakdown he exploded in anger.

Several months before, Louis Spears had spirited General de Gaulle away from France to London where he formed his Free French movement out of a small and disparate group of fellow exiles. Vice-Admiral Emile Muselier he made Commander-in-Chief of the Free French Navy. Captain André Dewavrin was appointed his chief of intelligence, with no previous experience in intelligence and no links with Vichy. De Gaulle preferred this. 'As soon as he was appointed', he recalled, 'a sort of cold passion for his job took hold of him'. Neither Dewavrin nor Muselier inspired confidence in Whitehall and both reinforced Churchill's reservations about de Gaulle. Desmond Morton wondered 'if we could not find a potential Napoleon from among the French Armed Forces. I doubt if de Gaulle is more than Marshal Murat'. He also dismissed Muselier, with his tinted moustache and rakish cap, as an 'adventurer'. Dewavrin, code-named Passy after the Paris Métro station, quickly became known as de Gaulle's private Gestapo and MI5 believed that he practised torture on suspected traitors at his London headquarters. Passy himself described Muselier contemptuously as 'a buccaneer guiding his brigantine toward some luckless merchantman'.

MI5's New Year's Day bombshell for Churchill was the claim that Muselier was a traitor. Their evidence – four letters written by the Vichy French air attaché in London – apparently revealed that it was Muselier (not de Gaulle with his loose talk as he kitted himself out in

Simpson's in Piccadilly) who had betrayed the ill-fated Dakar expedition of the previous autumn when de Gaulle had tried to raise his Free French flag in West Africa. Worse, Muselier was conspiring to hand over the submarine *Surcouf* to Vichy and had received money to sabotage the recruiting of sailors to the Free French Navy.

Refusing to consult de Gaulle, Churchill ordered Muselier's arrest and the head of de Gaulle's Navy was thrown into Pentonville prison. 'PM of course wants to hang him at once', observed Sir Alexander Cadogan at the Foreign Office, adding that the case against Muselier was weak and that Churchill had reacted prematurely.

He was right. It soon emerged that the affair had been a plot from within Passy's security service to discredit Muselier and that the documents shown to MI5 had been forged. De Gaulle told Spears that unless Muselier was released within twenty-four hours relations between Free France and Britain would be broken off. Churchill graciously apologised to de Gaulle in person. Muselier, somewhat bemused, returned to his desk.

Although this bizarre affair blew over quickly, it had serious consequences. De Gaulle harboured lingering suspicions that Passy's forgers had been planted by British intelligence and that it was all part of some 'dreary affair of intelligence'. From then on he resented anything to do with SIS or SOE in France. For his part Churchill mistrusted de Gaulle's claims to the exclusive loyalty of the French resistance. When it appeared that General de la Laurencie, the anti-Gaullist head of the *Libération* resistance network, could be smuggled out to London by SIS, Morton persuaded Churchill to keep de Gaulle in the dark. Churchill then agreed that Morton should carry out a secret survey of attitudes towards de Gaulle in France and the Vichy-controlled colonies. Morton argued that de Gaulle screened French resistance leaders paraded before British ministers for their loyalty and charisma, whereas British secret agents could not, for obvious reasons, break cover. Morton also demanded to see the identity of SOE and SIS secret agents and all intelligence material about France. Could he send a letter to those concerned saying he had the Prime Minister's personal authority? he asked. 'Please do so', replied Churchill.[1]

The Muselier affair also deepened Churchill's scepticism about MI5. Only the day before it presented its 'proof' of Muselier's guilt, Sir David Petrie had begun an internal inquiry prompted by

Desmond Morton's report that the security service was on the verge of collapse. Churchill's suspicions about MI5 and its tendency to get things wrong only grew as the war progressed; the one significant exception was its work in controlling double agents.

Meanwhile, Churchill delivered a powerful speech in London to representatives of occupied Europe. 'We shall aid and stir the people of every conquered country to resistance and revolt', he promised, 'and derange every effort which Hitler makes to systematise and consolidate his subjugation. He will find no peace, no rest, no halting place, no parley.' Translating rhetoric into action was another matter. Churchill told Hugh Dalton that resistance in Europe could embarrass the enemy out of all proportion to the energy expended or loss incurred, but he was interested in results and so long as SOE had little to show he kept his distance. The 'minister for ungentlemanly war', suspicious of Desmond Morton and under attack from bureaucratic rivals, became increasingly frustrated. An attempt to see Churchill in January failed, and a paper listing SOE's achievements specifically designed for Churchill's eyes was intercepted by the Foreign Office. 'It reads like a company prospectus', observed Cadogan, 'and I have a salt cellar by me when I study it.'

Finally Dalton was invited to a placatory lunch at Chequers where the guest of honour was Sir Robert Menzies, the Australian Prime Minister. Churchill was in an ebullient mood. He provoked Dalton by denouncing Labour's post-war nationalisation plans and ragged Menzies about Hitler's threat to deport 16 million Jews to Australia. Afterwards he dragged Dalton off for a long private chat about special operations.[2]

It was Dalton's first opportunity to let off steam about Whitehall hostility, demand more aircraft and extract some sign of personal approval. The results were mixed. Churchill's assurance of satisfaction lacked warmth and he was non-committal about visiting Baker Street. By contrast, he was enthusiastic about particular SOE operations. He liked Operation Claymore, an imminent Commando raid on the Norwegian Lofoten Islands in which SOE had an important supporting role. Its ostensible purpose was to sabotage fish-oil factories, round up local quislings and destroy the German garrison. Its most important aim, kept secret from SOE, was to capture Enigma material to help the code-breakers penetrate German naval ciphers.

Churchill also enthused about Operation Rubble, a recent SOE-mastered escape of Norwegian ships from the Swedish port of

Gothenberg carrying vital supplies of steel for the aircraft industry, and happily heard of a repeat performance. However, about an operation in the pipeline he was far more cautious.

This was Relator, a plan for guerrilla war in Spain in the event of a Nazi invasion. 'I want Spain kept neutral as long as possible', he insisted. He was also adamant that SOE should steer clear of any involvement with Spanish 'Reds'. Alan Hillgarth helped to reassure him. After another meeting with Churchill that January, he had returned to Spain as supervisor of SOE operations there. With strong anti-'Red' sympathies of his own, Hillgarth ensured that Churchill's instructions were obeyed.

By contrast Churchill felt no inhibitions about SOE plans for France. Operation Savanna was aimed at wiping out the pilots of the KG 100 pathfinder force in Brittany – in revenge for its role in guiding the *Luftwaffe* to Coventry. It failed only because the Germans made last-minute changes for transporting the crews to and from the airfield, but it demonstrated how easy it was to get agents in and out of France and Churchill was sufficiently impressed to recommend a medal for the mission's leader.

Churchill discussed two further items with Dalton before declaring it was time for his afternoon nap. In different ways they revealed the limits and the potential of special operations.

The first involved American attitudes towards Britain's blockade of Europe. Dalton wanted to hit the Germans as hard as possible by imposing a tight blockade, but the Lend-Lease Bill was still before Congress and Churchill had no desire to alienate Roosevelt on this or anything else, such as the freedom of the seas or policy towards neutral states. The issue had coalesced in a particularly sensitive case involving SOE the month before. Only with the opening of SOE archives in the 1990s has Churchill's part been revealed.[3]

The *Asaka Maru*, a 7,000-ton passenger-cargo ship, sailed from Japan in January 1941 bound for Lisbon and Bilbao. On board was a Japanese naval mission headed for technical discussions in Berlin. Intelligence intercepts in London quickly revealed that before returning to Japan the ship would load up in neutral Lisbon with vital war machinery including electrical transformers, Swiss-made Oerlikon guns, Italian optical goods, and consignments of strontium and cyolite (used in aluminium production) for Mitsui.

This posed a dramatic threat to the blockade. It was also political dynamite referred straight to Cabinet level. Rumours of war with

Japan were rampant and Cadogan described the affair as looking 'ugly'. The War Cabinet's Far Eastern Committee urgently instructed Lord Halifax in Washington to raise the affair with the Americans and imposed a censorship blanket. The full War Cabinet agreed that the economic warfare arguments pointed in favour of seizing the ship. But in the volatile state of relations with Japan this could spark war and would be disastrous for relations with the United States if it appeared to have been provoked by Britain. It was decided to consult first with Roosevelt and in the meantime confirm details of what the *Asaka Maru* proposed to take aboard in Lisbon.

Such, at least, was officially recorded in the War Cabinet minutes. As so often, much was left out. Churchill, who presided over the meeting, had a bolder idea. As Dalton cryptically recorded in his diary that night: 'A hint [was] dropped to me from the chair.' He hurried back to his office and issued orders. Less than forty-eight hours later he sent directly to Churchill, marked 'Immediate and Most Secret', a plan for the clandestine destruction of the *Asaka Maru*.

Code-named Operation Marchioness, it presented two options. One was to purchase a ship in Gibraltar in the name of a fictional Yugoslav, man it with a hand-picked crew including a sabotage expert, and in radio liaison with SOE agents in Lisbon fake a break-down and enter the Tagus River for repair. Here, they would 'acci-dentally' ram the *Asaka Maru*. 'Possibly', Dalton helpfully footnoted for Churchill, 'some inflammatory material might be placed in the bows of our ship.' The second option was to send to Lisbon, dis-guised as a diplomatic courier, a specially trained agent supplied with sabotage material and plenty of money to arrange for incendiary devices to be smuggled on board and limpet time bombs placed on her hull. Both options could be pursued simultaneously, reported Dalton. Should he now proceed?

Churchill was clearly tempted – this was the sort of covert action that appealed to him – but by now signs were showing that Roosevelt feared a showdown with Japan and was opposed to drastic measures. As soon as Churchill read Dalton's plan he decreed that any action against the *Asaka Maru* should be put on hold, to be reactivated if Roosevelt changed his mind – but he did not, and while the ship's return was closely monitored by British global intelligence, it safely reached Japan in April.

If Churchill's anger over the *Asaka Maru* was frustrated by

Roosevelt, the other clandestine operation he discussed with Dalton at Chequers went ahead. 'We spoke of the Danube', Dalton confided to his diary, '[Churchill] expressed supreme contempt for Prince Paul.'

Prince Paul was the Regent of Yugoslavia, his nephew King Peter being too young to assume the throne. Like other neutral Balkan states such as Romania and Bulgaria, Yugoslavia had come under increasing pressure since Hitler's triumphs in France and the Low Countries. Berlin sought these countries as satellites, Britain urged them to stand firm. SOE secretly subsidised anti-German Balkan politicians and plotted sabotage against German economic interests. The most significant was oil, extracted from the Romanian oil fields at Ploesti and transported to Germany by rail through the Balkans or on oil barges up the Danube. In January Churchill approved an ambitious SOE plan to disrupt these oil supplies by undermining the pro-German Romanian dicator, blocking the Danube at the so-called 'Iron Gates', and attacking oil tankers at Varna and Constanza. Prompted by Ultra revelations of forthcoming Nazi plans in the Balkans, Churchill told Dalton that this was the 'acid test' for SOE.

By this time Ultra had revealed that Hitler reluctantly planned to attack Greece to support Mussolini, whose October 1940 invasion of the country had been stalled by the valiant Greek resistance; now, as unfinished business, it threatened the southern flank of Hitler's planned attack on the Soviet Union. Churchill had boldly offered Athens direct military help. Prince Paul, terrified that a British move would prompt a German descent on Belgrade, condemned Churchill's offer as 'rash and mistaken'. Churchill shrugged this off. Prince Paul, he growled, resembled 'an unfortunate man in a cage with a tiger, hoping not to provoke him while steadily dinner time approaches'. Soon, as the Yugoslav Regent edged towards signing a pact with Hitler, Churchill denounced him as 'Prince Palsy'.

Churchill now learned of a secret plan to deal with Prince Paul presented by Dalton. If and when the Regent signed a deal with Hitler, SOE undercover agents in Belgrade would support a *coup d'état*. Already they were in contact with dissident senior Royal Yugoslav Air Force officers and secret subsidies were being fed to anti-government newspapers and politicians.

Churchill thoroughly approved. Three weeks after the Chequers meeting Prince Paul signed Hitler's pact and London gave the go-ahead to SOE Belgrade. Within forty-eight hours Army and Air

Force officers launched a successful coup. The Regent abdicated in favour of the young King Peter and General Simović, Air Force Chief of Staff, formed a new government. Churchill was jubilant. 'Yugoslavia has found its soul', he declared. Dalton and SOE basked in the glory of their first dramatic and visible success.

It was all short-lived. A furious Hitler savagely bombed Belgrade and invaded Yugoslavia. His troops quickly overran Greece and forced the evacuation of the British expeditionary force. Britain had lost its last foothold in Europe, apart from Gibraltar, and some of SOE's best networks on the Continent. As for the Balkans, it was the beginning of a nightmare of Nazi occupation, repression, and resistance and civil war. 'You big nations are hard', a bitter Prince Paul told the American ambassador in Belgrade, 'you talk of honour, but you are far away.' SOE's mission to redeem the debt was to become one of its most controversial tasks.[4]

Over the winter of 1940/41 the flow of intelligence from SIS, photo-reconnaissance and human sources steadily expanded. Much of it was of exceptional value. One regular high-grade human source, known as A54, was a high-ranking *Abwehr* officer whose reports on German plans and order of battle reached SIS thanks to Czech intelligence. But Churchill remained electrified by the immediacy and authenticity of Ultra. It had confirmed his scepticism about Hitler's invasion plans, exposed the inbuilt caution of his intelligence professionals, and handed him a useful tool in negotiations with Roosevelt. In March 1941 it also helped produce Britain's first great naval victory with the defeat of the Italian fleet at Matapan, a blow of psychological and practical importance in securing the Mediterranean. Elsewhere Ultra could only mitigate defeat.

Ultra began to produce intelligence about an enemy campaign in the Balkans as early as October 1940 by revealing a massive build-up of German forces in Romania. But what was the reason, who was the likely victim and when would the attack come? Ultra revealed nothing of this. Hitler's real goal was to subdue Greece and protect his southern flank for his attack on Russia, but Churchill feared a major attack through Turkey on the Middle East. Only in late December did Ultra detect German forces infiltrating Bulgaria, reveal massive troop movements through Hungary, and refer to a target date of mid-January. Not surprisingly, Churchill concluded that this was the date for an attack on Greece, a formal British ally by treaty. He ordered General Archibald Wavell, his Commander-in-Chief in the Middle East, to fly to Athens and offer immediate reinforcements.

Wavell's forces were in hot pursuit of the Italians in North Africa and he immediately challenged London's assessment of German intentions when his analysts suggested that the German move was bluff to stop his advance in Libya. This was wrong; as was London about Hitler's timing. Not until mid-February, after crucial break-throughs on the German railway and *Abwehr* ciphers, did Ultra point to a more likely date of March and to Greece as the certain victim. Churchill felt obliged to assist Britain's ally and ordered Wavell to halt his advance and divert his forces. Wavell, still sceptical, obeyed. The two men now changed roles. Flying to Athens, Wavell became more optimistic while Churchill became less so. Ultra had revealed the arrival in North Africa of General Rommel. Should the desert army be reduced after all? But Ultra revealed nothing of Rommel's plans, whereas the political commitment to Greece was clear. Early in March the first British troops left Cairo for Greece. A month later Hitler's forces attacked.

General 'Jumbo' Wilson, the commander of British forces in Greece, was provided with more than 150 Enigma messages detailing German positions and plans. One of his intelligence officers was 'Monty' Woodhouse, later to head the SOE mission to the Greek resistance and a key figure in the 1953 SIS–CIA coup against Musaddiq. Ultra's information, he recalled, was 'astonishingly accurate', but although it enabled the British to read the German Order of Battle every evening, 'we could not do anything about it, having virtually nothing to hit back with'. Sir David Hunt, later a private secretary to Churchill and then an RAF intelligence officer in Greece, was also Ultra-indoctrinated: 'I remember the impression of impending doom as we watched those overwhelming forces rolling towards us.' By the end of April Greece had surrendered and 50,000 British and Dominion troops had been evacuated, mostly to Crete.[5]

Churchill's hopes about Ultra climaxed in Crete, its first major test in a land battle.[6] To hold the island would be vital for Britain's position in the Middle East and would deliver a much-needed domestic tonic, as well as evidence to Roosevelt and Stalin of Hitler's vulnerability. By early May Ultra had provided full operational details of the German attack including an airborne landing by troops under the command of one of Hitler's favourite generals, Kurt Student. The intelligence was a gift, Churchill told Wavell, that provided a 'heaven-sent' opportunity to deliver the enemy a heavy blow. He took more personal pains over the battle for Crete than he did over any other operation of the war. In the War Room, Group-Captain Winterbotham, the SIS Air Liaison Officer with Bletchley Park, carefully explained the details on a specially prepared map.

The local force commander was an authentic Churchillian hero, 'the kind', one historian has written, 'usually found in the pages of the *Boys' Own Paper*'. This was General Bernard Freyberg, the British-born commander of the New Zealand Division. Idolised by his troops, he was, in the words of one of his subordinates, 'as simple as a child and as cunning as a Maori dog'. Churchill had been an unabashed admirer since the First World War when Freyberg became a living legend by swimming ashore at Gallipoli to light false beacons to deceive the Turks about the invasion beaches. The next year on the Western Front he won the Victoria Cross. Churchill glowingly described him as a 'Salamander': a man who thrived in the fire of battle.

Crete was lost in a matter of days and Freyberg's reputation never fully recovered. What had gone wrong? The answer lay partly in Freyberg, but most of all in the labyrinthine secrets of Ultra. For unlike the false claims for Coventry, Crete provides a solid example of a sacrifice produced by the need to protect the security of Churchill's 'golden eggs'.

The single most crucial episode in the battle for Crete, the moment at which the balance of advantage swung decisively in German favour, came only twenty-four hours after their initial parachute landings when they captured the airfield at Maleme. With this securely in their hands, they were able to fly in the reinforcements that secured their victory. With full operational details of the German attack in hand, why was Maleme not better defended?

Freyberg first learned about Ultra at midday on 30 April following a hastily convened staff conference at a villa between Maleme and Canae. Wavell, who had flown in from Cairo, had just told him of his appointment as commanding officer on the island and of the impending German attack. Strolling amongst the olive trees, he explained what Ultra intelligence was and how precisely it would reach him. Two specific orders followed. First, he was to tell no one on Crete about Ultra. Second, he was *never* to take action on the basis of Ultra alone lest the Germans suspected that Enigma was being read.

That Freyburg alone on Crete knew the full Ultra secret placed a heavy burden on him, magnified by ignorance of his own intelligence officers of the true source. The direct Ultra link with Crete was in place even before he took charge, through Group-Captain Beamish, the Air Officer commanding on the island, whose wireless set communicated directly with Bletchley Park. Urgent decrypts were sent to him using unbreakable one-time pads, then circulated to the intelligence staff who were told that it came from a spy in German HQ, Athens. Many British officers were convinced that it came from none other than the *Abwehr* chief himself, Admiral Canaris, who was suspected of being a double agent. Churchill maintained the illusion of a human source in his post-war memoirs. 'Our agents in Greece', he wrote, 'were active and daring.'

It was under this cover, and carrying the reference OL (for Orange Leonard, a supposedly human source) 302, that on 7 May, on Churchill's orders, Freyberg's HQ received the detailed summary of German operational orders for their attack decrypted just the day before. Freyberg faced a terrible dilemma. The impending attack was far heavier than he anticipated, and the weight of the attack from the air as compared to that from the sea was twice so. His initial troop deployments were wrongly placed to encounter such a massive attack aimed at the airfields, particularly Maleme. The obvious answer was to move more troops to the airfield. The intractable objection was that this would break the golden rule laid down by Wavell: no action on the basis of Ultra alone.

Churchill knew that Freyberg was receiving Ultra in summarised form. As he himself responded most enthusiastically to the original Enigma texts, he thought that seeing them would also energise Freyberg. Why not send a special officer to Crete by air armed with all the intercepts and show them to Freyberg? The messages would then be burned and the officer concerned made answerable for their destruction in case engine failure forced a landing. Freyberg himself would then make the requisite decisions without revealing the reasons to his staff.

This panicked Stewart Menzies, to whom the protection of Britain's most powerful asset was of paramount importance. To send raw Enigma intercepts to Crete on the eve of an invasion was folly. No record exists of what next transpired but 'C''s biographer claims that he threatened to resign. Instead, a compromise was reached. The Ultra-indoctrinated Acting Director of Operations at GHQ

Middle East in Cairo flew to Maleme to brief Freyberg on the latest Ultra reports. He also carried a letter from Wavell, as well as certain word-of-mouth instructions. The letter, mostly seeking Freyberg's opinions of subordinates, ended with the admonition: 'Be very careful of SECURITY. Crete is certain to have many enemy agents. Especially keep all knowledge of OL [Orange Leonard, i.e. Ultra] to yourself.' The intelligence appreciation specially emphasised that 'the entire [German] plan is based on the capture of the aerodromes'. And, most crucial of all, Wavell's oral instruction stressed again that despite the latest information *action could not be taken on intelligence derived solely from Ultra.*

Freyberg's reaction was immediate. If the rule continued to be enforced, he warned, then Crete was lost; Ultra, and Ultra alone, clearly revealed that his forces were wrongly placed to counter the German attack. The message was passed on to Wavell who the next day sent Freyberg by special messenger a letter which he burned after reading. 'The authorities in England', as Freyberg later recalled, 'would prefer to lose Crete rather than risk jeopardising Ultra.' A week later the Germans attacked. Woodhouse, who had been evacuated from Greece, breakfasted with him at dawn on the veranda of his villa. 'The sky was exquisitely blue – a perfect early summer day', he recalled, 'but momentarily looking up I was startled to see the sky full of gliders and parachutists. Freyberg did not let it spoil his breakfast. He looked up, grunted, and remarked: "Well, they're on time".' The next day Maleme fell, five days later Freyberg reported his position as hopeless, and by 30 May the battle was lost. Some 15,000 British and Dominion troops were killed, wounded or captured. Those not rounded up went on to join the SOE-supported resistance that harried the Germans until they withdrew three years later. The Germans lost 7,000 killed. They never again attempted an airborne landing against enemy-occupied territory.

This recently revealed Ultra evidence and the testimony of Freyberg's son throws extraordinary light on the fall of Crete and explains why, on the day he received Wavell's letter, Freyberg cancelled a planned move by the 1st Greek regiment to an area immediately west of the Maleme airfield – a decision that has long mystified historians of the battle and that was never explained by Freyberg, who died in 1963 still protecting Ultra's secret. Even more astonishing is that Churchill himself was apparently ignorant of the choice being made between Ultra and Crete. From everything he said it is clear that he expected Freyberg, once in possession of Ultra, to be given a free hand. Yet, as is evident from Wavell's orders, the standing order forbidding action on the basis of Ultra alone was never lifted.

To the end of his life Freyberg assumed that this was Churchill's decision. On the contrary it seems to have been made by the security-conscious Menzies *without reference to Churchill*. Only this can explain why Churchill continued to complain, after the fall of Crete, about the slowness of Wavell and Freyberg to act on the intelligence they received. What may also have confused him and others was that Middle East command had only just begun to receive Ultra and the ground rules for its use remained inconsistent. None of this entirely absolves Freyberg of blame. A reinforcement of Maleme could well have been explained – and hence Ultra protected – by reference to the conspicuous failure of the Germans to bomb the airfield, a decision that revealed an obvious intention to use it themselves. But what remains clear is that Ultra, unlike Crete and its hapless defenders, emerged from the débâcle intact and that Churchill's enthusiasm for it remained undimmed. He now rapidly turned his jaundiced eye back to Wavell and the North African desert.

By the end of April 1941 Rommel's Afrika Korps had rolled back British advances in Libya to reach the Egyptian frontier. Wavell ordered that Tobruk should be held at all costs and a series of increasingly desperate attacks prompted the German High Command to send out General Paulus to investigate Rommel's tactics. He reported that the troops were thoroughly exhausted, needed reorganisation and re-equipping, and that no further major action should be taken without careful review. The report was transmitted in the *Luftwaffe* Enigma cipher on 2 May. The text was in front of Churchill two days later. Here was irrefutable evidence of Rommel's weakness. Churchill, champing at the bit for action, had already overruled the Admiralty and sent a convoy of tanks, code-named *Tiger*, through the Mediterranean to Egypt. It arrived with the loss of only one ship in Alexandria just days after he read Paulus's message. The conclusion seemed clear. 'It is time to deliver a decisive battle in Libya', Churchill urged Wavell, 'and go on day after day facing all necessary losses until you have beaten the life out of General Rommel's army.' Wavell typically exuded caution, and it was with relief that Churchill finally learned that the offensive, code-named Battleaxe, was to begin on 15 June. Yet, like Crete, it was to belie the golden promises so temptingly suggested by Ultra. Only three days after its launch Wavell had to tell Churchill that it had failed.

Ultra did not reveal that Rommel was enjoying significant intelligence successes of his own in intercepting British Army tactical codes. Thus forewarned, he had placed his frontline troops on full alert and had continued to read British signals throughout the battle. Furthermore, Churchill's beloved 'Tiger' tanks also proved inadequate. They arrived badly equipped for desert war and were still not ready by the time Battleaxe began; nor could their armour or firepower match that of the Germans. For Churchill, who was facing mounting domestic criticism, the failure finally precipitated his removal of Wavell.[7]

13

Special Intelligence, Special Friends

For Churchill the fall of Greece and the loss of Cyrenaica in Libya caused a 'sudden darkening of the landscape'. In Parliament Lloyd George made a severely critical speech and the house divided, with an overwhelming vote of confidence in Churchill. Three days later, on the night of 10 May 1941 and a full moon, the chamber itself was destroyed in the *Luftwaffe*'s heaviest and most devastating air raid on London so far. Fifteen hundred civilians were killed and twelve thousand made homeless.

That night there also flew in from Germany the unlikely figure of Rudolf Hess, Hitler's deputy and second only to Herman Goering in the line of succession. Piloting a Messerschmitt 110, he parachuted out close to Glasgow near the family seat of the Duke of Hamilton, whom he had met at the 1936 Berlin Olympics and hoped would take him to King George VI. The astonished Duke immediately telephoned Churchill. Getting Sir John Colville on the line, he confessed that he felt he was living in an E. Phillips Oppenheim spy novel. When he finally reached Churchill, who as customary on nights of the full moon was staying at Ditchley Park, he found the Prime Minister relaxing with a Marx Brothers movie. 'Hess or no Hess', declared the incredulous Churchill, 'I am going to see the Marx Brothers.' Interrogated by Sir Ivone Kirkpatrick, a senior diplomat with German experience, Hess revealed that his mission was to negotiate a compromise peace. Its aim was a British–German alliance against the Soviet Union; its essential prerequisite the removal of Churchill.

So bizarre was this episode that mystery and speculation have surrounded it ever since, fuelled by a delay in releasing the relevant British files and Hess's 1987 suicide in Berlin's Spandau Prison to where he was consigned for life at the Nuremberg trials. The notion that it was not Hess at all who flew to Britain but a double belongs in the realm of fantasy. Only slightly less fanciful is the theory that his flight was plotted with the active connivance of the Secret Intelligence Service and Stewart Menzies himself.

Churchill told Parliament that Hess's flight was a case 'where imagination is sometimes baffled by the facts as they present themselves', and he ordered that Hess should be kept in solitary confinement and fitted by 'C' with 'the necessary appliances [listening and recording devices], to get anything worthwhile out of him – 'the public will not stand any pampering except for intelligence purposes with this notorious war criminal.' He carefully read the transcripts of an interview with Hess conducted by a psychiatrist and declared it contained 'the outpourings of a disordered mind' and read like 'a conversation with a mentally defective child who has been guilty of murder or arson'. He also privately hinted to Roosevelt that more than Hess's eccentricities were at work. If Hess indeed hoped to contact a British peace party, he told the President, then it was clearly an encouraging sign of ineptitude on the part of German Intelligence. This explains why Churchill adamantly stuck to his line, enunciated during the 1939 Venlo episode, of having nothing to do with Nazis allegedly seeking peace. He refused to see Hess, or to cover up the fact of the mysterious flight – a strategy that, had Hess been part of an *Abwehr* plot, would have badly backfired when leaked to the world.[1]

There was nothing puzzling about the reactions to the sensation. In the United States speculation about peace negotiations took on a new lease of life and Roosevelt asked for any revelations from Hess about Nazi subversive or military plans for the United States that could be used for propaganda. But Churchill had to disappoint the President. Hess shared his master's dismal opinion of Americans and said little except to disparage their likely support for Britain. Besides, Churchill preferred that Hess's adventure not be romanticised by the press, but he agreed there was advantage in letting the story run for a while to keep worry alive in Germany, and especially amongst the armed forces, about what Hess might reveal.

Otherwise well judged, the strategy seriously backfired in Moscow. Behind the Kremlin walls the always-suspicious Stalin brooded more darkly than ever over Churchill's probably treacherous intentions towards the Soviet Union.

Churchill relieved Wavell of his Middle East command on Saturday 21 June 1941. Later that day he travelled to Chequers where one topic dominated discussion over dinner that evening: Hitler's intentions towards the Soviet Union. An attack was certain, Churchill insisted, and when it came, which would be soon, he would do all he could to help the Russians. That night Hitler launched Operation Barbarossa. Along a front that stretched from the Baltic in the north to the Black Sea in the south, three Army groups punched their way through Stalin's unprepared defences and headed for Leningrad, Moscow and Stalingrad. The bloodiest conflict in European history had begun.

Churchill later recorded that he became convinced that Hitler intended to attack Russia just before the *coup d'état* in Yugoslavia when Ultra revealed the transfer of three German armoured divisions from the Balkans to Cracow. The report, he said, 'illuminated the whole Eastern scene like a lightning flash'. These divisions were not for use in the Balkans, as had long been assumed, but for the east. He had already imagined such a move by Hitler. Less than a week after the collapse of France, he had told Jan Christian Smuts, South Africa's Prime Minister, that if Hitler failed to beat Britain he would probaby recoil eastwards even without attempting invasion. Early in the New Year he again speculated that Hitler might turn east. He was remarkably prescient. Hitler had ordered preliminary studies and preparations for an attack on Russia as early as July 1940 and he issued his Barbarossa directive exactly one week before Christmas. Churchill's reading of the intelligence was better than that of his professional advisers, imprisoned as they were by the *idée fixe* that Hitler would never turn east before defeating Britain. They interpreted a massive build-up of German forces there as a war of nerves designed to squeeze Stalin. The Joint Intelligence Committee pictured the most likely outcome as a new German–Russian agreement more favourable to Berlin. Only in early June did it determine that something more vital was at stake. Finally, just ten days before the invasion, it concluded unequivocally that 'Hitler has made up his mind to have done with Soviet obstruction, and to attack'.[2]

Once convinced, Churchill immediately decided to tell Stalin. He passed on the intelligence disguising it as 'information from a trusted agent'. By making it personal, keeping it brief and ordering it to be delivered to Stalin personally, he hoped to increase its impact. But Stalin dismissed it as evidence of a Churchill plot to embroil him with Hitler and told Molotov to pass it on to the German ambassador in Moscow. Nor did he respond to several messages containing Ultra intelligence passed to him from Anthony Eden via Ivan

Maisky, his ambassador in London. One in particular, handed to Maisky personally by Sir Alexander Cadogan, ought to have warned him. Containing the precise disposition of German units massed on the Soviet border, it was dated 11 June 1941.

Stalin's faith in personal intuition bore a remarkable similarity to Churchill's, but there the comparison ends. The Soviet dictator, blinded by ideology, rejected any notion of a collegial intelligence community in which his intuition could be tested by open debate. He certainly did not lack first-rate sources. Both his ambassador and counsellor in Berlin were officers in Beria's NKVD secret police, with its networks of underground agents within Hitler's sprawling Reich. From Tokyo, Richard Sorge was regularly transmitting information to Moscow gleaned from inside the German Embassy that was chillingly precise about Hitler's intentions. Along the Soviet–German frontier local Red Army officers were able to see for themselves evidence of the military build-up.[3]

Yet to Stalin such intelligence was proof of a Western plot, probably assisted by some hardline *Abwehr* faction, to embroil him with Hitler. His chief GRU (military) intelligence adviser, F. I. Golikov, the officer personally responsible for passing the bulk of the intelligence to him – as Menzies was to Churchill – was as a survivor of the purges all too aware of Stalin's pathological paranoia. Reports that confirmed his master's suspicions he carefully classified as 'reliable'; the others he described as 'doubtful'. And while punctiliously passing to Stalin the German operational plan for Barbarossa, he noted that it was 'merely the work of *agents provocateurs* aiming to embroil Germany and the Soviet Union in war'. Only five days before the attack, a Soviet agent working inside *Luftwaffe* headquarters in Berlin reported that the assault could be expected at any moment. 'You can tell your "source" . . . to fuck off', Stalin told his controller. To the end, paranoid about Western intentions, threatened by demons of his own creation, his hands still bloodied by his massive purges, Stalin sleepwalked his fatal path to the biggest intelligence disaster of the Second World War.

About the Soviet Union's capabilities Churchill knew virtually nothing, but he would do everything he could to deny victory to Hitler. For the veteran anti-Bolshevik and former patron of Savinkov and Reilly it was a poignant irony. Twelve hours after hearing the news of Barbarossa he told the British people over the BBC that he would help Russia in whatever way he could. Frankly surveying his own attitude since the 1917 Bolshevik Revolution, he spoke dramatically of Russian soldiers guarding their homelands against the 'hideous onslaught of the Nazi war machine with its clanking, heel-clicking, dandified Prussian officers'. Any man or state fighting Nazism, he concluded, would have Britain's aid.

This assistance included Ultra.[4] Within twenty-four hours he asked for an item to be sent to Stalin. This deeply alarmed Menzies. Ultra, he told Churchill, had revealed that the Germans were breaking Soviet ciphers and thus might learn indirectly about Britain's Ultra successes. Churchill overruled him but kept an eagle eye on the ground rules that insisted information should be passed on only in paraphrased form with the source concealed. When the Director of Military Intelligence demanded that information passed to subordinate Russian commanders should never be identified as coming from British sources, Churchill scrawled a note to Menzies in red crayon: 'Does this satisfy you?' Back came the reply in the famous green ink used by 'C': 'I am satisfied, as all drafts of wires to Moscow based on Most Secret material will be submitted to me.' Even then Churchill scrutinised the Moscow traffic. In September General Mason Macfarlane, head of the Military Mission in Moscow, passed Ultra information about German concentrations in the Smolensk sector to his Moscow contacts. 'I stressed secrecy and value of source', he told London. Churchill sent an urgent note to Menzies. 'Has he told them the source?' he asked. Only when Menzies assured him did he relax.

Thus began an extraordinary intelligence-sharing operation between London and Moscow that lasted until the end of the war and for its first few months overshadowed exchanges with Washington. Once the pattern of transmissions was securely established Churchill often demanded that a particular decrypt be sent or asked why an item had been withheld. 'Has Joe [Stalin] seen this?' became a regular refrain. Occasionally he pushed Menzies beyond the limits of professional comfort. By 1942 the lack of Soviet reciprocity, as well as continuing evidence of Soviet cipher insecurity, was leading the directors of air and army intelligence to cut back on what they sent to Moscow. But the battle for Stalingrad refuelled Churchill's demands. Menzies was again unhappy. The Germans were tightening their signals security, he pointed out, and to provide the Russians with information gleaned only from Enigma could be dangerous to Ultra. 'I am always embarrassed at sending the

Russians information only obtainable from this source, owing to the legibility of many Russian ciphers', he told Churchill.[5]

The ironies of Churchill's role as guardian of Soviet security were enhanced by his support for SOE's response to Barbarossa. Dalton at first prepared for a Red Army collapse and sent two of his men to Moscow to prepare sabotage plans against Caucasus oil production in case of German occupation. Then in August he approved a mission to Moscow to negotiate with the NKVD on subversive activities. In September a remarkable agreement on co-operation between the two secret services was signed in Moscow that included geographical spheres of interest, the stimulation of guerrilla warfare, a European-wide campaign of sabotage, and the dropping by SOE of Soviet agents into Western Europe in exchange for intelligence for use by SIS.

'Our negotiations . . . in Moscow are necessarily so secret that I would prefer to talk to you about them and not put anything on paper', Dalton told Churchill in late September. Churchill listened eagerly. Between 1941 and 1944, under the generic code name Pickaxe, twenty-five Soviet agents – a motley collection of political refugees, Comintern loyalists and hardened Communists – were successfully infiltrated behind enemy lines. Churchill, according to one eyewitness account, became personally involved in one of the first operations.[6]

Code-named Pickaxe II and launched in December 1941, it was to have a tragic and macabre ending. It involved two NKVD agents, Pavel Koubitski and Pyotr Kousnetzov, who arrived by boat at Scapa in November and were driven to Beaulieu, SOE's 'finishing school', in southern England. Douglas Dodds-Parker, later to become a Conservative MP and junior member of Churchill's post-war government, was in charge of arranging SOE transport for the operation and later claimed that it arose from a direct appeal by Stalin to Churchill. One day he was taken by Colin Gubbins to 10 Downing Street, where Churchill emphasised the importance of the mission and instructed them that they alone were to know the identities of the agents. Dodds-Parker then arranged with Colonel Ivan Chichaev, head of the NKVD mission in London, to sort out details, arrange dropping points, and check out clothing and equipment.

SOE files released fifty years later reveal that their cover stories, documents and W/T sets were vetted by SIS and that two days after Christmas 1941 they were driven to Stradishall airfield close to

Cambridge. Both were of German or Austrian nationality and their destination was Germany. Kousnetzov's real identity was Bruno Kahn, a German Communist and veteran of the Spanish Civil War, who impressed his SOE handler as an agent 'who would be a credit to any country for which he worked'. Their plane encountered snowstorms over Belgium. Shortly after midnight, attempting to land back at Stradishall, it crashed killing several members of the crew and severely injuring Kousnetzov/Kahn who spent weeks recovering at Ely Royal Air Force hospital under the guise of Ivan Roberts, a Ukrainian. As for 'Koubitski', he was one of the fatalities. This caused panic in Baker Street. 'It is essential', Hugh Dalton had told Churchill, 'that no wind of the [NKVD arrangements] should get out here.' The burial of an NKVD agent on English soil was likely to cause just such a leak. So, in the chilling words of the SOE file, 'his body [was] dropped by container into the sea'. Three thousand miles away in the White House, Churchill remained blissfully unaware of this inauspicious beginning, but Pickaxe operations continued for the next three years. As late as April 1944 a top SOE official was ordering all base commanders to do everything they could to help the NKVD.

As for broader SOE plans, Churchill's bold vision was yielding to harsh reality. Three weeks after the launching of Barbarossa, Dalton sent him a plan for setting in motion large-scale and long-term schemes for revolution in Europe. But it was already clear that the Europe Churchill urged him to set ablaze was a barely smouldering damp squib. People were still numbed by defeat, many had far from exhausted the option of co-operation with the occupiers, and Britain's ability to help was minimal. Grandiose talk of secret armies was abandoned and the focus shifted to sabotage campaigns linked with Allied strategy; in the meantime SIS was given priority over SOE in demands for aircraft. Churchill's acceptance of all this makes nonsense of the notion that he demanded reckless plans for European resistance. 'Our last reports have been most bare', Dalton wrote despondently in his diary that December, 'only tales of what has not been done.'[7] Yet this was the darkest hour before the dawn. Hitler's attack on the Soviet Union had already flung the Communist parties of Europe into the defence of the Soviet homeland. Across the Continent, from Caen to Kiev, their underground forces were mobilising for resistance.

By the summer of 1941 Churchill desperately needed a victory. Domestic discontent had to be quelled, Stalin assisted and Roosevelt reassured about Britain's ability to win. Only in the North African desert, where they now faced Rommel's Afrika Korps, could British forces directly strike at the Germans. For weeks Churchill had been demanding a counter-offensive in Libya with a date as early as September. General Sir Claude Auchinleck, Wavell's successor, resisted. Reluctantly Churchill agreed that the offensive, code-named Crusader, would be launched in November. The delay meant that anything threatening this date became intolerable – including inconvenient intelligence.

On 13 October a telegram from the New Zealand Prime Minister Peter Fraser arrived in London. The New Zealand 2nd Division had suffered heavy casualties in Greece and Crete, and Fraser was determined to suffer no more débâcles. What, he asked, were the expected air and tank strengths for Crusader? Particularly in the light of Crete, where they had suffered enormous casualties, he was worried that New Zealand troops would once again lack adequate air support.

The implied threat to withdraw New Zealand's Division from the Crusader offensive touched a raw Churchillian nerve. He had already lost a battle with the Australians over the relief of their forces holed up in the besieged city of Tobruk. Yet another political dogfight over the use of Dominion forces infuriated him. It was vital to offer Fraser cast-iron guarantees of British air superiority. But at this point his own Air Force Commander in the Middle East, Air Chief Marshall Arthur Tedder, intervened with a gloomy intelligence assessment that threatened to blow everything off course.

Tedder, who was later to serve as General Eisenhower's deputy for the D-Day landings, had no special reverence for Churchill. Simultaneously with Fraser's enquiry he reported that while Britain would be superior in mechanised forces for Crusader, it would be numerically inferior in the air. This was a bombshell, for it ran counter to Ultra-based intelligence on relative Middle East air strengths. Churchill was furious. Denouncing Tedder's estimate as alarmist, misleading and militarily untrue, and determined to keep Crusader on track and New Zealand on board, he immediately dispatched Air Chief Marshal Sir Wilfred Freeman, the Vice-Chief of the Air Staff, to Cairo to sort out the facts – and, if necessary, to sack Tedder. Nor was his temper improved when only days later Auchinleck told him that he was delaying Crusader for another three weeks. 'It is impossible to explain to parliament and the nation',

Churchill fulminated, 'how it is that our Middle East armies had to stand for 4½ months without engaging the enemy while all the time Russia is being battered to pieces.'

Getting the intelligence right, therefore, was of crucial political importance. Tedder – who also had access to Ultra – estimated 520 British against 790 Axis aircraft, of which 370 were Italian and 420 German. By contrast, Air Intelligence in London estimated that on any given date German strength in Cyrenaica, the crucial operational area for Crusader, would be only 192 aircraft and of these, only 30 would be serviceable single-engined fighters, vital in any German effort to deny Britain local air superiority.

In reality, the difference between London and Cairo was not all that great. Tedder had allowed for possible *Luftwaffe* reinforcements from Russia while London had restricted its gaze to actual German strength in Cyrenaica. Besides, but overlooked in the row, Tedder had spoken of only numerical, not strategic, inferiority. But in view of the heavy political burden being carried by Crusader his bare numbers proved politically unacceptable. Air Marshal Sir Charles Portal, the more politically astute Chief of Air Staff, realised this at once. The stakes were so high, he privately signalled to Tedder, that they should both try hard to ensure that nothing likely to contribute to success had been overlooked either in Britain or the Middle East. 'The Royal Air Force, Middle East', he told Tedder, 'must go into this battle with one thought only, and that is to win it at all costs. Nothing must be held back for insurance.'

On his arrival in Cairo Freeman met with Tedder, by now fully alerted to the storm he had created in London. It was mostly a question, Freeman assured him, 'of presenting the figures.' The two men agreed a revised comparison of air strengths sufficient to satisfy both Churchill and Fraser. In Cyrenaica there would be 660 British and 642 Axis aircraft, Freeman telegraphed London. Of the latter, only 385 were serviceable, of which 207 were German. Britain by contrast had 528 serviceable aircraft. To reach these figures, Freeman had excluded any reinforcements from Russia as well as all German aircraft based in Greece or Crete. Churchill approved the conjuring trick. He had what he needed: proof of Crusader's numerical air superiority and figures to keep New Zealand in play. He sent Freeman's figures to Fraser promising 'good air superiority', and the New Zealand Division duly remained at Auchinleck's disposal.

This incident demonstrated how the higher intelligence moved up the political ladder, and the greater the stakes, the more important became its packaging and presentation. Between Tedder's and Freeman's telegrams nothing had in fact changed in the balance of Allied and Axis air forces in the Middle East. 'The only difference was', Churchill noted, 'that the first version stated that we should be inferior, and the revised version that we should be superior. It is only the kind of difference between plus or minus, or black and white.' Managing the intelligence was what mattered.[8]

Churchill's first request on returning to the Admiralty in 1939 had been to ask how many U-boats existed. Hitler, by fortunate contrast, was slow to appreciate their potential and by the summer of 1941 Admiral Karl Doenitz, his U-boat Commander-in-Chief, could muster only about thirty or so in the Atlantic at any one time. But they were still wreaking enough havoc for an anxious Churchill to tell Roosevelt in May that British shipping losses could mount to some 4.5 million tons over the next year with the rate of sinkings outpacing new construction. That very month the Bletchley Park code-breakers made their first significant breakthrough into Germany's naval Enigma. By August every signal to or from U-boats at sea was being read, Allied convoys rerouted, and the number of sinkings had plummeted.[9]

Against this more hopeful Ultra background Admiral Godfrey arrived in the United States for discussions on closer intelligence co-operation. Accompanied by his personal assistant, Lieutenant-Commander Ian Fleming of later James Bond fame, he spent several weeks in Washington reviewing the American intelligence scene. He met privately with President Roosevelt, who reminisced enthusiastically about his visit to London in 1918 as Assistant Secretary of the Navy, and about the First World War triumphs of 'Blinker' Hall and British Intelligence. British spies, he told the astonished Godfrey, had daringly crossed the North Sea in flying boats and infiltrated the German–Danish border to bring back crucial intelligence that had helped win the war. It dawned on Godfrey that what he was hearing was some fantastic cover story concocted by Hall to conceal Room 40's code-breaking triumphs from Roosevelt. Astutely he did not dis-abuse the President, for he was also busy promoting 'Wild Bill' Donovan, in whose gung-ho enthusiasm and vitality he detected an American version of 'Blinker' Hall as a central figure in America's secret war. Soon after, Roosevelt approved Donovan's plan for the creation of the office of Co-ordinator of Information 'to collect and analyse all information and data which bear on national security'. Within months Donovan had transformed COI into the Office of Strategic Services, forerunner of the CIA, with added responsibility for subversion, sabotage and guerrilla warfare.[10]

Churchill gave added momentum for intensified transatlantic intelligence exchanges in his first meeting with Roosevelt. On 4 August he left on the battleship *Prince of Wales* bound for Newfoundland. To safeguard his own informational lifeline, he carefully arranged for summaries of military and diplomatic intercepts to be sent to him by air – 'in a weighted case', he added, 'so that they will sink in the sea if anything happens to the aeroplane'.[11] Five days later the battleship entered Placentia Bay where Roosevelt was waiting on board the heavy cruiser USS *Augusta*. The meeting failed to meet Churchill's highest hopes of winning American entry into the war and its highly visible outcome, the Atlantic Charter, was a fairly anodyne statement of war aims. Yet for the President of the still-neutral United States to meet personally with Churchill and agree on so much was even more remarkable. Unofficially Roosevelt also agreed that US naval patrols would now cover the Iceland–American leg of the transatlantic convoy route. Such close operational assistance inevitably increased intelligence exchanges.

Not long after his return from Newfoundland Churchill had another meeting with Alan Hillgarth to discuss a crisis in the Spanish bribery scheme. Spanish neutrality had hung in the balance through much of 1941 and Churchill remained keen to maintain the pressure on Franco, whose position, Hillgarth assured him, was far from secure. The scheme had been boosted with additional British funds in May but the American government had suddenly thrown a spanner in the works by freezing the Spaniards' Swiss bank account in New York. Hillgarth insisted that something had to be done to keep the Spanish generals on side and Churchill decided to make a personal appeal to Roosevelt. Chancellor of the Exchequer Kingsley Wood urged caution but Churchill was adamant. 'We must not lose them now after all we have spent and gained', he stated. 'Vital strategic issues depend on Spain keeping out or resisting. Hillgarth is pretty good.' The logjam was finally broken when Anthony Eden instructed Lord Halifax to ask the US Secretary of the Treasury Henry Morgenthau as a personal favour to Churchill to unblock the account. By early November the deed was done and the account unfrozen. 'Good', noted Churchill with satisfaction, passing on his personal thanks to Morgenthau.[12]

In the meantime the *Wehrmacht* continued its inexorable advance on the Eastern Front. By September Smolensk had fallen, Kiev was threatened and German troops were approaching Leningrad. Churchill again told Stalin he would do all he could to help and that his own intelligence revealed that winter would give the Russians vital breathing space. Churchill's information again came from Ultra which had begun to reveal growing German supply problems. Subsequently Bletchley Park had provided him with overwhelming evidence that, far from his expected victory celebration in Moscow, Hitler was facing an extended winter campaign.

The day he shared this intelligence with Stalin, Churchill paid his first (and only) visit to Bletchley Park. Accompanied by Desmond Morton and Stewart Menzies he talked to a selected group of thirty or forty cryptographers gathered outside Hut 6 which worked on German Air Force and Army ciphers. He first broke the ice by cracking a joke about how innocent they all looked, then praised their work and gave concrete examples of how it had helped him. He visited a few of the huts and was introduced to key figures such as Gordon Welchman, acting head of Hut 6, and Alan Turing, the eccentric and brilliant mathematician. One of the code-breakers, apparently oblivious to the visit, was hard at work in his office when the door opened and he saw Churchill's face peering in. Overcome, the man turned grey, then green, and was promptly sick. He was certainly not around to hear Churchill's remark to Menzies as they left: 'I know I told you to leave no stone unturned to find the necessary staff, but I didn't mean you to take me so literally!'[13]

Churchill's visit boosted morale. But it did even more. Encouraged by his interest, Welchman and his deputy, Stuart Milner-Barry, together with their opposite numbers in Hut 8, decided to alert him personally to long-standing grievances about supply and staff shortages. Urgency was lent to their efforts by a crisis that Menzies brought to Churchill's attention just a month after his visit. At the beginning of October the Germans separated the U-boat cipher from the main Fleet cipher of the German Navy. While Menzies expected that the latter would cause no increased difficulties, the U-boat cipher could – although, he added, Bletchley Park had succeeded on 7 October in reading a U-boat cipher from two days before. Churchill promptly acknowledged the message.

'Give my compliments to those concerned', he asked. So he was amicably focused on the code-breakers when on 21 October 1941 – Trafalgar Day, the significance of which they knew would not be lost on the historically conscious Churchill – they wrote a letter highlighting concerns about the pace of recovery of the naval Enigma keys, the solutions of North African *Luftwaffe* material, and the staffing levels for the *bombes*. To ensure it reached Churchill himself, Milner-Barry delivered it by hand to 10 Downing Street. Churchill reacted immediately. The next day, in one of his famous 'Action This Day' memoranda, he ordered that the code-breakers should have all they want 'on extreme priority'. Within a month, Menzies reported that he had appointed a special investigator to look into Bletchley Park's administration. The results were to be felt early the next year.[14]

Churchill's Newfoundland encounter with Roosevelt reinforced a growing transatlantic collaboration in secret warfare. 'C''s man in New York, William Stephenson, added special operations to his British Security Co-ordination empire located in the Rockefeller Center and within weeks of the Newfoundland meeting a top SOE official flew to the United States to discuss how to strengthen secret-service links with 'Wild Bill' Donovan. One decision was to build a secret-agent training school that could be used by the Americans. 'We think the Americans are going to come into the war and they have to learn about all this stuff', SOE's training supremo Colin Gubbins told the camp's first chief instructor. 'Your job is to help train them and tell them everything we know.' In considerable secrecy 'Camp X' – Special Training School 131 – was constructed on an isolated stretch of the Lake Ontario shore some sixty miles east of Toronto. Its first commandant and training staff arrived on Saturday 6 December 1941. Within twenty-four hours the world, and Anglo-American relations, were transformed by Japan's surprise and devastating attack on Pearl Harbor.[15]

14

Executive Action

On the evening of Sunday 7 December 1941 Churchill was dining with the American ambassador, John G. Winant, and Averell Harriman, Roosevelt's special envoy. He was dispirited and said little during the meal. Shortly after nine o'clock he switched on his wireless and barely caught an item announcing a Japanese attack on the Americans. Only when his butler confirmed the news was he galvanised into action and within minutes was talking to Roosevelt on the transatlantic line. The President told him of the assault on Pearl Harbor and his intention to seek a Congressional declaration of war on Japan. At first stunned by the momentous news, Churchill finally grasped its import. Anticipating Germany's declaration of war on the United States, he concluded that Hitler's fate was sealed and the war was won. 'I went to bed', he recalled, 'and slept the sleep of the saved and thankful.'[1]

Did he also dream contentedly of a conspiracy come to fruition? Almost as soon as the Japanese struck Hawaii, claims surfaced that Roosevelt had withheld intelligence of the coming attack in order to ensure America's entry into the war. More recently, voices have suggested that the real Pearl Harbor conspirator was not Roosevelt but Churchill. According to this claim, Churchill's astonished reaction at Chequers was a charade that masked the secret of advanced intelligence that he concealed in order to lure the United States into war.

Central to this startling theory is the claim that, prior to the Japanese attack, British and American code-breakers working separately at the British Far East Combined Bureau at Singapore and the US Navy's Station Cast at Corregidor had broken not only MAGIC, the Japanese diplomatic cipher, but also JN-25, the Navy's operational cipher. While the American decrypts had not been sent to the White House, the British ones reached Churchill and forewarned him of the attack. This not only places Churchill at the heart of an intelligence conspiracy, it also transforms Roosevelt from a dangerous schemer into Churchill's ignorant dupe.[2]

Yet this claim, too, is flawed. Churchill was certainly capable of manipulating intelligence to maximise the chances of American participation. He had already done so with invasion intelligence and was palpably desperate for American entry. But the theory flies in the face of Churchill's own patent desire to win American help. Why would he deliberately connive at the destruction of the US Pacific Fleet? Its use to protect British Far East interests was one of the pressing reasons he desired American entry into the war in the first place. It would have made far more sense, had he possessed advanced intelligence, to have passed it on to the White House and thus both save the US fleet and earn Roosevelt's gratitude in the war that would still have occurred. But most crucially, Churchill did *not* have advanced intelligence about Pearl Harbor. It is true that British Far East code-breakers had broken JN-25 before Pearl Harbor, perhaps as early as 1939, but it was superseded by an improved system, JN-25B, in December 1940, and then again in 1941 by two successive changes, JN-25B7 and JN-25B8. These new ciphers caused British and American code-breakers extensive problems, and only about 10 per cent of their material was being broken in December 1941. For all practical purposes it was unreadable. Moreover, the Japanese maintained an extremely high level of security. Knowledge of the plan in Tokyo was restricted to a handful of people and was distributed to the task force by hand. No prior reference to the raid on Pearl Harbor went out over the air, so that even if JN-25 had been fully readable it would not have helped. 'The day of infamy' was not only an American intelligence failure. It was also a brilliant Japanese security success.[3]

It is, however, true that British and American intelligence had long been predicting a Japanese attack, *somewhere*. Relations with Japan had deteriorated in 1941 and the MAGIC intercepts unambiguously revealed that Tokyo had opted for war. But this diplomatic material revealed nothing of operational detail. London and Washington believed that Japan's most logical target would be the Philippines and South-East Asia.

So Churchill knew that a Japanese attack was coming, but the details of where and when eluded him. He told Anthony Eden that Japan would most likely launch a limited attack against neutral

Thailand before taking on Britain or the United States. The Chiefs of Staff spent most of their meetings in the two days immediately preceding the attack discussing what to do when Japan attacked some *European* possession in South-East Asia, and how then to involve the Americans. On the day before the attack, too, in one of the three personal batches of Ultra that reached him, Churchill read a telegram from the Japanese Foreign Minister in Tokyo to his ambassador in London instructing him to destroy all except certain key codes, and burn files and secret documents. 'As these are precautions envisaging an emergency', read the message, 'you should communicate this to no-one but members of your staff and you should redouble your attention to your duties and maintain your calmness and self-respect.'[4] But neither this nor other intercepts Churchill read in the forty-eight hours before Pearl Harbor contained any hint of the target.

He was, indeed, still desperately seeking it up to the last minute. Since his visit to Bletchley Park he had made personal telephone contact with the producers of his 'golden eggs'. One of them was Malcolm Kennedy, a Japanese linguist who had joined GC & CS from military intelligence in the 1930s. Against all the rules he kept a diary that still survives. Bletchley Park was on high alert for Japanese material, and twenty hours before the attack Kennedy noted that Churchill 'is all over himself at the moment for latest information and indications re. Japan's intentions and rings up at all hours of the day and night, except for the 4 hours in each 24 (2 to 6 am) when he sleeps'. When Kennedy heard the news of Japan's attack on the wireless he recorded his 'complete surprise'. If he, working at Bletchley Park, did not know in advance of Pearl Harbor, how would Churchill?[5]

American entry into the war paved the way for the greatest intelligence alliance in history, an integrated and co-ordinated system that saw British, American, Canadian, Australian and other Allied codebreakers working side by side to defeat first the German, Italian and Japanese Empires, and then, during the Cold War, the Soviet Union. But it followed on neither immediately nor unconditionally from Pearl Harbor. Doubts and suspicions about sharing precious secrets lingered on both sides of the Atlantic. On the one hand, Churchill immediately sailed to North America, and at the Arcadia Conference held in Washington agreed with Roosevelt on a 'Europe First' strategy that gave priority to the defeat of Nazi Germany and laid the foundations of a joint UK–USA war machine including a Combined Chiefs of Staff and a Combined Intelligence Committee. He also travelled to Canada, hitherto Britain's most important wartime ally, and raised loyal spirits in Ottawa by referring scornfully to General Maxime Weygand's defeatist 1940 prediction that England would 'have her neck wrung like a chicken'. Pausing, he then growled: 'Some chicken, some neck.' Yet while he was raising a chuckle in Ottawa, his intelligence chiefs in London decided that 'for the time being, our sources of intelligence and most secret methods of acquiring it, should not be divulged to the Americans'. Clearly the Chiefs of Staff were not yet prepared to go beyond the limited cryptographic sharing agreed during the Sinkov visit ten months before.[6]

Churchill was less guarded. In a midnight tête-à-tête with Roosevelt at the White House, he confessed that British code-breakers had been reading State Department ciphers but that since Pearl Harbor he had ordered the work to stop. The experience suggested, he told the President, that the two allies should co-operate closely on guarding their own cipher security.[7] Having gone this far, it seems certain that he also briefed Roosevelt about British successes against Enigma, although how much detail he revealed is unknown and whether Roosevelt fully absorbed the impact is unclear. He had been slow to grasp the potential of MAGIC, seemed uninterested in how it was produced, and showed a greater fascination for cloak-and-dagger operations than for code-breaking.

Churchill's was an extraordinary confession. He had also been instrumental in ensuring that since the summer of 1941 Washington received Ultra material about U-boat policy towards American naval units in the Atlantic. Typically, this had roused opposition from the security-conscious Menzies, who feared what might happen if Ultra texts were distributed in the United States. Equally characteristically Churchill persisted, and as American involvement in patrolling the Atlantic deepened, they received an increasing flow of Ultra. Over the following twelve months Churchill bulldozed aside the inhibitions of intelligence professionals on both sides of the Atlantic. When General Dwight D. Eisenhower arrived in Britain as Commander-in-Chief of 'Torch', the Allied landings in North Africa, Churchill personally briefed him on the secrets of Ultra. It was Churchill, overruling Sir Alan Brooke, who assigned Eisenhower the British intelligence chief who accompanied him through D-Day to the end of the war. This was Major-General Kenneth Strong, who had learned the basics of his craft in the struggle against Michael Collins's guerrillas. Soon Churchill and Roosevelt began to draw each other's attention to intercepts that caught their eye. 'Make sure that President sees this at my desire', scribbled Churchill to Menzies on a sombre analysis from the Japanese ambassador in Berlin to Tokyo on German problems on the Russian Front. 'President Roosevelt has asked that this message shall be brought to the notice of the Prime Minister', noted a Bletchley Park code-breaker on a report from the same source ruling out any prospect of a separate peace deal between Hitler and Stalin.[8]

Churchill's view that American entry into the war guaranteed victory was, in the long run, correct. In the short term, however, the Atlantic scene darkened as Allied shipping losses rose dramatically and the American seaboard and the Caribbean became, in Churchill's words, 'a U-boat paradise'. Then catastrophe was added to misfortune. On 1 February 1942 the U-boat key suddenly became unreadable when the Germans changed their cipher. Christened 'Shark' at Bletchley Park, it defied their efforts for most of the next year. Simultaneously, German code-breakers mastered Britain's Naval Cipher No. 3, enabling them to gain a highly accurate picture of convoy traffic.[9]

For Churchill these setbacks, combined with the loss of Singapore, plunged him into a profound depression. To the British people he confessed that 'many misfortunes, severe torturing losses, remorseless and gnawing anxieties lie before us', while heavy criticism in the press and Parliament forced a government reshuffle. Charles Wilson, his doctor (later Lord Moran), found him one day in the Map Room staring at the wall chart dotted with markers representing U-boats. 'Terrible', he was muttering to himself, 'terrible.' Four weeks after the loss of 'Shark' he confessed to Roosevelt: 'When I reflect how I have longed and prayed for the entry of the United States into the war I find it difficult to realise how greatly our British affairs have deteriorated since December 7.' It was with considerable relief that in March 1943 he learned the code-breakers had decisively broken the 'Shark' settings and could once again read U-boat traffic.[10]

Bletchley Park was also marking up dramatic successes in breaking other German ciphers. By mid-1942 it was producing some 3,000 to 4,000 German decrypts a day, not to mention a huge amount of Italian, Japanese and diplomatic material. Ironically, this triumph had the effect of diminishing Churchill's personal role in the intelligence war. As his marginal notes on the files reveal, he continued to consume his daily 'golden eggs' but they represented a decreasing fragment of the overall intelligence picture. This, combined with the perfection of secure mechanisms for providing Ultra in real time to local commands, made it increasingly difficult for him to make a personal mark on the intelligence effort. Ultra, in the words of Ronald Lewin, 'now seeped through many branches of what had become a highly articulated politico-military system'.[11] The best Churchill could hope for was to bring to the attention of the Chiefs of Staff, or that of a theatre commander, items that caught his eye. Less and less, however, did they effect much change in policy, and he was increasingly bypassed by the very intelligence he had done so much to promote. The days of Room 40, when he and half a dozen Admiralty officers in one room could act on secret intelligence – or indeed the anxious months of 1940 when he and his Directors of Intelligence saw most of what the code-breakers produced – were by 1942 features of an era that had already passed.

February 1942 also saw a major personnel change at Bletchley Park, an aftershock from Churchill's October 1941 response to the personal appeal from the code-breakers. Commander Alastair Denniston was replaced by Sir Edward Travis, a naval specialist with managerial skills, who was able to handle the heavy demands of transforming GC & CS into a quasi-industrial operation. In compensation, Denniston was placed in charge of diplomatic deciphering set up at a separate site in London's Berkeley Street.[12]

At SOE, too, there was significant change. Hugh Dalton left during the February 1942 reshuffle to become President of the Board of Trade and was replaced by Lord Selborne, a Conservative and long-standing Churchill loyalist. Author of a book on Post Office reform and formerly director of cement at the Ministry of Works, he seemed an implausible figure to set Europe ablaze. But he was shrewd and tough, and Churchill referred to him affectionately as 'Top'. He was a powerful asset in SOE's bureaucratic struggles. That spring, quarrels with the Foreign Office, complaints from governments-in-exile and demands for greater co-ordination of plans with strategy coalesced to threaten SOE. With deep reluctance Menzies agreed to let SOE have its own ciphers and radio organisation, and become fully independent of SIS. Desmond Morton also joined the critics, but Churchill rejected their pleas and a Joint

Intelligence Committee proposal to merge SOE and SIS was dropped. Instead, Churchill told Morton to do his best to keep the peace between his two squabbling secret services. Prudently, Selborne began to send Churchill quarterly reports on SOE's achievements. 'As my Department works more in the twilight than in the limelight', he told him, 'I should like to keep you informed regularly of the progress of the brave men who serve in it.' The series was finally released in 1992, revealing that Sir John Peck, one of Churchill's private secretaries, judged SOE's achievements 'impressive'. Churchill read them closely, and knowing his liking for detail, Selborne first highlighted total acts of sabotage, followed by the numbers of agents, containers and W/T sets dropped in each quarter. Reports on activities in Germany and Italy were followed by occupied countries. It was a chance for SOE to boast – 'SOE continues to stoke the flames' – and to complain. 'Transport', Selborne noted more than once, 'is still a very seriously limiting factor.' Churchill carefully sidelined such comments. Above all, he demonstrated unfailing and genuine concern for the fate of individual agents. Had they been rewarded for their efforts, he would ask, or did SOE know their fate when captured?[13]

After the initial shock of occupation, Europe was beginning to stir. The previous autumn the first SOE officer had penetrated Yugoslavia. Captain Bill Hudson, a mining engineer who spoke Serbo-Croat, was a man 'who might have stepped off the jacket of a boys' adventure book'. Landing on the Montenegrin coast from a submarine, he made contact first with Communist then royalist partisans who briefly formed a united front. Dalton hastened to tell Churchill that it was the first time that underground work had resulted in open rebellion against the Germans, and requested wireless sets, arms and 50,000 gold sovereigns per month. Churchill ordered all-out help, and the 'Knights of Saint George', already generously deployed in Spain, went to work in the Balkans to help pry loose from the arms of Italian soldiers valuable weaponry for the guerrillas.[14] In the spring of 1942, as Anglo-American thoughts turned to the eventual liberation of Europe and SOE received its first directive about resistance for D-Day, Churchill's imagination ran riot. His response to a bestselling novel by the American writer John Steinbeck revealed even more about his hopes for resistance.

The previous October, Steinbeck had met Robert E. Sherwood, the Pulitzer prize-winning playwright and newly appointed head of the United States Foreign Information Service, to discuss anti-Nazi propaganda. After meeting European refugees who intrigued yet horrified him with their tales of double agents, collaborators and resistance heroes, he sat down to write. Barely two weeks after Pearl Harbor he delivered a completed manuscript to his New York publisher. In March 1942, under the title *The Moon is Down*, it appeared in bookstores across the United States and in Britain.

It was a powerful fable of resistance to foreign occupation in a small European country. 'I placed the story in an unnamed country', Steinbeck later explained, 'cold and stern like Norway, cunning and implacable like Denmark, reasonable, like France.' Most readers assumed it was Norway, and Steinbeck did nothing to disabuse them. When he toured Scandinavia immediately after the Liberation he received a hero's welcome, but the key to the book's success was its universality. Clandestine editions quickly circulated throughout occupied Europe. Its story was simple. Assisted by a local collaborator, a battalion of invaders overrun a small town where they hope to keep open a coal mine. At first all is peaceful; then one of the miners impetuously kills an enemy soldier and is executed in the square. The townspeople become sullen, small acts of defiance and sabotage begin. The occupying troops become isolated and demoralised, and the mayor is taken hostage. Resistance escalates, young men flee across the sea to Britain and the mayor is taken away to be shot. In a dramatic climax he tells the commander of the enemy battalion, 'Free men cannot start a war, but once it is started, they can fight on in defeat.'[15]

Readers responded deeply to Steinbeck's assertion of democratic values, and his remarkable empathy for their predicament, hopes and fears. Churchill was amongst the most enthusiastic, his imagination particularly caught by a scene that precipitates the novel's climax. Two young men of the town escape to Britain. Before they leave, the mayor instructs them to ask for 'simple weapons, secret weapons, weapons of stealth, explosives, dynamite to blow up rails, grenades, if possible, even poison . . . Let the British bombers drop their big bombs on the works, but let them also drop us little bombs to use, to hide, to slip under the rails, under tanks. Then we will be armed, secretly armed.' A few weeks later British planes drop thousands of small explosive devices to the population of the town, where they are collected and hidden by adults and children like Easter eggs.

Churchill seized on Steinbeck's idea and asked Selborne whether similar small arms and sabotage devices could be dropped to civilian populations all over Europe. This was typically bold and visionary, but it ignored the reality of SOE policy. Its just-issued 1942 directive had stressed the importance of discouraging isolated civilian direct action for fear of provoking German reprisals. Selborne replied that such a plan should be initiated only on the eve of landings in Europe when Allied forces could protect civilians. Churchill backed down, but his hopes for European resistance remained high.[16]

Concern about reprisals did not block SOE's major coup that spring, perhaps its most sensational during the war. This was the assassination in Prague of the ruthless SS leader Reinhard Heydrich, head of the German secret police, deputy to Heinrich Himmler, and convenor of the fateful Wannsee Conference that completed arrangements for the 'Final Solution'. He was also 'Protector' of Bohemia and Moravia, where his arrival in Prague heralded a dangerously effective campaign against Czech resistance. In May 1942 he was fatally wounded in a grenade attack on his car. Hitler gave him a state funeral and the assassination made headlines around the world. Nazi reprisals were brutal and widespread. The village of Lidice was razed to the ground, its menfolk murdered, the women sent to Ravensbruck concentration camp, and the children farmed out to German families for 'Aryanisation'. Nationwide arrests effectively liquidated Czech resistance for the rest of the war.

The assassins were two Czechoslovakian agents who had parachuted into the country as Churchill arrived in Ottawa following his Christmas meetings with Roosevelt. They carefully reconnoitred Heydrich's movements and struck as he journeyed from his country home to his HQ in Hradčany Castle. Betrayed by a fellow agent turned Gestapo informer and surrounded by German troops in the crypt of a Prague church, they were killed or committed suicide.

For many years after the war the British stressed that it was purely a Czech affair. Churchill even omitted any reference to it in his history of the war. Eventually, when General František Moraveć, the wartime head of Czech intelligence, produced his memoirs, it became obvious that the British had provided crucial logistical support. But what they knew about the details of the mission, codenamed 'Anthropoid', remained unclear. SOE files released in 1994 reveal conclusively that its top officials were fully aware of the target.[17] The dramatic elimination of such a hated symbol of Nazi terror would put heart into European resistance and a spanner into Hitler's machinery of repression. Hand-picked by Moraveć for a mission decided on by him and Edvard Beneš, the Czech leader in exile, the agents were placed in the care of Major Peter Wilkinson, the head of SOE's Czech section, and his deputy, Captain Alfgar Hesketh-Prichard. Carefully isolated from other agents, SOE gave them special training, provided them with two .38 revolvers, six percussion bombs, a Sten gun and a lethal hypodermic syringe. They were dropped into Czechoslovakia from a Special Duties Squadron Halifax. 'The two agents', reported Hesketh-Prichard, 'have been trained in all methods of assassination known to us.'[18]

Colin Gubbins carefully rationed advanced knowledge of Anthropoid and kept Dalton in the dark, viewing him as a 'babbler' likely to promise Churchill what he might not deliver and thus weaken SOE's credibility. Even to Selborne, Gubbins broke the news only when it was too late to call it off. Whether Churchill learned of the target from Selborne remains unclear. Certainly he had no need to know given that assassination was one of SOE's many agreed tools and that 'plausible deniability' has always been a valued prerogative of leadership. On the other hand, given his close relationship with Selborne and the notoriety of Heydrich, the SOE Minister may have told him because Churchill was then negotiating with Molotov about a Second Front in Europe and such a coup, or even a hint of one to come, might have helped; Beneš did tell the Russians. But then again, a busted flush would have spoiled his hand. What is known is that after the fact Churchill fully approved of the killing. Wilkinson, later knighted after a distinguished diplomatic career and as Co-ordinator of Intelligence in the Cabinet Office, confirmed that news of SOE's role was received with approval by Churchill. Reportedly, too, when Roosevelt asked him if the British had been involved, he gave him a knowing wink. Gubbins definitely felt confident of Churchill's support to hope that the Anthropoid mission would be repeated elsewhere and the Germans themselves would learn what it was like to be victims of a reign of terror. Selborne described the killing as 'an act of justice' that would inspire the Czechs to renewed resistance.[19] The tragic reality was that the Czechs were the principal victims, and SOE soon found its Czech work so unfruitful that within a year it came close to shutting down this section altogether.

Meanwhile Churchill had been using Ultra to prod General Auchinleck into action against Rommel in the North African desert.

Following the Eighth Army's Crusader offensive in November, Rommel counter-attacked in January 1942, expelled British forces from Cyrenaica, and by February had advanced to Gazala, just west of Tobruk, thus deepening Churchill's black depression caused by Far East disasters and the loss of 'Shark'. Rommel resumed his offensive in May, captured Tobruk, and by July had reached El Alamein, just sixty kilometres from Alexandria, along the coast of Egypt. This marked the nadir of British fortunes in the Middle East. For Churchill, who received the news while in Washington with Roosevelt, the fall of Tobruk was not only a defeat but 'a disgrace', and he had to defend himself from a motion of censure in Parliament. The naval base at Alexandria was evacuated and the Cairo air reeked as secret documents were burned in a general panic. Reacting with customary vigour, Churchill replaced Auchinleck with General Harold Alexander and put General Bernard Montgomery, yet another veteran of old intelligence wars in Ireland, in command of the Eighth Army. Early in November, with his decisive victory over Rommel at El Alamein, Montgomery began the long march west that saw British forces enter Tunisia early in 1943.

In the halt between Rommel's advance to Gazala and his May offensive, Churchill had pushed Auchinleck to launch his own offensive. The General was cautious and would not attack without superiority in armour, but Ultra could provide little conclusive evidence. It could track Axis supply convoys across the Mediterranean because of Bletchley Park's access to the German Air Force cipher. But these intercepts revealed nothing of cargo manifests and estimates had to be made in a fog of uncertainty. Not surprisingly, as with air estimates prior to the Crusader offensive, those in Cairo and London were often at odds.

Churchill goaded Auchinleck with any weapon he could find. The most obvious was Ultra, from which he constructed a picture of a Rommel desperately short of supplies. 'What are your intentions?' he asked Auchinleck fiercely in late February, '. . . according to our figures you have substantial superiority in the air, in armour, and in other forces'. When Cairo replied that Auchinleck could not attack until June, Churchill seized on a *Luftwaffe* intercept to point out that the number of Axis tanks in Libya was barely half that which Auchinleck had previously suggested. Moreover, he argued, the enemy might reinforce faster than Auchinleck; simply waiting would not necessarily improve the position.

Yet Churchill had misunderstood this Ultra, failing to realise that the decrypt referred only to tanks in the forward area. He made a similar mistake in assuming that a further decrypt giving a number for Axis tanks represented the total available. Here he had over-enthusiastically reacted to another Bletchley Park victory, this time the breaking of 'Chaffinch', the Enigma key used by the German Army for communications between Rommel's HQ and his supply bases in North Africa. In April, a 'Chaffinch' intercept referred to 161 serviceable tanks, and Churchill asked Auchinleck to explain why only the day before he had reported some 265 serviceable German tanks in eastern Cyrenaica. 'I shall be glad to know', he asked, 'how this important correction strikes you.'[20]

Auchinleck, like Wavell before him, had to bite his tongue. Within twenty-four hours he carefully replied that Churchill's figures could not possibly be correct, and by then another 'Chaffinch' intercept had confirmed the mistake: there were over 400 Axis tanks. Churchill, not for the first time, had made the error of attempting to be his own intelligence officer. To his credit he acknowledged as much to Auchinleck. It was a salutary lesson, yet another reminder that Ultra was becoming a highly complex affair that required the subtle analysis of trained intelligence officers. One of those was David Hunt, who had arrived in the Middle East after intelligence work in Greece. He later strongly criticised Churchill's habit of reading Ultra at face value. 'He should have realised', Hunt noted, 'that although Rommel was an honourable and honest man he was not averse to exaggerating his difficulties if he thought it would speed up the despatch of reinforcements.'[21] It was a fair critique. Churchill learned from his mistake. By the end of the year he was explicitly acknowledging that in reading 'Boniface' he was dis-counting the enemy's 'natural tendency to exaggerate his difficulties'.

Having learned that playing the intelligence officer could be a mistake, Churchill conspicuously refrained from dealing the Ultra card in the momentous desert battles that culminated in Montgomery's victory at El Alamein. But he avidly read the Ultra intercepts, let his commanders know he was doing so, and ran his intelligence advisers in London ragged with his demands for the latest reports. 'The enemy is hard run for petrol and ammunition, and our air superiority weighs heavily upon him', he told General Alexander on the basis of Ultra five days after the offensive began. And when Rommel confessed to Berlin in another intercepted message that 'the gradual annihilation of the army must be faced', he immediately brought it to Alexander's attention. In a frenzy of excitement he sent for Stewart Menzies late the next evening to pore over more intercepts but sent him home when he saw that the guardian of Ultra was exhausted. Only three hours later he woke him by telephone to grill him about yet more intelligence in from the desert.[22] In marked contrast with his earlier habits, however, Churchill refrained from trying to issue operational orders, and when briefly tempted was firmly brought to heel by Sir Alan Brooke. Only once again in North Africa did he attempt to give operational orders based on his reading of Ultra, when he impatiently urged Montgomery to speed up his pursuit of Rommel, but his signals had no effect and he did not press the issue.

As Bletchley Park finally gained mastery over German North African ciphers, Churchill pushed security to its limits in ensuring that decrypts reached his commanders. Throughout the exchanges between London and Cairo over German tank strengths he had queried not only Middle East intelligence estimates but also the procedures for getting decrypts to the local command. Four days after Rommel launched the offensive that took him to Tobruk, Churchill ordered Menzies to see that Auchinleck was provided with the full texts of the German situation reports as well as the normal Bletchley Park summarised reports. 'During the present battle', he instructed him, 'messages of strategic importance giving enemy intentions are to be sent to General Auchinleck personally, verbatim'. This was a momentous decision, lifting a ban that had been in place since Ultra came on stream requiring all intercepts to be paraphrased before transmission. If Churchill could not be his own intelligence officer, then at least the raw material should get through to the field.[23]

Simultaneously Churchill was urging Menzies to be generous with his supply of Ultra to Moscow. Once again Menzies firmly put his foot down. 'I am always embarrassed at sending the Russians information only obtainable from [Ultra]', he told Churchill, 'owing to the legibility of Russian ciphers.' It was a timely and forceful reminder of the importance of Ultra security, although Menzies sweetened the pill by announcing that he would now help the Russians to read hand-enciphered *Abwehr* intercepts.[24] His warning had its effect. Soon Churchill was rebuking Montgomery about permitting intercepts to feed rumours surrounding Rommel's health. As the Allies moved decisively on to the offensive in 1943, he became as hawkish on this issue as Menzies.

On the eve of Montgomery's Eighth Army offensive Churchill read an Ultra report revealing that the Germans were worried about Crete. He immediately sent a message to Alexander: 'Anything that can make them more nervous would act as good cover.' Two weeks later he met with three leading figures in British deception who were expert on making the enemy nervous: Lieutenant-Colonel John Bevan, Brigadier Dudley Clarke and Major Peter Fleming. The basic pillars for deception were tight security and first-rate intelligence. Churchill intuitively knew their importance. 'All kinds of Munchausen tales can be spread about to confuse and baffle the truth', he declared in 1940, inimitably throwing himself into the building of dummy ships and phoney targets. Such ploys were tactical and defensive, appealing as much to his schoolboy delight in gadgets and wizardry as any considered military theory of deception as a force mutiplier. By 1942 he had awoken to the vast potential of strategic deception. By creating imaginary threats, the Allies were able to confuse the enemy about their offensive plans. Critical to this was Ultra. It not only provided insights into enemy plans but also enabled the Allies to read how well the deception was working, and by exposing *Abwehr* intelligence operations opened the door to the Double-Cross system. By now, the system was fully tested and running. Watertight security guaranteed that no suspicion of duplicity troubled the Nazis.[25]

It was Archibald Wavell who galvanised Churchill into action. Having learned the value of deception in Palestine during the First World War, he had created 'A' Force in the Middle East, a deception unit under Brigadier Dudley Clarke, that marked up several triumphs against the Italians in the desert, and then in India had a deception staff headed by Major Peter Fleming, the explorer brother of Ian Fleming. As the first serious Allied discussions about invading Europe began in the spring of 1942 he urged Churchill to support a major strategic deception campaign.

Churchill immediately circulated Wavell's proposal. The London Controlling Section (LCS) was created in the deepest secrecy to prepare deception plans on a worldwide basis. Its head was a former City stockbroker and First World War holder of the Military Cross, Lieutenant-Colonel John Bevan. His deputy was Lieutenant-Colonel Sir Ronald Wingate, eldest son of 'Wingate Pasha', Kitchener's intelligence officer who had briefed Churchill on the River War over forty years before. It was an Anglo-American enterprise, with a permanent American member and an equivalent staff in Washington known as the Joint Security Control.

Located in the Cabinet Office complex, it became integral to Allied planning. Churchill rapidly came to trust Bevan, the two often cooking up deception plots in late-night sessions over brandy. 'Bevan and Churchill sparked each other off', noted one LCS member, 'and pulled out what were all the old tricks of Eton and Harrow and polished them up for the task at hand.'[26] The first significant test came with Operation Torch, the Anglo-American landings in Morocco and Algeria, when two aborted invasion plans were readapted for deception use: Jupiter for an invasion of Norway and Sledgehammer for France. 'All depends upon secrecy and speed', Churchill told Roosevelt. 'Secrecy can only be maintained by deception.' Briefed on the details, he insisted that to make doubly sure the Germans would not guess the target Casablanca should be called 'Dunkirk', Oran 'Calais', and Algiers 'Boulogne'. 'No one', he ordered, 'should use the guilty names in conversation.'

Other important intelligence preparations for Torch advanced that summer. In June 'Wild Bill' Donovan briefed the War Cabinet on Roosevelt's creation of the Office of Strategic Services (OSS) and hammered out a co-ordination pact on subversion and sabotage with SOE. Geographically, to be shared fifty-fifty were Burma, Malaya, Sumatra, Germany, Italy, Sweden, Switzerland, Portugal and Spain. The British were to have primacy in India, East and West Africa, and – at least until the American strategic role was better defined – in Western Europe. The Americans were to lead in the rest of Asia and the Pacific, Finland and North Africa, where an OSS headquarters was established after the landing. As with Ultra, the special relationship in covert action had to bulldoze aside many transatlantic obstacles.

The Torch landings began four days after Montgomery's stunning victory at El Alamein. Some 65,000 troops transported and protected by over 600 warships came ashore on the Moroccan and Algerian coasts. Two days later Admiral François Darlan, the Commander-in-Chief of French Vichy forces, ordered a general ceasefire. The operation was a major success for Allied intelligence, deception and security. The North Atlantic was crossed without mishap, and despite watching eyes on both sides of the Straits of

Gibraltar the Germans were taken by complete surprise. Ultra provided a valuable and reassuring window on German behaviour before the landings, the deception planners hinted successfully at forthcoming landings on the northern French coast, Norway, Sicily and Italy, and the convoys evaded detection until they were inside the Mediterranean. Above all Torch represented a triumph of security and counter-intelligence. The *Abwehr* had a highly organised system of observation posts in Spain and Spanish Morocco to watch traffic passing through the Straits and had also installed a sophisticated infra-red maritime tracking system for night-time surveillance. Code-named 'Bodden', it was known about through *Abwehr* decrypts and reports from Hillgarth and SIS in Spain. Churchill seriously considered a Combined Operations assault to take out the system but finally opted for diplomatic approaches to Franco. Then, with only weeks to go before the landing, an accident occurred that threatened the entire Torch enterprise and had Churchill scrambling for reassurance.

In late September a British aircraft bound for Gibraltar crashed into the sea off the coast of Spain. On board was a Royal Navy courier carrying a letter announcing the arrival in Gibraltar of General Eisenhower and mentioning a 'target date'; another letter also referred to an 'Expeditionary Force'. The courier's body was washed ashore near Cadiz and was handed over to the British Embassy. Churchill demanded to know whether this had compromised Torch to the Germans. The Inter-Services Security Board concluded that there was no evidence of any tampering with the documents, and *Abwehr* intercepts confirmed that the Germans had tried but failed to get their hands on the documents. But it had been a close-run thing. As the Allied convoys passed through the Straits, Churchill expressed heartfelt relief to Alexander in Cairo: 'Torch movements are proceeding with precision and so far amazing security.'[27]

Meanwhile SOE was forging ahead with its Balkan plans. To prepare for the El Alamein offensive Cairo HQ cast around for ways to slow down German reinforcements making their way to North Africa. The railway line from Salonika to Athens was particularly vulnerable where viaducts carried it across precipitous valleys in the Greek mountains. SOE Cairo radioed its Athens-based contact, code-named 'Prometheus II', asking his guerrilla contacts to blow up the line. After a crash course in parachute training and supplied with plastic explosive, SOE agents were dropped into Greece to contact the guerrillas. Code-named 'Harling', the operation was headed by Brigadier Eddie Myers with Monty Woodhouse as his second in command. Since witnessing the German parachute drop at Maleme he had spent a rigorous winter with the resistance in Crete. In late November, in co-operation with a guerrilla leader named Colonel Napoleon Zervas, the group successfully blew up the railway viaduct over the Gorgopotamos River. It came too late to help Montgomery, but demonstrated how guerrillas working with British secret forces could carry out an operation co-ordinated with Allied strategy. Churchill was quickly sent the details.[28] As planning began for the invasion of Sicily, his attention turned actively to resistance that could tie down the Germans, divert their attention from Sicily and hasten an Italian collapse. Guerrilla war aroused his strong romantic instincts and opened an avenue of action where he could act without too much deference to Roosevelt. As Ultra slipped from his grasp and American power increasingly shaped Allied fortunes, he seized on SOE as the secret weapon Britain could wield to shorten the war.

The year ended with Churchill as deeply engaged in the minutiae of intelligence as ever. Lunchtime on Christmas Eve found him chairing a special meeting of ministers to discuss the urgent question of Nazi espionage in Portuguese East Africa. U-boats had been sinking large numbers of Allied ships in the Mozambique Channel, and South Africa's Jan Smuts was demanding that the Portuguese expel Axis spies from their colony. Churchill was predictably keen for action. Doubtless remembering his youthful escape from the Boers to Lourenço Marques and his fear that the city was riddled with Boer spies, he declared Portuguese East Africa a hotbed of subversion. There was no doubt at all, he insisted, that enemy agents were assisting U-boat operations. Not content with demanding a stiff note to Lisbon, he overruled Eden's diplomatic caution to order SOE to disable the wireless sets of Nazi agents by subversive action. But before it could strike, SIGINT revealed that *Abwehr* agents operating out of South Africa itself were responsible. Reluctantly, the secret agents were called off.[29]

While Churchill was mobilising cloak-and-dagger in London, some fifteen hundred miles to the south drama was unfolding in Algiers, capital of French North Africa. At 3 o'clock that afternoon a 20-year-old Frenchman climbed out of a black Peugeot and entered the Palais d'Eté, a Moorish villa high up on the pine-studded hills over the Bay of Algiers that served as the official residence of the High Commissioner in North Africa, Admiral François Darlan. The young man waited patiently for Darlan to return from a lengthy lunch with Admiral Andrew Cunningham, Allied Naval Commander of the Torch expedition. When he arrived, he coolly shot him twice in the stomach with a 7.65 calibre pistol. Two hours later Darlan died at the Maillot Hospital. Over lunch he had confessed that he knew of at least four plots against his life.

Darlan's murder, wrote Churchill in his war memoirs, 'however criminal, relieved the Allies of their embarrassment at working with him'.[30] This was putting it mildly. Darlan, former head of the French Navy, one-time Foreign and Defence Minister to Pétain, and Commander-in-Chief of all Vichy forces, was universally detested as a symbol of collaboration. Churchill himself said he had 'an odious record'. Three days after Torch, Eisenhower's deputy, Major-General Mark Clark, signed a ceasefire agreement with him that guaranteed a bloodless occupation of North Africa. But the price, acceptance of Darlan as High Commissioner, sparked outrage. Shouts of 'Munich' were heard in Parliament, Darlan was denounced as America's first quisling, and French resistance fighters cried betrayal. The deal also threatened Churchill's link with Roosevelt. Robert Murphy, Roosevelt's personal emissary in North Africa, had long prepared for the deal, and Darlan's arrival in Algiers on the eve of Torch was not, as Churchill claimed, 'an odd and formidable coincidence'. Although public outrage forced Murphy and Eisenhower to describe the deal as a temporary expedient, they obstinately clung to it. Churchill was faced with a dilemma. Despite the storms in his relationship with de Gaulle, he had forged a bond with the leader of Free France that went back to the desperate days of 1940. Yet the alliance with Roosevelt was crucial to victory. At stake was the political future of France. By Christmas 1942 the choice was becoming clear: Churchill could either support Roosevelt and Darlan, or opt for a France that included de Gaulle. It was a crisis that cried out for special action. The assassination solved his problem.

Berlin and Rome were quick to point at the British secret service; Churchill was equally prompt to deny it. The day before Darlan's funeral in Algiers he chaired a Defence Committee meeting that discussed SOE activities in North Africa, particularly 'certain disquieting, although probably [sic] mendacious' reports that the British were responsible for Darlan's assassination. The laconic minutes simply note that Churchill ordered an inquiry. There is no subsequent record of what, if anything, transpired. The next day Admiral Cunningham was instructed formally to deny the charges. Whatever might be claimed, he was told, nothing could incriminate any branch of the British secret service, 'who do not indulge in such activities'.[31]

Perhaps so, but extensive evidence exists of an active behind-the-scenes effort to rid the Allies of Darlan. Churchill no more needed to order the killing of Darlan than did Henry II that of Thomas à Becket. Caught off guard by the chorus of disapproval over the deal, he quickly came to regret it and within a week told de Gaulle that Darlan should be shot. Anthony Eden told Lord Halifax in Washington that 'It's a question of Darlan or de Gaulle. We can't have both', while Sir Alexander Cadogan complained bitterly, 'The Americans and naval officers in Algiers are letting us in for a *pot* of trouble. We shall do no good until we've killed Darlan.' But Roosevelt refused to budge. 'If France one day discovers that because of the British and Americans the liberation consists of Darlan', de Gaulle bitterly told Churchill, 'you can perhaps win the war from a military point of view but you will lose it morally, and ultimately there will only be one victor: Stalin.' In his heart, Churchill knew de Gaulle was right.

In December General de Gaulle dispatched an emissary to Algiers, ostensibly to seek a *modus vivendi* with Darlan. This was General François d'Astier de la Vigerie, one of three brothers. Emmanuel led *Libération*, a resistance movement in France, while the other, Henri, was Secretary-General of the Police in Algiers, a royalist and former right-wing activist remembered as 'a brilliant and enigmatic *condottiere*' with contacts amongst paramilitary groups opposed to Darlan. François d'Astier's travel to Algiers was arranged by SOE, where Major-General Colin Gubbins had taken charge of North African affairs. Douglas Dodds-Parker, now finished with his SOE–NKVD liaison, and David Keswick, a senior intelligence officer with SOE in North Africa, believed that Darlan's continued rule in Algiers was inflicting appalling damage on Allied relations with French resistance and that he had to go.

As, by this time, did Churchill's personal intelligence adviser. Desmond Morton held no special brief for de Gaulle, but he understood the politics of France and he, too, decided that Darlan 'will not do'. Early in December he flew out to Gibraltar to confer with

Keswick who wired Gubbins in London that Henri d'Astier would be a suitable vehicle for getting rid of Darlan. Ten days later Baker Street alerted Keswick to General François d'Astier's impending arrival and told him he would have a reasonably free hand in deciding what to do, had been provided with $38,000, and that the one essential requirement was that neither the British government nor Fighting France should be implicated. Then, two days before General d'Astier's arrival, Eisenhower issued a warning that if SOE gave any help to anti-Darlan or pro-Gaullist elements he would immediately close down North African operations. The very future of SOE operations into France, not to mention relations with the United States, seemed at stake. On Christmas Eve, just hours before the assassination, Lord Selborne told Eden that any expediency in using Darlan had finally vanished.

Curiously enough, Stewart Menzies was also in Algiers for the assassination. He rarely left Churchill's side but in what Patrick Reilly, his personal assistant, described as the strangest episode of his term in SIS, Menzies encouraged him to take a short and unexpected leave. Only forty years later did Reilly learn that in his absence Menzies had flown to Algiers and that the proffered leave had been a deliberate ploy to prevent him knowing that he had gone. Ostensibly, the trip was to discuss the start-up of a new French intelligence service based in Algiers. It was perhaps no more than a formidable coincidence, therefore, that Menzies was enjoying Christmas Eve lunch on a sunny Algiers rooftop when Darlan was shot only a few hundred yards away.[32]

The assassin, Fernand Bonnier de la Chapelle, belonged to a small paramilitary group known as the Corps Franc d'Afrique based at Ain Taya, a camp about thirty miles outside Algiers run by SOE, where he was trained in small arms and demolitions and wore the Gaullist Cross of Lorraine as a shoulder flash. Later he transferred to another camp at the Club des Pins close to Algiers. Here he met Henri d'Astier, his son Jean-Bernard, and, through him, an Army padre called Father Cordier. Both OSS and SOE had given Bonnier pistols, but it was Cordier who provided him with the weapon that killed Darlan. Jean-Bernard d'Astier drove him to the scene.

Naively, Bonnier believed he would be hailed as a hero. Instead, hauled before an in camera court-martial, he was silenced by a firing squad less than forty-eight hours later and buried at an unmarked site in a coffin thoughtfully ordered before his trial. His hurried final confession was written on a visiting card he found in his pocket which bore the name of Henri d'Astier.

'Good Morning', announced the BBC in its first news bulletin of Christmas Day, 'a very Happy Christmas to you all. Last night, in Algiers, Admiral Darlan was assassinated.' In London Sir Robin Brook, SOE's controller for Western Europe, popped champagne corks with André Dewavrin ('Passy'), while Sir Peter Wilkinson recalled that the sentiment in SOE was that Darlan's death was the best thing that had happened since Heydrich's assassination.[33]

As for Churchill, whose closest intelligence advisers had been so deeply involved and for whom a severe political problem had been so abruptly eliminated, Christmas Day found him in an especially cheerful mood. He was sitting up in bed reading, one of his secretaries reported, looking 'like a benevolent old cherub'. Three days later he met with de Gaulle and General François d'Astier, and then appointed Harold Macmillan as Eisenhower's political adviser. No longer was Churchill prepared to allow Roosevelt to dictate the politics of Allied grand strategy. Three weeks after that, Colin Gubbins flew out to Algiers to ensure that SOE was equipped for the challenges ahead. As Allied eyes turned north to resistance in France, Italy and the Balkans, Churchill was determined to place a British stamp on the secret war.

15

Battle Joined

Over the next twelve months the tide of global war turned decisively against the Axis powers. Churchill now began to fear the growing power of his Allies. Roosevelt's presence at Casablanca marked the arrival of the Americans. The Red Army never looked back after Stalingrad. Across occupied Europe resistance intensified. Plans for victory became entangled with hopes and fears for peace that caught the secret services in their cross-currents. This became most apparent in the Balkans.

After his 1941 landing on the Dalmation coast, SOE's Bill Hudson had made contact with Colonel Draza Mihailović, leader of the chetniks. A Serb whose loyalty was to the Yugoslav monarchy, his strategy was to create a secret army to liberate the country when the Allies arrived. By contrast, the partisans under Josip 'Broz' Tito, General Secretary of the Yugoslav Communist Party, waged continuous guerrilla warfare. By the summer of 1942 Moscow was accusing Mihailović of collaborating with the enemy. The truth was that the chetniks and partisans were fighting a civil war in which each occasionally made deals with the Germans in order to strike at the other.

This provided the backdrop to Churchill's arrival in Cairo in January 1943 *en route* to Turkey following the Casablanca Conference. Bill Hudson's reports had galvanised him into action and he had summoned Hugh Dalton to a nocturnal meeting at Downing Street to tell him that everything humanly possible must be done to help the guerrillas. By the end of 1942 Churchill was aware that Mihailović was under deep suspicion.

Two days after arriving in Cairo Churchill lunched with Captain Bill Deakin, the Oxford don who had helped him with the Marlborough biography and who was now an intelligence officer in SOE Cairo's Yugoslav section. That evening, on Deakin's urging,

Churchill met with Brigadier Mervyn Keble, Chief of Staff to Lord Glenconner who headed SOE Middle East. 'Bolo' Keble was an ambitious regular army officer whose manner combined 'the quick in-out of a commando raid with the onward drone of a brigade of tanks'. He had previously worked for GHQ Intelligence and had concluded that in Croatia and Slovenia the most effective guerrilla campaign was being waged by the partisans. For months he had vainly been trying to persuade SOE London to send arms to Tito. Now Keble unburdened himself to Churchill who wanted to know more. He produced a lengthy memorandum advocating immediate aid to the partisans in Croatia and Slovenia. Unless Britain helped, he pleaded, the Russians or Americans would.

This Cairo encounter marked a turning point in Churchill's attitude towards Yugoslavia. In London he showed Keble's paper to Lord Selborne and told him to make closer contact with the resistance leaders. Selborne was profoundly unhappy at the notion of supporting Communists. But in April, after SOE received a directive stressing that an intensified campaign of sabotage and guerrilla activities in the Balkans was of the primary strategic importance, the first SOE agents, Communist Croats recruited in Canada, were dropped to make contact with the partisans.

Was there a sinister manipulation of intelligence that saw Britain abandon Mihailović in favour of Tito and help foist a brutal Communist regime on post-war Yugoslavia? Was Churchill an unwitting dupe or even willing puppet in a plot manipulated by Moscow and its moles deep within British intelligence? Such claims have surfaced since the death of Tito, challenging the post-war consensus that in supporting him Britain chose the authentic resistance rather than the collaborating chetniks. After a show trial, Mihailović was shot by a firing squad on a Belgrade golf course in 1946. That he deserved his fate has been long accepted by many historians. Revisionists vigorously reject this view.

Their central claim is that within SOE Cairo, intelligence about the partisans was deliberately inflated in order to force a change of policy. 'In the crucial decisions', writes one author, 'there can be little doubt that the Communists and pro-Communists working within the Western Intelligence apparatus made a crucial contribution.' A former SOE officer who worked with the chetniks has denounced Soviet moles for feeding 'tendentious and politically devious' material into reports used for policy-making decisions.[1]

Indubitably passionate supporters of Tito existed within British wartime intelligence, some of whom continued to defend his case in the post-war years. But when measured against the evidence the claims of conspiracy are thin. The crucial item is Keble's intervention. It has generally been assumed that Ultra was available to Keble in his previous Cairo post and that, by some administrative fluke, he continued to receive it after transferring to SOE. If this were so it would be fuel for the revisionists, for in reality very little Ultra material on Yugoslavia had reached Cairo by then, and suspicions that Keble largely invented his case on nebulous intercepts might be sustained. Yet it seems highly unlikely that Keble was accidentally kept on the Ultra distribution list. Far more plausible as his source were the intercepts of *Abwehr* hand ciphers which began to reach Cairo from London in 1942. This weakens the case that he invented his sources, although here too doubt must linger; fifty years after the war, they are still not available in the Public Record Office.[2]

However, not even the harshest critics deny that Tito's partisans were actively fighting the Germans. Was Churchill fooled into supporting them by some Communist-inspired group in Cairo? Basil Davidson, head of SOE's Yugoslav section, was enthusiastically pro-partisan, as was James Klugmann, a member of the Communist Party and post-war apologist for Stalin who worked under Davidson. Yet it was Deakin and Keble, neither remotely Communist, who made the crucial intervention with Churchill. Deakin later parachuted to Tito, survived several hazardous missions and certainly came to admire him. The ambitious Keble enlarged his Cairo empire by finding new resistance movements to support. But this was not Communism at work, it was Churchill. Once his imagination was fired by the partisans his enthusiasm became unstoppable, overriding Foreign Office qualms and protests by Selborne. Only at the end of the war did he recognise that Tito had dazzled him.[3]

Exhilarated but exhausted by his travels Churchill returned to London early in February 1943. Just over a week later his personal physician diagnosed pneumonia and he took to his bed. That night, guided by a full moon, six Norwegian agents parachuted into the mountains of southern Norway. Their mission, code-named 'Gunnerside', was to sabotage the Norsk Hydro plant at Vemork, the critical source of 'heavy water' (deuterium oxide) used by the Germans in their atomic-bomb programme. The world's first atomic pile had gone critical in Chicago just two months before; Churchill

feared the worst about Nazi scientific advance. For weeks the saboteurs had practised on a duplicate model of the plant constructed by
SOE technicians. They silently approached the building on skis, surprised the guards and planted explosives that wrecked the plant
along with some 3,000 lbs of heavy water. This, and a later bombing
by the American Air Force, effectively ended German heavy-water
production. It may have been the most important act of sabotage by
either side during the Second World War.

Still inspired by Steinbeck's novel of Nordic resistance, Churchill
was delighted by SOE's success. 'What rewards are to be given to
these heroic men?' he asked, noting with approval the list of DSOs,
MCs and MMs later sent to him. He read details in SOE's next quarterly report and particularly drew to Cherwell's attention the
comment by the German Commander-in-Chief Norway, that it was
'the most splendid coup' he had seen so far. It was a feather in the
cap for Baker Street and the tempo of resistance across Europe, particularly in the Balkans, was increasing. 'The number of enemy divisions being contained in these regions is most remarkable', Churchill
enthused, but an invasion of Europe was still distant and victory
depended on first-rate intelligence. Bletchley Park's final triumph
over Shark that month made the point. 'You don't have to worry
about the U-boats', he confided to W. P. Crozier, editor of the
Manchester Guardian, in an off-the-record chat, 'I think it is going to
come out alright.' If his heart was with the guerrillas, his head still
told him that Stewart Menzies and SIS were the pathfinders of
victory. Sabotage, subversion, secret intelligence and deception
would have to be carefully co-ordinated in a coherent and centrally
directed programme of secret service.[4]

Co-ordination was one thing, unity of control another. That same
month Churchill rejected the idea of a unified secret service that
would place SOE, SIS and MI5 under a single head. Its sponsor was
Alfred Duff Cooper, who had succeeded Lord Swinton as chairman
of the Security Executive. In a secret memorandum he argued that a
single service would reduce internal friction as well as the number of
ministers involved in intelligence matters. Although Churchill had
favoured such an idea after the First World War, he now rejected it.
It would be a mistake, he thought, 'to stir up all these pools' at such
a critical time. Another reason was the suspicion, fed to him by
Desmond Morton, that it embodied some predatory agenda by MI5
for the post-war secret service. And yet a third was its likely effect on

SOE's role, which was about to become crucially more important. Instead, Churchill created a Secret Service Co-ordinating Committee comprising the heads of MI5, SIS and SOE, and Morton as his personal representative. However it was doomed by inter-service rivalries and met only twice before Duff Cooper declared it dead.[5]

Churchill was neither surprised nor particularly disturbed by these intra-intelligence rivalries, taking the view that provided they did not seriously hinder the war effort such tensions could be healthy. It had become clear that a unified secret service could be a threat to ministers – as well as to the parliamentary system. Churchill was acutely aware of the enormous domestic powers MI5 had amassed. 'Every Department which has waxed during the war is now considering how it can quarter its officials on the public indefinitely', he curtly responded to Duff Cooper's proposal. 'The less we encourage these illusions the better.' Soon afterwards the Cabinet Secretary commissioned a heavily critical report on MI5 that condemned the lack of proper ministerial control, its abuse of powers and 'injustices to the public' – especially in vetting procedures and the treatment of aliens. 'Look what has happened to the liberties of this country during the war', Churchill complained bitterly to the *Manchester Guardian*'s editor. 'Men of position are seized and kept in prison for years without trial and no "have your carcase" [habeas corpus] rights . . . a frightful thing to anyone concerned about British liberties.'[6]

What particularly exercised Churchill was the case of Sir Oswald Mosley who was released from prison a month later on medical grounds. A huge political row broke out but Churchill defended the move on the grounds that 'the power of the Executive to cast a man into prison without formulating any charge known to the law, and particularly to deny him the judgement of his peers, is in the highest degree odious and is the foundation of all totalitarian government whether Nazi or Communist'. The Home Office vetoed the circulation of his comments, subversive as they were of Regulation 18B that he now firmly believed should be repealed. But, head of a coalition government, he was politically constrained by an informal alliance between the Labour Party and MI5. Bedfellows for once, neither wanted a relaxation of the stringent powers that kept the detested Mosley behind bars.[7]

Churchill also worried about MI5's approach to Communists. The Soviet alliance had done nothing to shake his anti-Bolshevism, nor did he nourish any illusions about the long-term revolutionary goals of the Communist Party. In May 1943, when Moscow dissolved the Comintern, Duff Cooper advised the War Cabinet that Communist Party principles remained unchanged and that government departments should treat it as carefully as before. Less than a month later the conviction of Douglas Springhall, National Convenor of the Communist Party, for recruiting agents in the Air Ministry and SOE to pass on secrets to the Soviets, hammered the point home.

Yet distinct from anti-Communism was the matter of riding roughshod over constitutional proprieties. The Springhall case galvanised MI5 into producing a list of suspected Communists working in sensitive positions and demanding their immediate removal. Churchill concurred, but he insisted that MI5's word alone on the guilt of suspects should not be accepted. Instead, he agreed with Desmond Morton that 'MI5 tends to see dangerous men too freely and to lack [a] knowledge of the world and sense of perspective'. He set up a secret panel, again with Morton as his personal representative, to 'vet' MI5 recommendations. The final say on the employment of suspects would rest with departments and ministers concerned, not MI5.[8]

The Security Service's response can only have intensified his disquiet about its growing imperial pretensions, ironically embodied in its wartime occupation of his birthplace at Blenheim Palace. Arguing that the panel's members knew little about underground Communist methods, it simply refused to bring any cases before the panel. This was the second time in six months that the intelligence bureaucracy had sabotaged an oversight committee which included his personal watchdog. The next year, prior to a review of post-war intelligence needs, MI5 began to dread how Churchill's entourage might wreak its revenge.

In mid-April 1943 Churchill was briefed by his Chief of Staff on Operation Mincemeat, described by Sir Ronald Wingate as 'the most brilliant and elaborate *ruse de guerre* in history', and certainly the best known deception tale of the Second World War.[9] Its object was to deceive the Germans about the forthcoming invasion of Sicily. The body of a man, apparently a British staff officer killed in a plane crash, was to be 'found' carrying documents suggesting that Sicily was merely part of a cover plan. Inspired by the real-life incident that had almost sabotaged Operation Torch, it was conceived by the Double-Cross planners in MI5, approved by Colonel John Bevan's

London Controlling Section, and later immortalised by Commander Ewen Montagu, one of the two officers in charge, in his post-war bestseller *The Man Who Never Was*.

Bevan had to convince Churchill that it should go ahead. In the underground bunker in Whitehall he found the Prime Minister in bed smoking a cigar and handed him a single sheet of paper outlining the plan. Churchill asked whether there was any chance the Spaniards might find out that 'Major Martin' (the fictional identity given to the corpse, in reality that of a Welsh drifter who had died in London after eating rat poison) had not in fact drowned. Bevan reassured him, but felt obliged to point out that the wind or tide might mean the body did not wash ashore at all. 'Well in that case', grinned Churchill, 'you'll have to take him for another swim.'

At dawn on 30 April the body was slipped into the sea from a British submarine off the coast of Spain. Three hours later a local fisherman found the body, it was impounded by the Spanish authorities, and copies of the faked dispatches ended up in *Abwehr* hands. The German High Command, already expecting an attack in the eastern Mediterranean, accepted them as genuine. Hitler ordered southern Greece, the Dodecanese islands, Sardinia and Corsica immediately reinforced. In London Ultra confirmed the operation's success by revealing German reinforcements in the Balkans and *Abwehr* preparations to evacuate its stations in Greece. Churchill was in Washington for the 'Trident' conference with Roosevelt. Here he received the news in a special message: '"Mincemeat" swallowed rod, line and sinker by right people and from best information they look like acting on it.' He was suitably delighted.[10]

By this time the Germans had been driven from North Africa and the next great prize lay in Italy and the Balkans. Talking to Roosevelt in the Oval Office of the White House Churchill told him that they should do everything to take the pressure off the Russians on the Eastern Front. He should remember that there were some 185 German divisions tied down with the Red Army. As they met, Hitler was massing his forces for a major strategic offensive against the Kursk salient. Once again Churchill proved more astute in his intelligence assessment than the professionals. The Joint Intelligence Committee predicted a localised effort, but Churchill told Stalin that he thought a major attack probable. He and Roosevelt agreed that all the available evidence should be sent to Moscow.[11] This was the last major intelligence exchange. Contacts continued until the end of the war, but diminished because of vastly improved Soviet intelligence methods and Moscow's reluctance to reciprocate. More momentous in 1943 was the strengthening intelligence link with Washington.

Five days before 'Major Martin' set out on his historic swim, the American code-breaking genius William Friedmann arrived in London at the head of a US Army delegation to a personal welcome by Stewart Menzies and extensive briefings on British code-breaking victories. Soon after, the head of Bletchley Park signed a deal in Washington for full Anglo-American collaboration on Army and Air Force signals intelligence. Still-classified parts of the agreement, known as BRUSA (Britain/United States), allowed for similar co-operation on diplomatic intercepts. The two navies had already signed a similar deal, as had MI6 with Donovan's counter-intelligence experts in the OSS. Taken together, these agreements bound Britain and the United States into the closest intelligence alliance history had ever seen.[12]

Churchill's personal Ultra files for 1943 reveal him persistently drawing to the attention of the Chiefs of Staff and commanding generals this or that item of 'Boniface'. So addicted was he that he refused to travel without it. When at the Casablanca conference he complained to Menzies about the lack of 'important messages', the problem was that no Special Liaison Unit had been provided. Churchill had to content himself with a morning telegram from Menzies and a copy of the regular evening 'Sunset' telegrams based on Enigma decrypts sent routinely by Naval Intelligence to the Admiralty delegation in Washington. After this Menzies ensured that for future overseas conferences Churchill was fully supplied; even then he remained querulous and demanding. In August, as he prepared to sail to the Quebec conference, he told his Private Office to make sure that he was kept fully informed about major developments. 'Particularly I must have good "C" stuff', he emphasised. 'At any moment a larger crisis may arise . . . Make sure that full pouches by air including "C" stuff await me at H[alifax]. There will be time for a long read up on the train.' His own impulsive decisions made things worse. The Quebec meeting over, he took off for an isolated fishing camp in the Laurentian mountains seventy miles from Quebec city. 'Please telegraph urgently details and times of future movements', his Private Office in London pleaded despairingly to his private secretary, 'in order transmissions of news may be arranged, particularly information from "C". Ironically his host at Quebec, Canadian

Prime Minister Mackenzie King, remained in the dark about Ultra. Only one Commonwealth Prime Minister knew the secret: Field Marshal Jan Smuts of South Africa. Churchill revered and trusted the old Boer fighter and personally revealed it to him.[13]

The lessons Churchill had learned about the pitfalls of being his own intelligence officer, not to mention the overwhelming volume of material, meant that his anxieties were now focused mainly on Ultra's security. In March 1943 he suffered his greatest scare. In Tunisia Rommel was fighting a bitter rearguard battle and Ultra picked up reports of an encircling attack on Medenine by three panzer divisions. Montgomery rushed up tanks and artillery, and Rommel was forced to abandon his offensive only six hours after it started. Churchill shared the intelligence battle from afar, reading the intercepts as they reached him daily in London. He knew better than to order Montgomery about, but at least he could insist on Ultra's security. 'Safeguard our precious secret so far as possible in your dispositions', he urged him. 'Tell even your most trusted commanders only the minimum necessary.' Yet, alarmingly, only three days after the battle, Ultra revealed that the Germans had concluded that Montgomery had known in advance of the strength, place and timing of Rommel's offensive. No evidence suggested that the Germans specifically suspected Enigma traffic, but Sir Alan Brooke was seriously worried that the Germans might tighten cipher security and blind the Allies. Then, a few days later, Ultra produced another revelation: the *Luftwaffe* suspected prior British knowledge of a major convoy to Tunisia successfully sunk by the Royal Air Force. Here indeed there was a failure of basic security, for no cover for Ultra had been provided by making sure of air sightings. Churchill reacted with vigour. Not content to leave the reprimand to his First Sea Lord, he personally chided the Commander-in-Chief Mediterranean and threatened to withhold Ultra altogether unless it was used 'only on great occasions or when thoroughly camouflaged'. Again the Germans dismissed Enigma as a suspect, but Churchill refused to relax his vigilance. It was time to have another tone-up of security, he told the Cabinet Secretary, 'especially to Boniface'. It was a significant indicator of how far the intercepts had escaped Churchill's control that Menzies was able to argue successfully that reducing the number of recipients would severely damage its operational value.[14]

Churchill also carefully monitored the Americans. Wholeheartedly though he approved of the BRUSA agreement he worried about their handling of Ultra. The year before, the *Chicago Tribune* had strongly hinted that America owed its victory at Midway to triumphs in signals intelligence, and in North Africa German penetration of ciphers used by the American military attaché in Cairo had provided Rommel with an open window on much British planning. Many of the American Special Security Officers responsible for explaining and interpreting Ultra intelligence were considerably junior to the commanders they briefed. Churchill could only too easily imagine that some 'cowboy' general would simply ignore their strictures about security. Privately, he ordered Group Captain Frederick Winterbotham to discreetly monitor the American's handling of Ultra. Complaints about security breaches by top American officials in Washington that endangered deception campaigns were taken up personally with Roosevelt.[15]

SOE's destruction of the Norsk Hydro plant reassured Churchill about Nazi atomic research, but in April 1943 he received alarming intelligence about another potentially lethal German scientific advance. This was Hitler's 'secret weapon', a long-range rocket that could strike directly at Britain. He had ordered its mass-production after the successful firing of a liquid-fuelled V-2 rocket at the Peenemunde testing station on the Baltic coast. Since then SIS had filed several helpful reports from secret agents and sympathisers in the resistance; here was a case where Ultra had little to offer. But what really jolted British intelligence was a conversation between two German generals captured after El Alamein. Deliberately brought together in a room wired for sound, one of them recalled a visit to a rocket-testing site and expressed amazement that London was not yet in flames.

To investigate, Churchill appointed his son-in-law Duncan Sandys. R. V. Jones, of *Knickebein* fame, directed his energy towards helping target SIS agents and RAF reconnaissance missions on the Peenemunde work. At Medmenham, the RAF's Photographic Interpretation Unit, a special section worked exclusively on intelligence for Sandys, although when Churchill made a visit the official interpreters had yet failed to detect any signs of a rocket in the blurred and grainy prints. Four days later, however, R. V. Jones did. Sandys was immediately notified and Churchill convened a full meeting of the Defence Committee in the Cabinet's underground rooms. Sandys laid out the evidence pointing to the advanced

German development of a rocket that could, he claimed, cause up to four thousand casualties killed and injured. There was even the risk that one could be launched before the RAF could deliver a knock-out blow on Peenemunde. Because of the short summer nights this could not be until mid-August. He was followed by Lord Cherwell. Churchill's chief scientific investigator was a sceptic who argued that the whole affair might be a hoax designed to draw attention away from Hitler's 'real' secret weapon, a pilotless aircraft. Finally Churchill turned to Jones. Recalling that the young scientist had been right about the *Knickebein,* he told him: 'I want the truth.' Jones obliged. The evidence, he pronounced, was stronger than that on the famous beams of 1940. The threat was real, although perhaps less imminent than feared by Sandys.

Churchill was persuaded. In mid-August, as he waited for Roosevelt in the citadel at Quebec, over 500 RAF bombers pounded Peenemunde. Although Werner von Braun, the driving force of the project, survived, over one hundred scientists and staff, along with several hundred slave labourers, perished. For the Allies the raid was a triumph that forced the Germans to shift development and pro-duction facilities and lost them a valuable two months, enough to prevent the V-weapon attack from damaging the Normandy land-ings ten months later. 'Operation Hydra has been a success', Sandys told his father-in-law triumphantly over the transatlantic line.[16]

The Trident conference set a target date of May 1944 for the inva-sion of France and agreed that after Sicily efforts should aim at elim-inating Italy from the war. This delighted Churchill. His gaze was irresistibly drawn to the Balkans and he took it as giving Britain a free hand in the Mediterranean. He enthused to Roosevelt that here thirty-four Axis divisions were held in play by rebels whose activities could be further intensified by Allied support. Within days Captain Bill Deakin and an SIS officer parachuted to Tito's guerrilla head-quarters in the mountains of Montenegro.

Churchill had rejected the advice of the Joint Intelligence Committee that British support should focus exclusively on Mihailović, but he was by no means ready to write off the Serb leader just yet. When a Japanese diplomatic intercept caught his eye, sug-gesting the Germans were far from happy at Italian relations with Mihailović, he demanded a summary of Ultra messages on the subject. It fuelled his suspicion – not to mention hope – that the Serb leader was playing a double-cross game with the Italians. Thus armed,

Churchill urged the Chiefs of Staff and a wavering Roosevelt to look boldly on action in the Balkans. 'In spite of his naturally foxy attitude', he told them, 'Mihailović will throw his whole weight against the Italians the moment we are able to give him any effective help.'

Whatever the Serb leader's intentions, the 'uncertain and flickering' light of Ultra revealed that chetnik fighting value was considerably less than that of the partisans.[17] To Churchill, that was what mattered. In June he brushed aside Selborne's anti-Communist reservations to order vastly increased supplies to the partisans and demanded more aircraft. 'This', he said, 'has priority even over the bombing of Germany.' On the eve of the Sicily landings he again ordered Menzies to provide a special report based on Ultra intelligence, 'showing the heavy fighting and great disorder going on in those regions and assembling also the intelligence about the number of Partisans &c., and of Axis troops involved or contained'. He then sent it to General Alexander exhorting him that 'Great prizes lie in the Balkan direction'. Early in July he took a drastic step to increase the standing of the mission with Tito. To the shock and dismay both of SOE and the Foreign Office he appointed Fitzroy Maclean as his special emissary to the guerrilla leader. 'What we want', he told Anthony Eden, 'is a daring Ambassador-Leader with these hardy and hunted guerrillas.'

There is no better evidence of Churchill's romantic passion for the guerrillas than his choice of Maclean. A warrior-diplomat whose father had been a friend of Churchill at Sandhurst, he enjoyed a privileged education at Eton and Cambridge, and a front seat in the stalls as a diplomat in Paris and Moscow during Europe's descent into war. His reputation as an adventurer-traveller and expert on the Soviet Union was made by daring forays into Soviet Central Asia. As an adept puller of strings he exited the Foreign Office via Parliament to join the SAS in the Western Desert. Here he made his name as a desert warrior in behind-the-lines exploits and became friends with Randolph, Churchill's boisterous son. He also made a strong impact on Churchill at an embassy dinner in Cairo in August 1942. 'No gentler pirate ever cut a throat or robbed a ship', wrote Churchill of Maclean, quoting from Byron. Behind Maclean's charismatic charm lay determined ambition.[18]

Summoned to Chequers, the 32-year-old Maclean suffered the traditional ritual of staying up late while Churchill watched films and cartoons. Towards midnight a message was brought to Churchill. 'As the squawking of Donald Duck and the baying of Pluto died away', recalled Maclean, Churchill rose to his feet to announce the dramatic news of the resignation of Mussolini. 'This', he told Maclean, 'makes your job even more important than ever. The German position in Italy is crumbling. We must now put all the pressure we can on the other side of the Adriatic.' Maclean asked about the political risks of supporting the Communist partisans. His task, Churchill told him, 'was simply to help find out who was killing the most Germans and suggest means by which we could help them kill more'. Politics would be a secondary consideration.

Responsible directly to Churchill, Maclean rode roughshod over SOE and the Foreign Office. Keble, still holding the SOE fort in Cairo, actively obstructed him, and Maclean prudently arranged to duplicate his messages to SIS. Finally, in mid-September, now a Brigadier and with a mission that included an OSS Major, he parachuted into the Yugoslav blackness. 'I fancied myself as a latter day Lawrence [of Arabia]', he wrote later, 'blowing up trains and bridges.' What he found instead was a kaleidescope of heroism and treachery, rivalry and intrigue.[19]

On the eve of his departure for Quebec Churchill demonstrated again his liking for daring and unorthodox men of action. Half an hour before sitting down to dinner with his wife and daughter he heard that Brigadier Orde Wingate had just arrived from Burma. Wingate's exploits in Abyssinia had already made him a living legend before Archibald Wavell chose him to organise guerrilla warfare behind Japanese lines in Burma. Here, the feats of his Chindits – long-range penetration groups supported by air – transformed him into a figure of controversy, but Churchill had no doubts. Considering him as a man of 'genius and audacity', he immediately asked to see him. Wingate arrived at Downing Street with little but a bush shirt and toothbrush. Over dinner he captivated Churchill with his tales of jungle fighting behind enemy lines. 'We had not talked for half an hour before I felt myself in the presence of the highest quality', recalled Churchill. He told him, 'You must come tonight and tell all this to the President.' Barely three hours later, and still in his tropical clothes, Wingate was on the night train to Scotland bound for the Clyde, the *Queen Mary* and Quebec.[20]

Early in the summer of 1943 Greek guerrillas under SOE command blew up the Asopos viaduct on the Athens–Salonika line to maintain the fiction of an imminent threat to southern Greece. This attack, like the Gorgopotamos raid six months before, was led by Brigadier Eddie Myers. Selborne described him to Churchill as a remarkable personality akin to Lawrence of Arabia who had submitted a 'thrilling' account of both operations. 'He is a quiet, modest, and very attractive man to meet, and I think very sensible', he reported, 'although he is not by any means a trained politician.' Churchill pored over the details, including photographs, and worried about Myers's politics. By now, Greek affairs had become infinitely byzantine. Myers's group consisted of guerrillas from EAM/ELAS, the Communist-dominated and anti-royalist resistance. This was anathema to Churchill, who felt strong loyalty to the Greek King George II, a cousin to the British monarch. He quickly acquired a visceral loathing for EAM/ELAS, denouncing them as little more than bandits. They should, he told Eden, 'be starved and struck at by every means in our power'. Behind all this lay Greece's considerable strategic significance for Britain's long-term position in the eastern Mediterranean, the lifeline to the Middle East and India. Early in October he asked Desmond Morton to summon Myers to Chequers for lunch. On hearing the news Eden warned Churchill that Myers was too sympathetic to the guerrillas. 'I will look after him', Churchill promised.

For Myers the lunch was acutely uncomfortable. Wedged between Churchill in his famous boiler suit on one side and Mrs Churchill on the other, he found himself simultaneously talking to Clementine about women's contribution to the war while listening to her husband's perorations about Greece. Over cigars, Myers showed Churchill aerial photographs of the Asopos Viaduct lying at the bottom of the gorge and Churchill chuckled delightedly. Profiting from the joviality, Myers prevailed on him to insert a few words into an overseas BBC broadcast Myers was to make that night to Greece promising that Britain had no intention of restoring the Greek King against the will of the Greek people. Half an hour later Churchill had second thoughts. 'No, I don't like any of this', he told Myers, 'it's too risky.' Nor could he accept Myers's view of the EAM/ELAS guerrillas. Several times he referred to them dismissively as 'Tom Wintringhams', after the Communist former military correspondent of the *Daily Worker* who had commanded a battalion of the International Brigades in the Spanish Civil War and whose articles on guerrilla warfare appeared regularly in the popular weekly *Picture*

Post. 'One point I could not get into Churchill's head', Myers complained, 'was that the [guerrillas] were not just "bandits" but that they represented all types of Greeks.' When he told Churchill that 80 to 90 per cent of Greeks were republicans, Churchill simply rejected his view. 'I won't be blackmailed by these bandits!' he protested. His final words were that he wanted a fair deal for the Greek King. 'I won't be stampeded', he declared. Three weeks later civil war broke out. Myers, who had hoped to rejoin ELAS, was posted elsewhere. From then on Churchill's combative anti-Communist views dictated the SOE line on Greece.[21]

Churchill had greeted Myers at Chequers with the ominous words: 'Ah, yes, your organisation has been meddling in the work of the Foreign Office and, if it had not been for me, they would have gone under.' Myers had no idea what he meant, but Churchill spoke the truth. At a stormy meeting of ministers only five days before he had saved SOE from extinction.

The crisis had been building since the spring over the priority to be given to special operations. At most the RAF was prepared to supply a few more aircraft for use in the Balkans, but for Western Europe, where resistance would not be fully operational until 1944, it dug in its heels. The dispute also became entangled in SOE's rivalry with SIS. Stewart Menzies was deeply suspicious about the security of SOE's European circuits. In part he was right. Belgian networks had been penetrated by the Germans in 1942, as (still unconfirmed) had Dutch operations, but it was the state of affairs in France that most bothered him.

The secret war in France reflected Churchill's general maxim that 'there is more in British policy . . . than abusing Pétain and backing de Gaulle'. SIS's closest links were with the pre-war intelligence service, many of whose members were serving Vichy. It ran networks in the occupied and non-occupied zones, and Menzies insisted on a ban on sabotage in the non-occupied zone in order to protect his assets. SOE worked with Gaullists and non-Gaullists. The former prefect Jean Moulin arrived in London from France in 1941 bringing news of growing underground resistance and parachuted back on New Year's Day 1942 as de Gaulle's personal representative. A year later he formed the *Conseil national de la Résistance* that rallied most resistance movements to the banner of de Gaulle. After the Germans entered the unoccupied zone, the ban on sabotage was lifted.

Churchill was a prime mover in the decision. 'It seems important', he said, 'to intensify operations in order to make the relations between the torpid French and the German invaders as unpleasant as possible.' This rang alarm bells with Stewart Menzies, who complained that it threatened his own networks along the Mediterranean coast and the Franco-Spanish frontier. His panic was calmed only by a promise that a general campaign of sabotage was not yet on the agenda and by SOE ordering its circuits to dampen down the rising tempo of resistance caused by the growth of the Maquis; this threatened longer term planning for D-Day.

One of Menzies' principal worries was the security of the Free French. Here he could count on Churchill, who was far from reconciled to de Gaulle and was under intense pressure from Roosevelt to drop him altogether. At Casablanca he and Roosevelt had contrived a public handshake between de Gaulle and the American-backed General Giraud, but it took the two Frenchmen months to form a French Committee of National Liberation in Algiers, after which Churchill declared the end of his relations with Free France. He even sent a secret circular to the British press denouncing de Gaulle for his 'undoubtedly Fascist and dictatorial tendencies'.

That summer his desire to propitiate Roosevelt's dislike for de Gaulle caused a serious crisis in relations with the French resistance. It relied heavily on British subsidies of 30 million francs per month. In June the amount soared to 80 million francs after a one-time payment to support the thousands of young men fleeing from forced labour. The decision outraged Desmond Morton, who wanted to take the leadership of the resistance away from de Gaulle. 'Otherwise', he argued, 'de Gaulle will use this great power, backed by our money, to advance his own political interests in France . . .' Churchill ordered that French resistance should not fall into Gaullist hands. 'Let me have your proposals', he wrote to Selborne, 'for carrying on the underground work without admitting de Gaulle or his agents to any effective share in it, and without letting any sums of money getting into their hands.'

This was a particularly fatuous intervention. Most resistance in France had long since rallied to de Gaulle and SOE depended heavily on these groups to fulfil their directives. Only relentless pressure by Eden, a powerful backlash in the press against Churchill's attempted manipulation, and a forceful response by Selborne that thousands of young Frenchmen could not be abandoned to the

Gestapo forced Churchill to back down. The threat to withhold further subsidies was soon lifted and the crisis blew over, but it threw alarming light on Churchill's volatile relations with de Gaulle and his uncertain grasp of resistance realities.[22]

In the meantime tragic dramas in France overshadowed the histrionics in London. Jean Moulin was arrested in a suburb of Lyons, and only his heroism in the face of Gestapo torture prevented a total collapse of Free French resistance. Three days later the Gestapo moved in on a small hotel in Paris and arrested Francis Suttill, a 32-year-old agent of SOE's 'F' Section. Code-named 'Prosper', he headed a circuit operating under the same name south of the French capital. His arrest followed the round-up of other agents in the circuit, which gave rise in London to suspicions of treachery, poor security and mismanagement. SIS was quickly aware of the disaster. 'C''s personal assistant later recalled how Claude Dansey, the assistant chief of SIS, came into his room and delightedly asked him if he had heard the latest news. 'What news?' he asked, thinking that the Allies had pulled off some coup against the Germans. 'SOE's in the shit', replied Dansey. 'They've bought it in France. The Germans are mopping them up all over the place.'[23] Menzies quickly submitted a damning report to the Joint Intelligence Committee and Churchill called a meeting of the Defence Committee. Here he listened while arguments that had raged in Whitehall corridors for most of the summer were rehearsed again. Selborne claimed that resistance across Europe was booming and unless supported by arms would wither and die. Charles Portal remained adamant that the RAF could spare no more planes in Western Europe. When they had finished Churchill weighed in with passionate support for the resistance. It was vital for the war effort, he insisted, and while terrible reprisals occurred they should all remember that 'the blood of the martyrs was the seed of the Church'. There was no question, as far as he was concerned, of either abolishing SOE or giving it to Menzies. This basic issue out of the way, he accepted that Bomber Command and SIS should continue to have priority for aircraft supply. He reaffirmed the decision after his return from Quebec.

Before leaving for Canada Churchill read in his report on special operations that in June the Germans had rounded up resistance leaders under the impression that an Allied invasion of France was imminent. 'They succeeded in capturing some important men', he read, 'and a very few British officers ... the incident shows once more the chronic French incapacity in security.' Boldly circling the words 'British officers', Churchill scribbled 'What happened to them?' His interest may have gone beyond normal concern, for it has been alleged that he met Francis Suttill before he left for France and misbriefed him deliberately about plans for an imminent Allied invasion. Suttill, in short, was sacrificed to a greater game of strategic deception in which Churchill played a personal hand.[24]

The Prosper affair contains many imponderables ripe for tales of conspiracy and double cross. Some facts are clear. There certainly existed a deception operation, code-named 'Starkey', a notional attack to take place early in September designed to keep German forces pinned down in the west. It is also clear that Colonel Maurice Buckmaster, head of SOE's 'F' Section, was ordered to accelerate preparations for invasion in case it turned out possible, after all, to mount one that year. And when Suttill arrived in France he took with him an 'alert' signal warning the whole Prosper circuit to stand by. At the heart of the question is whether or not this was a misunderstanding or something more deliberate.

If it was indeed planned, the deception staff in London would have relied on two possible routes for the information to flow to the Germans: careless talk and lax security by Suttill, or deliberate betrayal of Prosper to the Gestapo in the knowledge it would extract news of Allied 'plans' under interrogation. The role of duplicitous traitor in this conspiratorial scenario is played by Claude Dansey, who possessed the means in the enigmatic and sinister figure of Henri Dericourt. A skilled pre-war pilot, he was an Air Movement Officer for SOE in France, but he also maintained pre-war contacts with the Nazi security service while also working for Dansey and SIS. Where his true loyalties lay, and what precise role he played in the Prosper affair, remains a mystery. A post-war verdict of not guilty of treachery at a trial in Paris did nothing to dispel suspicion.

What about Churchill? Did he personally lend a hand to deception by briefing Suttill before he flew back to France? Buckmaster claimed as such shortly before his death. Churchill sent for Suttill because, he claimed, 'he wanted to increase the amount of sabotage operations and general unrest in France . . . he was encouraged . . . to run enormous risks, to forget his security training and produce violent explosions in and around the Paris area, so that Churchill could say to Stalin: Now look what we're doing.' He also claimed to have learned of all this (presumably after the fact) from Colonel John

Bevan, head of the London Controlling Section. A 1988 account, itself based in part on Buckmaster's evidence, told of Suttill driving from Baker Street to the Cabinet War Rooms in a staff car accompanied by Selborne. 'When Francis Suttill emerged from the Cabinet War Rooms he was a changed man', the account claims. 'He had been charged with what he believed was the greatest secret of the war – the date of the invasion.'[25]

Yet despite the apparently authenticating detail no convincing evidence exists to support it. Churchill was in London during the period in question and could have seen Suttill. Even if he did, it seems unlikely that he deliberately misbriefed him. If part of a deception plan, he would not have acted without the approval of Bevan, and it seems implausible that the man who masterminded 'Mincemeat' with such scrupulous care would have favoured a scheme riddled with potential hazards. There was no guarantee that Suttill, if captured, would talk, or that the story would reach the Germans in the form that the deception planners wanted. Nor would Churchill have knowingly risked long-term damage to SOE whose role for the *real* invasion he regarded as crucial. If he saw Suttill personally, then he may well have praised the resistance for holding down German troops in France, and from this Suttill might have concluded that an invasion was imminent, but a deliberately calculated sacrifice of Suttill for deception seems unlikely. Churchill's query about the fate of SOE officers in France arrested that summer reflects genuine concern, not some guilt-ridden secret. As for Suttill, he suffered the terrible fate of most captured secret agents. He was interrogated continuously for three days, denied sleep, food or drink, had one of his arms broken, and was murdered after a year's solitary confinement in Sachsenhausen.

In August 1943 Eisenhower began to prepare for the invasion of the Italian mainland. At Quebec Churchill and Roosevelt finally endorsed plans for Normandy but Churchill still hankered after action in the Balkans. The capitulation of Italy early in September only whetted his appetite. This and other contentious strategic and political issues were placed on the agenda for Tehran at the end of November. Three days after Kiev was recaptured by the Red Army, Churchill told an audience at the Mansion House that while the Western Allies had notched up several impressive victories, the outstanding event that year had been the liberation of two-thirds of occupied Russia by the Red Army. This mood of triumphalism was not shared by his professional intelligence advisers and Lord Selborne for one was now seriously worried. The longer the war lasted the more powerful Communist resistance would become, he told Churchill, and SIS and MI5 should initiate a study of Communism on a worldwide scale. Churchill merely initialled this before sailing for Cairo to meet with Roosevelt. As the battleship approached Alexandria he again lamented the failure to exploit events in the Mediterranean: 'the allies have also failed to give any real measure of support to the Partisans in Yugoslavia and Albania. These forces are containing as many divisions as the British and Americans put together . . .'[26]

Three major decisions at Tehran had particular import for the secret war. First was the agreement to launch Operation Overlord, the invasion of France, in the spring of 1944, a decision that gave a target date and place for the co-ordination of resistance movements and intelligence circuits. Second was the announcement to Stalin of a major Anglo-American deception campaign intended to deceive the Germans about the strength, timing and objective of the invasion of Europe. Finally the Allies agreed to supply Tito's partisans in Yugoslavia to the greatest possible extent.

The results were quickly felt. Back in Cairo Churchill met Deakin and Maclean with Tito's right-hand man, Vladimir Velebit. 'We found him installed in a villa out by the Pyramids', Maclean recorded, 'in bed . . . smoking a cigar and wearing an embroidered dressing gown.' Loosening them up with anecdotes about Stalin and an adolescent crack about the hazards of parachuting in a kilt, Churchill briefed them on the decision to give all-out support to Tito. As for Mihailović, he would be given one last chance with a request to blow up an important bridge on the Belgrade–Salonika railway line. If he failed, then the British mission would be withdrawn and all supplies to the chetniks stopped. Maclean then asked Churchill if there was a problem in supporting Communists. 'Do you intend', Churchill asked, 'to make Yugoslavia your home after the war?' Maclean replied no. 'Neither do I', said Churchill. 'And that being so, the less you and I worry about the form of government they set up the better . . . what interests us is, which of them is doing most harm to the Germans.' Two days later the decision was sanctified at a lunch held by the Minister Resident in the Middle East. Such was Churchill's enthusiasm for Tito that none of the guests felt inclined to speak up for Mihailović. Those who did harbour doubts were quickly put in their place. One was the young Julian Amery, son of the Secretary of State for India who was working for SOE's Balkan Division. He queried the apparent inconsistency of supporting a monarch in Greece and Tito in Yugoslavia. To this Churchill magisterially replied: 'I see you think that what I am proposing is inconsistent. It may be. But it is my policy and I still have some influence here.'[27]

Maclean returned to the partisans with a greatly enlarged mission. One of its members was the unlikely figure of Randolph Churchill. 'On operations', Maclean explained later, 'I knew him to be thoroughly dependable, possessing both endurance and determination . . . I felt too . . . that he would get on well with the Yugoslavs, for his enthusiastic and at times explosive approach to life was not unlike theirs.'[28] It was a shrewd move. Randolph's presence strengthened Churchill's own emotional commitment to Tito's cause. If he could not be there himself then he could, by filial proxy, relive his youthful days of guerrilla adventure in Cuba, India and South Africa. Maclean's reports on Tito confirmed what Ultra and *Abwehr* intercepts had long been suggesting and skilfully reinforced Churchill's strategic preferences. Ever since the Sicily landings he had been pressing for action in the Balkans. Denied this, and deeply frustrated by the American obsession with Overlord, he eagerly grasped at the Balkan guerrillas as a substitute. This did not automatically mean abandoning Mihailović. But when he received an *Abwehr* decrypt revealing a secret treaty between the Germans and chetniks in Montenegro, followed shortly afterwards by another revealing negotiations between Mihailović and the SS in Zagreb, the die was cast. In February 1944 British liaison officers with the chetniks withdrew. Three months later Mihailović was dismissed as Minister of War by King Peter.

By mid-1943 the preponderance of American power was severely limiting Britain's hand. Roosevelt's attempts to bypass Churchill and manoeuvre a separate summit with Stalin had caused a definite chill and Churchill, as his defiant comment to Amery in Cairo suggested, was determined to play a British game in the Mediterranean. His speech to Parliament after his return from Trident hinted at the turbulence beneath the surface. 'All sorts of divergences, all sorts of differences of outlook and all sorts of awkward little jars necessarily occur as we roll ponderously forward together along the rough and broken road of war.'[29]

The path was particularly rocky when it came to secret service. On the one hand Churchill happily shared intelligence with Roosevelt about their common great venture for Normandy. Hardly had he left Tehran than he received a lengthy MAGIC report on a visit made by Oshima to see German defences in France that reassured him about the feasibility of Overlord. Knowing that Roosevelt had seen little SIGINT material since leaving Washington, he ordered that it be brought to his notice. But elsewhere conflict bubbled over areas of subversive warfare. Despite the 1942 SOE–OSS agreement, the Americans were increasingly chafing at their exclusion from areas dominated by the British. In particular Donovan was determined to break what he called 'the British hammerlock' in the Balkans. Fitzroy Maclean's appearance in Yugoslavia brought matters to a head. For although his mission included an OSS officer, it was clear that command lay with Maclean who reported direct to Churchill. Nor did an arrangement that same month for joint missions mollify Donovan. Defiantly, he sent an officer to Italy to ferry supplies directly to Tito. The American crossed into Yugoslavia and made contact with the partisan leader. When an SOE officer tried to stop him, he told him brutally 'to go fuck himself'. Meanwhile Roosevelt made the extraordinary suggestion to Churchill that Donovan should take over all Balkan special operations. Churchill gave him a robust refusal but Donovan remained obstinate. In November 1943 he flew out to Cairo and announced that OSS would no longer co-operate with Maclean and would send its own independent missions to the partisans and chetniks. His subsequent incursions into Balkan resistance, not to mention those of Roosevelt, were to trouble Churchill throughout the final months of the war.[30]

Churchill spent Christmas 1943 recuperating from pneumonia at Eisenhower's requisitioned villa near Carthage. News from France did little to improve his mood. Hearing that de Gaulle had arrested three former Vichy politicians with anti-Nazi credentials, he bitterly denounced the Free French as ambitious intriguers carrying civil war into France. He promised that he would also personally see members of the French National Committee and the resistance movement itself to try to sort things out. Six months before D-Day affairs in France were beginning to dominate his thoughts on the secret war.

16

Behind the Lines

New Year's Day 1944 found Churchill in Marrakesh still conva-
lescing from pneumonia after the Tehran and Cairo conferences. Recuperating in the sun he conferred with Montgomery over
'Overlord', scrutinised plans for Anzio, consumed his daily Ultra,
and pondered the future of Poland, an issue made acute when Soviet
forces swept across its pre-war frontier in the first week of January.
He also held a tetchy meeting with de Gaulle.

Apart from Anzio, the topic that absorbed him most was
Yugoslavia. The meetings in Cairo had removed any lingering doubts
over Mihailović's collaboration with the enemy. Bill Deakin, for
example, had shown him a photograph of one of Mihailović's
commanders being entertained at a banquet by the Italian General
he was supposed to be fighting. Yet there remained the problem of
the royal Yugoslav government. Churchill hoped he could broker a
deal between the young monarch and Tito that would guarantee the
King his throne; the price would be the ditching of Mihailović. By
now Tito was once again on the run from the Germans and
Churchill felt that he needed encouragement. In the first of many
messages he told him that Britain's goal in Yugoslavia was 'to cleanse
the soil . . . from the filthy Nazi Fascist taint', not to dictate the
future government of the country. In future Britain would send aid
only to him but he would not cast King Peter aside. He hoped that
Tito would let him know through Fitzroy Maclean of anything he
could do to help. He signed the letter: 'Believe me, Yours faithfully,
Winston S. Churchill'. Two weeks later, with the letter in his pocket
and Randolph in tow, Maclean parachuted back to Tito.

During Churchill's stay in Marrakesh a shadow had fallen over
SOE in London. By this time Overlord planners had built the
French resistance into their preparations. In the run-up to D-Day

underground networks would sabotage strategic industries, power supplies, and rail and canal communications; create special groups for action on the day itself; control and supply spontaneous uprisings that would inevitably occur once liberation began; and help with 'Bodyguard', the strategic deception plan. All this would justify Churchill's patient support for SOE.

While he was hosting his 69th birthday dinner at Tehran in the convivial company of Stalin and Roosevelt, this sunny prospect was clouded by the abrupt suspension by the Royal Air Force of clandestine flights into Europe on the grounds that the Dutch SOE network had been penetrated by the *Abwehr* and over 40 SOE agents had parachuted directly into German hands. Behind the decision lay yet another Whitehall intrigue involving SIS, and the Joint Intelligence Committee launched another inquiry into SOE. Churchill was too preoccupied with events in Tehran and Cairo, and too ill with pneumonia in Tunis, to do anything about all this. It was eventually in Marrakesh that Desmond Morton handed him the JIC report marked 'Most Secret and Personal'. It called for radical change at the top, the separate direction of paramilitary activities, and the unification of intelligence and subversion.

The hand of Stewart Menzies was all too apparent. Morton also put in the knife. 'I have always held the view', he told Churchill, 'that on technical as opposed to political grounds at least part of the work for which SOE is now responsible should always have been carried out by "C".'[1] Churchill was by now used to Morton's prejudice and had been long resigned to the sniping between Baker Street and Broadway, the SIS headquarters. He decided to defer any decision until he returned to London. By the time he did so, in mid-January, passions had cooled and flights to Europe resumed. On Churchill's insistence there were no more challenges to SOE.

Dramatic evidence of his continuing faith in the clandestine war was provided later that month after he set up a committee with himself in the chair to review weekly preparations for Overlord. Lord Selborne provided him with plenty of ammunition. First was the case of Squadron-Leader Frank Griffiths of the 138 Special Duties Squadron. Piloting a Halifax and circling a dropping zone near the Swiss border the previous August, two of his engines had been knocked out by ground fire and the plane had crashed. Griffiths evaded capture and made contact with the local Maquis. They passed him from safe house to safe house until he crossed the Swiss border and reached Geneva. From there he had been smuggled back to Britain by the escape agency MI9 and had written up a colourful account of his adventures. Selborne mentioned it to Churchill who demanded to see it.[2] Barely had he done so than a formidable figure from the French resistance made an appearance. Emmanuel d'Astier de la Vigerie, whose brothers had been implicated in the Darlan assassination, was head of the resistance movement *Libération* and de Gaulle's Minister of the Interior. He had accompanied de Gaulle to Marrakesh and sparked Churchill's interest in the Maquis. He had just arrived in London and Selborne, still smarting from the attacks on SOE, saw him as a valuable weapon in dealing with Churchill. Thus he dined with Churchill at Downing Street and the next afternoon turned up to discuss air drops for the French resistance.

For Churchill it was an electric encounter. D'Astier was a charismatic figure whom he described to Roosevelt as 'a man of the Scarlet Pimpernel type'. As for d'Astier, he had quickly summed up Churchill. 'Like de Gaulle', he later recorded, 'Churchill was a hero out of the *Iliad*, the lone and jealous governor of the British war effort.' If anything was to be done it was through Churchill himself, not his 'secret services'.[3] Deliberately, he stressed how the Maquis was killing two German soldiers for every one of its own, and how some 20,000 eager fighters could be found between Grenoble and the Italian frontier. But they were heavily harrassed by the Germans and their French collaborators in the dreaded Milice. Worse, they were desperately short of guns and ammunition. Only one in five of the Maquis in the Haute-Savoie had a gun of any sort. What, d'Astier asked, could Churchill offer to help?

This was all Churchill needed. 'Brave and desperate men could cause the most acute embarrassment to the enemy', he declared, 'and it was right that we should do all in our power to foster and stimulate so valuable an aid to Allied strategy.'[4] With sufficient Allied aid, he enthused, the whole of south-eastern France could be turned into a second Yugoslavia; unspoken, perhaps, was also the thought that such an uprising could render redundant the American 'Anvil' landings in southern France to which he was so strongly opposed. But Churchill was not yet finished: another face-to-face encounter remained.

Wing Commander Forrest Yeo-Thomas, MC, was a natural Churchillian: turbulent, ungovernable, physically brave and robustly patriotic. Born into an English family long resident in France, he had fought in the First World War and narrowly escaped being shot by the Bolsheviks while fighting with the Poles. By 1939, after a chequered career in Paris as mechanic, accountant and audit clerk, he was a director of the Molyneaux fashion house. When Hitler invaded Poland he joined the Royal Air Force and after persistent efforts was recruited by SOE to work with 'Passy's' intelligence service. Twice he had gone behind enemy lines to help co-ordinate Gaullist networks and prepare them for action on D-Day. In England that January he was angry. Since Moulin's death German pressure had intensified and entire networks had been wiped out. The Maquis was desperately short of arms. 'Our present puny efforts are as likely to succeed as a man trying to fill a swimming pool with a fountain pen filler', he fulminated to a group of Air Ministry brass hats. Frustrated, he eventually poured out his anger to the one person of influence he knew, Major-General E. D. Swinton, Churchill's First World War ally over tank warfare. Impressed, Swinton wrote a personal letter to Churchill urging him to see Yeo-Thomas: 'You are the only one in a position to handle [this] without delay.' Early in February Yeo-Thomas found himself at 10 Downing Street.[5]

Churchill greeted Yeo-Thomas in the Cabinet room, his chair tilted back, the inevitable cigar in his mouth. He came to the point. 'I'm a busy man', he grunted, 'what have you got to say? I can give you five minutes.' Yeo-Thomas was given almost a full hour. He instantly entranced Churchill with his tales of men and women risking torture and death, 'carrying messages through the crowded, police-ridden streets of Paris and waiting for agents in the darkness in the windy wilderness of central France'. When he had finished Churchill grilled him about the Maquis. How were they organised? What did they need besides arms? Clothing? What sort of clothing? How much? How many aircraft would it take? Yeo-Thomas told him at least 100, with a minimum of 250 sorties a month. 'I shall see you get a hundred to start with', promised Churchill. Desmond Morton, sitting in, must have been silently apoplectic. His discomfort can only have increased when d'Astier arrived for his second meeting. To de Gaulle's right-hand man Churchill repeated the pledge he had just made to Yeo-Thomas: 'I am going to increase substantially the number of aircraft doing parachute operations to the Resistance, 'and greater supplies and more armaments are going to be sent.'

No sooner had an elated Yeo-Thomas left than Churchill dictated his orders to Lord Selborne and the Air Ministry. 'I want extra efforts made to improvise additional sorties to the Maquis . . . Even if fairly successful the February programme is not enough. Pray start at once on a programme for the March moon.'[6] D'Astier had told him that stocks of ammunition were far below what was reasonable, even for the few weapons that the Maquis in fact possessed. They also needed concentrated food and vitamins. On all this SOE should consult with the French. March supplies, Churchill ordered, should be double those of February.

Typically, his enthusiasm caused temporary chaos. As the SOE official historian later noted, it led Churchill for a few days to busy himself with the details of organising operations 'that he would better have left to . . . junior staff officers'. Eventually, too, he had to yield to the priorities of General Eisenhower when making choices between the resistance in northern France and the Maquis in the south-east. 'The mountain people have not had enough', he declared, but this romantic view was largely irrelevant to the needs of D-Day.[7]

Most important of all, Churchill stamped on further attempts to obstruct SOE in the run-up to D-Day. Stewart Menzies was quick to complain that the campaign to arm the Maquis was diverting aircraft from his own intelligence operations. Churchill reacted with impatience: 'Someone has been stirring him up.' Only a tiny fraction of the air effort was affected and did not involve the small Lysander planes used by SIS, but by now he accepted that the warfare between the two rival secret services was 'a lamentable, but perhaps inevitable, feature of our affairs'. The programme for arming the Maquis went ahead and Morton had the job of keeping Menzies both informed and happy. 'Otherwise', Churchill wryly observed, 'he becomes distressed if he thinks airplanes are being diverted from his service.'[8]

Three days after Yeo-Thomas walked out of Downing Street Churchill greeted 'Wild Bill' Donovan at Chequers. The OSS chief was in good form. He had just arrived from Anzio and gave Churchill an eyewitness account that presaged well for British–American intelligence co-operation in the battles ahead. Two weeks later Churchill presented Parliament with his first survey of the war since Tehran. After reviewing the campaign in Italy, progress in the bombing of Germany and the victories of the Red Army, he turned his gaze to behind enemy lines. Throughout conquered Europe, he told the packed and attentive Commons, there existed a unity of hatred and a desire to revolt against the Germans such as had never been seen before. But Europe was also suffering the 'disease of defeat', where the basic principles of national life had broken down. In these conditions, he said, 'indomitable patriots take different paths; quislings and collaborationists of all kinds abound; guerrilla leaders, each with their personal followers, quarrel and fight'. Because of these complexities the safest course for Britain was to judge all parties and factions dispassionately by the test of their readiness and their ability to fight the Germans and thus lighten the burden on Allied troops. It was on these grounds that British support in Yugoslavia had switched from Mihailović to Tito, 'an outstanding leader, glorious in the fight for freedom', whose partisans were now the only people doing any effective fighting against the Germans. By contrast, Greece presented a sharp and dismal picture. Here was the saddest example of the disease of defeat, where the Germans watched with 'contemptuous complacency' as treachery and violence tore the resistance apart. Powerful elements in the resistance (he did not mention EAM/ELAS by name) were less concerned with driving out the enemy than in 'seizing the title deeds of their country'. The suffering Greek people wanted liberation from bondage. 'They shall not wait in vain', he promised.[9]

Matters were far more complex and troubled. Throughout the Balkans a growing Anglo-American intelligence rift was casting its shadow and Churchill's meeting with Donovan at Chequers concealed severe tensions. Donovan tried hard to assert American influence against Churchill's determination to maintain a political monopoly in the Mediterranean. On the eve of Tehran he had even persuaded Roosevelt to propose that he should take over as the Allied intelligence supremo. 'Being a fearless and aggressive character', Roosevelt urged Churchill, 'he might do much good.' Churchill stamped on the idea. Pointing out that Britain already had some eighty SOE missions in the Balkans, many of them led by senior officers with considerable experience, he told the President that he did not see any centre in the Balkans from where Donovan could 'grip the situation'.

All came to a head with Churchill's decision to abandon Mihailović. Many Americans thought that this was a bad mistake. 'If we follow too closely the lead being taken by our British cousins', complained the head of OSS intelligence in Bari, 'we are letting go by default a force very well disposed to the United States . . .' Senior

OSS officers in the field told Donovan much the same. Not surprisingly, he insisted that if OSS agents were to operate with Maclean the mission should come under the joint American–British command of the Combined Chiefs of Staff in Washington.[10]

Against this background Churchill returned from Marrakesh only to be alerted by the Cabinet Secretary that the Americans were attempting to penetrate British ciphers. His first reaction was to consider approaching Roosevelt directly. Recalling his confession to Roosevelt after Pearl Harbor that Britain had ceased to attack American ciphers, he wondered whether it 'Would not be well for me to suggest to the President a self-denying ordinance by which, on a gentleman's agreement, both the British and American Governments would refrain from trying to penetrate each other's ciphers?' His second reaction was to ensure that particularly sensitive messages to the British mission in Washington now passed through specially secure channels provided by SIS. Finally he ordered that his personal communications with Maclean were kept firmly out of American hands. Donovan, he complained, 'is shoving his nose in everywhere. We are hardly allowed to breathe.' In a 'Most Secret' cipher telegram sent by one-time pad to General Wilson, Supreme Commander in the Mediterranean, he asked anxiously: 'Are you sure that my telegrams to you through this channel never pass through American hands and are kept strictly secret?'[11]

Meanwhile Donovan returned to Washington and won Roosevelt's support for keeping OSS intelligence (as opposed to operational) missions with Mihailović. Plans to send another OSS mission into chetnik territory began and Roosevelt told his intelligence chief that it should be made clear to the British that the Americans intended to keep their freedom of action. SOE Cairo learned of this in early April and immediately informed London. Churchill demanded that Roosevelt veto the OSS mission, and to be doubly sure secretly instructed SOE Cairo to delay 'by every reasonable means' any arrangement to fly the Americans into Yugoslavia. By all means be courteous, he told them, but be sure to deny them transport. He need not have worried. Roosevelt backed down and ordered Donovan to cancel the mission. 'The hatchet men had done their job at the highest level', came the bitter complaint from OSS officers in Cairo.[12]

Churchill felt equally as strongly about Greece, but here he held the left-wing guerrillas in contempt. When Sir Alan Brooke suggested that it would help D-Day deception plans if resistance in Greece could be intensified and Myers allowed back, Churchill exploded. 'Giving them weapons will not increase their efforts against the Germans', he protested, 'but only secure the domination of these base and treacherous people after the war.' As for Myers, he flatly forbade his return. 'He is the chief man who reared by hand this cockatrice brute of EAM-ELAS', he declared. 'There is no comparison between them and the bands of Marshal Tito. They are a mere scourge on the population, and are feared by the Greek villagers more than the Germans.' But many of the OSS agents were hostile to the Greek monarchy and sympathetic to the left. Even those who were not often had no truck with Churchill. 'The British', declared one American officer in Cairo, 'were not interested in Greek liberation . . . but in naked imperial interest.'

The cousins were drifting apart. In Algiers, Harold Macmillan observed the divergence. The Americans, he noted, 'either wish to revert to isolationism combined with suspicion of British imperialism, or to intervene in a pathetic desire to solve in a few months . . . problems which have baffled statesmen for many centuries'. Two weeks later, after a long talk with his American opposite number Robert Murphy, he noted gloomily that Washington and London were not as close as they had been. 'The honeymoon stage between the President and Prime Minister is over', he wrote. Within hours Anglo-American forces under General Dwight D. Eisenhower were to land on the Normandy beaches.[13]

Determined to resist American influence in the Balkans, Churchill was no less adamant about Britain's interests in the Far East. Here his goal was the restoration or expansion of colonial rule after Japanese defeat. By contrast Roosevelt envisaged independence for the colonised peoples of Asia and the dissolution of Britain's Empire. Both men agreed not to let the issue damage their joint efforts in Europe, but beneath the surface tensions were particularly acute between the Allies' secret services. SOE in the Far East was known as Force 136. The immense distances, the special challenges of jungle warfare, and the need for agents who could mingle unseen with local populations made special operations particularly hazardous. Officered largely by businessmen, merchants and colonial officials keen to re-establish British influence, SOE did its best. As the war progressed, one historian has written, it 'began to resemble empire trade in khaki'. By contrast OSS was fuelled by American anti-imperialism. 'Why should American boys die to re-possess colonies for the British and their French and Dutch allies?' asked the political adviser to General 'Vinegar Joe' Stilwell, commander of the China–Burma–India theatre.[14]

The spring of 1944 found Churchill gazing with particular interest at Burma, anxious to see action in a British sphere of influence. In March the Japanese launched an offensive across the Indian border towards Imphal and Churchill urged Mountbatten to counter-attack. 'What is Wingate doing?' he asked. The maverick soldier was already at work. That month several hundred men of his second Chindit Expedition penetrated by glider into Burma and across the Irrawady River. Soon they were joined by Chindits trekking overland from the Naga hills, as well as Ghurkas and Kachins. 'All our columns are inside the enemy's guts', Wingate told his men, and he ebulliently told Churchill that the Japanese had made mistakes which might prove fatal: 'Get Special Force four transport squadrons and you have all Burma North of twenty-fourth parallel plus a decisive Japanese defeat.' Churchill leapt at the proposal and promised to praise his efforts in his next broadcast on the BBC. But within hours tragedy struck. Wingate's plane crashed in the jungle, killing him instantly. Churchill was shattered. In Wingate he had seen a latter-day Lawrence of Arabia, a romantic hero raising revolt behind enemy lines. Now all he could do was tell Mountbatten that he was 'deeply grieved at the loss of this man of genius who might have been a man of destiny'.[15]

Longer-term politics also dictated Churchill's view of plans for Japanese-occupied Indo-China, the heartland of France's Asian empire. Guerrilla training had already begun to recapture Indo-China for the French, but Roosevelt's anti-colonialism redoubled in vigour when it came to this issue. 'After a hundred years of French rule in Indo-China', he declared to Stalin at Tehran, 'the inhabitants are worse off than before.' He vetoed any moves to strengthen Gaullist hands in Asia and especially the dispatch of a French mission to Mountbatten's headquarters in Colombo. Both Mountbatten and Force 136 thought this a bad mistake that would play into Japanese hands. They asked Churchill to persuade Roosevelt to lift the ban.

He refused point-blank. An exasperated Lord Selborne told Churchill bluntly that he was standing in the way of all SOE plans for Indo-China. Why not let the French mission go to Colombo without telling the Americans? Even Anthony Eden grew impatient. If the

French were officially frozen out, he warned, they would simply find another way to make their mark. Again Churchill refused. One reason was his dislike of de Gaulle, but more important was Roosevelt who had been more outspoken to him on the evils of French colonialism in Indo-China than on any other subject. 'I imagine it is one of his principal war aims to liberate Indo-China from France', he told Eden just days before D-Day. 'Do you really want to go and stir all this up at such a time as this?' But he reserved his final blow for SOE. It was a mistake to suppose one should always be doing something, he said. 'The greatest service SOE can render is to select with great discrimination their areas and occasions of intervention.'[16] He was to maintain his veto on special operations in Indo-China until well after D-Day.

Churchill's outburst was not confined to Asia. Conflicts over the resistance in Greece and his personal backing for Maclean in Yugoslavia highlighted the growing conflict between the political forces released by the resistance and Churchill's long-term aims. By the spring of 1944 he was becoming deeply anxious about Communism in Europe. The warm glow of Tehran had dissipated. The Red Army was about to enter Hungary and had long crossed into Poland. That Stalin regarded it as a future satellite was becoming clearer by the day. Churchill welcomed Soviet victories over the *Wehrmacht* while dreading their political impact. 'It is perfectly clear that to argue with the Russians only infuriates them . . .', he told Eden gloomily. 'Although I have tried in every way to put myself in sympathy with these Communist leaders, I cannot feel the slightest trust or confidence in them.' Nor was he reassured by obvious signs of Soviet bad faith on sensitive aspects of the secret war. After Tehran John Bevan had travelled to Moscow to brief the Russians on the Bodyguard deception plan. The Russians responded with proposals for diversionary raids on the north coast of Norway and Finland. Churchill accepted the plan and agreed to provide Moscow with detailed maps and photo-reconnaissance data along with a photographic interpretive expert. But after a series of delays in Moscow, General Burrows, head of the British military mission, concluded it was nothing but a ruse by the Soviet General Staff to obtain details of British intelligence about the target area.[17]

It was in a volatile mood of despair and exhilaration that Churchill erupted in May over special operations in Romania. Back in 1940, when he had spoken so glibly of 'Setting Europe Ablaze', neutral

Romania had been a happy hunting ground for Britain's secret agents plotting to blow up oil fields or to block the Danube. Now it was different. Romania under Marshal Ion Antonescu had sided with Hitler and the Red Army's advance into Bessarabia meant that Romania's future lay in the Soviet bloc. Three days before Christmas 1943 a small SOE team headed by Gardyne de Chastelain, a former oil engineer, parachuted into the country on Operation 'Autonomous'. Its primary mission was to contact the leader of the National Peasant Party and persuade him to press for a surrender to the Russians, but the team fell into the hands of the Romanian government and was interned in Bucharest. Here Antonescu protected them from the Germans, seeing in their W/T set and ciphers a way of communicating secretly with the Allies that might prove useful in the future.

At the end of April Churchill was enjoying a warm spring day at Chequers. Guests included Jan Smuts and SOE's Bill Hudson. The pleasantries were interrupted by a telegram from Molotov claiming that SOE was plotting with Antonescu behind Moscow's back. Declaring that 'Bolsheviks are crocodiles', Churchill robustly rejected Molotov's claims but seized the chance to lay the foundation of his famous 'percentages deal' with Stalin by which Romania was traded off for Greece. But he vented his real spleen on SOE for precipitating a crisis in Anglo-Soviet relations. 'It does seem to me that [it] barges in in an ignorant manner into all sorts of delicate situations', he protested. 'They were originally responsible for building up the nest of cockatrices for EAM in Greece . . . It is a very dangerous thing that the relations of two mighty forces like the British Empire and the USSR should be disturbed by obscure persons playing the fool far below the surface.' Such was his anger that he even threatened to dissolve SOE and a ban was placed on future operations into Romania. He soon simered down when he heard that Moscow had been informed about the mission weeks in advance, but it reinforced his view that special operations existed to serve policy, not make it. That same month he refused to discuss a possible post-war role for SOE. 'The part your naughty deeds in war play', he told Lord Selborne, 'in peace cannot at all be considered at the present time.' And to Harold Macmillan, who was keen to see subversive war continued into the peace, he pronounced that SOE in the Middle East should be dealt with firmly. 'They are a fertile sprout of mischief and overstaffing', Churchill declared.[18]

Churchill's decision to make personal contact had delighted Tito. Now a self-declared Marshal, head of a provisional government and receiving an increasing flow of Allied arms, Tito could look forward to victory over both the Germans and the chetniks. Churchill hoped that success would dilute his Communism and make him friendly to Britain. Throughout the spring and summer of 1944 he worked hard to strengthen the personal link and give the partisans solid support.

The linchpin of the strategy was Maclean, who refused to use SOE communications links, a quirk that caused delays and confusion. Churchill added even more. When he learned that Maclean was visiting Algiers he requested that they use code names that Churchill devised himself in all telephone calls. Fruit and vegetables were the theme of the day. General Wilson, the portly Commander-in-Chief Mediterranean universally known as 'Jumbo', was 'Pumpkin'. The Communist Tito was 'Raspberry', the prickly King Peter 'Gooseberry', and the unpalatable Mihailović was christened 'Cabbage'. Churchill's sweet-and-sour son Randolph became 'Apple'. When the call came through farce took over. Through an error Maclean had not received the code names. On picking up the telephone he heard Churchill's voice booming down the line asking if he had yet spoken to Pumpkin. 'Clearly one of us was off his head', Maclean concluded after this had been repeated once or twice. 'I hoped it wasn't me.' Fortunately for both, but after more confusion, it transpired that Churchill's penchant for spycraft may have been unnecessary as they were speaking on a scrambled line.[19]

Five weeks before Overlord, Maclean arrived in London with Vladimir Velebit to discuss how resistance in Yugoslavia could form a united campaign to attack the Germans. Churchill had several meetings with Maclean, and King Peter agreed to form a new government without Mihailović. This, hoped Churchill, would permit the Serbs to join with Tito and expel 'the filthy Hitlerite murderers . . . till not one remains'. He also had a long meeting with Velebit. 'A remarkable man', he declared. The next day, as Velebit prepared to return to Bosnia, Churchill sent Tito yet another message and added a wistful comment: 'I wish I could come myself but I am too old and heavy to jump out of a parachute.' Later, when he finally met Tito face to face, he repeated his regret. 'Yes I know', replied the partisan leader, 'but you did the next best thing and sent us your son.' Churchill's eyes filled with tears.[20]

In Randolph's adventures with the partisans Churchill fought guerrilla war by proxy. His son spent several months in 'Titoland', first in Bosnia at partisan HQ with Tito and Maclean, then in Croatia, before finally helping to celebrate the liberation of Belgrade. Aged 33 Randolph was still slim, blond and good-looking, but his character was already set, his personality and reputation a matter of public renown. Loquacious, opinionated, irascible, often drunk, he was too like his father for their relations to be anything but stormy. A sometimes brilliant political journalist, he had staunchly supported and frequently embarrassed his father during the 1930s, twice failing to win a parliamentary seat.

None the less Churchill loved him, and sending him to Tito was a stroke of genius. It removed Randolph from the fleshpots of Cairo and dinner tables of London, gave him a sense of purpose, and allowed his undoubted courage to show. It also signalled that he was serious about the Partisans. Above all, it came closest to giving Churchill what he wanted above all else: the feeling that he too was personally fighting the Nazis in hand-to-hand combat.

Randolph's exploits with the partisans are largely remembered through the acerbic pen of the novelist Evelyn Waugh, who spent several weeks with him in Croatia. The two men brought out the worst in each other. Waugh could be as drunken and boorish as Randolph. On one occasion, in order to shut Randolph up, Waugh wagered he could not read the Bible from begining to end. The silence lasted only to the end of Genesis. 'God, what a shit God is', exploded Randolph. Maclean added his own gloss. Randolph, he told Churchill, had thrown himself energetically into remedying the partisans' phenomenal ignorance of the Allied war effort. 'He is living in a wooden shack with the Intelligence Officer, a pig, and six Bosnian peasant girls', he added, 'and seems quite happy.' Randolph spoke no Serbo-Croat and hated Communism.

Yet he also trekked through the mountains, narrowly escaped death in a plane crash, and came close to capture by the Germans. His very arrival made a deep impression, as Vladimir Dedijer, another of Tito's lieutenants, remembered. While Randolph was being escorted to Tito a German plane flew overhead. The partisan escort wondered how he would react, but he remained standing 'as still', Dedijer said, 'as the Rock of Gibraltar'. And he was the Prime Minister's own son. 'For the Yugoslav Highlanders', Dedijer recorded, 'the best proof that Britain had decided to change its policy and back the Partisans.' An OSS officer who came to know

Randolph well succeeded in penetrating his abrasive mask. 'He had courage beyond bravery', he remembered, 'because he had to force himself to the front, and he did so constantly.' Above all Randolph possessed insatiable curiosity and a remarkably retentive memory.[21]

Churchill devoured Randolph's reports. 'The more you can write to me the better', he urged, 'especially descriptive letters, so that I can picture your daily life.' Randolph obliged with graphic accounts that enabled his father to place himself imaginatively at the heart of the action. One was a 5,000-word report in diary form of a hazardous two-week trek from western Bosnia to Croatia that involved crossing the main road from Bihac to Knin. 'It is one of the most important Hun lines of communication', he told Churchill.

> We set out at 7 when it gets dark. The Germans only dare use this road by day. Four or five hundred vehicles were counted on it today. At night they retire inside strongly-wired pillboxes which are dotted every four or five kilometres along the road. The company goes ahead, secures the crossing of the road, and about 10 o'clock, in bright moonlight, we get safely across, cutting the telephone wires as we go. This is well worth doing. The repair party is so often ambushed that it needs an escort of 200 Huns to protect it each time repairs are necessary. Across the road, we start climbing . . .[22]

To such vivid prose he added serious political analysis. There were two reasons why the British should support Tito, he told his father. First, they were the only Yugoslavs fighting the Germans; second, whether Britain helped Tito or not, he would be the post-war master of the country. Backing Tito in Serbia, the heartland of chetnik support, would not, as some protested, result in civil war. It already existed. The best that could be done to limit the killing was 'to make one side so strong that the other is beaten very quickly'. Churchill had the reports printed and circulated in Whitehall. He also dismissed the danger to Randolph's life or the risk that he might fall into German hands. 'I do not want his relationship to me and the fact that the enemy are specially after him to be a bar to his doing what is most serviceable', he told Maclean.

In May the worst almost happened when German parachutists of the SS Brandenburg Division swooped on Tito's HQ at Drvar and achieved total surprise. Randolph was lucky to escape. He just had time to pull on a pair of trousers and his flying jacket over his pyjamas, grab his gun, and join his fellow British officers' retreat into the hills. All he suffered were sore feet, his boots having been taken away to be cleaned. 'Except for this', he enthusiastically reported to Churchill, 'the whole affair was great fun.'

Was it more sinister than that? Conspiracy theories have inevitably flourished around the episode. Did Ultra provide Churchill with advance intelligence about the attack, knowledge that he deliberately concealed because he – and perhaps more especially Stewart Menzies – now considered Tito a threat to British plans for the Balkans? Alternatively, did he dare not use it through fear, once again, of revealing the Ultra secret to the Germans? Or was British intelligence so poor that it failed to pick up the evidence at all? Finally, did detailed knowledge of Tito's presence in Drvar leak out via the OSS to Mihailović, and thence to the Germans?[23]

None of these theories survive the light of evidence. The last can be dismissed first: the Germans had long known of Tito's presence in Drvar and needed no leaks in Washington to tell them. As for what Churchill knew in advance, a familiar story emerges. Ultra certainly indicated a forthcoming German operation against the Partisans, but not specifically Drvar or Tito as the target. Such warnings were frequent. As for intelligence officers on the ground, they had no access to the reports. As for motive, Churchill was still enjoying his honeymoon with Tito and had no possible motive for getting rid of him. Randolph could certainly throw awkward tantrums at dinner, but this was hardly a reason to let him be killed or captured.

Drvar was more significant. It forced Tito on to the run and into British arms. In early June he was evacuated to Bari. Immediately he insisted on moving to the island of Vis which was Yugoslav territory, albeit protected by a British garrison. Churchill, calculating that this would give him useful political leverage, agreed. The partisan leader sailed for Vis on 6 June 1944. Allied forces were already on the beaches of Normandy.

Churchill played a role in guarding the D-Day secret. In March he issued a stern reminder to Cabinet members of the dangers of unauthorised disclosures of information. The only safe rule, he laid down, was never to mention policy discussions even in the form of guarded allusions. A ban was placed on access to huge areas of the coastline, postal censorship was tightened, greater security applied to the vetting of ships' crews sailing from the UK, and a ban placed on travel to Ireland. He was typically nervous about the latter. After the Dublin government rejected a plea from Roosevelt to break ties with

Tokyo and Berlin he pressed for even stronger measures. These included immobilising the only Aer Lingus service capable of reaching Europe, and banning Irish travellers from using British and American airlines using Shannon airport. In April, neutral and Allied diplomats – except Americans, Russians and Dominion – were forbidden to send or receive uncensored communications or to leave Great Britain. And so deep were concerns about the security of the Free French that he decreed that no information that could possibly compromise Overlord should be passed to them. Under the insistent prompting of Stewart Menzies he also issued another order: every precaution should be taken to prevent leakage through secret agents sent from Britain to the Continent who might have operational knowledge that could be deliberately or inadvertently transmitted to the enemy.[24]

How far Churchill was prepared to go is suggested by the case of Air Commodore Ronald Ivelaw-Chapman, a former Director of Plans at the Air Ministry. Given command of a top-secret squadron identifying German radar installations in north-west Europe, he decided to show solidarity with his men in their hazardous missions. On a May night just four weeks before D-Day he was shot down over France and picked up by the resistance who secluded him in a safe house. Six days later an escape and evasion network headed by a Free French officer confirmed his identity and presence by radio to London. By this time Churchill had already ordered extreme precautionary measures. Ivelaw-Chapman knew far more than was healthy about the timing and location of D-Day. Churchill told Desmond Morton that Ivelaw-Chapman was to be recovered at all costs – or else be eliminated. Planning began to bring him out of France by Lysander, but before this could happen, or the Gestapo could capture him, Overlord made Churchill's order redundant.[25]

While this minor drama was being played out Churchill finally heard from the Joint Intelligence Committee that two essential conditions for Overlord had been met: German fighter forces in north-west Europe were now lower than a year before and their offensive divisions in reserve did not exceed twelve full-strength first-quality divisons. But Ultra also revealed that since April the Germans had been on standby for the expected invasion and that Hitler had cancelled leave for all those under Field Marshal von Rundstedt, his Commander-in-Chief West. Had the Germans suspected when and where the landings would take place? In mid-May

Churchill suffered extreme anxiety when Ultra revealed that the German Air Force in north-west Europe had guessed the landings would be along the Normandy coast. He anxiously harried Stewart Menzies and Sir Alan Brooke for reassurance that the estimate was not shared by the German High Command. Fortunately Ultra revealed a different estimate by von Rundstedt that provided some comfort. None the less, haunted by memories of the Dardanelles, Churchill ordered that efforts should continue to confuse the *Luftwaffe* outlook. In its last pre-D-Day assessment of German appreciations the Joint Intelligence Committee concluded that they had failed to guess the area of the main assault. But as usual Churchill was not content to leave it all to the professionals and seized on particular raw intercepts that rang alarm bells. Thus he responded to a lengthy intercept in late May revealing German plans for their U-boats by demanding a personal report by the First Sea Lord on the countermeasures being planned. Conscious of security to the last, he gave General de Gaulle only forty-eight hours' notice of the liberation of France.[26]

17

Shadows of Peace

After holding Churchill spellbound with his exploits Forrest Yeo-Thomas parachuted back to France but was picked up a few weeks later by the Gestapo and over the next few weeks endured brutal interrogation at its Paris headquarters. On the morning of 6 June 1944, isolated in a freezing punishment cell, he heard a voice from the cell above. 'Your comrades have landed', it said. 'Vive la France!' Throughout the prison he could hear strains of the Marseillaise. Tears pouring down his face, he stood to attention and sang God Save the King. The hour for the resistance had come.

The night before, clustered around their clandestine wireless sets, resisters had heard the BBC broadcast its customary *messages personnels*: pre-arranged signals alerting them to the arrival of a Lysander, the dropping of supplies, the return of an agent. This time the messages put them on alert for the invasion. Circuits attacked railways, cut telephone lines and blocked roads. Their impact was graphically illustrated in the fate of the 2nd SS Panzer Division whose three-day journey from Toulouse to Normandy suffered continuous resistance attack. It arrived seventeen days late. In reprisal it carried out a notorious massacre of over six hundred civilians at Oradour-sur-Glane, a small town outside Limoges. Herding the women and children into a church and the men into barns, troops set the buildings alight and shot those trying to escape. Three weeks later the mastermind of the slaughter, SS Major Otto Dickman, stepped out of his Normandy bunker and was instantly killed by a shell splinter. The date was 30 June. It was also the official end of Operation Neptune, the assault phase of Overlord. Over 800,000 Allied soldiers were now ashore in France.

Churchill followed the fighting with avid attention. Within twenty-four hours of D-Day he was delighted to read an Enigma decrypt revealing that attacks on German aircraft fuel had forced Berlin to break into its armed forces strategic oil reserve. 'I regard this as one of the most important pieces of information we have yet received', Charles Portal told him. On the other hand, his anxiety level rose sharply at an intercept about German plans for concentrated bombing attacks on cross-Channel shipping. Alerted by further intercepts, RAF bombers carried out a successful pre-emptive attack on the key *Luftwaffe* base outside Bordeaux.[1]

Six days after D-Day Churchill scrambled out of a landing craft, toured the Normandy bridgehead, and was on deck when the destroyer HMS *Kelvin* fired a salvo at the enemy, the fitting climax to what he told Roosevelt had been 'a jolly day'. That night, back in London, his exuberance was punctured when a German flying bomb (V-1) landed in Bethnal Green killing six civilians. Hitler had finally launched his long-feared 'secret weapon'.

Churchill later paid a rare and generous tribute to the vital role of intelligence in blunting the V-weapon offensive through its estimates of the size and performance of weapons, the likely scale of the attack, and the location of launching sites and production centres. He was unable to mention Ultra, but went out of his way to thank the European resistance. 'Agents of every country', he recorded, 'had helped us often with the greatest gallantry.' One outstanding example was Jeannie Rousseau, code-named 'Amniatrix'. A 23-year-old member of the 'Alliance' network in France, she provided the so-called 'Wachtel Report' that was read by Churchill during the first meeting about the V-1 and V-2 he chaired after the 1943 Peenemunde raid. Eventually arrested by the Gestapo, she miraculously survived Ravensbruck. As for Churchill, he ensured that Stewart Menzies was ordered to use as many secret agents as he could in the war against the V-weapons.[2]

Convincing Hitler that the main invasion was yet to come in the Pas de Calais remained a deception priority for weeks after D-Day. Churchill intervened to bolster the strategy. In July he read a top-secret MAGIC message from Ambassador Oshima to Tokyo that Berlin believed General Patton would shortly cross the Channel to cut off their forces in Normandy. Neither the Japanese nor the Germans knew that Patton's First US Army Group was a construct of the deception planners combining real and imaginary units into a putative invasion force some 150,000 strong. Much of the fiction was sustained by double agents who throughout the anxious days after the Normandy landings fed a stream of disinformation through networks of imaginary agents about the forces in south-east England poised for a further assault. Churchill also knew from Ultra that General Jodl, head of the German High Command, was still prepared for another invasion force.

Churchill was delighted at this further evidence of Bodyguard's success. After sending Oshima's message to Eisenhower, he suggested that Patton's army might do more good by remaining in Britain than crossing over to Normandy, which some of its real units were designated to do. 'Uncertainty is a terror to the Germans', he added. 'The forces in Britain are a dominant pre-occupation of the Huns.' This was a typically spontaneous response with a short trajectory. It was far too late to stop the transfer of units to France, where they were badly needed. In any case, the planners were already bending their energies to maintaining the fiction of a second landing. Within a week the Germans had concluded that the progress of fighting in Normandy made a second landing unlikely, and the deception came to an end.[3]

Churchill was more assertive over a naval intercept revealing that Hitler had decided to establish the Apennines as 'the final blocking line' in Italy. It arrived at a crucial moment. Churchill was still fighting a rearguard action against the American-driven decision to transfer troops from Italy for Operation Anvil, the projected landings in the South of France. The subsequent erosion of General Alexander's forces in Italy had become a running sore on Churchill's relations with Roosevelt. He now sent Roosevelt one of his longest messages urging him not 'to wreck one great campaign for the sake of another. Both can be won.' To clinch the argument, he ordered Menzies to send a copy of the intercept to Roosevelt.

To his chagrin, Roosevelt failed even to mention Ultra in his equally lengthy reply. Instead he stressed the need to honour the Tehran agreements with Stalin and how his own political survival would be threatened by any setback to Overlord. 'History will never forgive us', he told Churchill, 'if we lose precious time and lives in indecision and debate. My dear friend', he concluded, 'I beg you let us go ahead with our plan.'

Roosevelt's immovability forced Churchill to back down. However, when the two men met at Quebec that September he again drew to the President's attention items of Ultra highlighting the Italian campaign. This time Roosevelt agreed not to weaken

Alexander's forces further, but Ultra was incidental to his decision. Anvil had been a striking success, and withdrawing forces from Alexander was no longer on the agenda. Roosevelt had done no more than Churchill in treating intelligence as the handmaiden to and not the dictator of strategy.[4]

On 20 July, as British and Canadian forces battled to capture Caen, Churchill flew to Cherbourg, inspected the severely damaged port, visited an unfinished V-1 launching site, and sailed from Utah beach to Arromanches, the main British D-Day landing point. The next day he visited Montgomery's headquarters and eagerly watched an artillery bombardment of German positions.

Meanwhile dramatic events had been unfolding in Germany. Hitler was at his headquarters in East Prussia, where a bomb hidden in a suitcase exploded under the map table killing four of the officers present. By the time Churchill arrived in Cherbourg Claus von Stauffenburg, who had planted the bomb, had reached Berlin and Operation Valkyrie, the plot to overthrow the Nazi regime, was underway. It quickly faltered at news of Hitler's survival and before darkness fell the first executions had begun. Stauffenburg headed the list. Over the next few weeks more than five thousand were to follow.

Bletchley Park had quickly picked up evidence of the attempted coup. As usual Churchill had arranged for Ultra to travel with him. At Montgomery's HQ he received his delivery and Brigadier Edgar Williams, Montgomery's chief intelligence officer, watched as he excitedly shuffled through the intercepts and began to mumble rhetorical phrases about the overthrow of the Nazis. Williams recognised the names of many of those involved in the plot but Churchill did not. That there had been a failed attempt on Hitler's life was clear; but the significance of the names entirely escaped him. By himself Churchill 'had not the slightest idea of what was going on', and could make no sense of the raw intelligence on the most dramatic crisis in the history of the Third Reich.[5] But this hardly mattered provided he made no attempt to move without expert advice. What counted was his drive that energised the entire intelligence machinery. A graphic example occurred during his visit to General Alexander's HQ later that summer.

In August Churchill flew to Corsica and embarked on the destroyer HMS *Kimberley* where he enjoyed a grandstand view of American troops landing on the south coast of France. Stimulated by the whiff of gunsmoke he hurried to Italy to observe a new offensive by the 8th Army against the Gothic line. Travelling with Alexander, he scrambled through an olive grove to a small chateau where he could hear the sound of rifle and machine-gun fire a mere 500 yards away. 'There were quite a lot of shells flying about, and land mines all over the place. He absolutely loved it', remembered Alexander. Accompanying him in Italy was a Special Liaison Unit officer with the latest Ultra intercepts, the first man Churchill had demanded to see when he had arrived. Then, from the battle front, Churchill ordered him to bring up the latest batch of intelligence. The security-conscious SLU officer thought it 'crazy' to travel around with Ultra papers and refused point-blank. Then he awaited 'the lion's roar' of anger. 'I want you', Churchill shouted on his return, but when the security reasons were explained Churchill meekly accepted them and instead invited the gratified officer to join him for dinner.[6]

No intelligence officer need worry that Churchill ignored his product. Nor did he show undue deference to his professional staff. Early in September he and his Chiefs of Staff embarked on the *Queen Mary* for Quebec and his sixth wartime meeting with Roosevelt. The liberation of Europe was well under way. Canadian forces were about to capture Ostend and British troops were poised to enter Antwerp and Brussels. American forces stood on the German frontier and Brussels radio wildly reported that Germany had surrendered. A mood of euphoria infected the Chiefs of Staff, bolstered by highly optimistic intelligence forecasts. Kenneth Strong, Eisenhower's British intelligence chief, had already declared that the enemy in the West had 'had it'. The Joint Intelligence Committee had always been optimistic. At an on-board staff conference it confidently predicted the enemy's final defeat by December.

Churchill's was the lone dissenting voice. A decrypt handed to him as he stepped aboard revealed that Hitler was determined to neutralise the fall of Antwerp. Churchill was the first to appreciate its strategic significance. The Western Allies, he pointed out, still had to secure a major port other than Cherbourg and could soon find their progress limited. In this event the Germans could consolidate behind the Siegfried Line and offer stiff resistance. For that reason he thought his intelligence advisers were far too optimistic. 'It is at least as likely that Hitler will be fighting on 1 January', he argued, 'as it is that he will collapse before then.' His refusal to accept the official estimate provoked a major shipboard row, but events were to justify his caution.[7]

By now de Gaulle had made his triumphant walk down the Champs Élysées. The resistance had significantly helped the liberation and Churchill's passion for the Maquis remained undiminished. 'Good, press on', he responded when Lord Selborne told him that arms for over 100,000 men had been dropped. Even the sceptical Desmond Morton was impressed by SOE's performance. The resistance had largely followed directives, he reported to Churchill, and so far had done a far better job than he had expected. 'Excellent', replied Churchill. 'Let me know in what way I can best accelerate despatch of weapons to the Maquis.' All this sat uncomfortably with his continuing hostility to de Gaulle. 'I look forward indeed to the day when we shall have representatives of a clean France, decent, honest Frenchmen with whom we can work, instead of the émigré de Gaullists', he told Anthony Eden only a week after D-Day.

Churchill's enthusiasm for the resistance climaxed in mid-June with news of a general rising throughout southern France. In the Vercors, a high plateau south-west of Grenoble, the Maquis had raised the tricolour to secure a safe base from which to harass the Germans. Churchill reacted to the news by urging that every effort should be made to supply arms and whatever else was necessary to extend the uprising, but little of this made sense to those on the spot. Eisenhower's Chief of Staff promised American supply drops but poured cold water on the idea of a resistance stronghold. As did the Chiefs of Staff. Instead Churchill had to content himself with limited drops. In mid-July the Germans brutally crushed the rising and savage reprisals followed. As for French resistance in general, Churchill's interest rapidly diminished once Overlord was secure. It had fulfilled its military purpose and – like de Gaulle – he viewed its political radicalism with mistrust.[8]

An emotional issue now surfaced over the arming of Jewish resistance to the Holocaust. Churchill was pro-Zionist and one of the few British politicians to grasp the centrality of anti-Semitism in Nazi ideology. Intelligence reports had alerted him to the killing of Jews immediately Hitler's forces invaded the Soviet Union in June 1941 and began to carry out mass shootings of civilians that served as a prelude to what became known as the Holocaust. The hand cipher of the German non-Party uniformed police, the *Ordnungspolizei* (ORPO), responsible for 'order' in the newly occupied areas, had been broken by Bletchley Park even before the war, and at least one significant SS Enigma key had been decrypted in 1940. As Hitler's armies marched across Russia, police commanders from all sectors of the battle front reported regularly to their headquarters on the mass executions by radio using their cipher, which was, unbeknown to them, being broken by the Military Section at Bletchley Park. The decrypts were sent in German to Military Intelligence, but it also provided a weekly summary in English. 'C' – Stewart Menzies – sent a copy to Churchill.

All this was revealed in 1981 in the official history of British intelligence,[9] and historians have long-since established that the Holocaust began with the killings of Jews which accompanied Operation Barbarossa, many months before the establishment of notorious extermination centres such as Auschwitz-Birkenau or Sobibor. But the first public release of the texts of the intercepts in the United States and Britain in 1996 and 1997 graphically demonstrates in chilling detail the full nature of the material on which the reports Churchill read were based. On 18 July 1941, for example, Erich von dem Bach-Zelewski, the ORPO commander in Belorussia, reported to the ORPO chief in Berlin, General Kurt Dalegue, that in 'yesterday's cleansing action in Slonim, carried out by Police Regiment Centre, 1,153 Jewish plunderers were shot'. Three weeks later he reported that he had ordered the entire male population of another town to be evacuated. 'Up to today, midday, a further 3,600 have been executed', he added, 'so that the total of executions . . . up to now amounts to 7,819. Thus the figure of executions in my area', he concluded, 'now exceeds 30,000.' The intercepts made clear that competition existed between sector police chiefs over the execution totals and that the principal targets were unmistakably Jews, although some analysts believed that the term was also used to cover the killing of non-Jews as well on the grounds that this made it more acceptable for the Nazis.[10] Dalegue soon worried that this unceasing flow of radio reports might be intercepted by the enemy and in mid-September 1941 ordered that in future they should be sent by courier; at the same time the ORPO hand cipher was changed. It took British code-breakers little time to crack it, and from then on it was read until almost the end of the war. Despite Dalegue's orders it continued to carry reports of the killings.

Churchill was deeply shocked and distressed by this intelligence and in August 1941, as the reports poured in, he took the first major step that eventually led to the Nuremberg trials. Britain could do nothing at that stage to stop the killings, but he could announce, and denounce, Nazi crimes to the world. In a live radio broadcast from Chequers on 24 August, therefore, in praising the heroic resistance of the Russians, he revealed that as Hitler's armies advanced whole districts were being exterminated and that literally scores of thousands of executions in cold blood were being perpetrated by German police troops. There had been no such methodical and merciless butchery on such a scale, he said, since the Mongol invasions of Europe in the sixteenth century. The world was in the presence of 'a crime without a name'.[11] Short of revealing the texts themselves, which would have fatally compromised the code-breakers' work, this was a swift and significant denunciation of Nazi crimes even as news of them was still arriving. Churchill did not at this stage refer specifically to the Jews as the Nazis' main target, but by 1944 he was in no doubt that a full-scale Holocaust was under way. He supported escaping Jews to enter Palestine and agreed on the need for a Jewish state.

By this time most Polish Jews had been slaughtered, as had a further million from Russia and the Baltic states, while deportations from Western Europe to the extermination camps continued. Then German troops marched into Hungary where some 750,000 Jews had long enjoyed shelter. Their fate was now sealed, for Adolf Eichmann had drawn up plans for their extermination at Auschwitz. Deportations began in May, with 4,000 Jews per day arriving at the camp. Most were gassed on arrival. Throughout the spring and summer, as the Western Allies battled in Normandy and Italy, and the Red Army steadily advanced in the east, the cattle trucks inexorably emptied Hungary of its Jews.

The Jewish Agency desperately pleaded for Allied action. One plan was to bomb Auschwitz and the railway lines that led to it. Moshe Shertok, head of the Agency's foreign section and – as Moshe Sharrett – a future Israeli foreign minister, proposed the creation of Jewish SOE groups to fight with the resistance in the Balkans. The plan was quashed on political grounds by British authorities in Palestine who had no desire to help fuel the Zionist cause. Desperate, Shertok flew to London determined to reach Churchill through Randolph, who was resting in the Dorchester Hotel during a break from his gruelling life with the partisans. Writing Randolph a passionate letter about events in Hungary, Shertok told him they were moving with catastrophic rapidity and over 400,000 Jews had already been sent to the death camps. The deportation of the remainder was about to begin. But if SOE could drop one hundred trained men into Hungary, in small groups of around five to ten, they in turn could recruit and command others. 'The general aim and object . . . would be to turn victims into fighters . . .', he declared, 'and rouse them to resistance, sabotage activities and guerrilla warfare.'

Randolph contacted his father and within hours SOE's trouble-shooting David Keswick called on him at the Dorchester to discuss Shertok's plan. Simultaneously Desmond Morton telephoned Harry Sporborg, a City solicitor close to the top at Baker Street. Morton emphasised Churchill's strong personal interest in the affair. 'I would add that the Prime Minister is extremely sympathetic to Dr Weizmann and the Agency', he told Sporborg. 'For political reasons alone it would be of real assistance if you could give Dr Shertok to understand that you are taking the proposal seriously.'

Within days Shertok's plan won approval from Baker Street and was cleared with Washington. But despite Churchill's keen endorsement, by mid-September the plan had been abandoned. Memories of the April row with Moscow over special operations in Romania still rankled, and Hungary was seen as lying in the Soviet sphere. Special operations there could be politically explosive. More potent was the political objection to any sort of Zionist unit by training Jews selected by the Jewish Agency itself. Only Jews in the British Armed Forces who had already been trained by SOE, it was decided, should be used. These, tragically, were academic wrangles. By September the Hungarian Jews had been eliminated.[12]

Churchill's enthusiasm for Balkan resistance continued to run high. Tito's dramatic escape from Drvar to Vis raised his hopes of reconciling Tito with the King and goverment-in-exile, and uniting Yugoslav resistance. A promising step was the appointment of Prime Minister Ivan Subasić, the former Governor of Croatia. In mid-June he and Tito recognised each other's governments, but there remained the question of resistance in Serbia, where loyalty to Mihailović remained strong. The future of the monarchy also remained an issue.

Churchill hoped to settle everything in face-to-face talks with Tito. Their encounter took place in mid-August on the terrace of General Wilson's HQ at the Villa Rivalta overlooking the Bay of Naples. Tito wore a marshal's uniform with red tabs lent by the Russians, and glittering gold braid supplied by the Americans.

Churchill wore a simple open-necked shirt. The contrast of dress reflected military reality. Across the Adriatic Tito held all the military cards, his partisans poised for victory over both the Germans and chetniks. In the events that followed Churchill was amiable, toasted Tito, and stage-managed friendly photo-sessions. But behind the scenes Churchill was badly disillusioned. Tito hardly lived up to his romantic vision of a guerrilla leader and proved surprisingly resistant to his plans including a public disclaimer about imposing Communism and a promise not to use British arms for political purposes. Tito simply ignored them.[13] Churchill arrived back in London to news of another American incursion into Yugoslav affairs.

Roosevelt had capitulated to Churchill's demand to cancel an OSS intelligence mission to Mihailović, but Donovan convinced the President that it was a difficult task 'to turn off and on intelligence work' and won his consent to a smaller mission. Aware that this would infuriate London, Donovan kept its planning strictly secret. Chosen to head mission 'Ranger' was Lieutenant-Colonel Robert H. McDowell, a US Army intelligence officer who had worked with British intelligence during the First World War. After several unsuccessful attempts his team finally parachuted into Serbia in late August, only two weeks before the Red Army crossed the Yugoslav frontier and just days before Mihailović ordered a general mobilisation of his chetnik forces against 'all enemies'. The final battle for Yugoslavia was joined. McDowell, a sympathetic witness on the chetnik side, began reporting that the partisans were waging a civil war.

News of the Ranger mission quickly reached Tito, who protested to Maclean. He in turn alerted Churchill, who once again confronted Roosevelt. General Donovan, he protested, was running a Mihailović lobby just as King Peter had agreed to drop him and chetniks were joining Tito. If OSS continued, he warned, 'we lay the scene for a fine civil war'. Claiming that he had made a mistake, Roosevelt ordered McDowell withdrawn. Churchill had once again forced Roosevelt to change course in the shadow war.[14]

It was a Pyrrhic victory. Events in Yugoslavia were rapidly slipping away from him. In mid-September Tito boarded a Soviet Dakota that flew him to Moscow for talks with Stalin. Churchill erupted in anger and muttered darkly about 'Balkan brigands'. In November he confessed to Randolph that he had been much disappointed in Tito and denounced him to King Peter as 'nothing but a Communist thug'. Before the year was out he had made an even more startling confession to Anthony Eden. 'I have come to the conclusion that in Tito we have nursed a viper', he said. 'But up till recently he has been biting Huns. Now that he has started biting us, I feel much less sympathetic.'[15]

Churchill had always viewed the Greek guerrillas of EAM/ELAS as venomous. The truce arranged by Monty Woodhouse between the warring resistance factions had collapsed and Churchill was secretly wrapping up the deal by which he traded off Romania for Greece. There remained the troublesome question of SOE liaison officers with EAM/ELAS. Should the guerrillas be denounced and British officers removed, or would it be wiser to keep them in place until the Germans withdrew? Eden favoured denunciation and withdrawal. Lord Selborne argued that this meant abandoning Greece to the Communists and endangering the lives of his SOE men in the Greek mountains.

In the midst of this debate Woodhouse himself arrived in London. By now he was a veteran commanding several SOE missions with EAM/ELAS. After his encounter with Eddie Myers the year before, Churchill was far from keen on meeting what he feared might be yet another advocate for left-wing Greeks. But he eventually yielded to Eden's pressure and Woodhouse found himself being briefed at Baker Street for the encounter. Desmond Morton told him that Churchill would certainly not like what he had to say.

Woodhouse was driven to Chequers with Jack, Churchill's stock-broking brother. With Morton's warning ringing in his ears he was understandably nervous and his discovery that the other guest was Brigadier Armstrong, former head of the mission to Mihailović, was no great help. Over lunch, sitting on Churchill's right, Woodhouse found talking about the Greek guerrillas tricky. Whenever he seemed to be gaining a point Churchill would turn to Armstrong on his left and talk about Yugoslavia. At times he appeared to forget that Armstrong had been with Mihailović, not Tito. When his wife reminded him, he swept away the objection with an expansive gesture. 'On my right I have Balkan revolution, on my left Balkan reaction – what am I to do?' he asked rhetorically.

Up until that moment Woodhouse had obeyed the instructions drilled into him by Morton on what to say and what not to say, but it had got him nowhere. Finally, he confessed later, 'I disobeyed my orders'. Speaking as soldier to soldier, he boldly appealed to

Churchill's emotions by declaring that if Britain denounced EAM/ELAS and tried to withdraw, very few of his officers would escape alive. If they stayed, they could have a useful restraining effect on the excesses of the guerrillas. The ploy worked. Churchill pondered for a few moments. Then he placed his hand on Woodhouse's shoulder. 'Yes, my boy', he said, 'I quite understand.' The proposal to denounce EAM/ELAS was shelved.

Churchill generously told Woodhouse that his visit had not been wasted but Woodhouse later concluded that far more important was Churchill's hope that Stalin would control the Greek Communists. But this was to underestimate the power of the personal encounter. No sooner had he left than Churchill dictated a memo to Eden. 'I had a long talk today with Colonel Woodhouse, who is certainly a very fine fellow and most able', he stated. 'I agree with much regret that the missions should stay for the present.'

Two weeks later Ultra revealed an accelerating rate of German troop withdrawal from Greece. Within days the Greek Communists issued an ultimatum that they would co-operate with the British only if George Papandreou, the Prime Minister of the government-in-exile in Cairo, resigned. Churchill replied with yet another outburst against EAM/ELAS. Contemptuously denouncing 'the snarlings of the miserable Greek Banditti', he ordered his Chiefs of Staff to begin preparing for Operation Manna, the dispatch of up to 12,000 men to Athens with tanks, guns and armoured cars. He was setting the scene for an extraordinary drama that was to unfold that Christmas.[16]

The Communist guerrillas were not the only players in the Greek drama to receive a tongue-lashing from Churchill. General Donovan and his American secret warriors also suffered. The cause, once again, was Donovan's resentment at Churchill's attempt to keep secret operations in British hands. In Yugoslavia the trigger for dissent was the decision to abandon Mihailović and support Tito. In Greece it was Churchill's determination to see King George II return to his country.

During the debate in London over whether to withdraw missions from EAM/ELAS, Colin Gubbins had alerted Donovan to prepare to do the same with his American officers. Stephen Penrose, who ran American intelligence into Greece, told Donovan that the move would endanger his men and plunge organised resistance to the Nazis into chaos. Donovan protested to Secretary of State Cordell Hull that the British were interfering with his intelligence operations and again dictating American policy in the Balkans. Hull agreed that intelligence missions should continue but told Donovan that his men should stay out of Greek politics.

To expect that OSS officers, amongst whom were passionate Greek Americans, could stay neutral in what was becoming a civil war was asking the impossible. 'Cynically opportunist' was how the head of the Greek desk in the OSS Research and Analysis division in Cairo described British policy. The protests leaked back to Washington and surfaced dramatically in the *Washington Post* with a damning critique of Churchill and his policy in Greece by the columnist Drew Pearson.

News of this reached Churchill on the day he visited General Mark Clark who presented him with the Union Jack raised over Rome on the night of its liberation. Free French forces were poised to enter Paris and Eisenhower's troops had reached the mouth of the Seine. The Red Army was about to cross the Romanian frontier. Allied co-operation was yielding the fruits of victory, but the harvest was bitter-sweet. Churchill's visit to Italy had renewed his resentment over Anvil. In Warsaw the Red Army watched while the Germans brutally crushed the Home Army resistance. Despite Churchill's impassioned pleas Roosevelt declined to support a protest to Moscow or to defy the Soviet veto.

What was particularly galling about Pearson's attack was that only two days before, Roosevelt had agreed to the British plans for Operation Manna. To have won the President's rare consent for a vital political battle only to see it resisted by OSS was particularly intolerable. Churchill vented his anger to Harry Hopkins. 'Is this not the man', he asked in reference to Pearson, 'the President described the other day as being America's greatest liar or words to that effect?' Could nothing be done to correct his crude assertions about British policy towards Greece? If nothing could be done he had 'half a mind' to try his own hand in the matter. It was clear, he observed, that Pearson's article was part of the campaign against the British in Egypt being waged by Donovan's agency.

Letting off steam to Hopkins was not enough. Still fuming, he sent an unprecedented message to Donovan himself. Marked 'Private and Personal' and 'Off the Record', it angrily warned that attempts to obstruct British policy towards the Greek resistance could cause formidable trouble for the Americans. He hoped not to have to bring the issue before Roosevelt and thus make it an official quarrel between London and Washington, but unless Donovan could smooth the waters he would have no other choice. Two days later Roosevelt effectively answered by approving Operation Manna. He even offered American planes to help ferry British troops into Greece. It was another victory for Churchill in his increasingly acrimonious relations with Donovan's intelligence empire.[17]

On 1 August 1944 the Polish underground army in Warsaw rose in revolt against the Germans. Across the Vistula Soviet tanks were a mere twelve miles away and the sound of heavy artillery could be heard in the city. Forty thousand joined the revolt and within hours had seized much of Poland's capital. The uprising marked the beginning of what Churchill later called 'the martyrdom of Warsaw'.[18] The Germans counter-attacked with ferocity. 'Destroy tens of thousands', ordered Himmler. Outside the city, the Russians halted their advance and Stalin denounced the revolt as the criminal act of adventurers. Street-fighting forced the resistance into the sewers, the only link between increasingly isolated pockets of fighters. After eight weeks of heroic fighting the Poles surrendered. More than 15,000 resisters and up to 250,000 civilians had been killed. The Home Army had been destroyed and Warsaw lay in ruins. When Hitler finally withdrew his forces the Communists easily seized control of Poland's future.

Churchill observed the unfolding tragedy with frustration and growing anger. It was for Poland that Britain had gone to war. The Polish government-in-exile was based in London and thousands of Poles were fighting in the British Armed Forces. Both SIS and SOE had strong links with Polish intelligence, and much of the early vision of setting Europe ablaze had been inspired by Polish plans for Home Army resistance. Polish intelligence had rendered valuable dividends to the Allies. The Poles also enjoyed special privileges. They sent uncensored messages in their own ciphers and were largely unaccountable for their clandestine operations and the £35 million in gold and currency sent to the underground by secret courier.

Against this background Bor Komorowski, commander of the Home Army forces in Warsaw, appealed for massive air drops of supplies and weapons. Churchill pleaded with Stalin and Roosevelt. In vain he asked the Soviet dictator to allow American and British aircraft to use landing strips behind Soviet lines, and urged the American President to join him in ignoring Stalin's veto. Allied planes flew desperate sorties from England and Italy, but none of this was enough. Stalin's cynical lifting of his ban came too late to help.

Churchill was genuinely distressed by Poland's fate, but he had long been prepared for it. As soon as the Soviet Union had become an ally he recognised that Poland's future was negotiable. Quietly, SOE had dropped its support for the secret army and confined its supplies to assisting sabotage. When the Red Army crossed the Polish border early in 1944 Churchill reluctantly yielded to the inexorable politics of resistance. He embraced Polish claims for increased support to the underground as enthusiastically as he supported those of Emmanuel d'Astier and Yeo-Thomas for the Maquis. Supplies to the Home Army, he impetuously told the Polish Prime Minister Mikolajczyk, would be tripled over the next three months, but his expansive gesture came in the wake of tightening Whitehall control over SOE and a cutback in the Poles' special privileges. Although he successfully resisted pressure from the Joint Intelligence Committee for a handover of Polish ciphers, he did insist that copies of their messages to the Home Army be provided *en clair* and that SOE decisions on Poland remain anchored in London – a move aimed as much at excluding American influence as anything else. Nor was anything to be done to provoke Stalin. Over the next two months a combination of grand strategy and winter weather guaranteed that only two SOE flights found their way to Poland.[19]

Churchill was equally hard-headed in his personal encounters with Polish leaders. He fought Mikolajczyk head-on over the future Polish eastern border with Russia and stood up to a delegation headed by Zygmunt Berezowski, just smuggled out of the country, who told him that the resistance looked to Britain to back Poland's independence and territorial integrity. Again Churchill refused to accept Polish claims in the east and committed himself only to its independence. Berezowski protested that this was unacceptable as it would leave Vilna and Lvov outside Polish borders. If necessary, he declared, Poland would meet such an outcome with active resistance. At this, Churchill made a gloomy and fatalistic reply: 'A decision to resist, regardless of the consequences is the privilege of every nation, and it cannot be denied even to the weakest.' Three weeks later the JIC and SOE decided that any responsibility for an uprising would be left to the Poles. In short, some three months before the Warsaw uprising Churchill had already spoken its obituary. When it happened, he nobly did what he could. Stranded by his allies in Moscow and Washington, he could only watch the defeat of Poland's Home Army with anguish and grief. Several weeks later he did not even try to help the Slovak uprising. It, too, had roots of its own and he knew that little could be done to help it.[20]

Warsaw's fate was proof that Churchill was now the least of the Big Three and that the future lay with the large battalions of Roosevelt and Stalin. 'I have less and less influence', he confessed to old friend and confidant Jan Smuts. His painful awareness of Washington's global power and Stalin's reach only encouraged him to wave the British flag more vigorously and secure what he could of Western Europe. There was now an uneasy edge to his relations with Roosevelt and open disagreement with Stalin. These powerful undercurrents began increasingly to guide the direction of Britain's intelligence efforts.

Within a week of returning from Moscow in October 1944 Churchill turned his gaze once more to special operations. Britain's shadow warriors still had a vital role to play, but now it was less a case of setting Europe ablaze than of dousing the left-wing and nationalist fires that threatened Britain's long-term interests. In northern Italy, where the partisans were severely harrying the Germans, SOE in August alone had infiltrated over sixty officers. But only small arms were supplied, armed groups were kept to the absolute minimum, and careful plans were laid for the disarming of partisans immediately the Germans left. There was to be no repeat of the EAM/ELAS crisis in Greece, and Italy was to remain firmly anchored to the West. Similar concerns shaped secret operations in countries yet to be liberated such as Austria, Denmark and Norway.[21]

They also produced an abrupt about-turn over clandestine operations in Indo-China. Still nominally governed by the pro-Vichy French Army authorities, it lay vulnerable to a Japanese take-over. In April 1944 Churchill vetoed a Gaullist military mission to Mountbatten's South-East Asia command headquarters in deference to Roosevelt. Since then Colin Gubbins had enjoyed a congenial meeting in Algiers with the Gaullist General Blaizot, the mission's leader-designate, and planners in London had reiterated how vital Free French co-operation would be in promoting resistance to the Japanese. The French *Service d'Action* was busy laying plans for the parachuting in of arms and ammunition for 3,000 guerrillas.

Roosevelt remained implacably hostile, but after Quebec Churchill finally stood up to him. First he agreed that Blaizot could pay a purely personal visit to Mountbatten, then summoned Mountbatten for a top-level conference to discuss Far Eastern strategy. His frustration with Roosevelt boiling over, he agreed that Blaizot could stay in Kandy with a fully fledged mission. Three weeks later a Special Duties flight landed an emissary from de Gaulle to the Hanoi French command at a landing strip at Dien Bien Phu. Over the next few months an intensive supply effort by Force 136 dropped W/T sets, agents and weapons to create a Gaullist resistance force that would ensure the future of Indo-China for France.[22]

Throughout the late summer and autumn Whitehall mandarins fought each other over the peacetime control of special operations. Lord Selborne told Churchill that in the disturbed conditions of the post-war world the government that neglected special operations would be 'like an admiral who said he did not require submarines'. But he hastened to make clear that he did not want the job himself and was anxious to leave the government before the end of the year. Churchill thrashed all this out over a long lunch, agreeing that SOE had an important job and should come under the Ministry of Defence. But Anthony Eden reminded him that the Foreign Office already supervised SIS and insisted that nothing but chaos would ensue if two secret services not under the same direction worked in foreign countries in peacetime. Churchill also described this as an 'excellent arrangement', but within days the Chiefs of Staff forced him to accept it as merely a temporary measure. These bureaucratic skirmishes tested Churchill's patience. He had already agreed that Selborne could go at the end of the year. Now he changed his mind and prevailed on his old friend to stay until the war with Germany was over. That way, he could defer difficult decisions about the future of the secret services.[23]

There was more to this decision than Whitehall in-fighting. Although Churchill personally favoured a post-war role for subversion and sabotage, his coalition partner and leader of the Labour Party, Clement Attlee, did not. Attlee had been a sympathetic midwife at the birth of SOE when Britain had its back to the wall, heady talk of 'people's war' in Europe was in vogue, and even Churchill dreamed of revolution behind enemy lines. It was radically different now. The war was all but won, the coalition's days were numbered, and Labour was deeply unhappy about Churchill's line on

Greece. During a noisy debate that December Labour voices denounced Britain for opposing the forces throughout Europe that had been 'the backbone of the resistance'. The up-and-coming young firebrand Major Denis Healey thundered at the Labour Party conference that British foreign policy was to protect the ruling class from 'the just wrath of the people who have been fighting underground against them for the past few years. There is a very great danger', he concluded, 'that we shall find ourselves running with the Red Flag in front of the armoured car of Tory imperialism and counter-revolution.' With sentiment like this running strong, Attlee was set against anything resembling 'a British Comintern'. This threat of Labour revolt, added to the sniping in Whitehall, convinced Churchill that discussion of post-war cloak-and-dagger was best left dormant.[24]

The future of the spy-catchers at home proved even more contentious. Churchill had become profoundly uneasy about the wartime increase in their powers, but attempts to rein in MI5 and the Security Panel had been sabotaged from within. In the meantime professional rivalries between SIS and MI5 inevitably surfaced as they jostled for post-war advantage and Stewart Menzies referred ominously to the dangers of an 'internal Gestapo'. As rumours spread in late 1944 of a major review of the British intelligence community, voices in the Security Service began to express dread about the impact of Churchill and claimed that he and his friends 'snooped around' too much in its work. This resistance to political control also affected higher levels. Sir Alan Brooke had lengthy conversations with the Minister of War and his chief liaison officer with MI5, and afterwards confided to his diary that there was a 'grave danger of [MI5] falling into the clutches of unscrupulous political hands of which there are too many at present'. Here again Churchill refused to tackle the issue so long as the war waged on. Before it was over the Labour Party came to power. Far from creating a socialist Gestapo, Attlee replaced Sir David Petrie with Sir Percy Sillitoe, an outsider from the Police Force who was strong on democratic values. Attlee also made the first visit of a British Prime Minister to MI5 headquarters. For all his close interest in its affairs, Churchill had never done so.[25]

Early in December 1944 civil war in Greece moved closer when EAM ministers resigned from the Athens government and violent demonstrations disrupted the city. Bolstered by his Moscow agreement with Stalin, Churchill determined on a showdown with the Communists. He told General Scobie, commanding British forces in Greece, 'Do not hesitate to act as if you were in a conquered city where a local rebellion is in progress.'

This provoked a storm of criticism in Washington and at home. Three days later he braved an onslaught in the Commons from Emanuel Shinwell and Aneurin Bevan for destroying Greek democracy. Churchill skilfully widened the debate into a survey of Europe as a whole. British policy had been 'to arm anyone who could shoot a Hun', regardless of their politics, but liberation did not give them the right to use these weapons to seize power by violence, murder or bloodshed, nor to shoot those they found 'politically inconvenient' under the guise of purging collaborators with the Germans. Not only Greece, but also Italy and other states in Western Europe were at risk. 'We are told', he said, 'that because we do not allow gangs of heavily armed guerrillas to descend from the mountains and install themselves . . . in power in great capitals, we are traitors to democracy. I repulse that claim . . . He then coined what was to become his well-known phrase about democracy: it was 'no harlot to be picked up in the street by a man with a tommy gun'.[26]

Churchill's romance with guerrillas was over, but his penchant for direct action was not. On Christmas Eve he impetuously flew to Athens. Riding the streets in an armoured car carrying a pistol, he finally confronted the 'miserable Greek banditti'. At a conference dimly lit by hurricane lamps and interrupted by the noise of rockets being fired by RAF Beaufighters, and under the unbending gaze of Colonel Popov, head of the Soviet military mission, three 'shabby desperadoes' – delegates of ELAS – sat down with representatives of the Greek government and other political parties to find a negotiated solution to the crisis. Churchill found it all 'intensely dramatic'. Putting to one side his violent rhetoric, he warmly welcomed the ELAS delegates – one of whom, General Mandakas, had only reluctantly handed over his Mauser at the door – and shook hands with each of them in turn. Hitherto expressionless, each gave him a smile and a short bow.

The solution he sought involved a regency under Archbishop Damaskinos. Twenty-four hours later negotiations broke down and two of the ELAS delegates asked to see Churchill for a private meeting. Only with considerable difficulty was he dissuaded on the grounds that this would undermine Damaskinos. Harold Macmillan, one of the central characters in this extraordinary episode, described it as 'a sort of super Sidney Street'. He also detected the former journalist in Churchill's desire to meet the guerrillas. Reluctantly Churchill returned to London where he twisted the Greek King's arm to declare a regency. Within days the fighting in Athens had ended.[27]

Churchill began 1945 in a depressed and sombre mood. Stupendous Red Army advances in the East had not been matched by Anglo-American progress in the West. V-2 rocket attacks on Britain were causing significant casualties, Poland was clearly fated to become a Soviet satellite, and the Balkans, except for Greece, lay open to Communism. Tito had virtually wiped out his chetnik rivals and on New Year's Day Churchill dismissed him as a 'well-drilled Communist'. The Yalta conference in early February, with its paper agreements on Poland and democracy in Europe, only temporarily lifted his mood. Hardly had he returned from the Crimea than he was talking gloomily of the 'shadows of victory'. What, he wondered ominously, would lie 'between the white snows of Russia and the white cliffs of Dover' once Germany was defeated? News of the Soviet arrest and deportation of Home Army resistance fighters in Poland soon confirmed his darkest fears.[28]

His hopes for Britain's secret services increasingly focused on how they could salvage the future. During the first three months of 1945 agents were dropped into Germany and Austria, supplies increased to the partisans in northern Italy, and sabotage continued in Norway, Denmark and the Netherlands. Along with their anti-German directives were guidelines to preserve Western Europe from disorder and revolution. 'I hope we may still save Italy from the Bolshevik pestilence', he told Eden as SOE liaison officers discouraged partisan talk of a national insurrection. Counter-sabotage instructions for Norway and elsewhere highlighted the need for uninterrupted industrial production and civil order in the transition from war to peace. In the Far East, Force 136 prepared for a return to the pre-war imperial order.

So long as the war was to be won Churchill kept a close eye on Ultra. The failure in December of JIC to warn of Hitler's counter-offensive in the Ardennes confirmed his belief that he should see the raw material himself. As usual, he paid special attention to items he found useful for his own political or strategic agenda. One such item surfaced in mid-March.

By this time British and American forces were poised for their major offensive across the Rhine, and the Red Army was within fifty miles of Berlin. Churchill again flew off for an eyewitness view. At Eisenhower's HQ he crossed the Rhine in a launch and was narrowly dissuaded from making himself a target for snipers. He described the whole affair, like his visit to the D-Day beaches, as 'a jolly day'. Typically Churchillian, it obscured his genuine distress at the strained faces of German civilians which intensified his fears about Soviet intentions. Dismemberment of Germany, so loosely discussed at Yalta, now seemed unwise.

On the eve of his departure he received an intercept from 'C'.[29] It was a MAGIC message from Berne to Tokyo referring to Nazi plans for a last-ditch stand in southern Germany. Intelligence reports from Eisenhower's HQ referred darkly to a 'German Maquis-to-be'. In reality they originated with a German deception, strongly promoted by Goebbels and swallowed by the OSS in Switzerland, to deter the Allies from insisting on total victory. Churchill asked JIC for its opinion. On the one hand, continued *Wehrmacht* resistance at Lake Balaton in Hungary and in Italy seemed consistent with such a plan. On the other, there might be nothing in the rumours at all. The committee agreed with his scepticism and dismissed reports from agents about the construction of underground buildings. Military intelligence separately pointed out that German plans for the dispersal of military staffs from Berlin revealed by Ultra referred exclusively to Thuringia.

Churchill quickly grasped the assessment's significance. If there was to be no southern redoubt, then Anglo-American forces could focus on reaching Berlin. He bombarded Roosevelt and Eisenhower with messages stressing the political significance of occupying the German capital and safeguarding the country's future, but Eisenhower's intelligence continued to warn of a final Nazi stand in the mountains of the south. Determined to pre-empt it, Eisenhower shifted the axis of his advance further south than originally planned. This had the effect of leaving Berlin to the Russians. Churchill could only warn and plead. 'I moved among cheering crowds', he wrote later of these closing days of the battle for Germany, 'with an aching heart and a mind oppressed by foreboding.'[30] He had no choice but reluctantly to accept Eisenhower's decision.

A week later Roosevelt collapsed and died at Warm Springs, Georgia. Churchill's genuine grief could not conceal that their relationship had recently come under strain. Disagreements over strategy masked deep political gulfs in how to deal with the Soviets, as well as in Anglo-American relations in the post-war world. Although Churchill endeavoured to keep them off their personal agenda, imperial issues ranked high. South-East Asia in particular was a minefield fought over by British and American intelligence agencies. Amongst the casualties was Churchill's relationship with General Donovan. Colonel Edmund S. Taylor, the OSS liaison officer at Mountbatten's South-East Asia command headquarters, warned Donovan that unless they were lucky 'Baker Street and Broadway [SIS] will proceed to squeeze us out of this part of the world'.[31]

Given his frustrations with Churchill over the Balkans, it was scarce wonder that Donovan was becoming bitter. Shortly before Christmas Rex Benson, a cousin of Stewart Menzies working for SIS in Washington, found himself at a dinner party with the OSS chief. Donovan was smarting over humiliation in Greece, he recorded, and 'went for Winston and his intolerance and dictatorship proclivities'.[32] Rivalries in Asia during the final months of the war with Japan soon guaranteed that Churchill came to feel much the same way about Donovan. After the American capture of Manila in March 1945 the Japanese seized control in Indo-China and ruthlessly neutralised the French Armed Forces. Long-prepared-for resistance plans by SOE and the Gaullists were quickly crushed, and the survivors fled north towards the Chinese border demanding American ammunition drops. But Roosevelt, who had starved them of support throughout the war, refused. Churchill had no more love for de Gaulle than the President, but he knew where to draw the line. 'It will look very bad in history', he told Roosevelt, 'if we were to let the French forces in Indo-China be cut to pieces by the Japanese . . .' It was too late. By August the Japanese had virtually eliminated the Gaullists and cajoled local authorities in Indo-China into declaring their independence. Three weeks after Hiroshima Ho Chi Minh, Communist leader of the VietMinh, seized power in Hanoi after considerable help from OSS.

Churchill's angriest clash with General Donovan came in the week of Roosevelt's death. Anxious to keep Hong Kong out of Chinese or American hands, the Colonial Office saw SOE as a useful ally, but

General Wedemeyer, Commander of the American-controlled China theatre, wanted nothing to do with British cloak-and-dagger. Neither did Donovan. The issue came to a head in April when Lord Selborne asked Churchill for his view. 'What do you say?' Churchill asked Eden. 'On the whole I incline against another SOE–OSS duel, on ground too favourable for that dirty Donovan.' He shrewdly realised that in contrast with the Balkans, Britain's secret services in China would be operating at a disadvantage.[33]

Donovan's men were not Churchill's only worry about the political future in the Far East. In Burma, Field Marshal Slim's 14th Army captured Mandalay and was poised to take the capital, Rangoon. To help his military advance and harass the Japanese Slim turned to Aung San, leader of the country's largest resistance force, the Burma National Army. This immediately sparked controversy. Aung San was a left-wing nationalist dedicated to winning Burma's independence from Britain. Even worse in British eyes, he had actively collaborated with the Japanese in their invasion of his country. Now, with the turning tide of battle, he was prepared to shift allegiance. Force 136 had already begun to provide him with arms, ammunition and financial aid in return for guerrilla support and intelligence about the Japanese. Eden was quick to see alarming analogies with EAM/ELAS in Greece. 'The tone of this', he reported to Churchill, 'is reminiscent of too much we have had from SOE in the past. Surely we should not boost these people so much. They will give great trouble hereafter.'

Churchill agreed, but he was too late. In Burma Aung San had already sparked a national uprising, and in April Mountbatten gave the go-ahead for Slim to meet face-to-face with the Burmese leader. A week after the end of the war in Europe Slim accepted his offer of support, but he made clear that he could not accept him as an Allied Commander representing the provisional government of Burma. Rangoon was captured the next month. Two years later, in London, Aung San signed the declaration that granted Burma its independence.[34]

Two weeks after VE Day the Labour and Liberal parties left the wartime coalition. Closeting himself at Chequers with Randolph and Desmond Morton, Churchill opened the election campaign with a broadcast that badly misfired. Speaking from his study, he delivered a broadside against socialism that shocked even some of his closest allies. Socialism, he declared, was inseparably interwoven with totalitarianism and the abject worship of the State, an attack upon the right of ordinary men and women to breathe freely 'without having a harsh, clumsy, tyrannical hand clapped across their mouths and nostrils'. No socialist system, he went on, could be established without a political police, and any socialist government would have to fall back on some form of Gestapo, 'no doubt very humanely directed in the first instance'.

The reference did him no good with the electorate. It was certainly an attack on Labour's plans for state control of the economy, but he also had two other targets in mind. The first was the Soviet secret police which, even as he spoke, was ruthlessly eliminating from Poland the politically inconvenient remnants of the Home Army resistance. Poland's fate lay heavily on his conscience and he was already lamenting the 'Iron Curtain' that had been drawn across Europe. The second target was closer to home. The massive wartime expansion of MI5's power had increasingly troubled him and Stewart Menzies had already expressed fears of a Gestapo. After VE Day Churchill ensured that Regulation 18B permitting the detention of suspects was abolished by Order in Council, but he knew that top officials in the Special Branch and MI5 had wanted either to retain it permanently or to see it extended for several months. For the rest of his political life Churchill was to have a jaundiced view of the Security Service. It was no coincidence that across the Atlantic his friend Harry Hopkins had helped unleash a press campaign denouncing 'Wild Bill' Donovan's plans for a post-war OSS as a 'Super Gestapo' that planned to spy on the 'World and Home Folks'.[35]

Ten days after VE Day Churchill sat down and wrote a fulsome letter of thanks to Sir Stewart Menzies for all his wartime intelligence work. He could make no public acknowledgement, nor could he refer to Bletchley Park and Ultra. Nevertheless, he told 'C', 'The services rendered, the incredible difficulties surmounted, and the advantages gained in the whole course and conduct of the war, cannot be overestimated . . . Will you, within the secret circle, convey to all possible my compliments and gratitude to a large band of devoted and patriotic workers.' Amongst the names that Menzies submitted for special honours was Commander Edward Travis, head of Bletchley Park since 1942. Signals intelligence fed Churchill's hunger for information throughout the war. It had also been an

Allied as well as British operation. Around the globe British, American, Canadian and Australian code-breakers had worked together as an integrated team. This wartime collaboration was to become a Cold War intelligence alliance. Travis was its British architect and in March began a remarkable round-the-world tour that oversaw a shift of code-breaking resources to the Pacific War and agreed on a framework for the post-war attack on Soviet ciphers. Soon after, Churchill ordered that no secret defence information should be given to any foreign power except the Americans 'from whom we get a great deal of information in return'. In September 1945, as Churchill licked the wounds of his electoral defeat, President Harry Truman signed a top-secret memorandum that authorised continued American collaboration with British code-breakers. At the end of the year Churchill reiterated the importance he attached to this central core of the special relationship when he urged Ernest Bevin, Labour's Foreign Secretary, to continue the Anglo-American alliance and the Combined Chiefs of Staff. 'From this', he said, 'should flow the continued interchange of military and scientific information and Intelligence . . .' In a world of measureless perils and anxieties, he insisted, it was 'a rock of safety'.[36]

18

Private Intelligence

Barely three weeks after the Japanese surrender, a 26-year-old cipher clerk working for the GRU (Soviet military intelligence) left the Soviet legation in Ottawa carrying a bundle of documents hidden beneath his coat. Lieutenant Igor Gouzenko, son of a Red Army civil-war hero, had decided to defect. His ticket to freedom was the irrefutable proof in his smuggled package that Moscow had been running a large-scale espionage network in North America focused on atomic research. The British High Commission in Ottawa had a Soviet mole, and scientist Alan Nunn May had been passing atomic secrets to Moscow.

The Gouzenko affair was a wake-up call to those still basking in wartime Russophilia. Gouzenko and his family were secreted in a former SOE–SIS training school on Lake Ontario, and British and American intelligence experts were called in to debrief the frightened but talkative defector. Canadian Prime Minister Mackenzie King journeyed to Washington to brief Harry Truman and then to London to agree with British intelligence on a co-ordinated line in handling the crisis. None of the Allies wanted the affair to damage relations with Stalin, especially as discussions about the future of Germany were still under way. Instead, a swift and drastic 'surgical operation' would be mounted in all three countries against the agents incriminated by Gouzenko.[1]

Churchill had accepted an invitation from Harry Truman to give a public lecture the following March at Westminster College in the small town of Fulton, Missouri, Truman's home state. He remained no less hostile to Communism, but wartime encounters with Stalin and Molotov had taught him that the men in the Kremlin were hard-headed realists rather than ideological fanatics. He believed that they would recognise and respect tough talk.

Churchill was therefore particularly receptive when Mackenzie King arrived at his London home to deliver a private briefing on the Gouzenko affair. He listened intently and poured out his own thoughts on the Russians. He fully supported a co-ordinated Western response but deprecated any attempts to hush things up. The world ought to know about Soviet espionage; the Communist movement was spreading everywhere. His parting shot was to urge King to do all he could to cement the Anglo-American alliance. 'It must not be written', he emphasised, 'it must be understood.'[2]

The Gouzenko affair confirmed Churchill's darkest views of Soviet and Communist behaviour. In January 1946 he set sail on the *Queen Elizabeth*, polishing his Fulton speech into a clarion call for Western vigilance against Moscow's ambitions. After holidaying in Florida and Cuba – the first time he had returned since his encounters with the guerrillas fifty years before – he arrived in a sombre Washington in early March. Soviet troops had failed to meet a deadline for quitting Iran, and from Moscow George Kennan, the United States chargé d'affaires, had sent his historic analysis of Soviet policy. Its message of containment, of the need for Western firmness and cohesion, harmonised with Truman's own thinking and echoed Churchill's by now well-developed line for Fulton. Not surprisingly, the President thought Churchill's text admirable.

Yet it was not just the Americans who joined the chorus. Lester B. Pearson, Canada's ambassador in Washington – and future Prime Minister – also had his say. The first interim report of the Canadian Commission of Inquiry into the Gouzenko affair had been released and suspects rounded up across the country. Paying Churchill a visit, Pearson found him still in bed, propped up with pillows, and 'looking pink and white as always, with a big cigar in his mouth'. Asked to read the Fulton text, Pearson found it 'very strong stuff indeed' and told Mackenzie King that he was impressed. Afterwards Churchill phoned King himself and was brought up to date on the latest Gouzenko news including the forthcoming publication of the final damning report unmasking Soviet espionage. 'Do not hold anything back', he emphasised again. The next day, in London, Alan Nunn May was arrested and charged under the Official Secrets Act. Twenty-fours later in Fulton, Churchill followed his own advice. Pulling no punches, his speech, broadcast live, provided the inaugural Western address of the Cold War. The Canadian Cabinet listened in as he spoke and King told him afterwards that it was the most courageous statement made by any man at any time.[3]

Entitled by Churchill 'The Sinews of Peace', the speech has become a classic largely remembered for the global currency it gave to the image of the 'Iron Curtain' imprisoning the great capitals of Central and Eastern Europe, and its plea for a 'special relationship' between the British Commonwealth and the United States. Less well remembered is Churchill's priority demand for a United Nations international armed force drawn from the air squadrons of member states, and his call for 'a good understanding' on all issues to be reached with Moscow that year under the aegis of the United Nations. And generally overlooked is his sombre view of the menace that also threatened on the Western side of the Iron Curtain. Italy and France harboured large Communist parties. Elsewhere around the globe Communist Fifth Columns were established and working 'in complete unity and absolute obedience to the directives they receive from the Communist centre'. Except for the British Commonwealth and United States, where they were still in their infancy, they constituted a growing challenge and peril to the West.

Implicit in Churchill's Fulton speech, with its nightmare of Kremlin-dominated police tyrannies in Eastern Europe and Fifth-Column subversion around the globe, was his demand for the continuation of the Anglo-American intelligence relationship he had forged with Roosevelt. Even as he spoke these hopes were coming to fruition, for most of that February and March Stewart Menzies had presided over a top-secret Anglo-American conference in London to thrash out the details of the SIGINT co-operation deal signed the year before. By the time Churchill returned from Fulton the negotiators had signed a document known as the UKUSA Treaty, laying out the details of how Britain and Commonwealth nations would co-operate with the United States to produce the 'golden eggs' of signals intelligence for the emerging Cold War. It remains highly classified.[4]

In opposition during the 1930s Churchill had relied on Desmond Morton for inside news from the secret services, but Morton was now a spent force, shunted aside by Menzies, MI5 and the Foreign Office into a series of harmless fact-finding missions. Early in 1946 he left for Brussels as Treasury representative on the Inter-Allied Reparations Agency. He kept in touch with Churchill, received letters addressed 'My dear Desmond', and even found time for the odd joke. When he entered London's Middlesex Hospital for a kidney-stone operation Churchill sent him flowers. Thanking him, Morton wondered how he had known that his 'unimportant self' was ill. 'Your intelligence service', he replied, 'is clearly working as efficiently of old.'[5] The barbed comment showed how far apart the two had grown. Churchill soon found another source who could keep him up to date with secrets of state.

Shortly before Christmas 1948 Churchill lunched at Chartwell with Alan Hillgarth, the naval intelligence officer whose exploits in Franco's Spain had so impressed and inspired him. With Spain's neutrality assured Hillgarth had moved on to head naval intelligence in the Eastern theatre where he worked with high-grade Japanese intercepts. The war over he left the Navy, schemed vainly with his old naval intelligence friend Ian Fleming to publish an English-language newspaper in Tangier, and finally settled on an estate in Tipperary, Ireland. Here he indulged a passion for forestry while retaining an active interest in Spanish affairs, and acting as UK representative for his old intelligence contact Juan March and his international financial ventures. Hillgarth also kept alive his wartime friendship with Churchill. He visited him in Switzerland in 1946, kept him up to date with personal and family matters, and briefed him on current affairs in Spain. A frequent visitor to London, where he was a member of the Army and Navy Club, he also nourished old service and intelligence contacts. Many like him were wary of the Labour government and its attitude towards the Soviet and Communist threat. This was what brought Hillgarth to Chartwell. At the heart of his concern was Soviet espionage and the general state of British intelligence.

In contrast to 1919, victory in the Second World War did not result in the mothballing of Britain's intelligence community. Even before atomic bombs obliterated Hiroshima and Nagasaki, Stalin's ruthless drawing of the Iron Curtain across Europe had transformed Moscow from ally to potential enemy. Whitehall kept in place the integrated intelligence structure created by Churchill and early in 1946 Stewart Menzies put his signature to the Anglo-American UKUSA Treaty. As the Armed Forces shrank, so the Chiefs of Staff highlighted the need for strengthened intelligence to warn of a Soviet attack. SOE fell victim to peace, but 'dirty tricks' quickly revived as weapons in the Cold War armoury and attempts were kindled again to 'set Europe ablaze', this time behind the Iron Curtain. With the 1948 Communist coup in Prague and the Berlin blockade, seasoned shadow warriors found themselves mobilised for new missions. The Foreign Office's Russia Committee and Information Research Department hatched counter-subversive and covert propaganda campaigns, and Whitehall mandarins created a Cold War planning staff to direct all anti-Soviet measures 'short of shooting'. SOE veterans recruited by SIS's new Special Operations Branch quickly found themselves up to their old tricks in a futile effort to topple the Communist regime of Enver Hoxha in Albania. Counter-insurgency campaigns were fought in places like Malaya, Greece and Palestine.[6]

At home the increasingly chilly Cold War climate heightened security concerns. The Gouzenko affair and conviction of Alan Nunn May had a powerful impact. Thousands of copies of the official Canadian report were snapped up. In June 1947, as the Marshall Plan was being unveiled and three months after President Harry Truman's historic Truman Doctrine speech, Clement Attlee created a special Cabinet committee on subversive activities chaired by himself as Prime Minister. Soon after, the 'negative vetting' of civil servants began, a procedure that involved the checking of personal records against MI5 and Special Branch files. Britain's secret services were now on the front line.[7]

It was a battle concealed from the public gaze, however, and many observers feared that Britain was too soft on the Soviets. Reluctant to acquire the stigma of being a new Gestapo or Soviet secret police, MI5 deliberately kept a low profile. Churchill was deeply concerned about a Soviet-inspired Fifth Column. The lesson he drew from the Prague coup was that even democracies could succumb to determined subversive attack.

He was therefore receptive to the warning that Alan Hillgarth brought to his Kent home in December about the burgeoning size of the Soviet Embassy in London. There were, he learned, some 150 employees, plus another 70 including the trade delegation and its affiliates. By contrast, the equivalent British figures in Moscow were 85 and 1 (the Commercial Counsellor). In addition, the Soviets had a number of representatives with various firms who enjoyed diplomatic privileges including unrestricted travel throughout Britain. 'All these people are a pest', Hillgarth told Churchill, 'poking their noses into everything.' What was worse, MI5 did not have the manpower to watch them and even the Soviet Air Attaché travelled unobserved around the country. Quite apart from all this the Russians were freely buying up British machinery such as diesel generators even as the Attlee government fretted about the number of Soviet submarines. 'No one', complained Hillgarth, was concerned to fight 'this quiet, cold-blooded war of brains in the background. The facts exist. No one will use them.'[8]

Hillgarth's visit marked the start of a remarkable period that ended only with Churchill's return to Downing Street in October 1951, during which Hillgarth became a regular and unofficial source on defence and intelligence matters. In many respects it echoed the 1930s, with Churchill in opposition receiving secret information from disaffected or worried insiders who saw him as a valuable sympathiser prepared publicly to voice their concerns within his own political agenda. And as in the 1930s, this was both supplement and alternative to information he received from official sources. Attlee was generous in providing him with secret briefings, wartime colleagues still in harness frequently met and discussed policy with him, and papers from the Joint Intelligence Committee and its staff were no strangers to his desk. He also kept in touch with Stewart Menzies, who was still running SIS.

Whether Churchill learned from Hillgarth what he already knew was largely irrelevant. What was important was that he had an independent and trusted source. Just as before the war he had carefully protected his sources, so he indulged in some *Boys' Own Paper* skulduggery to conceal what he was up to with Hillgarth. The following July, after a private dinner between the two of them at his Hyde Park Gate home, Churchill promised to send any telegraphed queries to Hillgarth disguised with the code name 'Sturdee'. Within a few weeks he was deploying the stratagem to request an update on the Soviet Embassy figures.[9]

Churchill's principal concern that summer was international security. In April the North Atlantic Treaty was signed in Washington and in May the Soviets lifted the Berlin blockade. Longer-term strategy towards Moscow was now urgently on the agenda and had become the heated focus of that year's defence debate. In July, with Lord Cherwell once again acting as his private 'statistical section', Churchill led a senior Conservative delegation for a private briefing from Attlee on Soviet military power and Britain's defences. There followed acrimonious exchanges between the Prime

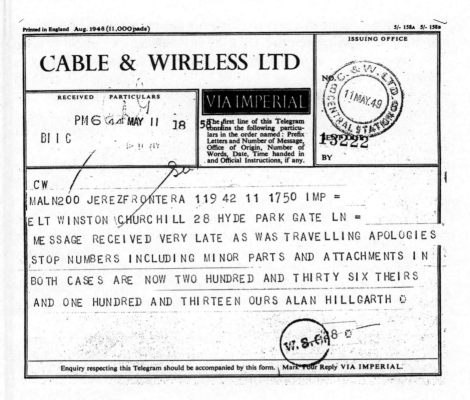

Printed in England Aug. 1948 (11,000 pads)   5/- 158A   5/- 158B

CABLE & WIRELESS LTD

ISSUING OFFICE

RECEIVED   PARTICULARS

PM 6 ⟨44⟩ MAY 11   18

BI I C

VIA IMPERIAL

5 The first line of this Telegram contains the following particulars in the order named : Prefix Letters and Number of Message, Office of Origin, Number of Words, Date, Time handed in and Official Instructions, if any.

NO. C. & W. LTD 11 MAY 49 CENTRAL STATION

BY

CW

MALN200 JEREZFRONTERA 119 42 11 1750 IMP =

E LT WINSTON CHURCHILL 28 HYDE PARK GATE LN =

MESSAGE RECEIVED VERY LATE AS WAS TRAVELLING APOLOGIES

STOP NUMBERS INCLUDING MINOR PARTS AND ATTACHMENTS IN

BOTH CASES ARE NOW TWO HUNDRED AND THIRTY SIX THEIRS

AND ONE HUNDRED AND THIRTEEN OURS ALAN HILLGARTH ⊡

Enquiry respecting this Telegram should be accompanied by this form. Mark Your Reply VIA IMPERIAL.

Alan Hillgarth provides to Churchill an update on the number of
employees in the Soviet Embassy in London and the British
Embassy in Moscow, respectively.

Minister and Churchill about British jet-fighter strength. Churchill
drew on Hillgarth's figures about Soviet Embassy personnel – 'far
more, I am assured, than our police and other agents can supervise'[10]
– to suggest that the Soviets were learning more than they should
about British fighter production. Another of his concerns was the
use that the American Air Force could make of British airfields. He
hoped, he told Attlee, that East Anglian airfields – so recently used
for the strategic bombing of Germany – would quickly have their
runways extended to service US heavy bombers.

It was precisely on the issue of Anglo-American strategy that
Hillgarth also reported on the impact in Whitehall of a recent top-
secret visit to Britain by the American Joint Chiefs of Staff. Anglo-
American joint-strategic planning was still in flux and the British

knew little of American preparations for atomic warfare. The Berlin blockade had prompted the US National Security Council to send B29 Superfortress atomic bombers – albeit unarmed – to bases in Britain from where they could strike Moscow, and the first American Strategic Air Command base was established in East Anglia. But when the American Defence Secretary visited London late in 1948 the Chief of the Air Staff, Air Marshal Arthur Tedder, confessed that the Royal Air Force did not know what plans the Americans had for the use of the atomic bomb in war. This was a shocking admission from the man who had been Eisenhower's deputy as Supreme Commander a mere three years before.

Hillgarth's report reflected the confusion. The Joint Chiefs' visit, he told Churchill, had 'shaken everyone up' by revealing that there existed no joint Anglo-American plan to counter Russian aggression. The Americans would simply drop atomic bombs in a campaign of 'pure improvisation' and Britain's defence chiefs felt they were getting no clear backing from the Cabinet. Hillgarth's inside sources were no more complimentary about the Foreign Office. Here they focused on its Russia Committee, whose chairman, Gladwyn Jebb, had headed the wartime Post-Hostilities Planning Committee where Churchill dubbed him 'gibbering-jabbering Jebb'. 'It meets once a fortnight', reported Hillgarth, 'but does nothing and the Service member can't get it to do anything.' The service member, as Churchill well knew, was none other than Tedder, who was keen to adopt all steps short of a shooting war to counter the Soviet offensive around the globe. But his relations with Churchill had never recovered from the Middle East air intelligence contretemps of 1943, and Churchill had written a corruscating memorandum about his work as Eisenhower's deputy. Hillgarth proved a useful channel of communication and buffer between them.

While Hillgarth concluded that overall intelligence about the Soviet Union was generally unsatisfactory, knowledge of the Soviet Air Order of Battle was improving and there was a steady flow of information from defectors. It was clear that the Soviet Union had not yet recovered from the war and that the figure of eight years before it could be ready for another might be a considerable underestimate. Russia would certainly go 'to almost any length to avoid a new war'.[11]

These words confirmed what Churchill had long argued about Moscow's attitude towards a new world conflict. It certainly bol-

stered his confidence when five months later he startled the world
with a bold and controversial call for an East–West summit. On 14
February 1950 – the day that Moscow signed a thirty-year friendship
pact with the new Communist regime in Peking – he delivered a
fighting speech in Edinburgh. The election campaign had begun,
and Churchill directed his principal barrage at the socialists. But after
shifting to his familiar theme that the American quasi-monopoly of
the atomic bomb was the best guarantee of peace, he electrified his
audience with a demand for immediate high-level talks with the
Kremlin. What was needed, he urged, was a supreme effort to bridge
the gulf between two worlds: 'It is not easy to see how things could
be worsened by a parley at the summit.' Labour dismissed the appeal
as an election stunt, but it marked the beginning of a deeply felt
endeavour he was to pursue when he became Prime Minister the
next year. War, he protested, was now no longer a romance. It could
mean nothing less than the massacre of human beings 'by the
hideous force of perverted science.'[12] That he could call so assuredly
for talks rested in part on his confidence in the intelligence provided
by Hillgarth.

Four months later the outbreak of the Korean War cast a pall of
gloom, and in the House of Commons Churchill spoke in alarmist
tones about the vast Red Army advantage in tanks and armoured
divisions in Europe. The Russians also knew the weaknesses of the
Western Allies. 'Apart from agents', he noted, 'there are Communists
all over Germany who see the troops living among them day after
day . . .'[13]

His depression was deepened by a sombre report delivered by
Hillgarth soon afterwards. He revealed that proposals to deny key
strategic materials to the Russians were being held up by the government's continuing reluctance to alienate Moscow and by its desperate pursuit of trade at any price. Nothing had been done, Hillgarth
complained, to prevent visiting Soviet technicians from visiting
British factories. The government was also hesitant to take the
necessary measures against Communists in Britain. Ernest Bevin,
while deeply concerned that the Trades Union Congress and teaching professions had been infiltrated by Communists, thought little
useful could be done short of outlawing the Communist Party, which
was politically impossible. Generally speaking, Hillgarth claimed,
knowledge of Russia remained lamentably weak. Intelligence on the
Soviet Air Force was out of date, there was no real knowledge of

atomic-bomb progress or stocks, and there was 'frighteningly insufficient' intelligence about Soviet ground missiles or bacteriological warfare.

Hillgarth's explanation for this intelligence failure was a severe restriction on photo-reconnaissance flights over Soviet territory, a veto that he claimed was caused by political fears of provoking the Soviets. But Hillgarth's inside sources thought these fears exaggerated. 'The Russians expect us to do these things', he declared. 'If they shot down even a number of PR aircraft they would not be pushed to war.'[14] Churchill took note. One of his first steps on becoming Prime Minister was to lift the ban.

Hillgarth painted an even gloomier picture of British intelligence in April 1951 when he reported that subversive propaganda remained weak and the Chiefs of Staff were still meeting political resistance in their efforts to ban exports to Moscow of strategic materials. Intelligence on what was happening in Russia was in fact worse than before. In contrast to their brilliant successes against the German Enigma, British code-breakers had cracked no significant Soviet ciphers. Nor did it look as though they would, 'since the Russians are cleverer than the Germans'. A few minor codes had been penetrated and some even bought, but nothing that carried important signals traffic. Some naval and air call signals were being read to provide a sketchy Order of Battle, but the material was, in Hillgarth's words, 'unfinished and unreliable'. Defectors had dried up, photo-reconaissance remained vetoed, submarines were forbidden to cruise off Soviet ports, and agents could glean nothing of importance except relatively low-grade snippets from Eastern Europe. Even the Korean War had proved a disappointment from the intelligence angle. Apart from some marine mines, no Soviet weapons or equipment 'other than junk' had been captured.

Despite all this Hillgarth felt able to pass on some general conclusions. The Soviet Union's new cruisers and submarines were all designed for inshore and coastal work and its Air Force was concentrating on fighters. Bombers were few and Moscow had no strategic air force in the modern sense. Its only long-range bombers were copies of B29s, and there was no sign of jet-propelled bombers. In general the Russian Navy was being designed as an aid to its Army, the Air Force was essentially defensive, and military preparations were not being made for a war of aggression. 'The inference from what we do know', Hillgarth told Churchill, 'is that Russia depends on all means of attack short of a shooting war and on a collapse of her opponents' economy. But it would be best to know.'

Hillgarth's basic explanation for these intelligence shortcomings was particularly significant in the light of Churchill's wartime addiction to the 'golden eggs' of the Bletchley Park code-breakers. If intelligence were sparse and unreliable, Hillgarth concluded, the explanation was that too much reliance had been placed on SIGINT. This was a source that no longer produced the answer, and no one had yet admitted to the need for a radical reassessment of intelligence methods. Yet without a knowledge of the enemy, rearmament – escalating rapidly in the Korean aftermath – would be wasteful and ineffective. 'Even a giant', Hillgarth concluded, 'is blind in the dark.'[15]

This was the last of his secret briefings to Churchill. Six years after the war his sources were either retiring or being dispersed, and soon Churchill was back in power, able to read the most secret of official intelligence reports. But he had not forgotten his wartime reliance on Ultra and appreciated the significance of Hillgarth's point about British failures to crack Soviet ciphers. Throughout the war Churchill and his advisers had dreaded the moment when they might lose Ultra. Now his successors were working more or less blind against the Soviets. Shortly after reading Hillgarth's report, he sent it – having first removed Hillgarth's name – to Stewart Menzies. 'I will mention it to you when we meet next', he promised. Before the month was out Menzies was lunching at Chartwell.[16] Churchill's return to Downing Street was still five months in the future. None of the visits to Chartwell by Hillgarth or Menzies was ever recorded in the visitor's book. Like Desmond Morton's in the 1930s, they were strictly off the record.

The other great international issue that fuelled Churchill's energy during these early Cold War years was European unity. At Zurich in September 1946 he appealed for a United States of Europe with a Franco-German partnership at its heart. The Prague coup heightened his sense of urgency. Addressing a conference at The Hague in April 1948 attended by such European luminaries as Léon Blum, Jean Monnet, Paul-Henri Spaak and Alcide de Gasperi, he called for the creation of a European Assembly. 'Europe', he declared, 'has only to arise and stand in her own majesty, faithfulness and virtue, to confront all forms of tyranny, ancient or modern, Nazi or

Communist, with forces which are unconquerable, and which if asserted in good time may never be challenged again.'

While there has been considerable debate about the depth and meaning of Churchill's commitment to a United Europe, a significant intelligence dimension to his involvement has largely escaped notice. In March 1949 he again set sail on the *Queen Elizabeth* for the transatlantic crossing to the United States. The ostensible reason was to speak at the Massachusetts Institute of Technology in Boston, but in New York he also delivered his most blistering attack on Communism since the 1920s. It was, he thundered, even more dangerous than Nazism because the small hierarchy in the Kremlin controlled 'a church of Communist adepts whose missionaries are in every country as a fifth column'. If their gamble paid off, he concluded, 'They will be the Quislings with power to rule and dominate all the rest of their fellow countrymen.' These were headline-grabbing phrases, but behind the scenes he was working with practitioners of intelligence to ensure the decisive defeat of the quislings he had so publicly denounced. Ironically, the mission brought him together with his former ally and opponent from the OSS, 'Wild Bill' Donovan.

Donovan's hopes of heading American peacetime intelligence had been thwarted by Truman's dissolution of the OSS at the end of the war, but by 1947 the National Security Act created the Central Intelligence Agency (CIA) and soon OSS veterans were back at work. Donovan himself retreated to private law practice on Wall Street but he continued to exert influence in Washington. In August of that year, as the Marshall Plan was unfolding, he bumped into Truman's Defence Secretary, James V. Forrestal, on the steps of Columbia University's library. Donovan had just returned from France where he had been profoundly disturbed at the power of the French Communist Party and its continuous campaign of 'psychological warfare', a Fifth Column of the kind that Churchill was denouncing. Donovan poured out his anxieties to the hardline and sympathetic Forrestal and urged that the United States should respond by pouring in money to help anti-Communists in the trade unions and boost the democratic press. The White House heard the message and soon CIA money was flowing into France, Italy and other Western countries with powerful Communist parties and labour unions.

Most of the funds were channelled through unofficial and pri-

vately sponsored agencies headed by prominent American citizens.
Donovan was one of them. To him, European unity was one of the
vital buttresses against Communism, the political cornerstone on
which the defence and the solvency of the Western world was being
built. In 1948, in the shadow cast by Prague and Berlin, he created
and became Chairman of the American Committee on United
Europe (ACUE). Its Vice-Chairman was the former OSS head of
station in Switzerland, Allen Dulles. The deceptively avuncular
Dulles was simultaneously recommending reforms for the CIA and
building the post-war intelligence career that would take him to the
top of the agency in 1953. Day-to-day administration of the committee was in the hands of Thomas Braden, another OSS veteran. He
too was to have a CIA future, becoming head of its International
Organisations Division in 1951.[17]

There was a double agenda in Donovan's creation of ACUE. Its
aim was not only to fight for European unity but also to help
Churchill. Rivalry had broken out between the European Movement
associated with Churchill and a pressure group headed by Count
von Coudenhove-Kalergi, a prominent inter-war campaigner for
European federalism. In the summer of 1948 Duncan Sandys, who
served as President of the Churchill group, arrived in New York to
seek backing for its efforts. To avoid splitting their support between
two rival groups Donovan and Dulles threw their weight behind
Churchill and Sandys.

By the time Churchill arrived in New York the next year, he was
clear in his mind about what he needed from Donovan: moral
support and money. He also told Donovan that the European
Movement would have to include representatives of the captive
nations behind the Iron Curtain and that there could be no permanent peace in Europe while ten of its capitals remained in
Communist hands. Churchill found the old OSS chief a more than
willing ally. Donovan also gave him the responsibility of dispersing
American funds through the International Secretariat of his
European Movement. Churchill returned to Britain as the North
Atlantic Treaty was being signed in Washington, and over the weeks
that followed he put in place the necessary financial arrangements to
fund the European campaign. Once Donovan had sent detailed
information about the short-term finance available, he passed day-
to-day management to Sandys. The benefits were immediately felt.
The European Movement had been staring bankruptcy in the face

and Sandys urgently requested £80,000 to keep it afloat. The CIA funds channelled via Donovan and Dulles prevented its collapse during the first two decisive meetings of the Council of Europe at Strasbourg in 1949 and 1950. But Churchill and Sandys kept knowledge of the source of their money confined to a small inner circle.

There was irony in this CIA funding of Churchill and his European Movement. The financial rescue package enabled the Belgian Paul-Henri Spaak to emerge as President of the European Assembly at Strasbourg, and over the following year his enthusiastic federalism encountered growing resistance in Britain. Opposition was strongest in the Labour Party, where Denis Healey and Hugh Dalton, so recently the 'minister of European resistance', set European fury alight with a stridently anti-federalist pamphlet. But Churchill and Sandys, not to mention the Conservative Party itself, also grew sceptical about Spaak's vision of a federal future for Europe and a growing rift again threatened to tear the European Movement apart. In June 1950 Donovan and Thomas Braden flew to Europe on a mission to sort out the mess. This time they sided against Churchill and threw their support behind the Continental federalists. Sandys was ousted as President of the European Movement and the secretariat moved to Brussels. Churchill, Donovan confessed, had in the end been 'a great disappointment' from the federalist standpoint.[18]

19

Cloak-and-Dagger

Churchill returned to power with the Conservative General Election victory of October 1951. He repeated his Edinburgh call for a summit to ease Cold War tensions, and within days was planning another visit to Washington where he hoped to re-establish the intimate relationship with the United States that had been the keynote of his wartime policy. As usual, defence and international affairs consumed most of his energy.

On the intelligence front repairs to the special relationship were urgently needed. Just days before Churchill's Edinburgh speech Dr Klaus Fuchs, a refugee scientist from Hitler's Germany who had worked at the wartime Los Alamos atomic laboratories and more recently at Britain's Atomic Energy Research Establishment at Harwell, had been sentenced to fourteen years in prison for passing secrets to Moscow (he had also, ironically, passed on secrets about the American programme to the British). Then, a year later, as Churchill was raising Hillgarth's final report on the state of British intelligence with Sir Stewart Menzies, the disappearance of two British diplomats, Guy Burgess and Donald Maclean, hit the head-lines. Behind the scenes there was panic in Whitehall. Maclean in particular was privy to highly sensitive Anglo-American secrets and his defection precipitated a transatlantic crisis. Maclean had been identified as a Soviet agent through patient American efforts on the Soviet 'Venona' decrypts. That the British had let him slip through their fingers was incomprehensible, or even sinister, to the CIA and FBI. If the London–Washington intelligence axis was to survive, each had to trust the other's security. Washington had long been pressing MI5 and MI6 for tighter measures. Reluctantly, Attlee's government had agreed to the 'positive vetting', involving detailed probes of personal backgrounds to weed out potential security threats, of all civil servants holding sensitive posts. It was one of the Labour government's last decisions. It fell to Churchill to introduce it in January 1952.[1]

Churchill's Opposition rhetoric about Communist Fifth Columns suggested that once in office he would launch a vigorous purge of subversives, especially if doing so meant salvaging the transatlantic alliance. The mood in Washington was now hawkish. Senator Joseph McCarthy had launched his campaign to purge alleged Communists and their supporters from American life. Since then McCarthyism had spread like a virus into the American body politic, claiming the innocent and the guilty alike. But Churchill was determined to avoid a witch-hunt. For all his anti-Communist outbursts he remained attached to the principles of free speech and was determined to ensure that purges of the civil service remained limited and discreet. Behind this low-key prudence also lingered his antipathy to MI5 dating back to the war. Part reaction to his own 1940 enthusiasm for the internment of aliens, part suspicion of MI5's potential as a threat to parliamentary democracy, the mistrust was mutual. MI5 had quietly sabotaged Churchill's attempts to limit its powers during the latter stages of the war, and under Attlee it had suffered the imposition of the policeman Sir Percy Sillitoe as its Director-General. Attlee had taken the straightforward view that MI5 was 'under the direct control' of the prime minister of the day. By 1951 MI5 was fighting back and the Cabinet Secretary recommended that the Prime Minister's role in its affairs should be reduced, with the Director-General responsible to the Home Secretary. This reflected unhappiness about Attlee, but also pre-empted interference by Churchill. While the new directive preserved a direct line of communication between the MI5 Director-General and the Prime Minister by allowing, 'on appropriate occasions', for the former to appeal to the latter over the head of the Home Secretary, it specifically laid down that ministers should not concern themselves with details. Moreover, MI5 should carry out work only if it was convinced that it involved the public interest and the defence of the realm, and not some partisan political agenda. While all this sounded very good, it muddied the issue of responsibility at the top and gave MI5 a remarkably free hand to act with little political accountability, an aspect that Churchill had long deplored.

MI5 fears of the possible impact of Churchill's entourage on its affairs proved unfounded. He seemed curiously indifferent to the

Burgess–Maclean defection. 'I don't think he was much interested', recalled Sir John Colville, his principal private secretary, many years later. 'In fact I had to press him to ask the Cabinet Office to provide a Note on the incident. I think he merely wrote them off as being decadent young men, corrupted by drink and homosexuality.' This did not prevent Churchill from believing that homosexuality itself might pose a security threat. This was not for the usual blackmail reasons but because, he argued, homosexuals often felt themselves 'alien and apart' from the mainstream of the country. If the Burgess–Maclean affair convinced him of anything, Colville claimed, it was his already 'not very high' opinion of the Foreign Office. This was borne out by his one parliamentary intervention in the affair when he fiercely questioned Herbert Morrison, Ernest Bevin's successor at the Foreign Office, about the dates the two traitors had been promoted to their last Foreign Office posts.[2]

As for MI5 itself, Churchill may have felt reassured by the continued presence of Sillitoe who had policed some of Britain's toughest cities. The first meeting between the two men dated back to 1945 when Sillitoe was Chief Constable of Kent, the county in which Churchill had his home at Chartwell. Churchill had learned at Yalta that he and Roosevelt shared a hobby, the keeping of tropical fish, and promised to send him several rare breeding specimens. To his dismay the fish ponds at Chartwell proved empty. The Special Branch was called in and Sillitoe made himself available for consultation. While Churchill uselessly threw in handfuls of fish food, he spotted a grey heron flapping away from a distant corner of the ponds. 'I think, sir', he ventured, 'that we have just seen one of the thieves.' Churchill agreed, drew thoughtfully on his cigar and disarmingly confessed that with a war going on he could quite understand why people had better things to do than protect his fish.

Such an easy camaraderie was swept aside when Sillitoe was replaced in 1953 by Sir Dick White, an MI5 veteran of wartime work on the Double-Cross system. On one of the rare occasions when Churchill summoned him, things did not go well. Incautiously, in a general chat about public figures, White expressed his dislike for Brendan Bracken, whom he had known at school. It was an odd mistake for the MI5 chief to make given that Bracken was one of Churchill's closest friends. 'I got a special glare from the old man', he told his biographer. 'It was not my finest hour.'[3]

Oddly enough, it was precisely memories of his own finest hour that prompted Churchill to take his one firm initiative against a potential Fifth Column: the revival of the Home Guard. By the early 1950s the Joint Intelligence Committee was predicting that war with the Soviet Union could be followed by devastating missile attacks on Britain accompanied by invasion – even though this was unlikely before the middle of the decade. As for pro-Soviet saboteurs, the threat would have to be contained by the immediate detention of the leadership of the British Communist Party. As in 1940, visions of paratroopers (this time Soviet) landing in Britain assisted by domestic subversives deeply troubled Churchill's imagination, and within a month of his return to office a Bill allowing for a million-man 'Dad's Army' was tabled in Parliament. However, in the age of nuclear bombs it was a hopeless anachronism and after five months a mere 22,000 men had volunteered, but he persisted in supporting the scheme. Only after his resignation was it finally, with relief, dropped by his successors.[4]

MI5 was not alone in fearing what Churchill might get up to with secret intelligence that came his way. The dogged institutional memory of the Foreign Office carried many wartime scars of intelligence encounters with him. He and Anthony Eden were often at odds on current international issues. This was particularly true over the Middle East, where Churchill strongly disliked Eden's policy of reducing troop commitments in Egypt. Their disagreement produced one startling example of the deliberate withholding of intelligence from Churchill.

Not surprisingly, knowing his penchant for reacting to raw intelligence, those responsible in the Foreign Office for distributing SIS reports to Downing Street began to exercise an unofficial censorship by withholding certain items. This was either at Eden's express order, or, more likely, with his knowing connivance. Anthony Montague Browne, one of Churchill's principal private secretaries and himself a Foreign Office official, noticed that both the quantity and the quality of the secret intelligence papers being sent to Churchill was diminishing. After a protest, the quantity increased, but not the quality. One delivery, he recalled, contained 'some rather *Boys' Own Paper* clandestine photographs'. One weekend at Chequers Montague Browne told Churchill what was happening and there was a predictable explosion: 'Send for "C" and I'll sack the shit.' 'C' by this time was Major-General Sir John Sinclair, whose unhappy tenancy of the position was to end abruptly three years later following a botched attempt to spy on the Soviet cruiser *Ordzhonikidze* in Portsmouth harbour. It took all Montague Browne's diplomatic skills to prevent Churchill from summoning Sinclair and instead direct his anger at the Foreign Office, rather than SIS. In the end Churchill merely sent a petulant note to Sinclair asking that the 'disagreeable information' sent his way not be written in blue ink on blue paper but, as befitted the subject, in black on white.[5]

That Churchill was eager to reassert his power over secret intelligence was also made obvious to R. V. Jones, the wartime prodigy of scientific intelligence. Since 1945 Jones had built a successful academic career at the University of Aberdeen. When Churchill returned to Downing Street Jones came back to London as Director of Scientific Intelligence. His job was to anticipate the application of science to warfare by potential enemies, which meant directing intelligence collection and assessment as well as maintaining an awareness of British advances in the field. He was simultaneously made scientific adviser to the Government Code and Cipher School – the successor to Bletchley Park – and appointed to the Joint Intelligence Committee. But he quickly became frustrated by bureaucracy and 'drift', irritated by inter-service rivalries and resentment of the Ministry of Defence, and exasperated by the separation between scientific and atomic intelligence. Eventually he appealed to Churchill directly, quoting Churchill's own words after he had left the Admiralty in 1915: 'I had vehement convictions and small power to give effect to them. I had to watch the unhappy casting away of great opportunities and the feeble execution of plans I had launched and in which I heartily believed.' All Churchill did was refer him to Harold Alexander, now Minister of Defence, but Alexander was ineffective and in June 1954 Jones, disillusioned, returned to academia.[6]

The most dramatic demonstration of the military power of science during Jones's stay in London was the successful test of Britain's first atomic bomb at Monte Bello island off the Australian coast. Churchill threw himself energetically into its planning and set up the Apex Committee with himself in the chair. One of his worries was that the Soviet Union might try to sabotage the test, so a series of deceptions was set in motion to suggest it would take place at a date later than planned. Churchill particularly delighted in Operation 'Spoofer', involving the booking of airline tickets to Australia in the name of Sir William Penney, head of the atomic project, on a false date. Churchill's close attention to detail was not matched by the KGB: it appears not even to have noticed.[7]

Although Stewart Menzies retired as head of SIS in 1952, there was sufficient overlap for the two wartime veterans to resume familiar ways. One of the earliest fruits of the renewed alliance came six months after Churchill took office.

In April 1952 three RB-45C Tornado bombers of the United States Air Force took off from their air base in Norfolk for a highly sensitive mission that was to remain secret for the next forty years. Equipped with sophisticated radar, they were on a high-speed, high-altitude mission deep behind the Iron Curtain. All American markings had been removed and replaced by Royal Air Force roundels, and the crews included RAF pilots and navigators. One Tornado flew north over the Leningrad region. The second simultaneously covered an area just short of Moscow. The southernmost flight photographed targets over Belorussia and the Ukraine. To penetrate so deep and remain so long over Russian territory it was refuelled in mid-air on both outward and inward journeys by an accompanying KB-29 tanker. While the reconnaissance bombers took detailed photographs, airborne listening aircraft and ground-based listening posts recorded Russian reactions to gauge the nature of Soviet air defence organisation and readiness. All three aircraft returned safely to base. It was the first such mission and more were to follow. Churchill had finally lifted the ban, so frequently deplored by Alan Hillgarth, on intelligence missions over the Soviet Union.[8]

In doing so he was responding to American requests. Even as American and Red Army soldiers embraced on the Elbe River in 1945 US Intelligence was giving top priority to the capture of *Luftwaffe* documents revealing flight paths suitable for the bombing of Soviet military and industrial targets. US Air Force and Navy reconnaissance Soviet-territory overflights had been occurring since at least 1947 with the approval of Truman. Most took off from Alaska, others from Germany. In 1951 planning began for British-based flights. Reconnaissance was urgently needed to identify targets and their likely responses for the American strategic nuclear-deterrent force rapidly being built up in the aftermath of Korea. Soon the Americans had more than forty bases scattered across southern Britain with some 50,000 personnel. Preparations for the overflights began when selected RAF personnel were sent for training to the United States the month before Churchill returned to power. In March 1952 a successful probe flight to test Soviet reaction took place down the central air corridor to Berlin. There was a long delay after the April flights, with at least one projected mission cancelled, but in April 1954 Churchill approved another three-prong penetration over Soviet territory. Three things are clear about these secret flights. First, Churchill insisted on approving them personally. Second, he cancelled them if he thought there was any risk of upsetting the Russians. Third, despite his powerful commitent to building good relations with the Kremlin, if the circumstances were right he was prepared to take the risk.

If Churchill was a sometimes cautious shadow warrior against the Russians, his old enthusiasm for lighting subversive fires elsewhere remained undimmed. By this time Eisenhower was in the White House and Allen Dulles had taken over at the CIA. Both were covert-action enthusiasts. Churchill was swift to take advantage of the change of mood.

Only weeks before Churchill became Prime Minister Dr Mohammed Musaddiq, Prime Minister of Iran, had given the staff of the Anglo-Iranian Oil Company's refinery at Abadan a week to leave the country. Churchill bullishly told Clement Attlee that if he chose to use force he would have his full support, but this was not on the agenda and Abadan was duly abandoned. During what became widely described as a 'warmonger' election campaign Churchill denounced the decision. Musaddiq had won a triumph, he thundered in his opening election address, and had measured accurately the will-power of the men he had to deal with in Whitehall. The whole affair was a melancholy story of 'inadvertence, incompetence, indecision and final collapse', yet another sad episode in what Britain's enemies rejoiced in calling 'the decline and fall of the British Empire'. The electors would soon have their chance to prove them wrong. 'Do not fail', he added. 'The chance may not come again.'[9]

Churchill's return as Prime Minister soon saw him involved in one of the most extraordinary cloak-and-dagger episodes in his long involvement with secret service. In August 1953, two months after the Coronation of Queen Elizabeth II sparked visions of a brave new Elizabethan age, a joint SIS–CIA inspired coup toppled Musaddiq from power and restored the Shah to his Peacock Throne. It was a fitting finale to the career of this Victorian man of action who had come to embrace the transatlantic alliance as the rock of Britain's safety in the post-imperial world.

Iran meant oil, and it filled post-war British coffers with desperately needed currency.[10] The Anglo-Iranian Oil Company was over 50 per cent owned by the British government, and its Persian Gulf oil refinery at Abadan was the largest in the world. For Britain, Anglo-Iranian stood as a powerful witness to its technical prowess and was its largest single overseas asset with the physical plant alone valued at over £100 million. It also provided a potent symbol of British prestige in the Middle East.

Churchill had a strong emotional commitment to Britain's role in Iran, the last Middle East country where oil remained an exclusively British affair. As First Lord of the Admiralty in 1914 he had been instrumental in acquiring 51 per cent ownership in the company for the British government and in signing a thirty-year contract for it to supply oil to the Royal Navy. The deal, he enthused, was 'a prize from fairyland far beyond our brightest dreams'. Throughout the following decades Britain continued to treat Persia as its fiefdom. In the Second World War, displeased with the Shah's pro-German views, British forces invaded the country jointly with the Russians, deposed the Shah, and installed his pliable young son Mohammed Reza Pahlavi on the throne. Seven years later the financially strapped Labour government imposed a limit on all company dividends that heavily dented Iran's income from Anglo-Iranian, hardened growing nationalist protests against British influence, and fuelled demands for the company's nationalisation. Mohammed Musaddiq emerged as the most vociferous and anti-British member of Iran's Parliament, the Majlis. In March 1951 the Shah reluctantly appointed him Prime Minister. The 70-year-old scion of a wealthy landed family, Musaddiq once told the Shah that the British controlled everything in Iran. Determined to end their influence he immediately, and to massive popular acclaim, nationalised Anglo-Iranian. In retaliation the company closed down its operations and before long Musaddiq was expelling its remaining staff.

Churchill was not alone in his call for a forceful response. Behind the scenes plans had been made for a landing at Abadan and a small attack force had been assembled at the mouth of the Shatt-el-Arab in Iraqi waters (Iraq was still a British client state). Foreign Secretary Herbert Morrison was eager to move but failed to carry the Cabinet. SIS had bribed a local Iranian commander to offer no more than token resistance to the landing force. In Tehran the head of the SIS station was another wartime acquaintance of Churchill, the veteran of SOE exploits in Greece and visitor to Chequers in 1944, Monty Woodhouse.

After his Greek adventures Woodhouse had declined to take charge of the SIS's post-war Special Operations Branch.[11] But after war broke out in Korea he joined SIS and was soon in Tehran. He arrived shortly before the Abadan expulsions to find a politically volatile situation in which one of the biggest dangers seemed to be a coup by the Tudeh, the country's Communist Party. Clothed in nationalist garb, it gave its support to Musaddiq and enjoyed clandestine support from the Soviet Union. Woodhouse quickly concluded that preventing a Soviet coup would require American help. SIS had valuable human assets in the country but the Americans alone had the financial and technical resources that were needed. 'I soon realised', he confessed, 'that liaison with my CIA colleague could be the key to success.' So far the Americans had been reluctant to get involved in a British–Iranian quarrel fuelled by nationalism and fearful that Musaddiq's departure would lead to something worse. Woodhouse set out to convince them that there was a serious Communist threat and that with Musaddiq in power nothing could be done. He also took hands-on control of covert relations with 'the Brothers', two leading members of the Rashidian family, wealthy Anglophiles who provided the key to the unfolding plot. In case of sudden Soviet invasion, he also built up the nucleus of a resistance movement on SOE lines with local tribal leaders.

With Woodhouse laying the groundwork in Iran, Churchill's government spent much of 1952 in fruitless negotiations with Musaddiq. In October 1952 talks collapsed, diplomatic relations were broken off and Embassy staff, including the SIS team, were expelled. Woodhouse discussed a coup with Anthony Eden who vetoed the idea but offered a loophole. If a coup were to succeed, Eden observed, it would have to have American support. Woodhouse took the hint. After setting up a secret operational base in Cyprus he flew to Washington with two other top SIS officials.

They arrived in the American capital only days after Dwight D. Eisenhower's victory in the 1952 Presidential Election. Eisenhower, a hawk in dove's clothing, was a firm believer in covert action to thwart the Communists. His designate Secretary of State was the openly aggressive John Foster Dulles and his brother Allen was to head the CIA when Eisenhower entered the White House. So Woodhouse found sympathetic ears. Prudently he had taken along a detailed plan for a coup, Operation Boot, that stressed the Communist threat and Musaddiq's inability to resist a Soviet take-over. Allen Dulles and Frank Wisner, the CIA Director of Plans, were enthusiastic, but the State Department and the Truman White House were lukewarm and no one was prepared to take a decision before the new administration assumed office. In London the cautious mood infected Eden and early in 1953 he ordered an end to 'Boot': SIS could not indefinitely finance the Brothers' plans for a coup.

Barely had Eden taken the decision than the scene rapidly changed. The Brothers simply replaced SIS subventions with money of their own and went on plotting. Political passions in Iran intensified as Musaddiq alienated religious and parliamentary leaders as well as the Shah. Riots began in the streets, the Chief of Police was assassinated, and in March 1953 Musaddiq rejected yet another Anglo-American plan for a settlement of the oil dispute. While the rest of the world was digesting the news of Stalin's death, Woodhouse received a message from the CIA that it was ready to go ahead with plans for a coup. Soon afterwards both the State Department and Foreign Office confirmed they were on board. With SIS still excluded from Iran, detailed operational planning, now code-named 'Ajax', began under the designated CIA field commander. He, too, was already known to Churchill.

Kermit Roosevelt of the CIA had been present at the White House Christmas party of December 1941 during Churchill's visit to Washington after Pearl Harbor. He had graduated from teaching at Harvard to 'Wild Bill' Donovan's OSS, where he worked in Cairo and composed its official War Report. He was a natural recruit for the CIA and by the early 1950s was a major figure in its Middle East affairs, a quiet activist thoroughly convinced of the value of covert operations. In this he shared the optimism of the new CIA Director Allen Dulles and his covert-action lieutenant Frank Wisner. 'All three', it has been noted, 'were gregarious, intrigued by possibilities, liked to do things, had three bright ideas a day [and] shared the optimism of stock market plungers.'[12]

For all the Americans' enthusiasm and SIS certainty, however, Eden remained in two minds about the project, blowing hot and cold according to his febrile mood. By now recurring bouts of illness had severly weakened his grip and in April he underwent a serious gall-bladder operation. It failed, as did a second one that almost killed him. Early in June he flew to Boston for American surgery and was out of action for the rest of the summer. 'Fortunate chance', to use Woodhouse's words, had come to the aid of SIS. In Eden's absence Churchill took control of the Foreign Office and Woodhouse quickly felt the change.

Churchill was desperately keen to get rid of Musaddiq. 'Churchill enjoyed dramatic operations', recalled Woodhouse, 'and had no high regard for timid diplomatists.' David Hunt, Alexander's former wartime intelligence officer in the Middle East, was then working at Downing Street. He later suggested that by the time he returned to office in 1951 Churchill had lost most of his interest in intelligence matters but that Iran was the one great exception.[13] No sooner had Eden left for Boston than Churchill gave Operation Boot the green light.

Meanwhile Kermit Roosevelt had surreptitiously crossed the Iraqi border into Iran. Besides ensuring that the Brothers and other con-spirators remained onside, his principal mission was to persuade the Shah to play his role by signing royal decrees dismissing Musaddiq and appointing as his successor General Zahedi – ironically a figure denounced during the war as pro-Nazi and the target of a kidnap mission by Fitzroy Maclean that resulted in him spending the rest of the war in a Palestinian jail.

Roosevelt's mission was accomplished in true cloak-and-dagger style. Smuggled into the Royal Palace under a blanket on the back seat of a car, and following this up with midnight meetings on the edge of the desert outside Tehran, Roosevelt convinced the Shah that he would have the full backing of Washington and London. As proof that he was their personal emissary he arranged for Eisenhower and Churchill to send special signals to the Shah. Eisenhower inserted a particular phrase into a speech he made and Churchill persuaded the BBC World Service to alter its usual time signal on its Persian-language broadcast – the announcer changed 'It is now midnight' to 'It is now [pause] exactly midnight'.

Events came to a climax in mid-August. With the Shah waiting on the sidelines at a summer retreat on the Caspian Sea, carefully orchestrated CIA 'rent-a-crowds' filled the Tehran streets and Colonel Nematollah Nassiry, Commander of the Imperial Guard, led a detachment of troops to Musaddiq's house bearing the Shah's dismissal decree. Then disaster struck: word of the plot had leaked out and Nassiry was arrested. Zahedi went into hiding and the Shah, assuming all was lost, fled to Rome. Tehran descended into chaos, the Tudeh clamoured for a Republic, and statues of the Shah were smashed. Churchill, according to Woodhouse, 'hit the ceiling'.

Out of potential disaster Roosevelt was able to craft triumph. Skilfully exploiting his media contacts, he publicly circulated the Shah's decrees and mobilised support for him into a massive street protest that ended in bitter fighting leaving 300 people dead. Musaddiq fled, Zahedi emerged from the American Embassy, and the Shah returned in triumph from Rome. 'I owe my throne to God, my people, my army – and to you!' he exclaimed to Roosevelt, presenting him with a gold cigarette case.

Roosevelt then flew to London for his historic encounter with Churchill. Eisenhower was no less fascinated. At a White House debriefing Roosevelt heard John Foster Dulles 'purring like a giant cat' and saw the President held spellbound. 'I listened', Eisenhower confided to the secrecy of his diary, 'and it seemed more like a dime novel than a historical fact.'[14] By the end of the year London and Tehran had reopened diplomatic relations and Woodhouse had moved on to other SIS tasks, but some things had changed for good. Anglo-Iranian was renamed British Petroleum, lost its monopoly on Iranian oil and soon joined an international consortium in which American oil companies held a 40 per cent share of the stock. The era that had begun with Churchill's financial coup on the eve of the First World War was finally over.

Churchill resigned as Prime Minister in April 1955 and played no part in the SIS assassination plans of his successor, Anthony Eden, against President Nasser of Egypt. But before leaving office he gave the green light to more overflights of the Soviet Union and in the spring of 1954 approved one of the great success stories of Cold War espionage, Operation Gold. At a joint SIS–CIA conference held in London the allies agreed to build a tunnel from the American sector of Berlin into the Soviet sector to tap the landlines used by the Soviet military and intelligence headquarters at Karlshorst. Becoming operational just two months before Churchill resigned, it provided thousands of messages that confirmed what Churchill had long believed: Moscow had no great plans for conquest and was open to co-existence.[15]

In his retirement the secret war cast one last symbolic shadow across Churchill's life. Early in 1960 he and Clementine planned a Baltic cruise as guests of Aristotle Onassis on board his luxury yacht, the *Christina*. The highlight was to be a visit to Leningrad, which Clementine had visited and admired in 1945. But in May an American high-altitude U-2 reconnaisance flight on a spying mission was shot down deep over the Soviet Union. In the crisis that followed a summit meeting between Eisenhower and the Soviet leader Nikita Khrushchev was cancelled and East–West relations rapidly cooled. Leningrad suddenly became an impolitic port of call and the *Christina* headed for the warmer climes of the Mediterranean and Adratic, where it called in at the Yugoslav port of Split. Here, waiting to greet Churchill, was Marshal Tito who had a seaside villa near by. Over the next two days, past quarrels with the Yugoslav leader now forgiven, Churchill spent agreeable hours fuelled by caviar, wild boar, lobster, foie gras, cigars and slivovitz, and reminisced happily over the guerrilla war that had so vividly captured his spirit in the days of his greatest adventure.[16] Five years later he was dead. Prominent amongst the mourners at his funeral were former resistance fighters from occupied Europe. Today, in the nave of the Church at Bladon outside which he lies buried, and next to fading photographs of the nineteenth-century church, a bronzed plaque presented by the French resistance still honours his memory.

Churchill stood head and shoulders above his political contemporaries in grasping the importance of intelligence and harnessing it to his cause. Secret service, with all its romance and melodrama, trickery, deception, plot and counter-plot, certainly appealed to the schoolboy within him. Yet more important were the measurable and pragmatic benefits it brought him as politician, statesman and war leader. Secret intelligence was power that gave him leverage over political colleagues, military advisers and allies, as well as strategic and tactical advantage over enemies. Covert action, special operations and deception offered valuable additions or alternatives to conventional military force, especially when Britain was weak and on the defensive.

All this he learned very early in his life, and his enthusiastic nurturing and promotion of British intelligence during the Second World War grew from roots that took hold long before the First, and were grounded in vivid personal experience. As soldier and journalist vigorously engaged in imperial wars during his youth, he witnessed how good intelligence was vital to the conquered and conqueror alike, and how conventional military forces could be vulnerable to the calculated stratagems of the weak and the occupied. Within a decade, as an ambitious and powerful politician, he was applying the lessons to Britain's impending struggle with the Kaiser's Germany, and his long-forgotten briefing in 1909 on Britain's new Secret Service Bureau by Major-General John Spencer Ewart provided a foretaste of what was to follow. For the rest of his political career Churchill was to make it his business to know and cultivate those who ran Britain's intelligence agencies, and to see in the secret service an essential tool of statecraft. He wielded it powerfully if sometimes clumsily in the First World War through the Admiralty's Room 40, and the experience provided a valuable testing ground for the Second World War. Here, in the priority he gave to intelligence and his insistence that it be co-ordinated and ruthlessly harnessed to the operational demands of war, his long and passionate involvement with secret service fully and finally bore fruit.

In some respects Churchill was both the best and the worst of men to handle intelligence. His long political experience meant that from early on he was exceptionally well acquainted with the principal intelligence techniques, had valuable contacts within the various secret services, and quickly grasped the importance of signals intelligence. Yet by character excitable and impulsive, he was often mesmerised by the original texts of intercepts, irresistibly drawn too deeply into their tactical and operational use, and failed to appreciate that they formed only a small part – albeit a very important one – of the complete intelligence picture. In his arrangements for Room 40 during the First World War he poured over the intercepts with minute attention and segregated SIGINT from other intelligence to make it the monopoly of a tiny élite in the Admiralty remote from those who had to act on it at sea. During the decade that followed the Russian Revolution he frequently took Bolshevik intercepts at face value and overreacted accordingly. He often did the same with Ultra in the Second World War, particularly during its first two years when, desperate for success, he tried to conduct the North African campaign from Downing Street in competition with his generals. Intelligence officers and professional military advisers, not surprisingly, found this difficult.

Yet Churchill also instinctively understood that intelligence is far too important to be left to the professionals. His insistence on seeing the raw material provided a constant reminder that policy came first, and that intelligence was not an end in itself and did not belong to those who produced it. It was a commodity, to be deployed or withheld for purposes that only he as leader could decide. Often, as with Hitler's attack on the Soviet Union or the likelihood of Allied victory in 1944, his own strategic assessments were more accurate than those of the professionals. He leaned heavily on his advisers and listened to them carefully, but never permitted himself to be imprisoned by them. By temperament acutely aware of the deadly power of institutional inertia and *déformations professionnelles*, he always valued independent and trusted sources such as Desmond Morton and Alan Hillgarth. Infuriating though this often was to the secret services, it was a fundamentally healthy instinct, a reminder that the experts were not always right. And, while it was not always apparent at the time, Churchill was no more captive of these individuals than he was of others. Desmond Morton acquired a fearsome wartime reputation for sabotaging SOE, for example. Yet, for all his closeness, Churchill often overruled or ignored him. No one ever had Churchill in his pocket.

Perhaps the strongest criticisms of Churchill's dealings with secret service have been directed against his allegedly romantic attraction for cloak-and-dagger and his enthusiasm for special operations. There is some truth in this, as shown by his extraordinary dealings with Boris Savinkov and Sidney Reilly in the 1920s, and his fascination for resistance figures of the Second World War. Yet his respect for personal heroism and his taste for unreliable adventurers must be distinguished from his sometimes ruthlessly pragmatic use of special operations where *realpolitik* was never far from the surface. The assassinations of Heydrich and Darlan make the point, and while it would have been difficult to distinguish a Communist guerrilla in the hill of Bosnia from his counterpart in Greece, Churchill's support of one and denunciation of the other reflected hard-headed calculation about their respective political merits. Indeed, when it comes to special operations, in Yugoslavia, far from being a romantic, Churchill was a realist who abandoned Mihailović and his chetniks when he concluded they could not deliver what he wanted. Likewise, for all his apparently romantic and quixotic support, he lost interest in the French Maquis once their usefulness in the D-Day invasion had passed. As for the charge that he carelessly encouraged

Europeans to rise in revolt against the Germans because of some romantic conception of resistance, none of the major uprisings that provoked terrible reprisals – such as Warsaw, the Vercors or Slovakia – owed anything to exhortations by Churchill or even decisions by SOE. Poles, Frenchmen, Slovaks, not to mention other nations oppressed by Nazi brutality, all had their own agendas and national destinies to determine that owed little or nothing to London and Churchill. True, he was emotionally moved by Steinbeck's powerful fable of resistance, *The Moon is Down*, and as with Ultra his interventions with SOE could be impulsive, clumsy and erratic. But his consistent support for special operations sprang from more than a fascination with cloak-and-dagger and was based on a profound conviction that, as an underdog, Britain in 1940 had to mobilise every form of warfare that it could, however unconventional. And when the United States and Soviet Russia joined the war as powerful and competing allies, he saw special operations as a way of imposing a British stamp on the resistance and preserving British influence in the post-war world – a strategy that inevitably created friction with both Moscow and Washington. In 1940 he certainly overestimated the likely military contribution of resistance to eventual victory. But when he created SOE it was in the desperate period following the collapse of France, the expulsion of the British Army from the European continent, and the neutrality of both the United States and the Soviet Union. How, at that moment, could Britain's conventional forces promise victory?

Undeniably there was a darker side to Churchill's attraction for the clandestine powers of the state. His exaggerated obsession with German spies before the First World War, fed by a xenophobic MI5, led him to adopt measures that needlessly damaged the innocent while catching the guilty and eroded some important liberal principles. His overreaction to Bolshevik intercepts after the Russian Revolution even saw him resort to MI5 in what amounted to a personal vendetta against George Lansbury and to a dangerously close alliance with elements in the secret services and elsewhere that wildly talked the language of treason. Two decades later his widely shared obsession with an internal Fifth Column, this time fuelled by unexpected German victories in Europe, and lingering fears and memories of Irish subversion at home, again saw him opt for a drastic curtailment of civil liberties unwarranted by the evidence.

Yet against all this, Churchill provided his own best antidote.

Alongside his keen appreciation for national security he nurtured a powerful respect for the British constitution, the liberties of the individual, and habeas corpus. Exasperated though he was by Lloyd George's policies towards Bolshevik Russia, he refused in the end to indulge Sir Henry Wilson's talk of treason in 1920, and when advised by MI5 of the weak legal grounds against Lansbury eventually dropped his campaign against the Labour leader. And if he exhibited few retrospective regrets about the spymania of 1914, during the Second World War he quickly accepted that the drastic internment of aliens and Regulation 18B in 1940 had violated some basic principles of liberty, and began to denounce MI5 for its 'witch-hunting' activities. For the rest of the war, while delighted with its successes in running double agents, he fretted continually about MI5's increased domestic powers and tried vainly to bring it to heel. Here his fears of a British 'Gestapo' were sincere and heartfelt, but neither then nor later did he ever come to grips with the difficult issue of the democratic accountability of the secret services he had done so much to promote. It would be anachronistic to expect otherwise, for it has taken the end of the Cold War, some quarter of a century after his death, for the balance between national security and civil liberty to tilt in favour of the latter.

Out of the debris of 1940, with defeat staring Britain in the face, Churchill seized on the long-familiar weapons of secret service to fashion the modern British intelligence community that helped so significantly to deliver victory in 1945. He also inspired and helped to create with Roosevelt the transatlantic intelligence alliance that formed a vital backbone of defence during the Cold War. Nothing was perfect in this construction and Churchill revealed his personality flaws as vividly here as elsewhere. Yet the breadth of his vision, the strength of his purpose, and the depth of his experience in the world of intelligence was extraordinary and decisive. Throughout his long political career he had exhibited consistent support for Britain's secret service. As Prime Minister in war and peace, he finally reaped the reward.

Notes

Full details of all works cited appear in the Bibliography.

Introduction
1. Kermit Roosevelt, *Countercoup: The Struggle for the Control of Iran*, 199–200.
2. For example, Michael Handel (ed.), special issue on 'Leaders and Intelligence' in *Intelligence and National Security*, Vol. 3, No. 3, July 1988.
3. John Keegan, *The Mask of Command*, as quoted in Michael Herman, *Intelligence Power in Peace and War*, 325.
4. Ronald Lewin, *Churchill as Warlord*, 75.
5. Isaiah Berlin, *Personal Impressions*, 12.

Chapter 1: Adventure
1. Winston Churchill, *My Early Life*, 91.
2. Randolph S. Churchill, *Winston S. Churchill*, Vol. I, *Youth*, 43.
3. Ibid., 271.
4. Ibid., 266.
5. For his dispatches from Cuba, see *CV*, Vol. I, Part 1, 604–18.
6. Churchill, *Savrola: A Tale of Revolution in Laurania*.
7. Churchill, *The Malakand Field Force*, 295.
8. Ibid., 43.
9. WO 106/290; for Churchill on Stanton, see *CV*, Vol. 2, 787.
10. Churchill, *The Malakand Field Force*, 276–7.
11. Churchill, *The River War*, Vol. 2, 143.
12. Ibid., 166.
13. Ibid., 73.
14. Churchill, *London to Ladysmith via Pretoria*, and *Ian Hamilton's March*, *passim*.
15. G. W. Steevens, 'The Youngest Man in Europe', in *Churchill by his Contemporaries*, ed. Eade, 66.
16. J. B. Atkins, *Incidents and Reflections*, 122.
17. Norman Rose, *Churchill: An Unruly Life*, 54–5, 88.; *CV*, Vol. 3, Part 1, 178–283.
18. For Churchill's view on Sidney Street, see his 'The Battle of Sidney Street', in *Thoughts and Adventures*, 41–8. Also Donald Rumbelow, *The Houndsditch Murders and the Siege of Sidney Street*, 187–91.
19. Alexander MacCallum Scott, *Winston Spencer Churchill*, 1–2.
20. A. G. Gardiner, *Pillars of Society*, 55–63.

Chapter 2: Secret Service
1. Churchill, *The World Crisis 1911–1915*, 193–4.
2. The minutes of the subcommittee on foreign espionage are to be found in CAB 16/8. See

also Nicholas Hiley, 'The Failure of British Counter-espionage against Germany 1907–1914', in *Historical Journal*, Vol. 28, No. 4, 835–62.

3. See Churchill's speech at Saddleworth, 4 October 1901; House of Commons, 21 March 1902, 24 February 1903, 12 March 1903, 16 July 1903, in Robert Rhodes James, *The Speeches of Winston Churchill*, Vol. I, 99–102, 142, 171–2, 177–8, 202.

4. R. S. Churchill, *Churchill*, Vol. II, *Young Statesman*, 219; Paul Addison, *Churchill on the Home Front*, 82–3.

5. Diary of Lieutenant-General J. Spencer Ewart, Scottish Record Office, RH4/84/3, entries for 9 February, 9 November, 15 November 1909; see also WO 106/47A.

6. Ewart, Diary, 17 December 1909.

7. The papers of the two CID subcommittees on postal and press censorship, and on aliens, are in CAB 4/5. See also Bernard Porter, *The Origins of the Vigilant State: The London Metropolitan Police Special Branch Before the First World War*, especially 167–70.

8. Ewart, Diary, 27 April 1910.

9. *Parliamentary Debates, House of Commons*, Vol. XVI, 10 April 1910, cols 2355–360; Sir Robert Anderson, 'The Lighter Side of My Official Life', *Blackwood's Magazine*, Vol. CLXXXVII, January–March 1910.

10. *House of Lords*, Vol. IX, 25 July 1911; *House of Commons*, Vol. XXIX, 18 August 1911. J. E. B. Seeley, *Adventure*, 145; Lord Hankey, *The Supreme Command*, Vol. I, 115.

11. 'Report and Proceedings of the Standing Sub-Committee . . . on the Treatment of Aliens in Time of War', 14 August 1913, 8, CAB 4/5 (138).

12. HO 45/10629/199699.

13. Ibid.

14. 'Report and Proceedings of the Standing Sub-Committee Enquiry regarding Press and Postal Censorship in Time of War: Postal Censorship', 22 January 1913, 5, CAB 4/5 (53).

15. Hankey, *The Supreme Command*, Vol. I, 115.

16. 'Report . . . Press Censorship', 21 January 1913, 7, CAB 4/5 (38).

17. Churchill to Hurd, 12 December 1911, in Churchill Papers (Char), Churchill College, Cambridge, 13/1.

Chapter 3: Spy Fever

1. 'Report of the Home Ports Defence Committee: Protection of the Welsh Coalfields', 6 February, 1912, ADM 1/8264.

2. Churchill, *The World Crisis 1911–1915*, 51–2; see also WO 32/7187.

3. Granet to Churchill, 15 August 1911, Char 12/10.

4. General Macready to Home Ports Defence Committee, 30 January 1912, ADM 1/8264; Sir Nevil Macready, *Annals of an Active Life*, 161–5.

5. For Freeth and Pearson, see Home Ports Defence Committee Report, *passim*.

6. *CV*, Vol. II, Part 2, 1120–22.

7. Churchill to Grey, 22 November 1911, with minute by Grey, Char 13/1.

8. Churchill, *The World Crisis 1911–1915*, 68. A. J. Marder, *From the Dreadnought to Scapa Flow*, 252 *et seq.*

9. See John Bulloch, *MI5*, 31–71, and Christopher Andrew, *Secret Service*, 64 *et seq.*

10. Churchill, 'Pay of Men of the Royal Navy', 17 October 1912, CAB 37/112/ No. 114.

11. Marder, *From Dreadnought to Scapa Flow*, 353.

12. Churchill, *The World Crisis 1911–1915*, 153, 154–69.

13. John Gooch, 'The Bolt from the Blue', in *The Prospect of War*, 1–34; H. R. Moon, 'The Invasion of the United Kingdom: Public Controversy and Official Planning 1888–1918', PhD University of London, 1968, 106–107; and Churchill to Jellicoe, 8 October 1914, *CV*, Vol. III, Part 1, 180–82; Churchill to Kitchener, 19 October 1914, ibid., 204–205 *et seq.* For Sylt, see ibid., 290. See also ADM 116/1348–1351 'War Operations and Policy, Naval and Military'; and minute by Churchill, 1 August 1914, ADM 137/1013. Nicholas Hiley, 'The Failure of British Espionage Against Germany 1907–1914', in *Historical Journal*, Vol. 26, No. 4, 1983, 867–89.

14. Paul Kennedy, 'Great Britain before 1914', in Ernest R. May (ed.) *Knowing One's Enemies*, 172–204; Hiley, 'The Failure of British Espionage Against Germany 1907–1914'.
15. Churchill to Bethell, 1 October 1912, Char 13/13, 101–102.
16. John Savile and J. McConville, Tupper entry in *Dictionary of Labour Biography*, Vol. IV (1977), 203–205; Tupper's autobiography is E. Tupper, *Seaman's Torch: The Life Story of Captain Edward Tupper*. See also: W. C. Balfour, 'Captain Tupper and the 1911 Seaman's Strike in Cardiff', *Morgannwg*, 14 (1971), 62–80; Emanuel Shinwell, *Conflict Without Malice*, 48–53; Fenner Brockway, *Socialism Over Sixty Years*, 133–55; David Marquand, *Ramsay MacDonald*, 212–17. See also *The Times*, 28 July 1913.
17. Tupper, *Seaman's Torch*, 13.
18. Marquand, *Ramsay MacDonald*, 215.
19. Tupper, *Seaman's Torch*, 76.
20. Ibid., 93
21. Alexander MacCallum Scott, Diary, 30 July 1917, University of Glasgow MS 1465/8.
22. Tupper, *Seaman's Torch*, 196.
23. For Speyer, see *Dictionary of National Biography 1931–1940*; C. C. Aronsfeld, 'Enemy Aliens in England During the First World War', in *Jewish Social Studies*, Vol. XVIII, Part 4, October 1956, 275–83; *H. H. Asquith: Letters to Venetia Stanley*, ed. Brock, 292–5.
24. Churchill to Clementine, 28 July 1914, Spencer Churchill Papers, Churchill College, Cambridge.
25. Churchill, 'My Spy Story', in *Thoughts and Adventures*.
26. Stephen Roskill, *Admiral of the Fleet Earl Beatty*, 88.
27. Letters from Clementine to Winston, July and August 1914, in Spencer Churchill Papers 1/8. See also Mary Soames, *Clementine Churchill*, 102–11; William Manchester, *The Last Lion*, 479–80.
28. ADM 1/8425/175.
29. Churchill, 'My Spy Story', *Thoughts and Adventures*, 71–80. Oliver's version is in his unpublished 'Recollections' at the National Maritime Museum, Greenwich, .
30. Bayly to Churchill, 20 April 1913, in Char 13/19, No. 77; see also *CV* Vol. II, Part 3, 1728–9.
31. Sir David Beatty to Winston Churchill, *CV*, Vol. III, Part 1, 202.
32. Churchill to Jellicoe, 23 October 1914, ibid., 215–16; Churchill, *The World Crisis 1911–1915*, 393.

Chapter 4: SIGINT: 'The Intelligence that Never Fails'

1. Churchill, *The World Crisis 1911–1914*, 461–2.
2. Churchill to Bayly, 19 April 1913, *CV*, Vol. II, Part 3, 1728–9.
3. Patrick Beesly, *Room 40: British Naval Intelligence 1914–18*; for Oliver, see William James, *A Great Seaman*, and for Ewing, A. Ewing, *The Man of Room 40*; also R. V. Jones, 'Alfred Ewing and Room 40', in *Notes and Records of the Royal Society of London*, Vol. 34, 1979–80, 65–90.
4. David Kahn, *Seizing the Enigma*, 15.
5. Churchill, *The World Crisis 1911–1914*, 462.
6. Kahn, *Seizing the Enigma*, 22. See also FO 371/2095.
7. 'Lord Fisher and Mr Churchill', Hall Papers 3/5, 2, Churchill College, Cambridge. For Hall, see William James, *The Eyes of the Navy*, passim.
8. 'Lord Fisher and Mr Churchill', Hall Papers, 1.
9. Beesly, *Room 40*, 16.
10. *CV*, Vol. III, Part 1, 281.
11. 'Recollections of Rear-Admiral R. D. Oliver', OLV 12, Vol. 2, 102–103, Sir Henry Oliver Papers, National Maritime Museum, Greenwich.
12. Asquith to Venetia Stanley, 21 Dec 1914, *CV*, Vol. III, Part 1, 322.
13. Violet Bonham Carter, *Winston Churchill As I Knew Him*, 347.
14. Churchill, *The World Crisis 1911–1914*, 478.

15. Churchill to Jellico, 4 January 1915 (Draft: all references to 'priceless infn' deleted before dispatch), *CV*, Vol. III, Part 1, 368–9.
16. Churchill, *The World Crisis 1911–1914*, 129.
17. Ibid., 131.
18. Ibid., 132.
19. Andrew, *Secret Service*, 100.
20. 'Captain H. W. Hope's Notes on Fleet Movements and Submarine Reports (with remarks by the First Lord) 1914–1916', in ADM 137/4168.
21. For example, Colin Simpson, *Lusitania*, and Beesly, *Room 40*, 84–122. A contrary case is in Thomas A. Bailey and Paul B. Ryan, *The Lusitania Disaster*. See also ADM 137/1058, 'Loss of Lusitania', and ADM 116/1416, 'Official Enquiry into Loss of Lusitania', 3 vols; also ADM 137/112–13, ADM 137/1057; ADM 137/4353.
22. *CV*, Vol. III, Part 1, 501.
23. Churchill, 14 May 1915, ADM 137/1058.
24. Robert Rhodes James, *Gallipoli, passim*; Gilbert, *Churchill*, Vol. III, *The Challenge of War*, Part 1, 266 *et seq*; Michael Hickey, *Gallipoli, passim*.
25. Churchill, *The World Crisis 1915*, Appendix III, 547.
26. 'Lord Fisher and Mr Churchill', 4. For Eady and Whittal, see G. R. G. Allen, 'A Ghost From Gallipoli', *Journal of the Royal United Services Institute*, May 1963, 137–8; Stephen Roskill, *Hankey: Man of Secrets*, 158–61; Gilbert, *Churchill*, Vol. III, Part 1, 470–71.
27. ADM 137/4168.
28. Roskill, *Hankey*, 160. For the *Dresden* affair, see Beesly, *Room 40*, 72–9; Geoffrey Bennett, *Coronel and the Falklands*, 173–6; Heinz Hohne, *Canaris*, 30.
29. Gilbert, *Churchill*, Vol. III, Part 1, 574.
30. 'Lord Fisher and Mr. Churchill', Hall papers 3/5. Also Beesly, *Room 40*, 137, and Gilbert *Churchill*, ibid., 585–6.
31. R. W. Thompson, *Churchill and Morton*; John Colville, *The Churchillians*, 205–206.
32. Colville, ibid., 203–204; Sir Edward Spears, *Fulfilment of a Mission*, introduction by John Terraine, vii–x.
33. Colville, *The Churchillians*, 172; Gerard De Groot, *Liberal Crusader, passim*.
34. Anthony Cave Brown, *'C': The Secret Life of Sir Stewart Menzies*, 94–5.

Chapter 5: The Red Peril

1. David Kirkwood, *My Life of Revolt*, 65; 'David Kirkwood', *Scottish Labour Leaders 1918–39: A Biographical Dictionary*, ed. W. Knox, 161–3.
2. Nicholas Hiley, 'Internal Security in Wartime: The Rise and Fall of PMS 2, 1915–1917', *Intelligence and National Security*, Vol. 1, No. 3, September 1986, 395–415; Hiley, 'Counter-Espionage and Security During the First World War', *English Historical Review*, 101, July 1986, 635–6. Andrew, *Secret Service*, 174–202, 224–45; Basil Thomson, *The Scene Changes, passim*.
3. M. Swartz, *The Union of Democratic Control in British Politics During the First World War*, 160–98; Bernard Porter, *Plots and Paranoia*, 120–50.
4. Churchill to Beaverbrook, 23 February 1918, *CV*, Vol. IV, Part 2, 245.
5. Churchill, *The World Crisis: The Aftermath*, 74.
6. Andrew, *Secret Service*, 234.
7. Keith Jeffrey, 'The British Army and Internal Security 1919–1939', *Historical Journal*, Vol. 24, No. 2 (1981), 377–97.
8. Churchill, *The World Crisis: The Aftermath*, 63. Stephen R. Ward, 'Intelligence Surveillance of British Ex-Servicemen 1918–1920', *Historical Journal*, Vol. 16, No. 1, 1973, 179–88.
9. George Lansbury, *My Life* and *The Miracle of Fleet Street*; Raymond Postgate, *The Life of George Lansbury*.
10. Hiley, 'Internal Security in Wartime', 396.
11. Churchill, House of Commons, 8 July 1919, *House of Commons*, Vol. 117, Col 1581.
12. Gilbert, *Churchill*, Vol. IV, *World in Torment*, 915.

13. Churchill to Lloyd George, covering Churchill, 'Reduction of Estimates for Secret Services', 19 March 1920, in Lloyd George papers F/9/2/16, House of Lords Record Office. For GC & CS, see Keith Jeffery and Alan Sharp, 'Lord Curzon and Secret Intelligence', in *Intelligence and International Relations 1900–1945*, eds C. Andrew and J. Noakes, 103–26; for Bolshevik intercepts, see Richard H. Ullman, *Anglo-Soviet Relations 1917–1921: The Anglo-Soviet Accord, passim*; for the 1920 OSA, see Tony Bunyan, *The Political Police in Britain*, 13–14, and House of Commons, 22 November–10 December 1920, Cols 1537–83.

14. Michael Glenny, 'Leonid Krassin: the Years before 1917, An outline', *Soviet Studies*, XXII, 1970–71, 192–221; Ullman, *Anglo-Soviet Relations*, 89–93. Bull Papers, 5/8.

15. Lansbury, *Miracle of Fleet Street*, 138–56.

16. Ullman, *Anglo-Soviet Relations*, 258.

17. Lansbury, *Miracle of Fleet Street*, 150.

18. Ibid., 121–6.

19. Lansbury, *My Life*, 203–205.

20. Ibid., 255–6; Spears to Churchill, 16 April 1920, Char 16/66.

21. Churchill to Thwaites (DMI), 5 August 1920, WO 32/5719; Churchill to Thwaites, 20 August 1920, *CV*, Vol. IV, Part 2, 1175–6.

22. *Memoirs of a Conservative: J. C. C. Davidson's Memoirs and Papers*, ed. Robert Rhodes James, 272.

23. Ball to DMI, 23 August 1920 and Churchill minute 27 August 1920, WO 32/5719; FO 371/5445; and House of Commons, 28 October and 2 December 1920. I am grateful to Dr John Ferris for the WO reference.

24. Ullman, *Anglo-Soviet Relations*, 265–309.

25. Churchill to Lloyd George, 18 August 1920; Diary, Sir Henry Wilson, 24 August 1920, in *CV*, Vol. IV, Part 2, 1174, 1178–9.

26. Churchill to Lloyd George, 25 August 1920, *CV*, Vol. IV, Part 2, 1182–3.

27. Churchill to Lloyd George, 26 August 1920, Lloyd George Papers F/9/2/41; *CV*, Vol. IV, Part 2, 1184–7, 1188–9, 1196–7, 1205; Wilson to Churchill, 3 September 1920, Wilson Papers, Imperial War Museum, HHW 2/18C/14.

28. Churchill to Thwaites, 17 September 1920, *CV*, Vol. IV, Part 2, 1208.

29. Hankey, Diary, 18 November 1920, ibid., 1246; Norman and Jeanne Mackenzie, *The Time Traveller: The Life of H. G. Wells*, 327–8.

30. H. G. Wells, *Men Like Gods*, 20; also Gilbert, *Churchill*, Vol. IV, 441–2.

Chapter 6: Bolsheviks

1. For the following, see: Anita Leslie, *Cousin Clare*; Clare Sheridan, *Nuda Veritas, To the Four Winds, Russian Portraits*; John Pearson, *Citadel of the Heart*, 170–75; *The Times*, 2 June 1970.

2. Leslie, *Cousin Clare*, 103.

3. Sheridan, *Russian Portraits*, 15, 22–3.

4. Ibid., 30.

5. Leslie, *Cousin Clare*, 118.

6. Ibid., 125.

7. *The Times*, 22 November 1920, and issues to 27 November 1920.

8. Pearson, *Citadel of the Heart*, 170.

9. Leslie, *Cousin Clare*, 247–9.

10. Ibid., 111.

11. Sheridan, *To the Four Winds*, 95.

12. War Office Lists 1915–1917, Ministry of Defence Library; see also Andrew Lycett, *Ian Fleming*, 70–72 and *The Times*, 4 and 5 July 1930. I am grateful to Andrew Lycett for these references. Brown, *'C': The Secret Life of Sir Stewart Menzies*, 134–8, wrongly suggests that Clare's minder was Menzies.

13. Brown, *'C': The Secret Life of Sir Stewart Menzies*, 137.

14. Sheridan, *To the Four Winds*, 91.

15. Kamenev to Chicherin, 29 August 1920, Lloyd George Papers F/9/2/42.

16. Oswald Frewen, Diary, 24 September 1920. I am grateful to Jonathan Frewen for permitting me to consult this.
17. Sheridan, *Russian Portraits*, 134.
18. Gilbert, *Churchill*, Vol. IV, 305.
19. Spears to Churchill, 27 July 1919; Sinclair to Spears, 27 August 1919; MacCallum Scott to Sinclair, 4 September 1919; Churchill to Sinclair, 9 September 1919, Char 16/39, 16/40, 16/42A.
20. R. H. Bruce Lockhart, *Memoirs of a British Agent*, 182; also David Footman, 'Boris V. Savinkov: 1879–1925', *History Today*, 1958, 73–82; Richard B. Spence, *Boris Savinkov: Renegade on the Left*; Ted Morgan, *Maugham*, 229.
21. Churchill, *Great Contemporaries*, 125.
22. Churchill, *The World Crisis: The Aftermath*, 78.
23. Spence, *Boris Savinkov*, 283 *et seq*; Robin Bruce Lockhart, *Reilly: Ace of Spies*, 101–106; Andrew, *Secret Service*, 286–91; *CV*, Vol. IV, Part 2, 1138–9.
24. Sinclair to Spears, 21 February 1920 and Spears' reply, Spears Papers, Churchill College 1/310, and Char 16/65; Churchill to Lloyd George 17 October 1920, *CV*, Vol. IV, Part 2, 1219.
25. Churchill to Curzon, 29 October 1920, *CV*, Vol. IV, Part 2, 1227; Spence, *Boris Savinkov*, 241.
26. For Sinclair's dealings with Russia, see Char 16/40, 16/41, 16/42A and B, 16/63, 16/65, 16/66, 16/ 68A, 16/76, 16/77, 16/78, and Spears Papers, Churchill College, especially 1/301. Also see *CV*, Vol. IV, Part 2, 1010–12, 1028–9.
27. Michael Kettle, *Sidney Reilly*, 103.
28. Spence, *Boris Savinkov*, 321–3; David Watson, 'The Krasin–Savinkov Meeting of 10 December 1921', *Cahiers du monde russe et soviétique*, XXVII (3–4), juillet–décembre 1986, 461–70; Michael Heller, 'Krasin–Savinkov: Une Rencontre Secrète', ibid., XXVI (1), janvier–mars 1985, 63–8. I am grateful to David Watson for these journal references.
29. Churchill, 'Boris Savinkov', *Great Contemporaries*, 131–2; Kettle, *Reilly*, 103–105.
30. Kettle, *Reilly*, 115.
31. Ibid., 18–19; see also Bruce Lockhart, *Reilly, passim*.
32. Richard B. Spence, 'Sidney Reilly in America 1914–1917', *Intelligence and National Security*, Vol. 10, No. 1, January 1995, 92–121; Norman Thwaites, *Velvet and Vinegar*, 183.
33. Bruce Lockhart, *Reilly*, 88.
34. Sinclair to Churchill, 4 December 1919, Char 16/42A.
35. Sidney Reilly, *Adventures*, 173–4.
36. Kettle, *Reilly*, 97–102.
37. Bruce Lockhart, *Reilly*, 151.
38. Reilly, *Adventures*, 237–8.
39. Andrew, *Secret Service*, 302–12.
40. Char 22/143.
41. Lord Derby to Curzon, 10 April 1920, *CV*, Vol. IV, Part 2, 1071.
42. Churchill to Spears, 15 June 1919, Char 16/37. See also Char 16/38 and Spears Papers, 1/310, *passim*.
43. Char 16/66, 16/67; Spears Papers 1/76, 2/4.
44. Spears to Lockhart, 2 January 1967, Spears Papers 1/301.

Chapter 7: Guerrillas

1. W. H. Thompson, *Guard from the Yard*, 95, 109, 134–7; see also his 'Guarding Churchill', in *Churchill by his Contemporaries*, ed. Eade, 250–53; Martin Gilbert, *In Search of Churchill*, 292–8; *CV*, Vol. IV, Part 2, 1232.
2. Gilbert, *Churchill*, Vol. IV, 443–71; *CV*, Vol. IV, Part 2; Paul Addison, 'Churchill and Domestic Conflict: The Case of Ireland', unpublished paper kindly lent by the author; Churchill, *The World Crisis: The Aftermath*, 285 *et seq*. and 322–47; Sheila Lawlor, *Britain and Ireland 1914–1923*; Andrew, *Secret Service*, 246–58.

3. 'Conclusions of a Conference of Ministers ... 11 May 1920', CAB 23/21; Cabinet Minutes 21 May 1920, ibid.; Roskill, *Hankey*, 153; *CV*, Vol. IV, Part 2, 1085–6, 1090, 1095–6, 1128–9, 1149–50, 1194, 1212; see also Churchill's correspondence with Wilson, Wilson Papers HHW2/18B and C.

4. Andrew, *Secret Service*, 252; Charles Townshend, *The British Campaign in Ireland 1919–1921*, *passim*.

5. Andrew, *Secret Service*, 253.

6. Anthony Clayton, *Forearmed: A History of the Intelligence Corps*, 61; Eunan O' Halpin, 'British Intelligence in Ireland 1914–1921', in *The Missing Dimension*, eds Andrew and Dilks, 54–77.

7. O' Halpin, 'British Intelligence in Ireland', fn 90; see also David Neligan, *The Spy in the Castle*, *passim*.

8. Major-General H. H. Tudor, Confidential Report, 24 October 1922, CO 904/177 Part 2 [Correspondence of Colonel O. de l'E. Winter]. See also *The Times*, 15 February 1962 and Winter's autobiography, *Winter's Tale*; Sturgis, Diary, PRO 30/59/1, Vol. 1, 59–60.

9. Macready to Anderson, 8 April 1921, CO 904/188; Sturgis, Diary, 26 October 1920, PRO 30/59/2, Vol. 2, 51.

10. *CV*, Vol. IV, Part 2, 1214–15, 1221; Richard Bennett, *The Black and Tans*, especially 93–9.

11. Leslie, *Cousin Clare*, 163; Shane Leslie, *Long Shadows*, 228.

12. Sturgis, Diary, 9 December 1920, 'The military are very cock-a-hoop', PRO 30/59/2, Vol. III, 17; Cabinet, 29 December 1920, CAB 23/23,8; Gilbert, *Churchill*, Vol. IV, 470–71; Townshend, *The British Campaign in Ireland*, 140–41.

13. M. Forester, *Michael Collins: The Lost Leader*, *passim*; Tim Pat Coogan, *Michael Collins*, *passim*.

14. For Churchill and the Irish Treaty, see Gilbert, *Churchill*, Vol. IV, 663–83, 684–702.

15. For Collins's briefing on Churchill, by Crompton Llewellyn Davies, see Forester, *Michael Collins*, 220; for Churchill on Collins, see *The World Crisis: The Aftermath*, 369; also M. C. Bromage, *Churchill and Ireland*, 66.

16. Churchill, 'The Irish Treaty', *Thoughts and Adventures*, 191.

17. Bryan Folls, *A State Under Siege: The Establishment of Northern Ireland 1920–1925*, 106–107; Gilbert, *Churchill*, Vol. IV, 703–49.

18. Churchill, *The World Crisis: The Aftermath*, 355.

19. Ibid.

20. For Montgomery and Percival in Ireland, see Nigel Hamilton, *Monty: The Making of a General 1887–1942*, 154–63. For Strong, see his *Intelligence at the Top*, 1–5; for Gubbins, see Peter Wilkinson and Joan Bright Astley, *Gubbins and SOE*, 26–7; and M. R. D. Foot, 'The IRA and the Origins of SOE', in *War and Society, Historical Essays in Honour and Memory of J. R. Western 1928–1971*, ed. Foot.

21. Churchill, 'Lawrence of Arabia', *Great Contemporaries*, 155–67.

22. Ibid., 162.

23. Lawrence James, *The Golden Warrior*, 175.

24. Ibid., 275–81, 322–4.

25. Basil Liddell Hart, *T. E. Lawrence*, especially 438; see also Liddell Hart, *Memoirs*, 84, 353, 373; Robin Higham, *The Military Intellectuals*, 46–7; Brian Bond, *Liddell Hart*, especially 205–207.

Chapter 8: Private Networks

1. Gilbert, *Churchill*, Vol. V, *Prophet of Truth*, 48–9, 53–4; Andrew, *Secret Service*, 298–338; G. Gorodetsky, *The Precarious Peace*, 83, 176–7, 181–2, 215.

2. Andrew, *Secret Service*, 332.

3. Churchill to Curzon, 9 February 1921, *CV*, Vol. IV, Part 2, 1340.

4. Churchill to Baldwin, 5 February 1925, ibid., Part 1, 380.

5. Churchill, *The Second World War*, Vol. 1, *The Gathering Storm*, 596.

6. Deakin, quoted in R. W. Thompson, *Churchill and Morton*, 27; see also the Foreword by

Captain Stephen Roskill; Robert Rhodes James, *Churchill: A Study in Failure 1900–1939*, 302; Gilbert, *In Search of Churchill*, 119–20.

7. For the following, see: Gilbert, *Churchill*, Vol. V, *passim*; *CV*, Vol. V, Parts 1 and 2, *passim*; Gilbert, *In Search of Churchill*, 110–19.

8. *Parliamentary Debates, House of Commons*, Vol. 285, 1933–34, Cols 1193–200.

9. Uri Bialer, *The Shadow of the Bomber*, *passim*.

10. Donald Cameron Watt, 'Churchill and Appeasement', in *Churchill*, ed. Blake and Louis, 199–214.

11. Maurice Ashley, *Churchill as Historian*, quoted in Norman Rose, *Churchill: An Unruly Life*, 45.

12. Watt, 'Churchill and Appeasement'; James, *Churchill: A Study in Failure*, 279–359; François Kersaudy, *Churchill and De Gaulle*, 31; Rose, *Churchill: An Unruly Life*, 222–3.

13. *CV*, Vol. V, Part 2, 66; Part 3, 1051, 1446–8, 1452.

14. Wesley K. Wark, *The Ultimate Enemy: British Intelligence and Nazi Germany 1933–1939*, 236–7, and *passim*.

15. Andrew, *Secret Service*, 342 *et seq.*; Wark, *The Ultimate Enemy*, *passim*; John Ferris, '"Indulged in All Too Little?": Vansittart, Intelligence and Appeasement', *Diplomacy and Statecraft*, Vol. 6, No. 1, March 1995, 122–75.

16. Gilbert, *Churchill*, Vol. V, 555 n1.

17. Ibid., 952–3; Duncan Sandys Papers [DSND 1/12], Churchill College, Cambridge.

18. R. B. Crockett, 'Ball, Chamberlain, and *Truth*', *Historical Journal*, 33 (1990), 131–42; Andrew Davies, *We, the Nation*, 263–71; Addison, *Churchill on the Home Front*, 93–4; De Groot, *Liberal Crusader*, 149.

Chapter 9: In the Dark

1. Gilbert (ed.), *The Churchill War Papers*, Vol. 1, *At the Admiralty*, 515; F. H. Hinsley et al., *British Intelligence in the Second World War*, Vol. 1, 45–85.

2. A. J. Marder, *From the Dardanelles to Oran*, 122–3; *Churchill War Papers*, Vol. 1, 463–4, 679–80; Donald McLachlan, *Room 39*, 73; 'Naval Memories of John H. Godfrey', Vol. 5 (1) 1939–1942, Vol. 7 (1 and 2), 1903–1946, Vol. 8, *Afterthoughts*, in Godfrey Papers, National Maritime Museum, Greenwich; also file 'Working With Churchill', ibid., MS 81/005 Box A; Beesly, *Very Special Admiral*, *passim*.

3. Churchill, *The Second World War*, Vol. 1, 381–2; Churchill to Pound, 5 September 1939; Churchill to Godfrey, 6 September 1939, *The Churchill War Papers*, Vol. 1, 28–29, 37, 143–4, 309, 315, 354–5, 364–5; Robert Fisk, *In Time of War*, 112–33; M. C. Bromage, *Churchill and Ireland*, 136–48; Nigel West, *MI5: British Security Service Operations 1909–1945*, 309–28; Eunan O'Halpin, 'Intelligence and Security in Ireland 1922–45', *Intelligence and Security*, Vol. 5, No. 1, January 1990.

4. Beesly, *Very Special Admiral*, 132–6.

5. Churchill to Cadogan, 19 November 1939, *The Churchill War Papers*, Vol. 1, 390–1; *CV*, Vol. V, Part 3, 1303; Char 2/237; Beesly, *Very Special Admiral*, 138–9; cf. Brown, *'C':The Life of Sir Stewart Menzies*, 13–15 and Andrew Roberts, *The Holy Fox*, 189.

6. Churchill to Halifax, 1 November 1939, *The Churchill War Papers*, Vol. 1, 322–3; Callum A. MacDonald, 'The Venlo Affair', *European Studies Review*, Vol. 8, 1978, 443–64; Andrew, *Secret Service*, 434–9.

7. *The Churchill War Papers*, Vol. 1, 207–208; Kell, Diary, 5 October 1939, Imperial War Museum.

8. *The Churchill War Papers*, Vol. 1, 95, 236; 277–8, 308.

9. Kell, Diary, 23 December 1939.

10. Churchill, *The Second World War*, Vol. 1, 358.

11. Churchill to Pound, 23 October 1939, *Churchill War Papers*, Vol. 1, 281; see also 297, 299–303, 306, 350, 357.

12. 'German Espionage through UK Commercial Firms 1939–1940', HO 45/25497/700326/1–6; Brian Simpson, *In the Highest Degree Odious*, 77–8.

13. Memo by Churchill, War Cabinet 16 December 1939, *The Churchill War Papers*, Vol. 1, 522–5, also 548, 552; ADM 223/480, 481; Charles Cruickshank, *SOE in Scandinavia*, 34–40; Sir Brooks Richards, *Secret Flotillas*, 99.
14. *The Churchill War Papers*, Vol. 1, 209; David Jablonsky, *Churchill, the Great Game and Total War*, 78–80.

Chapter 10: Fifth Columns

1. Gilbert, *Churchill*, Vol. VI, *Finest Hour*, 372; 409–10.
2. Fisk, *In Time of War*, 121–4: David Stafford, 'Britain Looks at Europe 1940: Some Origins of SOE', *Canadian Journal of History*, Vol. IX, No. 2, August 1975; Hinsley et al., *British Intelligence in the Second World War*, Vol. IV, 47–65.
3. Gilbert, *Churchill*, Vol. VI, 326, 389, 492–3.
4. Ray Bearse and Anthony Read, *Conspirator: The Untold Story of Churchill, Roosevelt and Tyler Kent, Spy, passim*; Simpson, *In the Highest Degree Odious*, 112–52, 431–3; Joan Miller, *One Girl's War*, 16–32; Anthony Masters, *The Man Who Was 'M'*, 147–9; Peter and Lily Gillman, *Collar the Lot*, 115–29; Andrew Lownie, 'Tyler Kent: Isolationist or Spy?', in *North American Spies*, eds R. Jeffreys-Jones and Andrew Lownie, 49–78; Eric Homberger, '"Uncle Max" and his Thrillers', *Intelligence and National Security*, Vol. 3, No. 2, April 1988, 312–21.
5. Simpson, *In the Highest Degree Odious*, and Gillman, *Collar the Lot, passim*; Gilbert, *Churchill*, Vol. VI, 459 *et seq.*; Angus Calder, *The People's War*, 118–36; Hinsley et al., *British Intelligence in the Second World War*, 47–76; Addison, *Churchill on the Home Front*, 341–3; PREM 7/2.
6. Simpson, *In the Highest Degree Odious*, 248–50, 389–32, 408; John Colville, *The Fringes of Power*, 309–10.
7. Lord Swinton, *I Remember, passim*; J. A. Cross, *Lord Swinton*, 224–31; Croft to Churchill, 25 November 1940 and ensuing correspondence in PREM 7/6; see also Henry Page Croft, *My Life of Strife*, 325.
8. PREM 3/418/2, *passim*; Hinsley et al., *British Intelligence in the Second World War*, 97.
9. Ibid., 98–102.
10. Colville, *The Churchillians*, 205–206; Thompson, *Churchill and Morton*, 81.
11. Peter Wilkinson and Joan Bright Astley, *Gubbins and SOE*, 69–73.
12. Hugh Dalton, *The Fateful Years 1931–1945*; David Stafford, *Britain and European Resistance 1940–45*, 10–27; M. R. D Foot, *SOE in France*, 1–10; for the SOE 'Charter', see WP(40) 271 in ADM 223/480.
13. John Keegan, *The Second World War*, 484; see also Keegan, 'Churchill's Strategy', in *Churchill*, eds Blake and Louis, especially 333–4; and his review of Richard Lamb's *Churchill as War Leader: Right or Wrong?* in *Times Literary Supplement*, 22 November 1991.

Chapter 11: Ultra

1. Ronald Lewin, *Ultra Goes to War*, 183; Gilbert, *Churchill*, Vol. VI, 609–13; Hinsley et al., *British Intelligence in the Second World War*, Vol. 1, *passim*.
2. Hinsley, ibid., Vol. 1, 267–98, Vol. 2, 3–39.
3. Morton to 'C', 27 September 1940, HW1/1 [Government Code and Cypher School: Signals Intelligence passed to the Prime Minister, Messages and Correspondence], PRO London; Hinsley, 'Churchill and the Use of Special Intelligence', in *Churchill*, eds Blake and Louis, 407–26.
4. Lewin, *Ultra Goes to War*, 67; see also Robert Cecil, '"C"'s War', *Intelligence and National Security*, Vol. 1, 1986, 170–88; Brown, *'C': The Life of Sir Stewart Menzies*, passim.
5. Kathryn Brown, 'Intelligence and the Decision to Collect it: Churchill's Wartime Diplomatic Signals Intelligence', *Intelligence and National Security*, Vol. 10, No. 3, July 1995; Robin Denniston, 'Diplomatic Eavesdropping 1922–44: A New Source Discovered', ibid., 423–48; Denniston, *Churchill's Secret War*, 19–32; Eunan O'Halpin, '"According to

the Irish Minister in Rome . . .": British Decrypts and Irish Diplomacy in the Second World War', *Irish Studies in International Affairs*, Vol. 6, 1995, 95–105; I am grateful to Dr O'Halpin for kindly providing me with a copy of this.

6. Gilbert, *Churchill*, Vol. VI, 1154.
7. R. V. Jones, *Most Secret War: British Scientific Intelligence 1939–1945*, 134–49; Hinsley et al., *British Intelligence in the Second World War*, Vol. 1, 528–48; Gilbert, *Churchill*, Vol. VI, 583, 912–15.
8. F. W. Winterbotham, *The Ultra Secret*, 59–60; Gilbert, *Churchill*, Vol. VI, 609–27, 649–80, 769–86, 811–25, 878–90.
9. Churchill to Roosevelt, 26 October 1940, Gilbert, *Churchill*, Vol. VI, 869; for Churchill's management of intelligence, see Michael Handel, 'The Politics of Intelligence', *Intelligence and National Security*, Vol. 2, No. 4, October 1987, especially 8–10.
10. Robert E. Sherwood, *The White House Papers of Harry L. Hopkins, passim*; Gilbert, *Churchill*, Vol. VI, 981–1000.
11. Gilbert, ibid., 986, 993–4, 996; Sherwood, *The White House Papers*, 256–7.
12. Bradley F. Smith, *The Ultra–Magic Deals and the Most Secret Special Relationship*, 54–63.
13. Gilbert, *Churchill*, Vol. VI, 672.
14. 'C' to Churchill, 26 February 1941, C 506, and Churchill's reply, 27 February 1941, and A.G. Denniston to Menzies, 3 March 1941, HW1/2.
15. PREM 7/6.
16. Alan Hillgarth, dedication in *The War Maker*, 1926; see also: Denis Smyth, 'Alan Hillgarth', *DNB 1971–1980*, 409–10; Denis Smyth, *Diplomacy and Strategy of Survival, passim*; PREM 3/409/7; PREM 4/21/2A, 4/32/7, 7/4; FO 371/26890–907; ADM 223/409, 479–81, and /805 also contain much about Hillgart and Spain; see also Churchill, *The Second World War*, Vol. 2, 443; Gilbert, *Churchill*, Vol. VI, 585, 678, and Vol. VII, *Road to Victory*, 456; Viscount Templewood, *Ambassador on Special Leave*, 132–3; Beesly, *Very Special Admiral, passim*; Andrew Lycett, *Ian Fleming*, 109–10, 125–45. I am grateful to Mr Lycett for drawing my attention to the ADM 223 files.
17. Churchill to DNI [Godfrey], 26 September 1939, ADM 223/490.
18. Denis Smyth, '"Les Chevaliers de Saint-George": La Grande-Bretagne et la corruption des genéraux espagnoles', *Guerre Mondiales*, 162, 1991, 29–54. I am grateful to Professor Smyth for this and other information about Hillgarth, as well as to Alan Hillgarth's son, Dr Jocelyn Hillgarth.
19. Hyde, H. Montgomery, *The Quiet Canadian, passim*; Stafford, *Camp X: SOE and the American Connection*, especially 251–7, 271–92.
20. Richard Dunlop, *Donovan, America's Master Spy*, 421; Thomas F. Troy, *Donovan and the CIA, passim*; Brown, *The Last Hero*.
21. Brown, ibid., 152–3.
22. Alex Danchev (ed.), *Establishing the Anglo-American Alliance: The Second World War Diaries of Brigadier Vivian Dykes*, 24–65; Christopher Andrew, *For the President's Eyes Only*, 101.

Chapter 12: A Waiting Game
1. Morton to Churchill, 26 July 1940, PREM 7/2; Morton to Churchill, 14 January 1941, PREM 7/6; Elizabeth Barker, *Churchill and Eden at War*, 44–8.
2. Dalton, Diary, 2 March 1941, British Library of Political and Economic Science. Also, Churchill–Dalton correspondence re. SOE, 1941, in PREM 3/409/7, *passim*.
3. Dalton to Churchill, 12 February 1941, HS 1/350 [SOE files]; FO 371/ 27924–9; Dalton, Diary, 10 February 1941 and subsequent entries.
4. Dalton Diary, 2 March 1941; Dalton to Churchill, 30 April 1941, PREM 3/409/7; David Stafford, 'SOE and British Involvement in the Belgrade *coup d'état* of March 1941', *Slavic Review*, Vol. 36, No. 3, September 1977.
5. Hinsley et al., *British Intelligence in the Second World War*, Vol. 1, 347–73, 406–409; Ralph Bennett, *Behind the Battle: Intelligence in the War with Germany 1939–45*, 75–6.
6. For the following, see: Churchill, *The Second World War*, Vol. 3, *The Grand Alliance*, 228–57;

Gilbert, *Churchill*, Vol. VI, 1080–98; Callum MacDonald, *The Lost Battle: Crete 1941*, 137–61; Anthony Beevor, *Crete: The Battle and the Resistance*, 1–232; Bennett, *Behind the Battle*, 76–8, 280–84; Paul Freyberg, *Bernard Freyberg VC, passim*; Laurie Barber and John Tonkin-Covell, *Freyberg: Churchill's Salamander, passim*. C. M. Woodhouse, *Something Ventured*, 13; Hinsley et al., *British Intelligence in the Second World War*, Vol. 1, 415–21.
7. Hinsley, ibid., 399.

Chapter 13: Special Intelligence, Special Friends

1. Churchill to Eden, 13 May 1941, PREM 3/219/7; see also 3/219/5, 1–7, *passim*; Gilbert, *Churchill*, Vol. VI, 1087–8; cf. Peter Padfield, *Rudolf Hess, passim*.
2. Hinsley et al., *British Intelligence in the Second World War*, Vol. 1, 429–83, and his essay 'British Intelligence and Barbarossa', in *Barbarossa: The Axis and the Allies*, eds John Erickson and David Dilks, 43–75; Churchill, *The Second World War*, Vol. 3, 302; Gilbert, *Churchill*, Vol. VI, 1117–36.
3. John Erickson, *The Road to Stalingrad: Stalin's War with Germany*, Vol. 1, 58–9, 73–97; Christopher Andrew with Oleg Gordievsky, *KGB*, 207–17.
4. Hinsley et al., *British Intelligence in the Second World War*, Vol. 2, 58–61; Churchill/'C' exchanges, June 1941, HW 1/8.
5. 'C' to Prime Minister, 28 September 1941, HW 1/95.
6. HS 4/242, 243, 327, 328, 329, 334, 335, 341, 342; Douglas Dodds-Parker, *Setting Europe Ablaze*, 95, and letter to author, October 1995. See also Mark Seaman, 'Giving All and Taking Nothing – Aspects of SOE/NKVD Co-operation 1941–45', unpublished paper kindly furnished by the author. 'Dropped into the sea' – see Pickaxe Part II, Koubitski, Pavel, HS 4/341.
7. PREM 3/409/2,3; Stafford, *Britain and European Resistance 1940–1945*, 58–68.
8. Sebastian Cox, '"The Difference Between White and Black" – Churchill, Imperial Politics and Intelligence before the 1941 *Crusader* Offensive', *Intelligence and National Security*, Vol. 9, No. 3, July 1994, 405–47; Lord Tedder, *With Prejudice*, 176–84; Gilbert, *Churchill*, Vol. VI, 1216–47.
9. Hinsley et al., *British Intelligence in the Second World War*, Vol. 2, 163.
10. Bradley F. Smith, 'Admiral Godfrey's Mission to America June/July 1941', *Intelligence and National Security*, Vol. 1, No. 3, September 1986, 441–50.
11. Gilbert, *Churchill*, Vol. VI, 1154.
12. PREM 4/32/7, *passim*.
13. Gilbert, *Churchill*, Vol. VI, 1185; Brown, *'C': The Life of Sir Stewart Menzies*, 396–402; David Kahn, *Seizing the Enigma*, 184–9.
14. Hinsley et al., *British Intelligence in the Second World War*, Vol. 2, 174, 655–7.
15. Stafford, *Camp X, passim*.

Chapter 14: Executive Action

1. Churchill, *The Second World War*, Vol. 3, 509–12; Gilbert, *Churchill*, Vol. VI, 1267–9.
2. James Rusbridger and Eric Nave, *Betrayal at Pearl Harbor, passim*.
3. David Kahn, 'The Intelligence Failure of Pearl Harbor', *Foreign Affairs*, Vol. 70, No. 5, Winter 1991/92, 138–52; Richard Aldrich, 'Conspiracy or Confusion? Churchill, Roosevelt and Pearl Harbor', *Intelligence and National Security*, Vol. 7, No. 3, July 1992, 335–46; Louis W. Tordella and Edwin C. Fishel, 'A New Pearl Harbor Villain: Churchill', *International Journal of Intelligence and Counter-Intelligence*, Vol. 6, No. 3, Fall 1993.
4. HW 1/303.
5. John Ferris, 'From Broadway House to Bletchley Park: The Diary of Captain Malcolm D. Kennedy, 1934–1946', *Intelligence and National Security* Vol. 4, No. 3, July 1989, especially 439–40.
6. JIC (41) 40th, 30 December 1941, CAB 81/88.
7. Gilbert, *Churchill*, Vol. VII, 53.
8. Churchill to 'C', 9 February 1942, on Oshima to Tokyo, 18 January 1942, HW1/378.

9. Hinsley et al., *British Intelligence in the Second World War*, Vol. 2, 179.
10. Moran, *Churchill: The Struggle for Survival*, 35; Churchill to Roosevelt, 5 March 1942, quoted in Gilbert, *Churchill*, Vol. VII, 71; Hinsley et al., *British Intelligence in the Second World War*, Vol. 2, 750.
11. Lewin, *Ultra Goes to War*, 189.
12. Nigel West, *The SIGINT Secrets*, 219–22; P. W. Filby, 'Bletchley Park and Berkeley Street', *Intelligence and National Security*, Vol. 3, No. 2, April 1988, 272–84.
13. PREM 3/409/4 & 5, *passim*; Hinsley et al., *British Intelligence in the Second World War*, Vol. 2, 14–15.
14. 'Colonel Bill Hudson', obituary, *Daily Telegraph*, 21 November 1995; Dalton to Churchill, 11 December 1941, PREM 3/409/7; DO (41) 72nd, 15 Dec 1941, ibid.; Ralph Bennett, *Ultra and the Mediterranean Strategy*, 324–31; Mark Wheeler, *Britain and the War for Yugoslavia 1940–1943*, 117.
15. Donald V. Coers, *John Steinbeck as Propagandist: The Moon is Down Goes to War*; Jay Parini, *John Steinbeck: A Biography*; David Stafford, 'Churchill, SOE and Northern Europe', in *La Résistance et les européens du nord/Het Verzet En Noord-Europa*, Brussels/Bruxelles, 1994, 143–55.
16. Stafford, *Britain and European Resistance*, 100.
17. HS 4/18, 19, 22, 24; see also Callum MacDonald, *The Killing of SS Obergruppenführer Reinhard Heydrich*, *passim*.
18. Hesketh Prichard, 'Operation Autonomous', 22 January 1942, HS 4/39.
19. Wilkinson and Bright Astley, *Gubbins and SOE*, 107–108; Wilkinson to author, personal communication; Gubbins to Moravec, 30 May 1942, HS 4/39; Selborne, SOE quarterly report, March–June 1942, PREM 3/409/5.
20. Hinsley et al., *British Intelligence in the Second World War*, Vol. 2, 350–57.
21. Sir David Hunt, *A Don at War*, xviii.
22. David Dilks (ed.), *The Diaries of Sir Alexander Cadogan*, 488–9.
23. Hinsley et al., *British Intelligence in the Second World War*, Vol. 2, 359.
24. 'C' to Churchill, 22 November 1942, HW 1/1134.
25. Churchill to C-in-C Middle East, 23 September 1942, and related correspondence, PREM 3/117; Hinsley et al., *British Intelligence in the Second World War*, Vol. 5, *Strategic Deception*, ix–xiii, 3–44; Michael Handel (ed.), *Strategic and Operational Deception in the Second World War*, 1–91; Lewin, *Ultra Goes to War*, 299–301.
26. Anthony Cave Brown, *Bodyguard of Lies*, 270.
27. Denis Smyth, 'Screening "Torch": Allied Counter-Intelligence and the Spanish Threat to the Secrecy of the Allied Invasion of French North Africa in November 1942', *Intelligence and National Security*, Vol. 4, No. 2, April 1989.
28. Morton to Churchill, 1 December 1942, PREM 3/409/7; Woodhouse, *Something Ventured*, 21–51.
29. CAB 78/4, Misc 38 (42) 1st Mtg 24 December 1942; FO 371/34646.
30. Churchill, *The Second World War*, Vol. IV, *The Hinge of Fate*, 560; Gilbert, *Churchill*, Vol. VII, 283; Anthony Verrier, *Assassination in Algiers*, *passim*; A. L. Funk, *The Politics of Torch*, Appendix B; Richards, *Secret Flotillas*, 582–610; Charles Williams, *The Last Great Frenchman*, 195–205.
31. CAB 69/4, Defence Committee, 29 December 1942, DO (42) 20th.
32. Brown, *'C': The Life of Sir Stewart Menzies*, 447–53.
33. Wilkinson and Bright Astley, *Gubbins and SOE*, 118.

Chapter 15: Battled Joined

1. Michael Lees, *The Rape of Serbia*, 24–9, 62–4, 313–41; Nora Beloff, *Tito's Flawed Legacy*, 87; Lamb, *Churchill as War Leader*, 250–75.
2. Ralph Bennett, *Ultra and Mediterranean Strategy*, 330, and Appendix XII, 'Missing Links in the Chain of Yugoslav Evidence', 393–6; also his *Behind the Battle*, 215–17.
3. Lees, *The Rape of Serbia*, 336.

4. Churchill to Selborne, 14 April 1943, PREM 3/409/5; 'SOE Activities, Summary for the Prime Minister Jan–March 1943', ibid.; W. P. Crozier, *Diaries*, 347; Cruickshank, *SOE in Scandinavia*, 198–202.

5. Hinsley et al., *British Intelligence in the Second World War*, Vol. 2, 16–17, and Vol. 4, *Security and Counter-Intelligence*, 173–8, 187; PREM 3 418/5.

6. Crozier, *Diaries*, 138.

7. Simpson, *In the Highest Degree Odious*, 248–50, 389–91.

8. Hinsley et al., *British Intelligence in the Second World War*, Vol. 4, 288–9; also Churchill to Home Secretary, 30 January 1944, Char 20/52, M 48/4.

9. Ewen Montagu, *The Man Who Never Was*; Hinsley et al., *British Intelligence*, Vol. 5, 88–92; R. E. W. Wingate, *Not in the Limelight*, 203.

10. Gilbert, *Churchill*, Vol. VII, 407.

11. T. P. Mulligan, 'Spies, Ciphers and "Zitadelle"', *Journal of Contemporary History*, Vol. 22, 1987, 246–50; Hinsley et al., *British Intelligence in the Second World War*, Vol. 2, 624–7.

12. Smith, *The Ultra–Magic Deals*, 131–72.

13. Gilbert, *Churchill*, Vol. VII, 459, 485.

14. Ibid., 295, 360–61, 366; Churchill/Sir Edward Bridges exchanges, May 1943, PREM 4/68/6A; Hinsley et al., *British Intelligence in the Second World War*, Vol. 2, 596–7.

15. 'Deception: Indiscretions by Members of the US Administration and High Officials', and personal minute by Prime Minister, July 1943, PREM 3/117; also Lewin, *Ultra Goes to War*, 253.

16. Jones, *Most Secret War*, 424–76; Gilbert, *Churchill*, Vol. VII, 438, 474.

17. Bennett, *Ultra and the Mediterranean*, 345; Hinsley et al., *British Intelligence in the Second World War*, Vol. 3, Part 1, 137–62.

18. Frank McLynn, *Fitzroy Maclean*, *passim*; Fitzroy Maclean, *Eastern Approaches*, 303–533; Gilbert, *Churchill*, Vol. VII, 435, 440, 448, 454; Elizabeth Barker, 'Some Factors in British Decision-Making over Yugoslavia', in Auty and Clogg (eds), *British Policy towards Wartime Resistance in Yugoslavia and Greece*, 22–58.

19. Maclean, *Eastern Approaches*, 280–81; McLynn, *Fitzroy Maclean*, 120–37, 138–56.

20. Trevor Royle, *Orde Wingate*, 264.

21. Gilbert, *Churchill*, Vol. VII, 513; Selborne to Churchill, 6 July 1943, PREM 3/409/5; Selborne to Churchill, 17 September 1943, PREM 3/211/5; Brigadier E. C. W. Myers, 'The Andarte Delegation to Cairo: August 1943', in Auty and Clogg (eds), *British Policy*, 147–66; Richard Clogg, '"Pearls from Swine": The Foreign Office Papers, SOE and the Greek Resistance', ibid., 167–205.

22. Churchill to Selborne, 13 November 1942, PREM 3/409/7; Menzies to Churchill, 13 November 1942, HW 1/1094; PREM 3/184/6, June–July 1943, *passim*; Barker, *Churchill and Eden at War*, 84–5; Kersuady, *Churchill and De Gaulle*, 272–82, 283–99.

23. Brown, *'C': The Life of Sir Stewart Menzies*, 498–513.

24. 'SOE Activities: Summary for Prime Minister, Quarter April to June 1943', 25, PREM 3/409/5; for 'Prosper', see Robert Marshall, *All the King's Men: The Truth behind SOE's Greatest Wartime Disaster*, *passim*; Foot, *SOE in France*, 307–22.

25. Marshall, *All the King's Men*, 161.

26. Gilbert, *Churchill*, Vol. VII, 557–8.

27. Maclean, *Eastern Approaches*, 401–402; Amery, *Approach March*, 269–70.

28. Maclean, ibid., 407.

29. Gilbert, *Churchill*, Vol. VII, 428.

30. Kirk Ford Jr, *OSS and the Yugoslav Resistance 1943–1945*, 12–36; Franklin Lindsay, *Beacons in the Night*, 227–9; Bradley F. Smith, *The Shadow Warriors*, 235–40; Wilkinson and Bright Astley, *Gubbins and SOE*, 152–3.

Chapter 16: Behind the Lines

1. Morton to Churchill, 6 January 1944, 'Control of Special Operations in Europe', PREM 3/408/4.

2. Morton to Churchill, 27 January 1944, PREM 7/5; Griffiths, *Winged Hours, passim*; obituary, *Daily Telegraph*, 30 March 1996.
3. Emmanuel d'Astier de la Vigerie, *Les Dieux et les hommes*, 20–21; Foot, *SOE in France*, 353–4.
4. War Cabinet, 27 January 1944, CAB 80/78; d'Astier de la Vigerie, *Les Dieux*, 76–99; PREM 3/185/1.
5. Bruce Marshall, *The White Rabbit*, 92, 95–7.
6. Churchill minute, 2 February 1944, PREM 7/5.
7. Foot, *SOE in France*, 355.
8. Churchill to Ismay, 10 February 1944, Char 20/158; Churchill to Morton, 25 February 1944, Char 20/152.
9. *Parliamentary Debates, House of Commons*, 22 February 1944, Cols 689–96.
10. Wilkinson and Bright Astley, *Gubbins of SOE*, 143; McLynn, *Fitzroy Maclean*, 188–90; Gilbert, *Churchill*, Vol. VII, 690; Ford, *OSS and the Yugoslav Resistance*, 60–61; Macmillan to Churchill, 22 January 1944, Char 20/155; Brown, *The Last Hero*, 457.
11. Churchill to Bridges, 27 January 1944, Char 20/152; Churchill to Eden, 12 February and 8 March 1944, ibid.; Churchill to Wilson, 6 March 1944, ibid.
12. Ford, *OSS and the Yugoslav Resistance*, 39–41.
13. *Macmillan War Diary*, 5 June 1944; Wilkinson and Bright Astley, *Gubbins of SOE*, 172; Stafford, *Britain and European Resistance*, 152.
14. Richard Aldrich, 'Imperial Rivalry: British and American Intelligence in Asia, 1942–46', *Intelligence and National Security*, Vol. 3, No. 1, Jan 1988; also Christopher Thorne, *Allies of a Kind: The United States, Britain, and the War Against Japan 1941–45, passim*; Donald Cameron Watt, *Succeeding John Bull: America in Britain's Place 1900–75, passim*.
15. Churchill/Mountbatten exchanges, March 1944, Char 20/160.
16. Churchill to Eden, 21 May 1944, Char 20/160; Cruickshank, *SOE in the Far East*, 123–4.
17. PREM 3/117.
18. Stafford, *Britain and European Resistance*, 177–8; Ivor Porter, *Operation Autonomous: With SOE in Wartime Romania*, 99–164; Churchill to Eden, 22 May 1944, Char 20/152.
19. Maclean, *Eastern Approaches*, 444–5; for the list of code names, see FO to Algiers, 12 April 1944, Char 20/161.
20. McLynn, *Fitzroy Maclean*, 197–9.
21. Dedijer, quoted in Kay Hallie, *Randolph Churchill: The Great Unpretender*, 84; also Maclean, 'Randolph as a Commando', ibid., 88–92; John Blatnik, 'With Randolph in Yugoslavia', ibid., 92–7.
22. 'Report by Major Randolph Churchill MP', HQ Croatia, 12 April 1944, Char 1/381.
23. Brown, *The Last Hero*, 456–65; Ralph Bennett, 'Knight's Move at Drvar: Ultra and the Attempt on Tito's Life 25 May 1944', *Journal of Contemporary History*, Vol. 22, 1987, 195–208; McLynn, *Fitzroy Maclean*, 202–207.
24. Hinsley et al., *British Intelligence in the Second World War*, Vol. 4, 247–60; Vol. 5, 123–4.
25. M. R. D. Foot and J. M. Langley, *MI9: The British Secret Service that Fostered Escape and Evasion 1939–45 and its American Counterpart*, 214; R. Ivelaw-Chapman, *High Endeavour*, 93–113.
26. Gilbert, *Churchill*, Vol. VII, 775.

Chapter 17: Shadows of Peace

1. Hinsley et al., *British Intelligence in the Second World War*, Vol. 3, Part 1, 502–3; Part 2, 168.
2. Churchill, *The Second World War*, Vol. 5, *Triumph and Tragedy*, 42; Jones, *Most Secret War*, 523–80; Gilbert, *Churchill*, Vol. VII, 866–7.
3. Hinsley et al., *British Intelligence in the Second World War*, Vol. 3, Part 2, 216–17.
4. Gilbert, *Churchill*, Vol. VII, 822–31, 955–61.
5. Lewin, *Ultra Goes to War*, 190–91; Lamb, *Churchill as War Leader*, 286.
6. Lewin, ibid., 148–9.
7. Hinsley et al., *British Intelligence in the Second World War*, Vol. 3, Part 2, 368–9.

8. Gilbert, *Churchill*, Vol. VII, 811–12; Foot, *SOE in France*, 385 *et seq*.; Char 20/152; PREM 3/408/7.
9. Hinsley et al., *British Intelligence in the Second World War*, Vol. 2, Appendix 5, 'The German Police Cyphers', 669–73.
10. These intercepts were released in Britain in May 1997 and in the United States in November 1996. In the Public Record Office, Kew, they are in the HW 16 series.
11. Gilbert, *Churchill*, Vol. VI, 1174; HW 1/30.
12. Shertok to Randolph Churchill, 2 July 1944, Morton to Sporborg, 6 July 1944, and subsequent correspondence in HS 4/91 [SOE Hungary]; also Stafford, *Britain and European Resistance*, 179–81.
13. Gilbert, *Churchill*, Vol. VII, 893–4.
14. Ford, *OSS and Yugoslav Resistance*, 119–21.
15. Ibid., 154; Churchill to Eden, 19 December 1944, Char 20/153.
16. Woodhouse, *Something Ventured*, 84–6; Churchill to Eden, 15 July 1944, Char 20/153.
17. Churchill to Hopkins, 24 August 1944, Char 20/180; Brown, *The Last Hero*, 595–609.
18. Churchill, *The Second World War*, Vol. 6, 110.
19. Wilkinson and Bright Astley, *Gubbins and SOE*, 204–207.
20. Churchill, *The Second World War*, Vol. 6, 110–24.
21. Stafford, *Britain and European Resistance*, 144–98.
22. Cruickshank, *SOE in the Far East*, 124–5.
23. Wilkinson and Bright Astley, *Gubbins and SOE*, 221–23; Churchill to Eden, 25 November 1944, Char 20/153.
24. Paul Addison, *The Road to 1945*, 255.
25. Hinsley et al., *British Intelligence in the Second World War*, Vol. 4, 177; Richard J. Aldrich, 'Secret Intelligence for a Post-War World: Reshaping the British Intelligence Community', in *British Intelligence, Strategy and the Cold War*, ed. Aldrich, 15–49.
26. *Parliamentary Debates, House of Commons*, 8 Dec 1944, Cols 929–30.
27. Gilbert, *Churchill*, Vol. VII, 1117–36.
28. Churchill to Eden, 1 January 1945, Char 20/209; Gilbert, *Churchill*, Vol. VII, 1137–62.
29. Hinsley et al., *British Intelligence in the Second World War*, Vol. 3, Part 2, 714–18.
30. Churchill, *The Second World War*, Vol. 6, 391.
31. Richard Aldrich, 'Imperial Rivalry: British and American Intelligence in Asia, 1942–46', *Intelligence and National Security*, Vol. 3, No. 1, January 1988, 23.
32. Brown, '*C*: *The Secret Life of Sir Stewart Menzies*, 629.
33. Aldrich, 'Imperial Rivalry', 5.
34. Cruickshank, *SOE in the Far East*, 179–81.
35. Rhodri Jeffreys-Jones, *The CIA and American Democracy*, 30–31.
36. Churchill to Menzies, 19 May 1945, Churchill to Ismay, 21 May 1945, Char 20/209; Gilbert, *Churchill*, Vol. VIII, *Never Despair*, 166–7.

Chapter 18: Private Intelligence

1. J. L. Granatstein and David Stafford, *Spy Wars: Canada and Espionage from Gouzenko to Glasnost*, 47–75; Stafford, *Camp X: SOE and the American Connection*, 260–69.
2. Gilbert, *Churchill*, Vol. VIII, 162.
3. Reg Whitaker and Gary Marcuse, *Cold War Canada 1945–1957*, 68–9, 120–1.
4. Christopher Andrew, 'The Making of the Anglo-American SIGINT Alliance', *In the Name of Intelligence*, eds Peake and Halpern, 95–109; Thomas, *Armed Truce*, 506–13.
5. Morton to Churchill, 29 May 1947, Char 2/153.
6. Richard Aldrich (ed.), *British Intelligence, Strategy, and the Cold War 1945–51, passim*; Anne Deighton (ed.), *Britain and the First Cold War, passim*.
7. Peter Hennessy and Gail Brownfeld, 'Britain's Cold War Security Purge: The Origins of Positive Vetting', *Historical Journal*, Vol. 25, No. 4, 1982.
8. Hillgarth to Churchill, 4 December 1948, Chur 2/36; see also Hillgarth to Churchill, 20 November 1948, ibid.

9. Chur 2/36, 2/39.
10. Churchill to Attlee, 24 July 1949, Churchill Papers.
11. Hillgarth to Churchill, 12 September 1949, Churchill Papers.
12. J. W. Young, 'Cold War and Detente with Moscow' in *The Foreign Policy of Churchill's Peacetime Administration 1951–1955*, ed. J. W. Young, 55–60; J. W. Young, *Winston Churchill's Last Campaign: Britain and the Cold War 1951–55, passim*; R. R. James (ed.), *Churchill Speaks: Collected Speeches in Peace and War 1897–1963*, Vol. VIII, *1950–63*, 7936–44; *Scotsman*, 15 February 1950.
13. Gilbert, *Churchill*, Vol. VIII, 539.
14. Hillgarth to Churchill, 15 July 1950, Churchill Papers.
15. Hillgarth to Churchill, 31 March 1951, Churchill Papers.
16. Churchill to Major-General Sir Stewart Menzies, 12 May 1951, and Menzies to Churchill, 28 May 1951, Churchill Papers.
17. Richard Aldrich, 'European Integration, Political Elites, and the American Intelligence Connection', *passim*, and 'OSS, CIA and European Unity, 1948–1960: The American Committee on United Europe', *passim* – both unpublished papers kindly lent by their author.
18. Aldrich, 'OSS, CIA, and European Unity', 20; J. W. Young, 'Churchill's "No" to Europe: the Rejection of European Unity by Churchill's Post-War Government 1951–52', *Historical Journal*, Vol. 28, 1985, 923–31.

Chapter 19: Cloak-and-Dagger

1. Hennessy and Brownfeld, 'Britain's Cold War Security Purge'.
2. *Parliamentary Debates, House of Commons*, 9 July 1951, Cols 30–34; Colville, *The Churchillians*, 60; Anthony Montague Browne, *Long Sunset: Memoirs of Winston Churchill's Last Private Secretary*, 219–20.
3. Tom Bower, *The Perfect English Spy*, 146; Sir Percy Sillitoe, *Cloak Without Dagger*, 155–7.
4. S. P. Mackenzie, *The Home Guard: A Military and Political History*, 173; *Daily Telegraph*, 19 December 1996.
5. Browne, *Long Sunset*, 133–5.
6. R. V. Jones, *Reflections on Intelligence*, 7–34; also his *Most Secret War*, 66–7, 659–61.
7. Brian Cathcart, *Test of Greatness: Britain's Struggle for the Atom Bomb*, 173.
8. 'The Night the RAF "Bombed" Russia', *Daily Telegraph*, 7 February 1994, and BBC *Timewatch*, 9 February 1994.
9. Gilbert, *Churchill*, Vol. VIII, 640–41.
10. Wm Roger Louis, 'Musaddiq and the dilemmas of British imperialism', in *Musaddiq, Iranian Nationalism, and Oil*, eds James Bill and Wm Roger Louis, 228–60; Farhad Diba, *Mohammed Mossadegh: A Political Biography*, 179–97; William Blum, *The CIA: A Forgotten History*, 67–76; James Bill, *The Eagle and the Lion: The Tragedy of American-Iranian Relations*, 51–97.
11. Woodhouse, *Something Ventured*, 104–35; Nigel West, *The Friends*, 119–132.
12. Burton Hersh, *The Old Boys: The American Elite and the Origins of the CIA*, 331–5; Roosevelt, *Countercoup: The Struggle for the Control of Iran, passim*.
13. Sir David Hunt, letter to author, 27 August 1996.
14. Christopher Andrew, *For the President's Eyes Only*, 205; cf. Stephen Ambrose, *Ike's Spies: Eisenhower and the Espionage Establishment*, 213; Hersh, *The Old Boys*, 335.
15. Andrew, *For the President's Eyes Only*, 215.
16. Browne, *Long Sunset*, 293–4; Gilbert, *Churchill*, Vol. VIII, 1313–14.

Bibliography

Archives
1. Public Record Office, Kew
   (ADM) Admiralty
   (AIR) Air Ministry
   (CAB) Cabinet Office
   (CO) Colonial Office
   (FO) Foreign Office
   (HO) Home Office
   (HW) Government Code and Cipher School
   (HS) Special Operations Executive
   (WO) War Office
   Sturgis Papers
   Grey Papers
2. Churchill Archives Centre, Churchill College, Cambridge
   Churchill Papers [Chartwell/Churchill]
   Spencer Churchill Papers
   Bull Papers
   Croft Papers
   Hall Papers
   Hankey Papers
   Spears Papers
   Thurso Papers
3. Imperial War Museum
   Sir Henry Wilson Papers
   Kell Papers
4. House of Lords Record Library
   Lloyd George Papers
   Beaverbrook Papers
5. British Library of Political and Economic Science
   Dalton Papers
6. National Maritime Museum, Greenwich
   Sir Henry Oliver Papers
   Godfrey Papers
7. National Library of Scotland
   Richard Burdon Haldane Papers
   Aylmer Haldane Papers
8. Scottish Record Office
   Ewart Papers
9. University Library, Glasgow
   Diary of Alexander McCallum Scott

10. Wiltshire Record Office
    Walter Long Papers

Works of Winston S. Churchill
Savrola: A Tale of Revolution in Laurania (1897)
The Malakand Field Force (1898)
The River War (1899)
London to Ladysmith via Pretoria (1900)
Ian Hamilton's March (1900)
My Early Life (1930)
The World Crisis (5 Vols, 1923–31)
Thoughts and Adventures (1932)
Great Contemporaries (1937)
Marlborough (4 vols, 1933–38)
The Second World War (6 vols, 1948–54)

Official Biography
The official biography of Winston Churchill, begun by his son Randolph (RSC) and completed by Sir Martin Gilbert (MG), entitled *Winston S. Churchill*, consists of the following volumes:

Vol. I, *Youth 1874–1900* (RSC,1966)
Vol. II, *Young Statesman 1901–1914* (RSC,1967)
Vol. III, *The Challenge of War 1914–1916*, parts 1 and 2 (MG, 1971)
Vol. IV, *The Stricken World 1917–1922* (MG, 1975)
Vol. V, *The Prophet of Truth 1922–1939* (MG, 1976)
Vol.VI, *Finest Hour 1939–1941* (MG, 1983)
Vol. VII, *Road to Victory 1941–1945* (MG, 1986)
Vol. VIII, *Never Despair 1945–1965* (MG, 1988)

In addition, Martin Gilbert has produced a one-volume abridgement, entitled simply *Churchill, A Life* (1991).

Each of the volumes is accompanied by a separate *Companion Volume (CV)* of documents, also entitled *Winston S. Churchill*, as follows:

Vol. I, part 1, *1874–1896* (RSC, 1967)
——part 2, *1896–1900* (RSC, 1967)
Vol. II, part 1, *1901–1907* (RSC, 1969)
——part 2, *1907–1911* (RSC, 1969)
——part 3, *1911–1914* (RSC, 1969)
Vol. III, part 1, *August 1914–April 1915* (MG, 1972)
——part 2, *May 1915–December 1916* (MG, 1972)
Vol. IV, part 1, *Jan 1917–June 1919* (MG, 1977)
——part 2, *July 1919–March 1921* (MG, 1977)
——part 3, *April 1921–November 1922* (MG, 1977)
Vol. V, part 1, *The Exchequer Years* (MG, 1979)
——part 2, *The Wilderness Years 1929–1935* (MG, 1981)
——part 3, *The Coming of War, 1936–1939* (MG, 1982)

The most recent *Companion Volumes*, also edited by Sir Martin Gilbert, appear under the title *The Churchill War Papers*, Vol. I, *At the Admiralty September 1939–May 1940*, and Vol. II, *Never Surrender, May 1940–December 1940*.

In addition to this key primary source, there also exist the following collections of printed source material:

Charles Eade (ed.), *War Speeches by the Right Honourable Winston S.Churchill* (1942)
James, Robert Rhodes (ed.) *Churchill Speaks: Collected Speeches in Peace and War 1897–1963* (8 vols, 1981)
Cannadine, David (ed.) *Blood, Toil, Tears and Sweat: Winston Churchill's Famous Speeches* (1989)
Kimball, Warren (ed.), *Churchill and Roosevelt: The Complete Correspondence* (1984)
Michael Wolff (ed.) *The Collected Essays of Sir Winston Churchill* (1976)

Other Sources
Unless otherwise stated, London is the place of publication.

Books
Addison, Paul *Churchill on the Home Front 1900–1955*, 1993
——*The Road to 1945*, 1975
Aldrich, Richard J. (ed.) *British Intelligence, Strategy and the Cold War 1945–51* 1992
——and Hopkins, Michael (eds) *Intelligence, Defence and Diplomacy: British Policy in the Post-war World*, 1994
Ambrose, Stephen *Ike's Spies: Eisenhower and the Espionage Establishment*, Garden City, NY, 1981
Andrew, Christopher *For the President's Eyes Only*, 1995
——*Secret Service: the Making of the British Intelligence Community*, 1985
——with Gordievsky, Oleg *KGB*, 1990
——and Dilks, David (eds) *The Missing Dimension: Governments and Intelligence Communities in the Twentieth Century*, 1984
——and Noakes, Jeremy (eds) *Intelligence and International Relations*, Exeter, 1987
Annan, Noel *Changing Enemies: The Defeat and Regeneration of Germany*, 1995
Atkins, J. B. *Incidents and Reflections*, 1947
Auty, Phyllis, and Clogg, Richard, *British Policy towards Wartime Resistance in Yugoslavia and Greece*, 1975
Bailey, Thomas A., and Ryan, Paul B. *The Lusitania Disaster*, 1975
Barber, Laurie, and Tonkin-Covell, John *Freyberg: Churchill's Salamander*, 1989
Barker, Elizabeth *British Policy in South-East Europe in the Second World War*, 1976
——*Churchill and Eden at War*, 1978
Bearse, Ray, and Read, Anthony *Conspirator: The Untold Story of Churchill, Roosevelt and Tyler Kent, Spy*, 1991
Beesly, Patrick *Room 40: British Naval Intelligence 1914–18*, 1982
——*Very Special Admiral: The Life of Admiral J. H. Godfrey, CB*, 1980
——*Very Special Intelligence: The Story of the Admiralty's Operational Intelligence Centre 1939–1945*, 1977
Beevor, Anthony *Crete: The Battle and the Resistance* 1991
Beloff, Nora *Tito's Flawed Legacy: Yugoslavia and the West 1939–84*, 1985
Bennett, Geoffrey *Coronel and the Falklands*, 1962
Bennett, Ralph *Behind the Battle: Intelligence in the War with Germany 1939–45*, 1994
——*Ultra in the West: The Normandy Campaign of 1944–45*, New York, 1979
——*Ultra and Mediterranean Strategy 1941–45*, 1989
Bennett, Richard *The Black and Tans*, 1959
Berlin, Isaiah *Mr Churchill in 1940*, 1949
— *Selected Writings*, Vol. 4, *Personal Impressions*, 1980
Bialer, Uri *The Shadow of the Bomber: The Fear of Air Attack and British Politics 1932–1939*, 1980
Bill, James *The Eagle and the Lion: The Tragedy of American-Iranian Relations*, New Haven, 1988
——and Louis, Wm Roger (eds) *Musaddiq, Iranian Nationalism, and Oil*, 1988
Birkenhead, Earl of, *Churchill 1874–1922*, 1989
Blake, Robert, and Louis, William R. (eds) *Churchill*, 1993
Blum, William *The CIA: A Forgotten History*, 1986
Bond, Brian *Liddell Hart: A Study of his Military Thought*, 1977
Bonham Carter, Violet *Winston Churchill As I Knew Him*, 1965

Bower, Tom *The Perfect English Spy: Sir Dick White and the Secret War 1935–90*, 1995

Boyd, Carl, *Hitler's Japanese Confidant: General Oshima Hiroshi amd Magic Intelligence*, Kansas, 1993

Boyle, Peter G. (ed) *The Churchill–Eisenhower Correspondence 1953–1955*, 1990

Brendon, Piers *Winston Churchill: An Authentic Hero*, 1984

Brock, Eleanor and Michael (eds) *H. H. Asquith. Letters to Venetian Stanley*, Oxford, 1982

Brockway, Fenner *Socialism Over Sixty Years*, 1946

Bromage, M. C. *Churchill and Ireland*, 1964

Brown, Anthony Cave *The Last Hero: Wild Bill Donovan*, 1982

——*'C': The Secret Life of Sir Stewart Menzies, Spymaster to Winston Churchill*, 1987

——*Bodyguard of Lies*, New York, 1975

Browne, Anthony Montague *Long Sunset: Memoirs of Winston Churchill's Last Private Secretary*, 1995

Bruce Lockhart, R. *Reilly, Ace of Spies*, 1992

Bryant, Arthur (ed.) *Triumph in the West*, 1959

——(ed.) *The Turn of the Tide*, 1957

Bulloch, John *MI5*, 1963

Bunyan, Tony *The Political Police in Britain*, 1976

Calder, Angus *The People's War: Britain 1939–1945*, 1969

Calvocoressi, Peter *Top Secret Ultra*, 1981

Campbell, Duncan *The Unsinkable Aircraft Carrier: American Military Power in Britain*, 1986

Cathcart, Brian *Test of Greatess: Britain's Struggle for the Atom Bomb*, 1994

Charmley, John *Churchill: The End of Glory*, 1993

——*Churchill's Grand Alliance: The Anglo-American Special Relationship 1940–57*, 1995

Churchill: Four Faces and the Man, 1969, essays on 'The Statesman', A. J. P Taylor; 'The Politician', Robert Rhodes James; 'The Historian', J. H. Plumb; 'The Military Strategist', Basil Liddell Hart; 'The Man', Anthony Storr

Clayton, Anthony *Forearmed: A History of the Intelligence Corps*, 1993

Cockett, Richard *Twilight of Truth: Chamberlain, Appeasement and the Manipulation of the Press*, 1989

Coers, Donald V. *John Steinbeck as Propagandist: The Moon is Down Goes to War*, Tuscaloosa, 1991

Collier, Basil *The Defence of the United Kingdom*, 1957

Colville, John *The Fringes of Power: Downing Street Diaries 1939–October 1941*, 2 vols, 1985, 1987

——*The Churchillians*, 1981

Connell, John *Wavell, Scholar and Soldier*, 1964

——*Auchinleck: A Biography of Field Marshal Sir Claude Auchinleck*, 1959

Coogan, Tim Pat *Michael Collins*, 1990

Corbett, Sir Julian S. *History of the Great War: Naval Operations*, Vols II and III, 1921

Costello, John *Ten Days that Saved the West*, 1991

Croft, Henry Page, *My Life of Strife*, 1949

Cross, J. A. *Lord Swinton*, Oxford, 1982

Crozier, W. P. *Off the Record: Political Interviews 1933–1943* (ed. A. J. P. Taylor), 1973

Cruickshank, Charles *SOE in Scandinavia*, 1986

Dalton, Hugh *The Fateful Years 1931–45*, 1957

Danchev, Alex (ed.) *Establishing the Anglo-American Alliance: The Second World War Diaries of Brigadier Vivian Dykes*, 1990

D'Astier de la Vigerie, Emmanuel *Les Dieux et les hommes*, Paris, 1952

Davies, Andrew *We, the Nation: The Conservative Party and the Pursuit of Power*, 1995

De Gaulle, Charles *War Memoirs Vol I: The Call to Honour 1940–1942*, 1955

De Groot, Gerard *Liberal Crusader: The Life of Sir Archibald Sinclair*, 1993

Deighton, Anne (ed.) *Britain and the First Cold War*, 1990

De Mendelssohn, Peter *The Age of Churchill: Heritage and Adventure 1874–1911*, 1961

Denniston, Robin *Churchill's Secret War: Diplomatic Decrypts, the Foreign Offce and Turkey 1942–44*, 1997

Diba, Farhad *Mohammed Mossadegh: A Political Biography*, 1986

Dictionary of Labour Biography, Vol. IV, 1977
Dictionary of National Biography 1931–1940; 1971–1980
Dilks, David (ed.) *The Diaries of Sir Alexander Cadogan, 1938–1945*, 1971
Dodds-Parker, Douglas *Setting Europe Ablaze*, 1983
Donaghue, Bernard, and Jones, G. W. *Herbert Morrison: Portrait of a Politician*, 1973
Dunlop, Richard *Donovan, America's Master Spy*, Chicago, 1982
Eade, Charles *Churchill by his Contemporaries*, 1954
Edmonds, Robin *The Big Three: Churchill, Roosevelt and Stalin*, 1991
Erickson, John *The Road to Stalingrad: Stalin's War with Germany*, 1975
——and Dilks, David, *Barbarossa: The Axis and the Allies*, Edinburgh, 1994
Ewing, A. *The Man of Room 40*, 1939
Fay, Chester, Young, Lewis, and Stephen, Hugo *The Zinoviev Letter*, 1967
Feis, H. *Churchill, Roosevelt, Stalin: The War they Waged and the Peace they Sought*, 1957
Fisk, Robert *In Time of War: Ireland, Ulster and the Price of Neutrality*, 1983
Folls, Bryan *A State Under Siege: The Establishment of Northern Ireland 1920–1925*, Oxford, 1994
Foot, M. R. D. *SOE: An Outline History of the Special Operations Executive 1940–46*, 1984
——*SOE in France*, 1966
——*War and Society*, 1973
——and Langley, J. M. *MI9: Escape and Evasion 1939–45*, 1979
Ford, Kirk Jr *OSS and the Yugoslav Resistance 1943–1945*, Texas, 1992
Forester, M. *Michael Collins: The Lost Leader*, 1971
Fraser, David *Alanbrooke*, 1982
Freyberg, Paul *Bernard Freyberg VC, Soldier of Two Nations*, 1991
Funk, A. L. *The Politics of Torch*, Kansas, 1974
Gardiner, A. G. *Pillars of Society*, 1913
Gibbs, A. D. *With Winston Churchill at the Front*, 1924
Gilbert, Martin *In Search of Churchill: A Historian's Journey*, 1994
Gillman, Peter and Lily *Collar the Lot*, 1980
Gleichen, Albert Edward *A Guardsman's Memories*, 1932
Gooch, John *The Prospect of War*, 1981
Gorodetsky, G. *The Precarious Peace: Anglo-Soviet Relations 1924–27*, Cambridge, 1977
Granatstein, J. L., and Stafford, David *Spy Wars: Canada and Espionage from Gouzenko to Glasnost*, Toronto, 1990
Graves, Armgaard Karl *The Secrets of the German War Office*, 1914
Halle, Kay *Randolph Churchill: The Young Unpretender*, 1971
Hamilton, Sir Ian *Gallipoli Diary*, 2 vols, 1920
Hamilton, Nigel *Monty: The Making of a General 1887–1942*, 1981
——*Monty the Field-Marshal 1944–1976*, 1981
Handel, Michael (ed.) *Strategic and Operational Deception in the Second World War*, 1987
Hankey, Lord *The Supreme Command 1914–1918*, 1961
Herman, Michael *Intelligence Power in Peace and War*, 1996
Hersh, Burton *The Old Boys: The American Elite and the Origins of the CIA*, New York, 1992
Hickey, Michael *Gallipoli*, 1995
Higham, Robin *The Military Intellectuals in Britain: 1918–1939*, New Jersey, 1966
Hill, George *Go Spy the Land: Being the Adventures of IK8 of the British Secret Service*, 1932
Hillgarth, Alan *The Black Mountain*, 1933
——*Davy Jones*, 1936
——*The War Maker*, 1926
Hinsley, F. H., et al. *British Intelligence in the Second World War*, Vols 1–5, 1979–1990
Hinsley, F. H., and Stripp, Alan *Codebreakers: The Inside Story of Bletchley Park*, 1993
Hodges, Alan *The Enigma of Intelligence*, 1985
Holmes, Colin *Anti-Semitism in British Society 1876–1939*, 1979
Hohne, Heinx *Canaris*, 1979
Howarth, Patrick *Intelligence Chief Extraordinary*, 1986

Hunt, Sir David *A Don at War*, 1990
Irving, David *The Mare's Nest*, 1985
Ivelaw-Chapman, John *High Endeavour: The Life of Air Chief Marshal Sir Ronald Ivelaw-Chapman*, 1993
Jablonsky, David *Churchill, the Great Game and Total War*, 1991
James, Lawrence *Imperial Warrior*, 1993
——*The Golden Warrior*, 1990
James, Robert Rhodes *Churchill: A Study in Failure 1900–1939*, 1973
——*Gallipoli*, 1965
——(ed.) *Memoirs of a Conservative: J. C. C. Davidson's Memoirs and Papers*, 1969
James, Sir William M. *A Great Seaman: The Life of Admiral of the Fleet Sir Henry Oliver*, 1956
——*The Eyes of the Navy*, 1955
Jeffrey, Keith *The British Army and the Crisis of Empire*, 1984
Jeffreys-Jones, Rhodri *The CIA and American Democracy*, 1989
——and Lownie, A. *North American Spies*, Kansas, 1991
Jones, R. V. *Most Secret War: British Scientific Intelligence 1939–45*, 1979
——*Reflections on Intelligence*, 1989
Jones, Thomas *The Whitehall Diary* Vol. I: *1916–1925* (ed. Keith Middlemas), 1969
——*The Whitehall Diary* Vol III: *Ireland 1918–1925* (ed. Keith Middlemas), 1971
Kahn, David *Seizing the Enigma: The Race to Break the German U-boat Codes 1939–1943*, 1992
Keegan John (ed.) *Churchill's Generals*, 1991
——*The Second World War*, 1989
Kendall, Walter *The Revolutionary Movement in Britain 1900–21: The Origins of British Communism*, 1969
Kersaudy, F. *Churchill and De Gaulle*, 1981
Kettle, Michael *Churchill and the Archangel Fiasco*, 1992
——*Sidney Reilly – The True Story*, 1983
Kimball, Warren (ed.) *Churchill and Roosevelt: The Complete Correspondence*, Vols 1–3, Princeton, 1984
——*The Juggler: Franklin Roosevelt as Wartime Statesman*, Princeton, 1991
Kirkwood, David *My Life of Revolt*, 1935
Knightley, Philip *The Second Oldest Profession*, 1981
Krassin, Lubov *Leonid Krassin: His Life and Work*, 1929
Lamb, Richard *Churchill as War Leader: Right or Wrong?*, 1991
Lansbury, George *My Life*, 1928
——*The Miracle of Fleet Street*, 1925
Lash, J. P. *Roosevelt and Churchill, 1939–1941*, 1977
Lashmar, Paul, *Spy Flights of the Cold War*, 1996
Lawlor, Sheila *Britain and Ireland 1914–23*, Dublin, 1983
——*Churchill and the Politics of War 1940–1941*, Cambridge, 1994
Lees, Michael *The Rape of Serbia*, 1990
Leffler, Melvyn *A Preponderance of Power: National Security, the Truman Administration, and the Cold War*, Stanford, 1992
Leslie, Anita *Cousin Clare*, 1976
Leslie, Sir John *Long Shadows*, 1966
——*The Film of Memory*, 1938
Lewin, Ronald *Churchill as Warlord*, 1973
——*Ultra Goes to War*, 1981
Liddell Hart, Basil *Memoirs*, 1965
——*'T. E. Lawrence': In Arabia and After*, 1934
Lindsay, Franklin *Beacons in the Night: With the OSS and Tito's Partisans in Wartime Yugoslavia*, Stanford, 1993
Louis, Wm Roger, and Bull, Hedley *The 'Special Relationship': Anglo-American Relations since 1945*, Oxford, 1986

Lycett, Andrew *Ian Fleming*, 1995
MacDonald, Callum *The Killing of SS Obergruppenführer Reinhard Heydrich*, New York, 1989
——*The Lost Battle: Crete 1941*, 1995
McJimsey, George *Harry Hopkins: Ally of the Poor and Defender of Democracy*, Harvard, 1987
McKay, G. C. *From Information to Intrigue: Studies in Secret Service Based on the Swedish Experience 1939–45*, 1993
Mackenzie, Compton *Gallipoli Memories*, 1929
Mackenzie, Norman and Jeanne *The Time Traveller: The Life of H. G. Wells*, 1973
Mackenzie, S. P. *The Home Guard: A Military and Political History*, Oxford, 1995
McLachlan, Donald *Room 39: Naval Intelligence in Action 1939–45*, 1968
Maclean, Fitzroy *Eastern Approaches*, 1950
McLynn, Frank *Fitzroy Maclean*, 1992
Macmillan, Harold *The Blast of War 1939–1945*, 1967
——*War Diaries: Politics and War in the Mediterranean January 1943–May 1945*, 1984
Macready, Sir Nevil *Annals of an Active Life*, 2 vols, 1924
Manchester, William *The Caged Lion: Winston Spencer Churchill 1932–1940*, 1988
——*The Last Lion: Winston Spencer Churchill; Visions of Glory 1874–1932*, 1983
Marder, A. J. *Churchill is Back: Churchill at the Admiralty 1939–1940*, 1972
——*From the Dardanelles to Oran: Studies of the Royal Navy in War and Peace 1915–1940*, 1974
——*From the Dreadnought to Scapa Flow: the Royal Navy in the Fisher Era*, Vol. I (1961), Vol. II (1965)
Marquand, David *Ramsay MacDonald*, 1977
Marshall, Bruce *The White Rabbit*, 1952
Marshall, Robert *All the King's Men: The Truth behind SOE's Greatest Wartime Disaster*, 1989
Martin, Sir John *Downing Street: The War Years*, 1991
Masterman, J. C. *The Double-Cross System*, 1979
Masters, Anthony *The Man Who Was 'M': The Life of Maxwell Knight*, 1986
Maurice, Sir Fredrick Barton *Haldane: (I) 1856–1915 (II) 1915–1928*, 1937
May, Ernest R. (ed.) *Knowing One's Enemies: Intelligence Assessment before the Two World Wars*, Princeton, 1986
Middlebrook, Martin *The Peenemunde Raid*, 1982
Miller, Joan *One Girl's War: Personal Exploits in MI5's Most Secret Station*, Kerry, 1986
Montagu, Ewen *Beyond Top Secret Ultra*, 1978, New York
——*The Man Who Never Was*, 1965
Moran, Lord *Churchill: The Struggle for Survival 1940–1965*, 1966
Morgan, Ted *Somerset Maugham*, 1980
Neligan, David *The Spy in the Castle*, 1968
Nicolson, Nigel *Alex: The Life of Field Marshal Earl Alexander of Tunis*, 1973
North, John *The Alexander Memoirs*, 1962
Overy, Richard *Why the Allies Won*, 1995
Padfield, Peter *Rudolph Hess: The Fuhrer's Disciple*, 1991
Parini, Jay *John Steinbeck: A biography*, 1994
Parker, R. A. C, *Winston Churchill: Studies in Statesmanship*, 1995
Peake, Hayden, and Halpern, Samuel (eds) *In the Name of Intelligence: Essays in Honour of Walter Pforzheimer*, Washington DC, 1994
Pearson, John *Citadel of the Heart: Winston Churchill and the Churchill Dynasty*, 1991
Pelling, Henry *Winston Churchill*, 1974
Pimlott, Ben *Hugh Dalton*, 1985
——*The Second World War Diary of Hugh Dalton*, 1986
Plotke, A. J. *Imperial Spies Invade Russia: The British Intelligence Intervention 1918*, Connecticut, 1993
Porter, Bernard *Plots and Paranoia*, 1989
——*The Origins of the Vigilant State: The London Metropolitan Special Branch Before the First World War*, 1987

Bibliography

Porter, Ivor *Operation Autonomous: With SOE in Wartime Romania*, 1989
Postgate, Raymond *The Life of George Lansbury*, 1951
Reilly, Sydney George *The Adventures of Sydney Reilly: Britain's Master Spy*, 1931
Richards, Sir Brooks *Secret Flotillas: The Clandestine Sea Lines to France and French North Africa 1940–1944*, 1996
Robbins, Keith *Churchill*, 1992
Roberts, Andrew *Eminent Churchillians*, 1994
——*The Holy Fox*, 1992
Roberts, Walter R. *Tito, Mihailovic and the Allies 1941–1945*, New Brunswick, 1973
Rogers, Colin *The Battle of Stepney*, 1981
Roosevelt, Kermit *Countercoup: The Struggle for the Control of Iran*, New York, 1979
Rose, Norman *Churchill: An Unruly Life*, 1994
Roskill, Stephen *Admiral of the Fleet Earl Beatty*, 1980
——*Churchill and the Admirals*, 1977
——*Hankey: Man of Secrets*, 1970
Royle, Trevor, *Orde Wingate: Irregular Soldier*, 1995
Rumbelow, Donald *The Houndsditch Murders and the Siege of Sidney Street*, 1988
Rusbridger, James, and Nave, Eric *Betrayal at Pearl Harbor: How Churchill Lured Roosevelt into World War Two*, 1991
Sainsbury, Keith *Churchill and Roosevelt at War*, 1994
Scott, Alexander M. *Winston Churchill in Peace and War*, no date
——*Winston Spencer Churchill*, 1905
Seeley, J. E. B. *Adventure*, 1930
Seldon, A. *Churchill's Indian Summer: The Conservative Government, 1951–1955*, 1981
Sheridan, Clare *Nuda Veritas*, 1927
——*Russian Portraits*, 1921
——*To the Four Winds*, 1957
Sherwood, Robert E. *The White House Papers of Harry L. Hopkins: An Intimate History*, Vols I and II, 1948, 1949
Shinwell, Emanuel *Conflict without Malice*, 1955
Shuckburgh, Evelyn *Descent to Suez: Diaries 1951–56*, 1986
Sillitoe, Percy *Cloak without Dagger*, 1955
Simpson, Brian *In the Highest Degree Odious: Detention Without Trial in Wartime Britain*, Oxford, 1992
Simpson, Colin *Lusitania*, 1971
Slowikowski, Rygor *In the Secret Service: The Lighting of Torch*, 1988
Smith, Bradley F. *The Shadow Warriors: OSS and the Origins of the CIA*, 1983
——*The Ultra–Magic Deals and the Most Secret Special Relationship 1940–1946*, 1993
Smith, R Harris *OSS: The Secret History of America's First Central Intelligence Agency*, Berkeley, 1972
Smyth, Denis *Diplomacy and Strategy of Survival: British Policy and Franco's Spain* Cambridge, 1986
Soames, Mary *Clementine Churchill*, 1979
Spears, E. *Liaison 1914*, 1968
Spears, Sir Edward *Fulfilment of a Mission*, 1977
——*Prelude to Victory*, 1939
Spence, Richard B. *Boris Savinkov: Renegade on the Left*, 1991
Stafford, David *Britain and European Resistance 1940–45: A Survey of the Special Operations Executive, with documents*, 1980
——*Camp X: SOE and the American Connection*, 1987
Strong, K. *Men of Intelligence*, 1970
——*Intelligence at the Top*, 1968
Swartz, M. *The Union of Democratic Control in British Politics during the First World War*, Oxford, 1971

Swinton, Lord *I Remember*, 1948

Tangye, Derek *The Way to Minack*, 1968

Tedder, Lord *With Prejudice: The War Memoirs of Marshal of the Royal Air Force Lord Tedder GCB*, 1966

Templewood, Viscount *Ambassador on Special Leave*, 1946

Thomas, Hugh *Armed Truce*, 1986

Thompson, R.W. *Churchill and Morton*, 1976

——*The Yankee Marlborough*, 1963

Thompson, W. H. *Guard from the Yard*, 1938

——*I Was Churchill's Shadow*, 1951

Thomson, Basil *Queer People*, 1922

——*The Scene Changes*, 1939

Thorne, Christopher *Allies of a Kind: The United States, Britain, and the War Against Japan 1941–45*, 1978

Thurlow, Richard, *The Secret State: British Internal Security in the Twentieth Century*, 1994

Thwaites, Norman *Velvet and Vinegar*, 1932

Townshend, Charles *The British Campaign in Ireland*, 1978

Troy, Thomas F. *Donovan and the CIA*, Frederick, Maryland, 1981

——*Wild Bill and Intrepid: Donovan, Stephenson and the Origins of CIA*, New Haven, 1996

Tupper, E. *Seaman's Torch: The Life Story of Captain Edward Tupper*, no date

Tuttle, Dwight W. *Harry L. Hopkins and Anglo-American–Soviet Relations, 1941–1945*, New York, 1983

Ullman, Richard H. *Anglo-Soviet Relations 1917–21*, 1961–72

Verrier, Anthony *Assassination in Algiers: Churchill, Roosevelt, and the Murder of Admiral Darlan*, 1991

Wark, Wesley K. *The Ultimate Enemy: British Intelligence and Nazi Germany 1933–1939*, Ithaca, 1985

Warner, Philip *Auchinleck, the Lonely Soldier*, 1982

Watt, Donald Cameron *How War Came*, 1990

——*Succeeding John Bull: America in Britain's Place 1900–75*, 1984

Welchman, Gordon *The Hut Six Story: Breaking the Enigma Codes*, 1984

Wells, H. G. *Experiment in Autobiography*, 1934

——*Men Like Gods*, 1923

West, Nigel *The Friends: MI6 Operations 1945–1970*, 1990

——*The SIGINT Secrets*, 1991

——*MI5: British Security Service Operations 1909–1945*, 1981

——*MI6: British Secret Intelligence Operations 1909–45*, 1983

——*Secret War: The Story of SOE, Britain's Wartime Sabotage Organisation*, 1992

Wheeler, Mark *Britain and the War for Yugoslavia 1940–1943*, Boulder, 1980

Wheeler-Bennett, John *Action this Day: Working with Churchill*, 1968

Whitaker, Reg, and Marcuse, Gary *Cold War Canada: The Making of a National Insecurity State, 1945–1957*, Toronto, 1994

Williams, Charles *The Last Great Frenchman: A Life of General de Gaulle*, 1993

Wilkinson, Peter, and Astley, Joan *Gubbins and SOE*, 1993

Wilson, Sir Henry *Military Correspondence*, 1985

Wilson, Jeremy *Lawrence of Arabia: The Authorised Biography of T. E. Lawrence*, 1989

Wingate, R. E. W. *Not in the Limelight*, 1959

Winter, Colonel O. de L'E. *Winter's Tale*, 1955

Winterbotham, F. W. *The Ultra Secret*, 1974

Woodhouse, C. M. *Apple of Discord* 1948

——*Something Ventured*, 1982

Woods, Frederick *Artillery of Words: The Writings of Sir Winston Churchill*, 1993

Young, J.W. *The Foreign Policy of Churchill's Peacetime Administration*, 1988

——*Winston Churchill's Last Campaign: Britain and the Cold War 1951–55*, 1996

Bibliography

Young, Kenneth *Churchill and Beaverbrook*, 1966

Articles, Essays and Chapters

Aldrich, Richard, 'Conspiracy or Confusion? Churchill, Roosevelt, and Pearl Harbor', *Intelligence and National Security*, Vol. 7, No. 3, July 1992,
——'Imperial Rivalry: British and American Intelligence in Asia 1942–46', *Intelligence and National Security*, Vol. 3, No. 1, January 1988
——'Secret Intelligence for a Post-war World: Reshaping the British Intelligence Community', in *British Intelligence, Strategy and the Cold War* (ed. Aldrich)
Allen, Capt. G. R. G, 'A Ghost from Gallipoli', *Royal United Services Journal*, Vol. CVIII, No. 630, May 1963
Anderson, Scott, '"With Friends like These . . ." The OSS and the British in Yugoslavia', *Intelligence and National Security*, Vol. 8, No. 2, April 1993
Andrew, Christopher, 'Churchill and Intelligence', *Intelligence and National Security*, Vol. 3, No. 3, July 1988, 181–93
——'The Making of the Anglo-American SIGINT Alliance', in Peake and Halpern (eds), 95–111
Bennett, Ralph; Deakin, Sir William; Hunt, Sir David; Wilkinson, Sir Peter, 'Mihailovic and Tito', *Intelligence and National Security*, Vol. 10, No. 3, July 1995
Bennett, Ralph, 'Knight's Move at Drvar: Ultra and the Attempt on Tito's Life 25 May 1944', *Journal of Contemporary History*, Vol. 22, 1987, 195–208
Best, Antony, 'Constructing an Image: British Intelligence and Whitehall's Perception of Japan', *Intelligence and National Security*, Vol. 11, No. 3, July 1996
Bowden, T. 'Bloody Sunday – a Reappraisal', *European Studies Review*, Vol. 2, No. 1, 1972, 25–42
Boyd, Carl, 'Significance of MAGIC and the Japanese Ambassador to Berlin; (V) News of Hitler's Defence Preparations for the Allied Invasion of Western Europe', *Intelligence and National Security*, Vol. 4, No. 3, July 1989
Brown, Kathryn, 'Intelligence and the Decision to Collect it: Churchill's Wartime Diplomatic Signals Intelligence', *Intelligence and National Security*, Vol. 10, No. 3, July 1995
Cecil, Robert, '"C"'s War', *Intelligence and National Security*, Vol. 1, 1986
Cox, Sebastian, '"The Difference between White and Black": Churchill, Imperial Politics and Intelligence before the 1941 *Crusader* Offensive', *Intelligence and National Security*, Vol. 9, No. 3, July 1994, 405–47
Danchev, Alex, 'In the Backroom: Anglo-American Defence Co-operation 1945–51', in Aldrich, *British Intelligence, Strategy and the Cold War 1945–51*, 215–35
Denniston, Robin, 'Diplomatic Eavesdropping, 1922–44: A New Source Discovered', *Intelligence and National Security*, Vol. 10, No. 3, July 1995
Ferris, John, 'Whitehall's Black Chamber: British Cryptology and the Government Code and Cypher School 1919–1929', *Intelligence and National Security*, Vol. 2, No. 1, Jan 1987
——'From Broadway House to Bletchley Park: The Diary of Captain Malcolm D. Kennedy 1936–1946', *Intelligence and National Security*, Vol. 4, No. 3, July 1989
——'"Indulged in All Too Little"?: Vansittart, Intelligence and Appeasement', *Diplomacy and Statecraft*, Vol. 6, No. 1, March 1995
——'From Broadway House to Bletchley Park: The Diary of Captain Malcolm D. Kennedy 1934–46', *Intelligence and National Security*, Vol. 4, No. 3, July 1989
Filby, P. W. 'Bletchley Park and Berkeley Street', *Intelligence and National Security*, Vol. 3, No. 2, April 1988
Foot, M. R. D. 'Churchill and the Secret Services', *Address to the Churchill Society for the Advancement of Parliamentary Democracy*, Toronto, 1988
——'The IRA and the Origins of SOE', in *War and Society: Historical Essays in Honour and Memory of J. R. Western 1928–1971*, ed. Foot, 1973
Gardiner, L. Keith, 'Squaring the Circle: Dealing with Intelligence–Policy Breakdowns', *Intelligence and National Security*, Vol. 6, No. 1, Jan 1991, 141–53

Handel, Michael, 'Leaders and Intelligence', *Intelligence and National Security*, Vol. 3, No. 3, July 1988, 181–93

——'The Politics of Intelligence', *Intelligence and National Security*, Vol. 2, No. 4, October 1987, 5–66

Heller, Michael, 'Krasin–Savinkov, Une Rencontre Secrète', *Cahiers du monde russe et soviétique*, Vol. XXVI, 1, 1985

Hennessy, Peter, and Brownfeld, Gail, 'Britain's Cold War Security Purge: The Origins of Positive Vetting', in *Historical Journal*, Vol. 25, No. 4, 1982

Hiley, Nicholas, 'The Failure of British Espionage against Germany 1907–1914', *Historical Journal*, Vol. 26, No. 4, 1983, 867–89

——'Counter-espionage and Security during the First World War', *English Historical Review*, 101, July 1986, 635–61

——'The Strategic Origins of Room 40', *Intelligence and National Security*, Vol. 2, No. 2, April 1987, 245–73

——'Internal Security in Wartime: The Rise and Fall of PMS2, 1915–1917', *Intelligence and National Security*, Vol. 1, No. 3, Sept 1986

Hinsley, F. H., 'British Intelligence and Barbarossa', in *Barbarossa: The Axis and the Allies*, ed. Erickson and Dilks, 43–75

Homberger, Eric, '"Uncle Max" and his Thrillers', *Intelligence and National Security*, Vol. 3, No. 2, April 1988, 312–21

Hope, John G., 'Surveillance or Collusion? Maxwell Knight, MI5 and the British Fascists', *Intelligence and National Security*, Vol. 9, No. 4, Oct 1994, 651–75

Hoskins, Robert S., 'An Expanded Understanding of Eisenhower, American Policy and Overflights', *Intelligence and National Security*, Vol. 11, No. 2, April 1996

Jeffrey, Keith, 'The British Army and Internal Security 1919–1939', *Historical Journal*, Vol. 24, No. 2, 1981, 377–97

Jones, R.V. 'Intelligence and Command', *Intelligence and National Security*, Vol. 3, No. 3, July 1988, 288–98

Kahn, David, 'The Intelligence Failure of Pearl Harbor', *Foreign Affairs*, Vol. 70, No. 5, Winter 1991/92

Kaiser, David, 'Conspiracy or Cock-Up? Pearl Harbor Revisited', *Intelligence and National Security*, Vol. 9, No. 2, April 1994

Kennedy, Paul, 'Great Britain before 1914', in *Knowing One's Enemies*, ed. May

Kimball, Warren, and Bartlett, Bruce, 'Roosevelt and Pre-war Commitments to Churchill: The Tyler Kent Affair', *Diplomatic History*, Vol. 5, No. 4, Fall 1981, 291–311

Lownie, Andrew, 'Tyler Kent: Isolationist or Spy?', in *North American Spies*, eds Jeffreys-Jones and Lownie, 49–78

MacDonald, Callum, A., 'The Venlo Affair', *European Studies Review*, Vol. 8, 1978

Mulligan, T. P, 'Spies, Ciphers, and "Zitadelle": Intelligence and the Battle of Kursk 1943', *Journal of Contemporary History*, Vol. 22, 1987, 246–50

O'Halpin, Eunan, 'Intelligence and Security in Ireland, 1922–45', *Intelligence and National Security*, Vol. 5, No. 1, January 1990, 50–83

——'"According to the Irish Minister in Rome . . .": British Decrypts and Irish Diplomacy in the Second World War', *Irish Studies in International Affairs*, Vol. 6, 1995

Smith, Bradley F., 'Admiral Godfrey's Mission to America June/July 1941', *Intelligence and National Security*, Vol. 1, No. 3, September 1986

Smyth, Denis, 'Screening "Torch": Allied Counter-Intelligence and the Spanish Threat to the Secrecy of the Allied Invasion of French North Africa in November 1942', *Intelligence and National Security*, Vol. 4, No. 2, April 1989

——'"Les Chevaliers de Saint-George": La Grande-Bretagne et la corruption des généraux espagnoles', *Guerre Mondiales*, 162, 1991

Spence, Richard B., 'Sidney Reilly in America', *Intelligence and National Security*, Vol. 10, No. 1, Jan 1995, 92–121

Stafford, David, 'Britain Looks at Europe 1940: Some Origins of SOE', *Canadian Journal of*

History, Vol. IX, No. 2, August 1975

——'Secret Operations versus Secret Intelligence in World War Two: The British Experience', in *Men at War: Politics, Technology and Innovation in the Twentieth Century*, eds Travers and Archer, Chicago, 1982

——'SIGINT Secrets', *Canadian Military History*, 1995

——'SOE and British Involvement in the Belgian *coup d'état* of March 1941', *Slavic Review*, Vol. 36, No. 3, September 1977

——'Churchill, SOE and Northern Europe' in *La Résistance et les européens du nord*, Brussels, 1994

Tordella, Louis W., and Fishel, Edwin C., 'A New Pearl Harbor Villain: Churchill', *International Journal of Intelligence and Counter-Intelligence*, Vol. 6, No. 3, Fall 1993

Townshend, Charles, 'Bloody Sunday – Michael Collins Speaks', *European Studies Review*, Vol. 9, 1979, 377–85

——'The Irish Republican Army and the Development of Guerrilla Warfare 1916–1921', *English Historical Review*, Vol. XCIV, 1979, 318–45

Ward, Stephen R., 'Intelligence Surveillance of British Ex-Servicemen 1918–1920', *Historical Journal*, Vol. 16, No. 1, 1973, 179–88

Wark, Wesley, 'British Intelligence and Operation Barbarossa, 1941: The Failure of FOES', in *In the Name of Intelligence*, op. cit.

David Watson, 'The Krasin–Savinkov Meeting of 1 December 1921, *Cahiers du monde russe et soviétique*, Vol. XXVII, 3–4, 1986

Watt, Donald Cameron, 'British Intelligence and the Coming of the Second World War in Europe', in *Knowing One's Enemies*, ed. May

——'Churchill and Appeasement', in *Churchill*, ed. Blake and Louis

Index

Index